The Doomsday Machine

The Doomsday Machine

Confessions of a Nuclear War Planner

DANIEL ELLSBERG

BLOOMSBURY

NEW YORK · LONDON · OXFORD · NEW DELHI · SYDNEY

Bloomsbury USA

An imprint of Bloomsbury Publishing Plc

1385 Broadway	50 Bedford Square
New York	London
NY 10018	WC1B 3DP
USA	UK

www.bloomsbury.com

BLOOMSBURY and the Diana logo are trademarks of Bloomsbury Publishing Plc

First published 2017

ISBN: HB: 978-1-60819-670-8
       ePub: 978-1-60819-674-6

Library of Congress cataloging-in-publication data is available.

2 4 6 8 10 9 7 5 3 1

Typeset by Westchester Publishing Services
Printed and bound in the U.S.A. by Berryville Graphics Inc., Berryville, Virginia

To find out more about our authors and books visit www.bloomsbury.com.
Here you will find extracts, author interviews, details of forthcoming events and
the option to sign up for our newsletters.

Bloomsbury books may be purchased for business or promotional use.
For information on bulk purchases please contact Macmillan Corporate and
Premium Sales Department at specialmarkets@macmillan.com.

To those who struggle for a human future

The unleashed power of the atom has changed everything save our modes of thinking, and thus we drift toward unparalleled catastrophe.
—Albert Einstein, 1946

Madness in individuals is something rare;
but in groups, parties, nations, and epochs, it is the rule.
—Friedrich Nietzsche

Contents

Part II: The Road to Doomsday

Prologue

One day in the spring of 1961, soon after my thirtieth birthday, I was shown how our world would end. Not the earth itself, not—so far as I knew then, mistakenly—nearly all humanity or life on the planet, but the destruction of most cities and people in the northern hemisphere. What I was handed, in a White House office, was a single sheet of paper with a simple graph on it. It was headed "Top Secret—Sensitive." Under that was "For the President's Eyes Only."

The "eyes only" designation meant that, in principle, it was to be seen and read only by the person to whom it was explicitly addressed—in this case, the president. In practice, it usually meant that it was seen by one or more secretaries and assistants as well: a handful of people, instead of the scores to hundreds who would normally see copies of a Top Secret document, even one marked "sensitive," which meant that it was to be especially closely held for bureaucratic or political reasons.

Later, working in the Pentagon as the special assistant to the assistant secretary of defense, I often found myself reading copies of cables and memos marked "Eyes Only" for someone, even though I was not the addressee. And by the time I read this one, as a consultant to the Office of the Secretary of Defense, it was already routine for me to read Top Secret documents. But I had never before seen one marked "For the President's Eyes Only." And I never did again.

The deputy assistant to the president for national security, Bob Komer, showed it to me. A cover sheet identified it as the answer to a question that President Kennedy had addressed to the Joint Chiefs of Staff a week earlier. Komer showed their response to me because I had drafted the question, which Komer had sent in the president's name.

The question to the Joint Chiefs was this: "If your plans for general [nuclear] war are carried out as planned, how many people will be killed in the Soviet Union and China?"

Their answer was in the form of a graph. The vertical axis showed the number of deaths, in millions. The horizontal axis showed the amount of time, in months. The graph was a straight line, starting at time zero on the horizontal, with the vertical axis indicating the number of immediate deaths expected within hours of our attack, and then slanting upward to a maximum at six months—an arbitrary cutoff for the deaths that would accumulate over time from initial injuries and from fallout radiation. The representation below is from memory; it was impossible to forget.

The lowest number, at the left of the graph, was 275 million deaths. The number on the right-hand side, at six months, was 325 million.

That same morning, I had drafted another question to be sent to the Joint Chiefs over the president's signature, asking for a total breakdown of global deaths from our own attacks, to include not only the Sino-Soviet bloc but all other countries that would be affected by fallout as

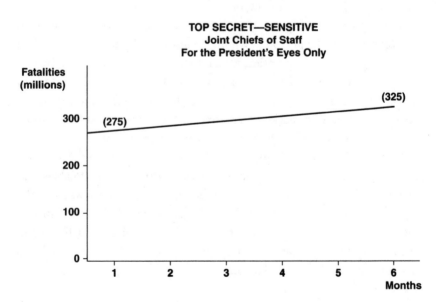

TOP SECRET—SENSITIVE
Joint Chiefs of Staff
For the President's Eyes Only

well. Komer showed it to me a week later, this time in the form of a table with explanatory footnotes.

In sum, another hundred million deaths, roughly, were predicted in Eastern Europe, from direct attacks on Warsaw Pact bases and air defenses and from fallout. There might be a hundred million more from fallout in Western Europe, depending on which way the wind blew (a matter, largely, of the season). But regardless of the season, another hundred million deaths, at least, were predicted from fallout in the mostly neutral countries adjacent to the Soviet bloc and China, including Finland, Sweden, Austria, Afghanistan, India, and Japan. Finland, for example, would be wiped out by fallout from U.S. ground-burst explosions on the Soviet submarine pens in Leningrad.

The total death toll as calculated by the Joint Chiefs, from a U.S. first strike aimed at the Soviet Union, its Warsaw Pact satellites, and China, would be roughly six hundred million dead. A hundred Holocausts.

I remember what I thought when I first held the single sheet with the graph on it. I thought, This piece of paper should not exist. It should never have existed. Not in America. Not anywhere, ever. It depicted evil beyond any human project ever. There should be nothing on earth, nothing real, that it referred to.

One of the principal expected effects of this plan—partly intended, partly (in allied, neutral, and satellite countries) undesired but foreseeable and accepted "collateral damage"—was summarized on that second piece of paper, which I held a week later in the spring of 1961: the extermination of over half a billion people.

From that day on, I have had one overriding life purpose: to prevent the execution of any such plan.

Introduction

There was a secret well-kept during the two years I was under indictment for copying the Top Secret Pentagon Papers and during the two years of Watergate investigations that followed—and for more than forty years since. On my defense team during the trial, it was known, aside from by me, only by my principal attorney, Leonard Boudin. Not by his associate lawyers; not by my co-defendant, Tony Russo; not even by my wife, Patricia.

During my trial in Los Angeles I was often asked by reporters, in particular Peter Schrag, who was writing a book about the case, "How much time did you spend copying? How long did it take?" I always answered vaguely and changed the subject. A realistic estimate would have indicated that it was a lot longer than was necessary to copy the Pentagon Papers alone. It would have led to a question that I wanted to avoid then: "What else did you copy?"

The fact is that from the fall of 1969 to leaving the RAND Corporation in August 1970, I copied everything in the Top Secret safe in my office—of which the seven thousand pages of the Pentagon Papers were only a fraction—and a good deal more from my several safes for files classified Secret or Confidential, perhaps fifteen thousand pages in all. I made several copies of each. I intended to disclose it all, not just the Pentagon Papers. That intent, along with the nature of these other documents, was the secret kept from the time of my copying until now.

Many of these other documents also had to do with Vietnam, including Top Secret work I had done in late 1968 and early 1969 for Henry Kissinger after president-elect Richard Nixon had named him as the assistant for national security affairs. But most of what else I copied—"the other Pentagon Papers"—consisted of my notes and studies on classified nuclear war planning, the command and control of nuclear weapons, and studies of nuclear crises. They included verbatim extracts or copies of critical documents, past war plans (none of which were, at the time, current), cables, and studies by me and by others, including some on nuclear policy by Kissinger's National Security Council staff.

Most of those who have heard my name at all in the past forty-seven years have known me only in connection with my release of the Top Secret study of U.S. decision-making in the Vietnam War that became known as the Pentagon Papers. They may also know that I came to have access to that study because I had helped produce it, and that I had earlier worked on Vietnam escalation in the Pentagon and then for the State Department in South Vietnam.

What is less known is that for years before that, I had worked as a consultant from the RAND Corporation at the highest levels of the U.S. national security system on completely different issues: deterring and averting—or if necessary, however hopeless the attempt, trying to control, limit, and terminate—a nuclear Armageddon between the superpowers. RAND (an acronym for Research and Development) was a nonprofit organization incorporated in 1948 to do mainly classified research and analysis for the Air Force.

In the spring of 1961 I drafted the Top Secret guidance issued by Secretary of Defense Robert McNamara to the Joint Chiefs of Staff (JCS) for the operational plans for general nuclear war. That January I had briefed McGeorge Bundy, President Kennedy's assistant for national security, on the peculiarities and risks of the existing nuclear planning in his first weeks in office in the White House. It was soon after that I was given access in the White House to the Top Secret estimate of casualties expected from our planned nuclear attacks.

The following year I was the only person to serve on two of several working groups reporting to the Executive Committee of the National Security Council (ExComm) during the Cuban missile crisis. A year later, just before I joined the Defense Department full-time at the highest civilian supergrade level[†] († indicates additional information is available in the endnote). I was the sole researcher in an interagency study of past

U.S. nuclear crises—including Korea, Cuba, Berlin, Quemoy, Lebanon, and Suez—with classified access several levels above Top Secret. All these functions gave me an unusual knowledge, at that time almost unique for a civilian, of the nature of the plans and operations of the nuclear forces and the dangers these posed.

It was a closely held secret, until now, that soon after I had begun to copy the Pentagon Papers and other Vietnam documents from my office safes at the RAND Corporation (to which I had returned from my government service in Vietnam), I had decided that it was even more important to release the *other* contents of my safes: those bearing on nuclear matters. I wanted to reveal to Congress, to my fellow citizens, and to the world the peril that U.S. nuclear policies over the last quarter century had created. Almost no other person known to me had the experience—let alone the will—to expose the breadth and intensity of those dangers, with documents as well as notes as detailed as mine. The documents, I felt, were essential to the credibility of what were otherwise almost unimaginable secret realities.

I told just one person what I was doing in this respect and what I intended to do: Randy Kehler, whose example of draft resistance had set me on this course a month earlier. He was due to report to prison shortly when I spoke with him in San Francisco in November 1969. I wanted to let him know, before he disappeared into prison, how much his example had meant to me and that it would have a tangible effect. And I wanted his advice as an activist.

His judgment was the same as mine on the relative importance of the nuclear data versus the Vietnam study that was later to be known as the Pentagon Papers. In fact, he urged me to forget about disclosing the latter at all. "By this time, we know all we need to know about Vietnam," he said. "What you reveal about that won't make any difference. From what you tell me, you're the one person who can warn the world about the dangers of our nuclear war plans. That's what you ought to put out."

I said, "I agree with you when it comes to the importance, but Vietnam is where the bombs are falling right now. If I put it all out now, including the nuclear material, the press won't pay any attention to the history about Vietnam. I think I have to give that as much of a run as I can first, for whatever difference it might make to shorten the war. Then I'll turn to the nuclear revelations."

On the basis of that tactical judgment, I had separated all the nuclear notes and documents from the Vietnam material and given them to my brother, Harry, to keep for me at his home in Hastings-on-Hudson, in Westchester County, New York.

I thought of these two sets of documents as essentially separate, to be subject to two distinct acts of disclosure, the nuclear documents later. From the time I was indicted in 1971, after nineteen newspapers had published parts of the Pentagon Papers in the face of four federal injunctions, I was saving the nuclear material for after my trial. That was why I didn't want to be asked "What else did you copy?" during the trial. I didn't want to be forced to release the nuclear documents until the Vietnam material had run its course.

I might also have waited until after the second trial we were expecting for the *distribution* of the Pentagon Papers. The charges in Los Angeles focused on the copying and retention of the documents by me and my friend and "co-conspirator" Tony Russo, who had made possible and initially helped me with the copying. A separate, secret grand jury was meeting in Boston to investigate the distribution and publication of the Pentagon Papers. It was preparing to indict me again—Tony was not involved in these later stages—along with *New York Times* reporters such as Neil Sheehan and Hedrick Smith, and perhaps others with whom I had shared some of the documents, including Noam Chomsky, Howard Zinn, and Richard Falk.

I expected that my third trial—for putting out the nuclear secrets I was determined to expose—was going to be the killer for me. I wouldn't beat that one. It would nail down the prosecutors' efforts to give me a life sentence—which had actually started with the first trial—and they would almost surely succeed this time, if not on the earlier attempts.

Things didn't turn out that way, for rather extraordinary reasons. First, after I had spent nearly two years in court facing a possible sentence of 115 years, the twelve felony counts in my initial trial were dismissed with prejudice (meaning, I couldn't be tried again on these charges), after exposure of White House criminal misconduct against me during the prosecution.

It turned out eventually that President Nixon had secretly been informed that I had copied material beyond the Pentagon Papers from his own National Security Council. He plausibly feared that I could reveal and document his secret threats to North Vietnam of escalations, including nuclear attacks, aiming essentially to win the war. To avert my possible exposure of his secret demands and threats—which had already prolonged the war for two years, widened it to Cambodia and Laos, and which would ultimately add twenty thousand American names to the Vietnam Memorial—he had set in motion a variety of criminal steps to keep me silent about his secret policy.

These crimes against me—including warrantless wiretaps, burglary of my former psychoanalyst's office seeking blackmail material, illegal use of the CIA, and an abortive effort to "totally incapacitate" me—when they were revealed, were a critical part of the impeachment proceedings that led to Nixon's resignation, which made the war endable nine months later. Since these same crimes would have tainted a second prosecution for distribution of the Pentagon Papers, the Boston grand jury was abruptly terminated, and the second trial was averted.

Yet in the end, it wasn't the White House, or its crimes, that stopped me from disclosing to the world in the mid-seventies, or after, the thousands of pages of notes and documents on a possible nuclear holocaust that I had begun to copy from my safe at RAND four years earlier. It was an act of nature: a tropical storm. An act of grace, my wife, Patricia, calls it, since—though it frustrated my deepest plans and caused me great anguish—it allowed me to sleep next to her, in loving embrace, for the last forty years instead of in prison.

After I had entrusted my nuclear papers to Harry, he kept them for almost two years, until June 13, 1971, in the basement of his home in Hastings-on-Hudson, where he lived with his wife, Sofia.

Then, when the *New York Times* and the *Washington Post* were enjoined from publication and a manhunt was on for me and Patricia, Harry buried this material in a compost heap in his backyard, in a cardboard box inside a green garbage bag.

During the next thirteen days, while the FBI was still searching for us—as Patricia and I, with the help of friends and a pickup team of antiwar recruits (a "Lavender Hill Mob," as I thought of them, in honor of Alec Guinness) were putting out other copies of the Vietnam history to seventeen more newspapers—Harry transferred them again. It was good that he did. The very next day, his neighbor told him that she had observed men in civilian clothes probing his compost heap with long metal rods.

Just in time, Harry had buried the box, inside its bag, in the town trash dump. He had dug out a space for it into the side of a bluff rising above the dirt road that bordered the dump. There was an old gas stove resting on the bluff just above the burial spot, to identify it.

But that summer, not long after I had been indicted, a near-hurricane (tropical storm Doria) hit Hastings-on-Hudson. The bluff and its contents collapsed over the roadway and down the slope below it. The stove was blown down and rolled a hundred feet or more from its last position. Harry didn't tell me right away, not until he had spent days and then weeks trying to find the lost box.

Then he and his friend Barbara Denyer and her husband spent weekend after weekend searching. At one point they rented a backhoe bulldozer to turn up the dirt in the dump. (The driver, a town employee, got in trouble when it came out that he had allowed the bulldozer to be used for a private purpose. Barbara had told him she was looking for a thesis manuscript that had been put in the trash by mistake.)

All this led to the discovery of more than one green garbage bag— perhaps a thousand of them, in the trash dump—but none with Top Secret documents inside. Denyer's husband quit the project—her weekend obsession had put a strain on their marriage—and eventually Harry did too, though Barbara continued to look for most of a year, sometimes with her daughter.

Meanwhile, I was on trial and not thinking much about the revelations still to come. Harry's heroic efforts kept me thinking that eventually the treasure would be found. That didn't wane until nearly the end of the trial, when he reported that much of the contents of the dump had been moved to become landfill for the foundation of a condominium nearby, which was about to be covered with concrete. There might no longer be any way to get at the missing box, he said, without using dynamite. A joke. The documents were lost.

Forty-five years have gone by, and most of what was buried then has remained secret. What a backhoe or dynamite could not pry loose, the Freedom of Information Act has not (with many important exceptions) freed from the safes where this information has wrongfully been sequestered for half a century. Yet a good deal of what was lost has since been declassified, in particular over the last thirty-two years by FOIA requests and tenacious appeals by William Burr for the National Security Archive of George Washington University, and even earlier by Fred Kaplan for his remarkably revealing account, *The Wizards of Armageddon* (1983), an exemplary work of investigative scholarship (using interviews as well as FOIA suits) on contemporary, classified history. Enough has been released by now to corroborate, in great part, the account that follows.

Moreover, taking advantage of the digital era, I will put all my files, memos, and notes, and my outtakes from this manuscript, on my website, ellsberg.net. And there are scores of important subjects closely related to what is presented here that I had neither time nor space to include in this book, especially dealing with developments and events after my own participation in the sixties. Many of those I aim to deal with on my website or elsewhere on the Internet.[†]

Those memos and documents that are referred to in this book can be found on my website under the heading Doomsday. That includes all my documents and notes still in my possession from my work at RAND, at the Pentagon, and in Vietnam in the fifties and sixties, including in particular very voluminous files on the Cuban missile crisis and the Quemoy crisis of 1958, and my drafts of the 1961 guidance for the JSCP and accompanying memos. There will also be on a continuing basis additional notes on this text, keyed to pages in the published edition, for which there is no room in the endnotes published here. I will be publishing there and/or elsewhere commentaries on current events to which the themes discussed here are relevant, the ongoing North Korean nuclear crisis for one.

*   *   *

From the account that follows, backed up by recently declassified documents (many cited in the endnotes) and the notes and files that will be available on my website, it should become clear why it seemed unquestionably worth my freedom, worth risking life in prison, to expose these truths almost half a century ago. I would certainly seize that risk today if I still had the same or comparable inside documentation that I had then. Lacking that, I have tried in many ways and venues (though not before in a narrative or a book of my own) to awaken audiences of Americans and others to the substance of what I then wanted to reveal: precisely because I do not believe it is just history. Tragically, I believe that nothing has fundamentally changed.

So far as I can tell from continuous and close reading of the open literature—which is incomparably more detailed and revealing than that of the sixties and seventies, but not, of course, the last word—a well-informed briefing of an incoming presidential assistant for national security in 2017 would be closely equivalent to the one I delivered to President John Kennedy's assistant McGeorge Bundy in January 1961 (see chapter 7), plus what I would have added for Bundy just a few years later. (Findings in the following pages on nuclear winter, however, were revealed only decades after that, as were key aspects of the Cuban missile crisis and some false alarms.) In partial summary of this book, I would tell that assistant (or President Trump himself, if he would accept a briefing) what I had learned, mostly in the late fifties and early sixties:

- The basic elements of American readiness for nuclear war remain today what they were almost sixty years ago: Thousands of nuclear weapons remain on hair-trigger alert, aimed mainly at Russian military targets including command and control, many in or near cities. The *declared* official rationale for such a system has always been primarily the supposed need to deter—or if necessary respond to—an aggressive Russian nuclear first strike against the United States. That widely believed public rationale is a deliberate deception. Deterring a surprise Soviet nuclear attack—or responding to such an attack—has *never* been the only or even the primary purpose of our nuclear plans and preparations. The nature, scale, and posture of our strategic nuclear forces has always been shaped by the requirements of quite different purposes: to attempt to limit the damage to the United States from Soviet or Russian retaliation to a *U.S. first strike* against the USSR or Russia. This capability is, in particular, intended to strengthen the credibility of U.S. threats to initiate limited nuclear attacks, or escalate them—U.S. threats of "first use"—to prevail in regional, initially non-nuclear conflicts involving Soviet or Russian forces or their allies.*

---

*Though there will be little Pentagon jargon in this book—and almost no footnotes—some matters of terminology will be recurrent. In particular, in technical language, a "first strike"—by one of the two superpowers, U.S. or Soviet Union/Russia—is distinguished from "first *use*" of nuclear weapons by any one of the now nine nuclear weapons states (NWS).

The former, first strike, refers to a full-scale attempt by a superpower—Soviet Union/Russia or the United States—to disarm as fully as possible the superpower opponent, to prevent or limit its retaliation, by initiating an attack mainly by long-range, relatively high-yield "strategic" weapons against all the enemy's military forces, especially its strategic nuclear forces in its homeland or at sea.

The latter term, "first use," by the United States or other nuclear weapons states, refers to any possible initiation of nuclear attacks *other than* a first strike, whether the opponent is nuclear-armed or is a non-nuclear-armed state (NNWS) (as was the case of U.S first use against Japan in 1945).

Nine states have some strategic weapons, though none but the United States and Soviet Union/Russia have ever had a "first strike" capability, the ability to attempt to disarm a nuclear-armed opponent. Along with their longer-range strategic weapons, all

- The required U.S. strategic capabilities have always been for a *first-strike* force: not, under any president, for a U.S. surprise attack, unprovoked or "a bolt out of the blue," but not, either, with an aim of striking "second" under any circumstances, if that can be avoided by preemption. Though officially denied, preemptive "launch on warning" (LOW)—either on tactical warning of an incoming attack or strategic warning that nuclear escalation is probably impending—has always been at the heart of our strategic alert.

- During the 2016 presidential campaign, Donald J. Trump was reported to have asked a foreign policy advisor, about nuclear weapons, "If we have them, why can't we use them?" Correct answer: We do. Contrary to the cliché that "no nuclear weapons have been used since Hiroshima and Nagasaki," U.S. presidents *have used* our nuclear weapons dozens of times in "crises," mostly in secret from the American public (though not from adversaries). They have used them in the precise way that a gun is used when it is pointed at someone in a confrontation, whether or not the trigger is pulled. To get one's way without pulling the trigger is a major purpose for owning the gun. (See chapter 20.)

  Moreover, our "extended deterrence" over allies in Europe or Japan rests on our preparedness and our frequently reiterated readiness to carry out threats of *first use* (initiation of limited nuclear attacks with short-range tactical weapons) and/or, implicitly, to carry out a disarming *first strike* on the homeland of the USSR or Russia, mostly with long-range strategic weapons, in response to large *non-nuclear* attacks by its conventional forces or those of its allies.

  As candidate in 2016, now President Donald J. Trump repeatedly asserted his unwillingness to take nuclear first-use threats "off the table" in *any* conflict, including with ISIS, or in Europe.

---

of them have had—and all but France and Britain retain—shorter-range, lower-yield "tactical" nuclear weapons with which to threaten or carry out first use against either a NNWS or a NWS opponent.

To launch a disarming, "damage-limiting" first strike on the expectation—possibly based on short-term "tactical warning" from radars or space satellites—of an imminent or ongoing first strike by the opponent is known as "preempting," or, ironically, "striking second first."

(He also said that he would be "the last to use nuclear weapons"—unless, evidently, he were the first.) In the first debate of the presidential campaign, he was asked: "On nuclear weapons, President Obama reportedly considered changing the nation's long-standing policy [i.e., changing it to no-first-use]. Do you support the current policy?"

Given two minutes to answer, Trump said, among other things: "I would like everybody to end it, just get rid of it. But I would certainly not do first strike.* I think that once the nuclear alternative happens, it's over. At the same time, we have to be prepared. I can't take anything off the table."

In her two minutes, Hillary Clinton managed not to repeat Trump's words about the table, or to respond to the question at all except to "reassure our allies . . . that we have mutual defense treaties and we will honor them." But clearly if she had been pressed, the former secretary of state would have given substantially the same answer as Trump did in all his interviews. Our mutual defense treaties have never excluded U.S. first use of nuclear weapons. (As a candidate in 2008, rebuking Senator Barack Obama for saying he would *not* use nuclear weapons against Pakistan, she said that no president should ever say what weapons he or she would or would not use.)

In the meantime, up through 2016, President Obama, under pressure to reject a no-first-use policy from his secretaries of defense, state, and energy as well as U.S. allies, complied with such advice both in his 2010 *Nuclear Posture Review* and in his last year in office. He was continuing a policy of threatening possible American initiation of nuclear war that has, outside public awareness, characterized *every* American administration since Truman's. Inheriting this policy and reiterating it, President Donald J. Trump continues to apply what Richard Nixon called the "madman theory," with, as some see it with unease, more plausibility than some of his predecessors.

- Posing as it does the threat of nuclear attack by the United States to every state that might potentially be in conflict with us (like North Korea), this persistent rejection by the United States of

---

*See footnote on page 12, on "first strike" versus "first use"; the question was about the latter.

a no-first-use commitment has always precluded an effective nonproliferation campaign. So it does at this time under President Trump. Indeed, it has encouraged proliferation in states hoping either to counter these American threats or to imitate them. But other aspects of U.S. nuclear policy as well have the same outcome, effectively promoting proliferation. Of course, our insistence on maintaining an arsenal of thousands of weapons, many on alert, a quarter century into the post–Cold War era, nullifies our advice to most other states in the world that they "have no need" or justification for producing a single nuclear weapon.

- With respect to deliberate, authorized U.S. strategic attacks, the system has always been designed to be triggered by a far wider range of events than the public has ever imagined. Moreover, the hand authorized to pull the trigger on U.S. nuclear forces has *never* been exclusively that of the president, nor even his highest military officials. (See chapters 3 and 7.)

As I discovered in my command and control research in the late fifties, President Eisenhower had secretly delegated authority to initiate nuclear attacks to his theater commanders under various circumstances, including the outage of communications with Washington (a daily occurrence in the Pacific) or a presidential incapacitation (which Eisenhower suffered twice). And with his authorization, they had in turn delegated this initiative, under comparable crisis conditions, to subordinate commanders.

To my surprise, after I had alerted the Kennedy White House to this policy and its dangers, President Kennedy continued it (rather than reverse the decision of the "great commander" who had preceded him). So did Presidents Johnson, Nixon, and Carter. So, almost certainly, has every subsequent president to this day, even though in the past several decades there may have been at least nominal "devolution" to *some* civilian outside Washington. This delegation has been one of our highest national secrets.

The same was true for the Soviet Union, now Russia. Public discussion of American plans for "decapitation" of Soviet command and control led to the institution and maintenance of a "Dead Hand" system of delegation that would assure retaliation to an American attack that destroyed Moscow and other command centers. This, too, has been treated as a state secret:

paradoxically, since on both sides the secrecy and denial diminish deterrence of a decapitating attack against it (see chapter 9).

An urgent reason for enlightening the world's public on this reality of the nuclear era is that it is virtually certain that this same secret delegation exists in every nuclear state, including the new ones: Israel, India, Pakistan, and North Korea. How many fingers are on Pakistani nuclear buttons? Probably not even the president of Pakistan knows reliably. Meanwhile, frequent leaked reports in the American press throughout 2016 and 2017 of U.S. contingency plans and exercises aimed in crucial part at decapitating North Korean leadership and command structure have, in my opinion, very probably had the effect in that country of creating a Soviet-like Dead Hand system for assuring retaliation to such an attack.

- Thanks to revelations from the former Soviet Union, there has been growing appreciation of the extreme dangers posed by the Cuban missile crisis. Yet my own highly classified study in 1964—following my high-level staff participation in the crisis— unearthed never-before-revealed details that, together with the new data, demonstrate that the risks were even higher than any previous account has concluded. Despite what I believe was the determination of both leaders to avoid nuclear war, events spiraled out of control, coming within a handbreadth of triggering our plans for general nuclear war. (See chapters 12 and 13.)

- The strategic nuclear system is more prone to false alarms, accidents, and unauthorized launches than the public (and even most high officials) has ever been aware. This was my special focus of classified investigation in 1958–61. Later studies have confirmed the persistence of these risks, with particularly serious false alarms in 1979, 1980, 1983, and 1995. The chance that this system could explode "by mistake" or unauthorized action in a crisis— as well as by the deliberate execution of nuclear threats—taking much of the world with it, has always been an unconscionable risk imposed by the superpowers upon the population of the world.

- Potentially catastrophic dangers such as these have been systematically concealed from the public. In 1961 I had learned as an insider that our secret nuclear decision-making, policy, plans, and practices for general nuclear war endangered, by the JCS estimate, hundreds of millions of people, perhaps a third of the earth's population. What none of us knew at that time—not the Joint Chiefs, not the president or his science advisors, not anyone else for the next two decades, until 1983—were the phenomena of nuclear winter and nuclear famine, which meant that a large nuclear war of the kind we prepared for then or later would kill nearly every human on earth (along with most other large species). (See chapter 18.)

It is the smoke, after all (not the fallout, which would remain mostly limited to the northern hemisphere), that would do it worldwide: smoke and soot *lofted* by fierce firestorms in hundreds of burning cities into the stratosphere, where it would not rain out and would remain for a decade or more, enveloping the globe and blocking most sunlight, lowering annual global temperatures to the level of the last Ice Age, and killing all harvests worldwide, causing near-universal starvation within a year or two.

U.S. plans for thermonuclear war in the early sixties, if carried out in the Berlin or Cuban missile crises, would have killed many times more than the six hundred million people predicted by the JCS. They would have caused nuclear winter that would have starved to death nearly everyone then living: at that time three billion.

The numbers of warheads on both sides have since declined greatly—by over 80 percent!—from their highest levels in the sixties. Yet by the most recent scientific calculations—confirming and even strengthening the initial warnings of more than thirty years ago—even a fraction of the existing smaller arsenals would be more than enough to cause nuclear winter today, on the basis of existing plans that target command and control centers and other objectives in or near cities. In other words, first-strike nuclear attacks by either side very much smaller than were planned in the sixties and seventies—and which are still prepared for instant execution in both Russia and America—would still kill by loss of sunlight and resulting starvation nearly all the humans on earth, now over seven billion.

There would be no limiting of damage to the superpower attacker—or to its allies, or the "enemy" population or that of neutrals throughout the globe—by its superpower adversary striking first rather than second (even without suffering retaliation), or by its preemption, "counterforce," or "decapitation" attacks, in short by any of the missions the great bulk of its weapons are specifically designed and intended to do. Damage to itself, and to everyone else, from its own first strike would be total, unlimited.

There is no sign that the findings of the latest scientific peer-reviewed studies of climatic consequences of nuclear war over the past decade have penetrated the consciousness of U.S. officials or Russian officials or have influenced in any way their nuclear deployments or arms-control negotiations.

There is good reason to doubt that either George W. Bush or Barack Obama—or, for that matter, George H. W. Bush or Bill Clinton in the previous twenty years since the original studies—was ever, once, briefed on the scale of this result of the large "options" he was presented with in nuclear command exercises. (Gorbachev has reported that he was strongly influenced by Soviet studies of this phenomenon, which underlay his desire to seek massive reductions and even the elimination of nuclear weapons in his discussions with Reagan, who made a similar attribution.)[†]

Whether or not President Donald Trump has been briefed on this (almost surely not), both he and several of his cabinet officials, along with leaders of the Republican majority in Congress, are famous deniers of the scientific authority of such findings, based as they are on the most advanced climate models.

*   *   *

At the conclusion of his famous satirical film of 1964, *Dr. Strangelove*, Stanley Kubrick introduced the concept of a "Doomsday Machine"—designed to deter nuclear attack on the Soviet Union by destroying all human life as an automatized response to such an attack. His Russian leader had fatefully installed the system before he had revealed it to the world, and it was now subject to being triggered by a single nuclear explosion from an American B-52 sent off by a rogue commander without presidential authorization.

Kubrick had borrowed the name and the very concept of such a hypothetical machine from my former colleague Herman Kahn, a RAND physicist with whom he had discussed it. In his 1960 book *On Thermonuclear War* and in popular articles in 1961, Kahn had said he was sure he could design such a device. It could be produced within ten years and would be relatively cheap, one of its main attractions as a deterrent system. It would cost closer to ten than to a hundred billion dollars, he guessed—only a fraction of the current budget for strategic weapons—since it could be emplaced in one's own country or in the ocean. It would not depend on sending warheads halfway around the world by expensive planes and missiles that would have to penetrate enemy defenses.

But, he said, it was obviously undesirable. It would be too uncontrollable—too inflexible and automatic—and it might fail to deter, and its failure "kills too many people": in fact, everyone, a result that the philosopher John Somerville later termed "omnicide." Kahn was sure in 1961 that no such system had been built, *nor would it be,* by either the United States or the Soviet Union.

The physicist Edward Teller, known as the "father of the H-bomb," went further to deny that omnicide—a concept he derided—was remotely feasible. In answer to a question I posed to him as late as 1982, he said emphatically it was *"impossible"* to kill by any imaginable use of thermonuclear weapons that he had co-invented "more than a quarter of the earth's population."

At the time, I thought of this assurance, ironically, as his perception of "the glass being three-quarters full." (Teller was, along with Kahn, Henry Kissinger, and the former Nazi missile designer Wernher von Braun, one of Kubrick's inspirations for the character of Dr. Strangelove.) And Teller's estimate was closely in line with what the JCS actually planned to do in 1961, though a better estimate (allowing for the direct effects of fire, which JSC calculations have always omitted) would have been closer to one-third to one-half of total omnicide.

But the JCS were mistaken in 1961, and so was Herman Kahn in 1960,[†] and so was Teller in 1982. Nobody's perfect. Just one year after Teller had made this negative assertion (at a hearing of the California state legislature which we both addressed, on the Bilateral Nuclear Weapons Freeze Initiative), the first papers appeared on the nuclear-winter effects of smoke injected into the stratosphere by firestorms generated by a thousand or more of the fifty thousand existing H-bombs used on cities. Contrary to Kahn and Teller, an American Doomsday Machine already existed in 1961—and had for years—in the form of pre-targeted bombers on alert in the Strategic Air Command (SAC), soon to be joined by Polaris submarine-launched missiles. Although this machine wasn't likely to kill outright or starve to death literally every last human, its effects, once triggered, would come close enough to that to deserve the name Doomsday.

* * *

Like discussion of covert operations and assassination plots, nuclear war plans and threats are taboo for public discussion by the small minority of officials and consultants who know anything about them. In addition to their own sense of identity as trustworthy keepers of these most-sensitive secrets, there is a strong careerist aspect to their silence. Such officials have been concerned to maintain their high clearances, their access, and their possibility of being consultants after they've left service. This seamless discretion, coupled with systematic official secrecy, lying, and obfuscation has created extremely deficient scholarly and journalistic understanding and almost total public *and congressional* ignorance.

In sum, most aspects of the U.S. nuclear planning system and force readiness that became known to me half a century ago still exist today, as prone to catastrophe as ever but on a scale, as now known to environmental scientists, looming vastly larger than was understood then. The present risks of the current nuclear era go far beyond the dangers of proliferation and non-state terrorism that have been the almost exclusive focus of public concern for the past generation and the past decade in particular. The arsenals and plans of the two superpowers represent not only an insuperable obstacle to an effective global anti-proliferation campaign; they are in themselves a clear and present existential danger to the human species, and most others.

The hidden reality I aim to expose is that for over fifty years, all-out thermonuclear war—an irreversible, unprecedented, and almost unimaginable calamity for civilization and most life on earth—has been, like the disasters of Chernobyl, Katrina, the Gulf oil spill, Fukushima Daiichi, and before these, World War I, *a catastrophe waiting to happen*, on a scale infinitely greater than any of these. And that is still true today.

No policies in human history have more deserved to be recognized as immoral. Or insane. The story of how this calamitous predicament came about and how and why it has persisted for over half a century is a chronicle of human madness. Whether Americans, Russians, and other humans can rise to the challenge of reversing these policies and eliminating the danger of near-term extinction caused by their own inventions and proclivities remains to be seen. I choose to join with others in acting *as if* that is still possible.

PART I

The Bomb and I

CHAPTER 1

How Could I?

The Making of a Nuclear War Planner

If the Doomsday Machine is ever to be dismantled, it would be well to have some understanding of how it came to be constructed and maintained. *How could we?* How could Americans—or, for that matter, Russians—ever have done this?

I plan to come at this question from several directions, but first I'll address it to myself. *How did I* come in my late twenties to be working on guidance for nuclear war plans—plans that I knew, if they were ever enacted, would kill hundreds of millions of humans (and, in reality, far more than that)?

That question is a loaded one for me. My eventual participation is especially ironic in view of my own earliest attitudes toward bombing and my unusual introduction to the nuclear age. An intense abhorrence of both population bombing and nuclear weapons went back to my childhood during World War II. A year before Pearl Harbor, when I was nine years old, newsreels of the London Blitz impressed me with the incomprehensible cruelty of the Nazis. The demolition and burning of cities filled with people of all ages seemed to express their demonic character.

In grade school after Pearl Harbor, we had air raid drills. One day my teacher handed out a model of a short, slim silver-colored incendiary bomb, which was used to spread fires. We were told it was a magnesium bomb, whose blaze couldn't be extinguished by water. You had to cover it with sand to keep oxygen from feeding the flames. In every room in our school there was a large bucket filled with sand for this purpose. I take it that this was a way of making us identify with the war effort, the likelihood of German or Japanese bombers penetrating as far as Detroit being quite small in retrospect. But the notion of the magnesium bomb made a strong impression on me. It was uncanny to think of humans designing and dropping on other humans a flaming substance that couldn't easily be extinguished, a particle of which, we were told, would burn through flesh to the bone and wouldn't stop burning even then. It was hard for me to understand people who were willing to burn children like that.

Later newsreels showed American and British bombers bravely flying through flak to drop their loads on targets in Germany. I believed what we were told—that our daylight precision bombing was aimed only at war factories and military targets (even if, regrettably, some civilians were also hit by accident).

My own father, a structural engineer in Detroit, was helping to send most of the American bombers. At the start of the war, he was the chief structural engineer in charge of designing the Ford Willow Run plant, a factory for making B-24 Liberator bombers for the Air Corps. He told me that it was the largest industrial building under one roof in the world. It put together bombers the way Ford produced cars, on an assembly line. The assembly line was a mile and a quarter long.

Once my father took me out to Willow Run to see the line in operation. For as far as I could see, the huge metal bodies of planes hanging from hooks were moving along tracks with workers riveting and installing parts as they moved. It was an exciting sight for a twelve-year-old, and I was proud of my father. His next wartime job was to design a still larger airplane engine factory—again the world's largest plant under one roof: the Dodge Chicago plant, which made the engines for B-29s.

I certainly didn't know that his bombers would, increasingly, be dropping incendiaries of the same kind we had handled in school—magnesium, or other substances like white phosphorus and napalm, with similar characteristics of clinging to flesh and burning inextinguishably. I doubt Dad knew that either. We never saw films of what was happening on the ground under our planes or in the firestorms in Hamburg, Dresden, or Tokyo.

And if I had been fully aware how commonly—particularly in the B-29 raids over Japan—we were imitating Nazi terror bombing practices, how would I have reacted? I don't really know. Perhaps any concerns would have been quieted by the thoughts that *they* had started the war and the bombing of cities, that retaliation was fair and necessary, and that anything that would help win a war against such atrocious foes was justified.

Those same thoughts might have reassured me about the use of atomic bombs on Japan, as they did for most Americans, if it hadn't been for an unusual classroom experience I had had in the last year of the war. Unlike nearly every other American outside the Manhattan Project, my first awareness of the challenges of the nuclear era had occurred some nine months earlier than the announcement of the destruction of Hiroshima, and in a crucially different context.

This occurred in a ninth-grade social studies class in the fall of 1944. I was thirteen, a boarding student on full scholarship at Cranbrook, a private school in Bloomfield Hills, Michigan. Our teacher, Bradley Patterson, was discussing a concept that was familiar then in sociology: William F. Ogburn's notion of "cultural lag."

The idea was that the development of technology regularly moved much further and faster than other aspects of culture: our institutions of government, values, habits, ethics, and understanding of society and ourselves. Indeed, the very notion of progress referred mainly to technology. What lagged behind, what developed more slowly or not at all, was everything that bore on our ability to direct technology and to *control* it wisely, ethically, prudently.

To illustrate this, Mr. Patterson posed a potential advance in technology that might soon be realized. It was possible now, he told us, to conceive of a bomb made of U-235, an isotope of uranium, which would have an explosive power a thousand times greater than the largest bombs being used in the present war. German scientists in late 1938 had discovered that uranium could be split by nuclear fission in a way that would release immense amounts of energy.

Several popular articles about the possibility of atomic bombs and specifically U-235 bombs appeared during the war in journals like the *Saturday Evening Post* and some sci-fi magazines. Though each of these articles led to secret investigations of security breaches within the Manhattan Project, whose existence was Top Secret, none of them actually represented leaks. In every case it turned out they had been inspired by earlier articles on the subject that had been published freely in 1939 and 1940, before scientific self-censorship and then formal classification had set in. Mr. Patterson had come across one of these wartime articles.

He brought the potential development to us as an example of one more possible leap by science and technology ahead of our social institutions.

Suppose, then, that one nation, or several, chose to explore the possibility of making this uranium isotope into a bomb and succeeded. What would be the probable implications of this for humanity? How would it be used by humans and states as they were today? Would it be, on balance, bad or good for the world? Would it be a force for peace, for example, or for destruction? We were to write a short essay on this due in a week's time.

I recall the conclusions I came to in my paper after thinking about it for a few days. As I remember, everyone in the class had arrived at much the same judgment. It seemed pretty obvious: the existence of such a bomb would be bad news for humanity. Mankind could not handle such a destructive force. It could not be safely controlled. The power would be "abused"—that is, used dangerously, with terrible consequences.

A bomb like that was just too powerful. Bad enough that bombs already existed that could destroy a whole city block. They were called "block-busters": ten to twenty tons of high explosive. Humanity didn't need the prospect of bombs a thousand times more powerful, single bombs that could destroy whole cities. Civilization, perhaps our species, would be in danger of destruction.

As I recall, this conclusion didn't depend mainly on who had the bomb, or how many had it, or who got it first. It would be a bad development, on balance, even if democratic countries got it first. After we turned in our papers and discussed them in class, it was many months before I thought of the issues again. I remember the moment when I did.

It was a hot August day in Detroit. I was standing on a downtown street corner, looking at the front page of the *Detroit News* in a news rack. A streetcar rattled by on the tracks as I read the headline: a single American bomb had destroyed a Japanese city. My first thought: "I know exactly what that bomb was." It was the U-235 bomb we had discussed in school and written papers about the previous fall.

I thought: *We got it first. And we used it. On a city.*

I had a sense of dread, a feeling that something very dangerous for humanity had just happened. A feeling, new to me as an American, at fourteen, that my country might have made a terrible mistake. I was glad when the war ended nine days later, but it didn't make me think that my first reaction on August 6 was wrong.

I felt uneasy in the days ahead, about the triumphal tone in Harry Truman's voice on the radio—flat and Midwestern as always, but unusually celebratory—as he exulted over our success in the race for the bomb and its effectiveness over Japan. This suggested, for me, that our leaders didn't have the full picture, didn't grasp the significance of the precedent they had set and the sinister implications for the future.

Unlikely thoughts for a fourteen-year-old American boy to have had the week the war ended? Yes, if he hadn't been in Mr. Patterson's social studies class the previous fall. All members of that class must have had the same flash of recognition of the bomb as they read the August headlines during our summer vacation.

And we were set apart from our fellow Americans in another important way. Perhaps no others outside our class or the Manhattan Project *ever* had occasion to think about the bomb—as we had, nine months earlier—without the strongly biasing positive associations that accompanied their first awareness of it in August 1945: that it was "our" weapon, an instrument of American democracy, developed to deter a Nazi bomb, a war-winning weapon and a *necessary* one—so it was claimed and almost universally believed—to have ended the war without a costly invasion of Japan.

Even if the premises of this last justification were realistic (and for many scholars of the subject whom I respect, they are not), the consequences of such beliefs in our public were bound to be fateful. Whether rightly or wrongly, we are the only country in the world that believes it won a war by bombing—specifically by bombing cities with weapons of mass destruction, firebombs, and atomic bombs—and believes that it was fully justified in doing so. It is a dangerous state of mind.

But given even a few days' reflection in the earlier period *before* a presidential fait accompli was framed in that fashion, you didn't have to be a moral prodigy to arrive at the sense of foreboding we all had in Mr. Patterson's class. It was as easily available to thirteen-year-old ninth graders as it had been to some Manhattan Project scientists, who also had the opportunity to form their judgments before the bomb was used.

The one with the earliest experience of recording such a judgment was Leo Szilard, who first conceived (and patented) the idea of a chain reaction in a heavy element like uranium. He was in London in 1933 as an émigré, having left Berlin just days after the Reichstag fire earlier that year, anticipating the Nazi dictatorship that would quickly emerge and foreseeing the subsequent European war.

On March 3, 1939, Szilard was the first person to see the flashes on an oscilloscope screen confirming his suspicion "that neutrons were emitted in the fission process of uranium and this in turn would mean that the large-scale liberation of atomic energy was just around the corner." He reports his reaction: "We watched them [the flashes] for a little while and then we switched everything off and went home. That night there was very little doubt in my mind that the world was headed for grief."

Nevertheless, later that year, expecting imminently the war he had long foreseen and fearing that Nazis might be first to exploit the potential of nuclear energy in a bomb, it was Szilard who induced Albert Einstein to send a letter, which he co-drafted, to President Franklin D. Roosevelt, urging what came to be the Manhattan Project. It was dated August 2, 1939. Hitler invaded Poland on September 1.

Almost three and a half years later, Szilard and Enrico Fermi constructed the first working nuclear reactor, which was necessary for the production of plutonium for a bomb. (The Germans never did get a reactor to work.) On December 2, 1942, Szilard recounts in his memoir, a chain reaction was actually initiated and controlled for a very brief period at Stagg Field on the University of Chicago campus. Someone brought out a scarce wartime bottle of Chianti and most present celebrated and congratulated Fermi. Szilard reports: "There was a crowd there and then Fermi and I stayed there alone. I shook hands with Fermi and I said I thought this day would go down as a black day in the history of mankind."

Yet despite this extreme, and fully justified, foreboding, Szilard was playing a critical role in bringing this ominous explosive power into the world. *How could he?* The answer is that he believed, even before others, that they were racing Hitler to the attainment of this power. It was German scientists, after all, who had first accomplished the fission of a heavy element. There seemed no reason to suppose that Germany could not stay ahead of any competitors in harnessing this unearthly energy to Hitler's unlimited ambitions for conquest. The specter of a possible German monopoly, even a temporary one, on an atomic bomb drove the Manhattan Project scientists—above all the Jewish émigrés from Europe like Szilard (Fermi had left Italy in 1938 because his wife was Jewish)—until the day of Germany's surrender.

In reality the race was one-sided. At virtually the same time, in June 1942, that the American team of theoretical physicists was tackling the problems of bomb design, Hitler had decided *against* a bomb effort, not for moral but for practical reasons: the unlikelihood that it could be delivered during the several years he had scheduled for the war. Nevertheless, ignorant of this German choice, the scientists in the United

States focused single-mindedly on achieving a usable weapon as quickly as possible.

Some of them saw it exclusively as a means for deterring Hitler from using such a weapon, if he got it. To possess such a deterrent seemed an urgent necessity, raising no moral issues for them. One of these scientists, Joseph Rotblat, after learning from a British associate in the fall of 1944 that there was no German program to deter, promptly resigned from the Manhattan Project. The only scientist to do so, Rotblat was induced, by threat of deportation, not to reveal his reasons for leaving, lest he inspire others to emulate him.

Others, including Szilard, remaining uncertain whether Hitler might unveil this war-winning weapon at the last moment, were prepared to use the weapon against Germany if it became available before Nazi surrender. But prior to that event, there had been almost no consideration or discussion within the Manhattan Project itself of what to do with or about this capability if it were not needed either to defeat Germany or to deter a German bomb. Only after this was unmistakably clear with the German surrender did Szilard and some of his colleagues turn to urgent efforts to avert a unilateral U.S. test of the bomb, or to refrain from dropping it on Japan—thus, hoping to avert an inevitable U.S.-Soviet nuclear arms race. But it was too late.

* * *

We come at last to the issue with which I began this chapter. The reasons for my own lower-level involvement in shaping nuclear policy—despite my early feelings of dread about the very existence of nuclear weapons—were strikingly similar to those of Joseph Rotblat and Leo Szilard. In the late fifties, I was given what seemed good reason to believe—on the basis of highly classified official information—that we were again in a desperate race with a powerful, totalitarian opponent comparable to Nazi Germany, working to deter a nuclear Pearl Harbor attack or to avert unanswerable nuclear blackmail. As we'll see, once again this apprehension was based on illusion. But the fears were real, and they seemed to have a plausible basis. How I came to share these fears and to act on them is a story with two parts.

First, like my older colleagues at that time and like so many among my generation in America, I had become a Cold Warrior over the preceding decade. I had taken some note when Churchill, one of my heroes since the Battle of Britain, proclaimed in March 1946 that an "iron curtain" had descended across the continent, dividing free Europe from tyrannical rule in the East. Less than a year after the defeat of the Nazis and their Japanese allies, he pointed to totalitarian control by Moscow of nearly all the capitals of Central and Eastern Europe, except, he said, Athens. It was to preserve precisely that exception that Harry S. Truman, the following March, called on Congress to supply aid to Greece, whose monarchy was facing a Communist-led insurrection.

My awareness of postwar foreign policy really began with this announcement of the Truman Doctrine in the spring of 1947, my junior year of high school. Truman proposed U.S. readiness to support "free peoples" anywhere from the imposition of "totalitarian regimes," a phrase he used four times in his speech. The phrase conveyed an essential equivalence between Communism and Nazism, and between Stalin and Hitler. It implied that the challenge we faced in World War II had not really ended in 1945. As a child of that war, and trusting Western leadership, I accepted that definition of the challenge and at sixteen, too young to have taken part in the earlier campaign, I was ready to rise to it.

As I followed the news in subsequent years about the Communist coup in Czechoslovakia in 1948, the Berlin blockade later that spring, the Stalinist regimes and political trials in Russia and Eastern Europe, and later the North Korean attack, I came gradually to accept all the Cold War premises and attitudes.

Looking back, the key premise was the equation of Stalin and his successors to Hitler. This was first of all in their internal totalitarian controls and ruthless repression of dissent, where the analogy (especially under Stalin) was valid. I've never lost my well-founded abhorrence of the domestic tyranny of Stalinist-style regimes—whether in the Soviet Union and Eastern Europe, China, North Korea, Vietnam, or Cuba.

More problematic, in retrospect—in fact, I would now say, flat wrong, recklessly so—was the presumption that such regimes, like Nazism, had an insatiable appetite for expansion, which they were determined to satisfy by military aggression where necessary and feasible. In particular, it was presumed that the Communist regimes in the USSR and Eastern Europe—now armed with nuclear weapons as well as superior conventional forces—posed a direct military threat to Western Europe and America even greater than Hitler's. Moreover, the equation of Communist regimes with Hitler ruled out any attempt at meaningful negotiations for the resolution of conflicts or arms control. Nothing other than full military preparedness for imminent warfare could influence or "contain" the Soviet threat to the "free world."

By the time I prepared to enter college, I was beginning to see myself, as I did for many years afterward, as a Truman Democrat: a liberal Cold Warrior, pro-labor and anti-Communist, like Senators Hubert Humphrey and Henry Jackson and like my Detroit hero Walter Reuther of the United Auto Workers.

I admired Truman's action in sending bombers filled with coal and food instead of weapons to resupply the people in Berlin during the Soviet blockade that began the month of my high school graduation. I supported his response two years later to naked Communist aggression in Korea. And I especially appreciated his decision to keep Korea a limited, conventional war, rejecting General Douglas MacArthur's recommendations to expand the war to China and to use nuclear weapons. Believing in the policy, I was prepared to go to Korea myself, though I had no eagerness for it.

After accepting student deferments until I finished Harvard and then for a year's graduate fellowship at Cambridge University, I felt an obligation to take the place that others had filled for me. On my return from Cambridge, I volunteered for officer candidate school in the Marine Corps in the fall of 1953; the first opening was the following spring.

When my two-year obligation in the Marines ended in the early summer of 1956 I requested Headquarters Marine Corps to extend it for up to a year because my unit—Third Battalion, Second Marines, in which I had been a rifle platoon leader, a battalion training officer, and a rifle company commander—was headed for a tour of sea duty in the Mediterranean with the Sixth Fleet. Gamal Abdel Nasser, the president of Egypt, had just nationalized the Suez Canal. With a Suez crisis looming, we had been alerted that our seaborne battalion might be in a war.

I had just been awarded a three-year term as a junior fellow in the Harvard Society of Fellows. But I didn't want to see the troops I'd trained and commanded go into combat without me. When headquarters granted my request to extend, I turned down the fellowship and went to the Mediterranean with my battalion.

This decade of ideological immersion as a Cold Warrior was a necessary part of what prepared me for the next decade of work as a government consultant and official on national security. But that wasn't what drew me to visit or then join the RAND Corporation in Santa Monica in the late fifties, thereby launching me on this career. As I knew, RAND did mostly classified research for the Air Force, largely on the use of nuclear weapons. Nothing could have repelled me more.

It was true that my three years in the Marines had left me with new respect for the military (especially the infantry), and with a greater readiness to apply intellectual concepts to problems of military strategy than I would have felt otherwise. But to work for the Air Force? On nuclear bombing plans? I'd picked the Marines to join over the Air Force very consciously because the Marines didn't bomb cities and had virtually nothing to do with nuclear weapons.

In any case, for years prior to my coming to RAND, I had expected to pursue an academic career as an economic theorist. On leaving the Marines in the spring of 1957, I had reapplied and was accepted in the Society of Fellows. It was perhaps the best postgraduate fellowship in the country, designed as an alternative to a Ph.D. For three years, junior fellows could pursue whatever line of study they wished, without supervision, with an office, research and travel expenses, and the salary of a Harvard assistant professor. They weren't allowed to take courses for credit and, in that period, were not encouraged to write a Ph.D. thesis or to get the degree.

I knew what I wanted to work on. Ever since my senior year in college I had become fascinated with the new field of "decision theory," the abstract analysis of decision-making under conditions of uncertainty. For my degree in economics I had written my senior honors thesis on the question of how to describe and understand, and perhaps to improve, the way people make choices when they are uncertain of the consequences of their actions. That included situations of conflict in which the uncertainty partly pertained to the choices of a rational adversary, the subject of so-called game theory.[†]

In the fall of 1957, I began to focus on choices in situations of extreme uncertainty, which I termed "ambiguity": sparse information, unprecedented or unfamiliar circumstances, lack of reliable frameworks for understanding processes, conflicting evidence or testimony, or contradictory opinions of experts. A great many situations had some or all these characteristics, military-political crises in particular. I felt that existing theories of appropriate behavior ("rational choice") in these circumstances were inadequate, in fact misleading, and I set out to demonstrate this and to invent better ones. I was also interested in the role of threats, which I felt that, along with uncertainty, most economists analyzing "bargaining theory" had long neglected.

Partly because all this had relevance to military decisions, one institution that had shown a special interest in such subjects was RAND, where mathematicians had made basic contributions. It was RAND's unclassified publications on decision theory that interested me, not its defense work, whatever that was.

In August 1957, at the end of a summer studying mathematical probability theory at Stanford University, I paid a visit to RAND, which led to an invitation from its economics department to spend the following summer there as a consultant. I accepted solely for intellectual reasons. Neither I nor anyone else, as far as I knew, had any sense of an impending nuclear or Cold War crisis that month.

That was shortly about to change for the public. But that change had already occurred, as I later learned, for the people in the RAND economics department. They had taken special note of something that hadn't yet drawn major attention outside the Department of Defense: a claim by the Soviet Union on August 26 that it had successfully tested an intercontinental ballistic missile (ICBM) at full range. On the basis of secret intelligence information they couldn't share with me when I visited, the economists at RAND knew that this claim was true.

Two months later, on October 4, 1957, when I was back at Harvard, the whole world learned about Sputnik, an earth-girdling artificial satellite sent up by the Soviet Union, which began broadcasting its "beep, beep" signal. It was a technical achievement that the United States was not immediately ready to match, and the global presumption of U.S. technical and scientific superiority was shattered. Though Eisenhower decried the concern about this new object in space (as he said publicly, it "does not raise my apprehensions, not one iota"), it actually did imply that Americans in the continental United States were becoming vulnerable in a way that had never been true in our previous history. By placing Sputnik in space orbit, the Soviets dramatically supported their claims two months earlier that they had rockets of intercontinental range.

As it happened, Project RAND's first reports to the Air Force, back in 1946 and 1947 (when Project RAND, embryo of the RAND Corporation, was part of Douglas Aircraft Company's engineering division), had been a proposal for a world-circling spaceship, which could be in orbit by 1952. The Project reports had foreseen the political impact: "The psychological effect of a satellite will in less dramatic fashion parallel that of the atom bomb. It will make possible an unspoken threat to every other nation that we can send a guided missile to any spot on earth." But at that time, General Curtis LeMay, then in charge of development for the Air Force, was far more attracted to threatening other nations with high-flying bombers than with missiles, and the proposal wasn't funded.

While the United States rushed its program to put something up in the fall of 1957, the Russians sent up their second, much larger satellite in November, this time with a dog, Laika, aboard. This second Soviet launch with a much larger payload—lofted like the first by their initial ICBM engine—demonstrated that Soviet rocketry had achieved both the thrust and the accuracy that could send missiles with thermonuclear warheads to targets in the United States within thirty minutes of launch. The next month, a vast global audience watched on television as an American missile rose four feet in the air, then sank back and exploded on the pad. The nose cone, with a miniature satellite aboard, detached and fell into surrounding brush, its little radio still beeping. ("Someone should put it out of its misery, shoot it," an observer suggested.) Newspapers derided "Flopnik," "Stayputnik," and "Kaputnik." (The first successful U.S. ICBM test at intercontinental range came in November 1958.)

By this time the national mood had changed abruptly. During the summer of 1958, while I was at RAND, the Eisenhower administration had found itself forced to respond to the humiliating Soviet lead in space by creating the Defense Advanced Research Projects Agency (DARPA) in the Defense Department, the National Aeronautics and Space Administration (NASA), and the National Defense Education Act, spending a billion dollars to improve science and mathematics education.

For my part, when I arrived in Santa Monica in June as a summer consultant what I had found myself addressing was not, after all, "decision theory" or "bargaining theory" in the abstract, but concrete decisions on which the future of peace and national or even human survival seemed to depend: how to deter the Soviet Union from exploiting its apparent superiority in missile capabilities to attack or coerce the United States.

The summer of 1958 was the high point of secret intelligence predictions of an imminent vast Soviet superiority in deployed ICBMs, the "missile gap." But even before those predictions, Top Secret RAND studies over the previous four years had concluded that the ability of the Strategic Air Command to retaliate against a Soviet surprise attack against our strategic bombers was far from reliable. These studies found great vulnerability even on the basis of Soviet bomber capabilities (which turned out later to have been greatly inflated by intelligence predictions of a "bomber gap," which preceded the missile-gap estimates). Earlier studies assumed only a minor role, if any, for Soviet ICBMs and submarine-based missiles. But the addition of even twenty to forty Soviet ICBMs ominously enhanced the possibilities of a disarming surprise attack. And thirty ICBMs were the *lowest* near-term estimate for Soviet missiles in the more recent RAND studies. The estimates by the Air Force and CIA of near-term Soviet ICBM forces looked toward several hundred, perhaps as early as 1959 (with a crash effort), almost certainly by 1960–61, with thousands in the sixties.

Eisenhower's reassurances and apparent calm about the challenge seemed to confirm the notion of him as a retired grandfather, out of touch with reality, focused only on his golf game. That was the image shared by everyone I came to meet at RAND. It was paired with the notion that our own sponsoring organization, the Air Force—which certainly didn't underrate the prospect of a vast Soviet superiority in ICBMs— didn't seem able bureaucratically to rise to that threat in an appropriate or effective way. That is, it was resisting or dragging its feet in adopting the recommendations that RAND had been making for several years at this point and which seemed all the more urgent after Sputnik.

To my new RAND colleagues, the projected Soviet ICBM buildup looked unmistakably like an urgent effort, with a startlingly high chance of success, to acquire the capability to disarm SAC's power to retaliate. Such a Soviet capability, and even the costly crash effort to achieve it, destroyed the basis for confidence in nuclear deterrence. At least, it did for anyone reading these studies who shared the widely accepted Cold War premise that the Soviets aimed ultimately at world domination. That included everyone I worked closely with at RAND. And in light of both the intelligence estimates that became available to me as I acquired security clearances and the views of my highly intelligent colleagues, it came to include me.

Within weeks of my arrival in 1958, I found myself immersed in what seemed the most urgent concrete problem of uncertainty and decision-making that humanity had ever faced: averting a nuclear exchange between the Soviet Union and the United States. On the basis of the RAND studies, the challenge looked both more difficult and more urgent than almost anyone outside RAND seemed able to imagine. In the last years of the decade, nearly all the departments and individual analysts at RAND were obsessed with solving the single problem of deterring a Soviet nuclear attack on U.S. retaliatory forces and society, in the next few years and beyond, by assuring that a large U.S. ability to retaliate with nuclear weapons would survive any such attack. The concentration of focus, the sense of a team effort of the highest urgency, was very much like that of the scientists in the Manhattan Project.

And the center of this obsessive ideation was the economics department, which I joined. In my first week as a summer consultant in 1958, I was assigned to be the rapporteur of a discussion group on responses to the strategic threat, which included Albert Wohlstetter, Harry Rowen, Andy Marshall, Alain Enthoven, and Fred Hoffman, the key strategic analysts in the economics department, as well as Bill Kaufmann from social science, and Herman Kahn from physics.

From my academic life, I was used to being in the company of very smart people, but it was apparent from the beginning that this was as smart a bunch of men as I had ever encountered. That first impression never changed (though I was to learn, in the years ahead, the severe limitations of sheer intellect). And it was even better than that. In the middle of the first session, I ventured—though I was the youngest, assigned to be taking notes, and obviously a total novice on the issues—to express an opinion. (I don't remember what it was.) Rather than showing irritation or ignoring my comment, Herman Kahn, brilliant and enormously fat, sitting directly across the table from me, looked at me soberly and said, *"You're absolutely wrong."*

A warm glow spread throughout my body. This was the way my undergraduate fellows on the editorial board of the *Harvard Crimson* (mostly Jewish, like Herman and me) had routinely spoken to each other; I hadn't experienced anything like it for six years. At King's College, Cambridge, or in the Society of Fellows, arguments didn't remotely take this gloves-off, take-no-prisoners form. I thought, "I've found a home."

And I had. I loved RAND, where I ended up spending ten years, in two hitches, the second when I came back from Vietnam in 1967. Much, I imagined, like members of a religious order would, I shared with my colleagues a sense of brotherhood, living and working with others for a transcendent cause.

In fact, those former Manhattan Project scientists who stayed on in weapons work, as well as their successors at the nuclear weapons labs, are often described by others (not admiringly) as a secular priesthood. In part that's a matter of their knowledge of secrets of the universe, arcana not to be shared with the laity: the sense of being an insider, the seductions of secrecy, to be counseling men of power. An article on the new "military intellectuals" likened RAND consultants in Washington and the Pentagon, moving invisibly across bureaucratic boundaries opaque to others, to the Jesuits of old Europe, moving between courts, serving as confessors to kings. But above all, precisely in my early missile-gap years at RAND and as a consultant in Washington, there was our sense of mission, the burden of believing we knew more about the dangers ahead, and what might be done about them, than did the generals in the Pentagon or SAC, or Congress or the public, or even the president. It was an enlivening burden.

Materially, we led a privileged life. I started at RAND, just out of graduate study, at the highest salary my father had ever attained as a chief structural engineer. Working conditions were ideal, the climate was that of Southern California, and our offices were a block from the Santa Monica Beach.

But my colleagues were driven men. They shared a feeling—soon transmitted to me—that we were in the most literal sense working to save the world. A successful Soviet nuclear attack on the United States would be a catastrophe, and not only for America. It was taken for granted that at some Russian equivalent of RAND in the Soviet Ministry of Defense or Strategic Rocket Forces, a similar team was working just as urgently and obsessively to exploit their lead in offensive forces, if not by a surprise attack then by compelling blackmail against the United States and its NATO allies. We were rescuing the world from our Soviet counterparts as well as from the possibly fatal lethargy and bureaucratic inertia of the Eisenhower administration and our sponsors in the Air Force.

The work was intense and unrelenting. The RAND building's lights were kept on all night because researchers came in and out at all hours, on self-chosen schedules. At lunch, over sandwiches on courtyard patios inside RAND, we talked shop—nothing else. During the cocktail interval at the frequent dinners that our wives took turns hosting, two or three men at a time would cluster in a corner to share secret reflections, sotto voce; the women didn't have clearances. After the meal the wives would go together into the living room—for security reasons—leaving the men to talk secrets at the table.

There were almost no cleared women professionals at RAND then. The only exceptions I remember were Nancy Nimitz, a Soviet specialist who was the daughter of Fleet Admiral Chester Nimitz; Alice Hsieh, a China analyst; and Albert Wohlstetter's wife, Roberta, a historian who was then working on a study of how the Japanese had achieved a surprise attack on our Navy at Pearl Harbor and our Air Force in the Philippines in December 1941. Her draft findings, which we all read intensely that summer, greatly influenced our thinking and our anxieties, as a premonition of exactly what we were trying to prevent.

My first summer there I worked seventy-hour weeks, devouring secret studies and analyses till late every night, to get up to speed on the problems and the possible solutions. I was looking for clues as to how we could frustrate the Soviet versions of RAND and SAC, and do it in time to avert a nuclear Pearl Harbor. Or postpone it. From the Air Force intelligence estimates I was newly privy to, and the dark view of the Soviets, which my colleagues shared with the whole national security community, I couldn't believe that the world would long escape nuclear holocaust. Alain Enthoven and I were the youngest members of the department. Neither of us joined the extremely generous retirement plan RAND offered. Neither of us believed, in our late twenties, we had a chance of collecting on it.

I remember one August night in particular, sitting in the office assigned to me, which looked out over the ocean. It was a moonless night, close to midnight. The ocean was dark outside my windows. I was reading an analysis of the optimal conditions, from a Soviet point of view, for a surprise attack. A key point, I read, would be for them to accompany ICBM and bomber attacks on SAC bases deep in our interior with carefully coordinated attacks by cruise missiles from submarines onto bases near our oceans and on command centers (outflanking our radar in the north and providing no warning, with only minutes of flight time).

Since their submarines had to be on the surface for this, and considering various weather conditions, the ideal time for the attack, I read, would be in August, about midnight on a moonless night. I looked out the window at the blackness of the sea, then I glanced at my watch. I literally felt a shiver and the hair on my neck rose.

In the circumstances described by these studies and by intelligence estimates (especially those of the Air Force), deterrence seemed imperative—and uncertain. According to these Top Secret estimates, we faced a powerful enemy making costly efforts to exploit the potential of nuclear weapons totally to disarm us and to gain unchallenged global dominance. No non-nuclear U.S. military capability could promise to survive such an attack and respond to it on a scale that would reliably deter an enemy so determined and ruthless. Nothing could do so other than a reliable capability for devastating nuclear retaliation: capability that would assuredly survive a well-designed nuclear first strike.

As Wohlstetter emphasized in his briefings to the Air Force, our ability to deter a Soviet attack on the United States was not measured by the scale of our offensive forces in place before the war, but by what the Soviets could foresee would be our "second-strike capability" to retaliate to their first strike. How much survivable destructive capacity would it take to deter them? That would depend on the circumstances and the alternatives, Wohlstetter suggested. Any potential alternatives to the Soviets' own first strike might, at a particular moment, look very ominous to the USSR: perhaps crushing defeat in a regional war, or a possible U.S. first strike in escalation of a conflict in Europe. Like us, the Soviets might be presented with a choice among grave risks. In the conclusion of RAND's Top Secret "vulnerability study" R-290, of which he was the principal author in 1956, Wohlstetter asserted that our then-programmed strategic force

> cannot ensure a level of destruction as high as that which Russia sustained in World War II—a destruction from which it has more than recovered in a few years. This is hardly the "crystal clear" deterrent we might need in some foreseeable circumstance.

The implication—never questioned by anyone at RAND while I was there—was that adequate deterrence for the United States demanded a survivable, assured second-strike capability to kill more than the twenty million Soviet citizens who had died in World War II. That meant we were working to assure the survival under attack of a capability for retaliatory genocide, though none of us ever thought of it in those terms for a moment. Truly, in view of my strong feelings against the indiscriminate bombing of cities by both sides in World War II, there was a terrible irony to my working for the Air Force on studies aimed at threatening the Russians with the ultimate in terror bombing if they should attack us. But there was a consistent logic to it. From the analyses by men who became my mentors and closest colleagues, I had come to believe—like Szilard and Rotblat a generation earlier—that this was the best, indeed the only way, of increasing the chance that there would be no large nuclear war in the near future.

When my former Harvard faculty advisor heard in 1959 that I was going back to RAND as a permanent employee, he told me bitterly that I was "selling out" (as an economist) for a high salary. I told him that after what I had learned the previous summer at RAND, I would gladly work there without pay. It was true. I couldn't imagine a more important way to serve humanity.

CHAPTER 2

Command and Control
Managing Catastrophe

For my own contribution at RAND, reflecting my long-term focus on decision theory, I chose to specialize in a subject that seemed up to this point understudied in relation to its importance: the command and control of nuclear retaliatory forces by senior military officers and especially by the president.

Most of my colleagues were studying the vulnerability, and how to reduce it, of strategic nuclear weapons, bases, and vehicles. I joined a few others who were examining the vulnerability and reliability of the military's "nervous system": command posts, information and decision-making processes at different levels, communications, warning systems, and intelligence.

It was widely accepted that the decision whether and when to initiate launch of U.S. nuclear forces against the Soviet Union under any circumstances should be made by the president, or the highest surviving authority. How he might arrive at that decision and how it would get implemented were concrete questions that demanded highly secret empirical knowledge. Nevertheless, I was especially drawn to study this particular command problem not only because of its obvious importance but also because it exemplified and drew on everything I had analyzed in my graduate study of decision-making under uncertainty. It would be the transcendent, and conceivably the last, decision under uncertainty ever made by a national leader.

Moreover, in my initial reading of the key RAND study R-290, "Protecting U.S. Power to Strike Back in the 1950's and 1960's," a word leaped out at me that had been the focus of my own thinking at Harvard that year: "ambiguity." The study, whose principal author was Albert Wohlstetter, alongside Harry Rowen and Fred Hoffman, noted that some of our plans depended on our having "strategic" warning of an imminent enemy attack—an intelligence warning received prior to any enemy weapons having been launched against us.

> But planning on strategic warning *is* dangerous, and this cannot be overemphasized. . . . If we are to be realistic and accurate before the event, the most positive answer we can ever expect to the question, "Are the Soviets going to attack us?" is "Perhaps." And the answers to the other important but vexing questions, "When?" and "Where?" will be even more uncertain. . . . The real question, however, is not only how early we will have these signals but how unambiguous they will be. We can state, unequivocally, that they will be equivocal. . . . The ambiguity of strategic warning complicates the problem of decision.

No other formulation of a decision problem—this one, the most important in human history!—could have caught my attention so forcefully. "Ambiguity" was not a term then used in academic discussions of risk and uncertainty. I was especially struck to see it in a classified study, because I was in the process of introducing it academically as a technical term, referring to subjective uncertainty when experience was lacking, or information was sparse, the bearing of evidence was unclear, the testimony of observers or experts was greatly in conflict, or the implications of different types of evidence was contradictory. (I conjectured—as was later borne out in many laboratory experiments—that such uncertainty could not be represented by a single, precise numerical probability distribution, either in subjects' minds or as reflected in their behavior, even though they did not regard it as "totally uncertain.")

The uncertainty of strategic warning described here seemed likely to fall into that category. And Wohlstetter went on to point out that the same problem arose even in the context of "tactical" warning: indications from long-distance ground radars or infrared satellites that enemy planes or missiles had left their launch sites, headed for the United States, before any of them had arrived on target.

The radars of the Arctic Distant Early Warning Line (DEW Line) had more than once, I soon learned, been fooled by a flock of high-flying geese into warning that Soviet bomber planes were coming toward us over the North Pole. In the pre-ICBM era, that still allowed hours in which to discover the error, and meanwhile to get our planes on alert off the ground. But just a year after I joined RAND, the higher-tech radar and computer system Ballistic Missile Early Warning System (BMEWS), designed to detect incoming ICBMs, in its first week of operation reported that a missile attack was under way. That called for decisions in under fifteen minutes.

On October 5, 1960, some of the highest industry officials associated with the Air Force's technical systems, including Tom Watson, head of IBM, were visiting North American Aerospace Defense Command (NORAD), inside Cheyenne Mountain, Colorado. Pete Peterson, later Nixon's secretary of commerce and at this time executive vice president of Bell & Howell, was sitting in the commander's chair on the command balcony confronting the huge world map. That bit of role playing was a little treat for honored visitors. In his book *Command and Control*, Eric Schlosser tells what happened that day, pretty much as I heard it at the time (as highly classified gossip) along with everyone else working on the issue.

> The first BMEWS radar complex, located at Thule Air Base, Greenland, had come online that week, and the numerical threat levels of the new warning system were being explained to the businessmen.
>
> If the number 1 flashed in red above the world map, unidentified objects were traveling toward the United States. If the number 3 flashed, the threat level was high; SAC headquarters and the Joint Chiefs of Staff had to be notified immediately. The maximum threat level was 5—a computer-generated warning, with a 99.9 percent certainty, that the United States was under attack. As Peterson sat in the commander's chair, the number above the map began to climb. When it reached 4, NORAD officers ran into the room. When it reached 5, Peterson and the other executives were quickly escorted out and put in a small

office. The door was closed, and they were left there believing that a nuclear war had just begun.

One of the businessmen in the room, Chuck Percy, then president of Bell & Howell and later a three-term senator from Illinois, "recalled a sense of panic at NORAD." That's the way I heard the story that month, from Air Force colonels—contrary to Pentagon assurances, when word leaked out, that the warning hadn't been taken seriously. One thing that led some at NORAD to find the warning somewhat more "ambiguous" than the computer's 99.9 percent certainty was that Khrushchev was in New York for the United Nations that week. It turned out that the BMEWS radar signals were bouncing off the moon as it rose over Norway. The designers, as I heard it in the Pentagon, had figured that the radar would reach the moon, but they didn't think the return echo would be so strong as to look like incoming missiles. Everyone makes mistakes.

What impressed me while reading Wohlstetter's passages above was not only that he had directed attention to the ambiguity of warning, he had also pointed to the cognitive and behavioral effects of this ambiguity. It would inevitably *delay* responses by the various command levels (as it should) and by the president himself. In the era of missiles, a delay of minutes could mean the destruction of a retaliatory capability, along with the commanders. But what were the president or lower levels of command to do, on the basis that "perhaps" an attack was on the way, or even on 99.9 percent certainty from a computer program that might possibly be overwrought?

Wohlstetter had successfully proposed a way of increasing the survivability of alert bombers on the basis of ambiguous or equivocal warning without committing us to war. Albert took credit for originating the "positive control" process as a partial answer to the problem of false alarms and poor information. This introduced a "launch on warning" (LOW) option with respect to bombers that was separable from the decision to execute the war plans, i.e., to send the bombers to target. The planes launched on warning under positive control were to fly to a predesignated rendezvous area, where they would circle unless they got an explicit, "positive" order to "Execute,"—i.e., to proceed to predesignated targets—or an order to return to the base.

If they received *no* order at all, they were to return to their base at the point when they had just enough fuel to do so safely. (This option doesn't exist for operational ballistic missiles, which can't be recalled once launched. President Reagan once made a public statement to the contrary for submarine-launched missiles. He really may not have known better. This is a dismaying confusion for a president to suffer.)

But how reliably were these safeguards observed in actual practice? No military secrets were more tightly guarded than the details of how, by whom, and under what circumstances decisions to execute nuclear war plans—both planes and unrecallable missiles—would really be arrived at and implemented. An opportunity to study these in the field, with high access—though not at the president's level—arose a few months into my research. The Commander in Chief, Pacific Command (CINCPAC), Admiral Harry D. Felt, called for a study of his problems of nuclear command and control in the Pacific to be done by the Office of Naval Research (ONR). I was glad to have RAND lend me to the study.

In the fall of 1959 I moved to Camp Smith in Oahu, Hawaii, CINCPAC headquarters, to join an ONR study group headed by Dr. John Wilkes. I didn't agree to stay for the whole year, since my wife wasn't prepared to move the family there with me, so I went for several months at first, then came back repeatedly during 1960 to help the group in the later stages of their study. Much of our work was at the headquarters of CINCPAC and of the Pacific Air Forces (PACAF) on Oahu, but we made extensive field trips throughout the Pacific theater. I observed operations and held discussions with commanders, planners, and operators in almost every command post in the Pacific.

The basic problem that CINCPAC most wanted our team to focus on was how to assure, if and when a decision were ever made to use nuclear weapons, that his own "Execute" message ordering the implementation of nuclear war plans would get out to the various forces in the Pacific in a reliable and timely way. This would have to be done before various command posts, communications in the theater, or his offensive forces were destroyed by a Soviet attack. But a problem that I took on personally to investigate was the obverse of that one: reducing the possibility of *unauthorized* action. How to assure that no subordinate would be inclined or able to launch the forces under his control in the absence of an authorization from his superiors or the president?

In principle, unauthorized action was simply forbidden. According to all the Top Secret war plans, an Execute order at any level of command to carry out a nuclear war plan had to be based on an immediate, explicit order from higher authority, ultimately from the president himself. However, there were provisions in the plans for taking various preparatory actions on local authority, and even for launching planes on warning of imminent enemy attack, to protect them from destruction. This was Wohlstetter's "positive control" process. Such a launch was not supposed to be tantamount to a decision to execute a war plan—to proceed to targets.

This procedure was also known as "fail-safe." If there were a failure from the base to transmit an intended signal, either to go ahead or to return, the planes were to act as if they had gotten a return signal. This response might be an error if there was actually a war on and communications were destroyed, but it was a safer error—less dangerous—than the mistake of going to target when no war was going on and communications were out for technical or atmospheric reasons.

The term "positive control," and its synonym "fail-safe procedure," meant that the pilots were to be trained and drilled to understand that they were never to go to target under any circumstances without a positive order—explicit and immediate—from a higher authority to do so. And an Execute order had to be "authenticated" as coming from the highest authorities, meaning it had to be accompanied by coded evidence and to come in such a manner that made its origins at the highest levels unmistakably clear.

But how reliably would their behavior conform to these instructions? How safe was this process, really? I had raised this question in the very first memo I had written on a Defense Department contract, just a month after I had come to the RAND Corporation as a summer consultant in 1958. It was titled "Strains on the Fail-Safe System" and it was addressed to Wohlstetter, the author of the fail-safe procedure, and to Frank Eldridge, the leading communications expert at RAND, one of the RAND analysts I had consulted. It reflected my own experience—ending just the year before—in a highly disciplined organization, the Marine Corps, and my reading of military history. I was aware that the behavior of conscientious officers would reflect not only what they had earlier been told to do under prescribed conditions but also their sense of the mission and their actual beliefs about the current situation, based on their immediate experience and observations.

To paraphrase my memo, what I foresaw was that the *lack* of a positive order to execute, following an order to launch that was accompanied or followed by strong signs of an enemy attack, would itself inevitably be ambiguous, perhaps no less so than the tactical warning that gave rise to the launch. The lack of any signal might mean that a return to base was desired. It was certainly supposed to be responded to as if it surely meant that, according to the written rules. Nevertheless, it might mean that an order to execute had been sent but had not arrived yet, and might not arrive in time for it to be carried out with the remaining fuel. Or that it would have been sent and received had not enemy nuclear attacks wiped out the commander or the transmitter or interfered with the transmission.

It could, in other words, be a very ominous indication, depending on what other evidence was available. For example, how often had pilots had the experience of getting to this point, of circling in a rendezvous area, without receiving a message to return and without, as it turned out, their base having been under attack? Ever?

If the whole procedure were practiced often enough up to this point, the pilots would come to expect on any given occasion, in the absence of any other evidence, that they were taking part in a drill. They would have acquired a habit of returning. They wouldn't feel any pressure to break that habit, to disobey their standing orders and to take off for their targets, even if they got no further orders. They would return to their base routinely.

But as I conjectured at RAND—and as I discovered when I was able to investigate this question in the field, in our CINCPAC study group— it was not at all clear that most pilots in the Pacific got a chance to acquire such a habit. In fact, although we heard different opinions on this, it seemed very unlikely.

As our group actually witnessed on a visit to Kadena Air Base on Okinawa, the first part of the launch-on-warning procedure was practiced frequently, in fact daily, at random times, up to the point when planes were ready to taxi for takeoff. At Kadena, the pilots weren't continuously in the alert planes or in the alert hut on the strip. They were allowed to be elsewhere, at the PX or in their quarters, each with his individual jeep and driver, because they practiced the alert at least once a day.

The officer in charge told our research group we could choose the time for that day's rehearsal. When our leader, John Wilkes, said later, "OK, now," the klaxons sounded all over the area, and almost instantly jeeps appeared on all the roads leading to the strip, rushing around curves, with pilots leaping out as they reached the strip and then scrambling into the cockpits, still tightening their helmets and gear. Engines starting in ten planes, almost simultaneously. Ten minutes.

That drill assured that the planes would be ready to take off in time when ordered. At that, practice had made perfect. But the later part of the exercise, to assure that they would fly to their rendezvous area and eventually come back from it unless they were ordered to proceed, was much more time-consuming and expensive in fuel and maintenance. It was obvious that it would be practiced much less often. We asked, was it ever rehearsed at all? Answers on that were vague and conflicting. It was understood that SAC, which had invented this procedure, did do full-scale rehearsals of it frequently, but it was not clear that theater forces ever did.

In fact, we learned at Kadena that the tactical alert planes there *never* actually left the ground in their daily drills, and that wasn't just for reasons of expense. They were barred even from taxiing from their alert pads to the point of takeoff. The reason, we were told, was the danger of accident, possibly a nuclear accident.

Each of the alert planes, single-person F-100s, was carrying a Mark 28 thermonuclear weapon outside the plane, beneath the undercarriage. These weapons, we were told, were designed to be carried inside a plane for greater safety. But there was no room for that in these tactical fighter-bombers.

Moreover, they were not "one-point safe." All H-bombs, thermonuclear fusion weapons like these, were triggered by a plutonium bomb of the type that destroyed Nagasaki. The plutonium core was surrounded by a spherical web of shaped charges of high explosive. When these all detonated simultaneously, they imploded the plutonium core inside, squeezing it to a density of greater than critical mass, leading to a nuclear fission explosion that in turn triggered the thermonuclear fuel.

"One-point safe" meant that the design ensured that if one of the high-explosive shaped-charge sections exploded accidentally, no significant nuclear yield would result. Or more precisely, there would be a "less than one in a million chance" of a nuclear yield greater than four pounds. Only if more than one went off—from being dropped, burned, or fired into, or from an electrical malfunction—might there be a partial nuclear explosion. That might be on the scale of the Hiroshima bomb.

Since these weapons were not one-point safe, there was a danger that if they were dropped or involved in a crash or a fire or an explosion and one or two sections of the high explosive detonated, it would mean not only the dispersal of radioactive contamination from the plutonium trigger over a large area but also a possible partial or total nuclear explosion. While the probability of the latter was small, the risk was not worth taking in a practice drill, which, after all, happened once a day.

Therefore, in these practice alerts, the pilots would jump into their planes and gun up the engines. But they didn't go to the point of racing down the runway, or even taxiing over to the runway from their pads, let alone taking off. When they were not on alert, the pilots, of course, often flew their planes without weapons. And apparently they also did training missions with actual weapons when not on alert. But we found it hard to get a clear answer whether pilots on actual standby alert ever took off, in a practice drill, from their alert pads with weapons aboard. Certainly not very often, if ever, we were told. Probably never.

That said to me that if they were ordered to take off from those pads, it would be an extraordinary, perhaps unprecedented, experience for the alert pilots. Even if it was in fact—unknown to them—only a drill, the first time or two that it happened would almost surely lead them to infer that "this was it." An enemy attack was under way or else they were leading a preemptive strike. At the least, they would have to infer that the indications of enemy attack were more serious than they ever had been before. It would be in that state of mind that they would head for their rendezvous areas, even if they received no Execute order to follow their launch order.

This particular consequence of the lack of regular rehearsal of takeoff under fully realistic simulated alert conditions didn't seem familiar to any of the nuclear control officers or pilots that I questioned. In fact, they all admitted that it had never occurred to them. They all seemed to hear my reasoning as new, interesting, and plausible. That was worrisome. They agreed: the first time, even the first few times, that alert pilots found themselves circling in a rendezvous area with bombs aboard waiting for an Execute or a Return message, they would be strongly inclined to expect the worst, simply because it was the first time they had ever gotten that far. They would believe the war was on, or was imminent, because the commanders who had launched them without precedent would appear to have thought so.

What if they had other reasons to think that as well? Suppose this launch came in a time of international crisis, either in the region or elsewhere in the world. Suppose there had been an earlier strategic warning of a heightened danger of war or attack. What if there was an actual war going on in the area, between China and Taiwan, or in Korea, or in Indochina? Or a serious crisis, such as actually occurred in 1954–55 and again in 1958 (soon after I wrote this memo), when the Chinese Communists on the mainland spent months shelling islands a few miles offshore that were occupied by Chinese Nationalist forces? In both these cases there was presidential discussion of using U.S. nuclear weapons to repel an attack or to maintain access to the offshore islands, Quemoy and Matsu. (In early 1958, nuclear warheads for Matador cruise missiles had arrived in both Taiwan and Osan, South Korea.)

What if there were, in the course of a launch on warning or soon after it, a massive explosion on an American airbase in the region, perhaps on this very base? On first thought, that might seem improbably coincidental, stretching too far for a worst-case scenario. On second thought, less so. As far as I could tell from many conversations, no one else in the area had had the first thought, let alone the second. But no one found it implausible after a brief discussion.

It was only necessary to recall why the alert F-100s, despite a command obsession with realistic drills and with meeting standards, rarely if ever rehearsed to the point of takeoff. It was precisely because of the serious danger of a crash and its possible nuclear consequences, with these particular bombloads. The other side of that reluctance, the very basis for it, was an estimate by commanders that if a number of these planes actually taxied to the runway and took off in a great rush, one or more of them might bump into another or otherwise turn over, burn and explode, and produce a huge explosion, spreading lethal radioactivity over a large area, and just possibly, a nuclear fireball.

That possibility itself wasn't remote from people's thoughts. It was why they didn't taxi. What they hadn't thought about was the next question. What would the effect of that event be on the minds of the alert pilots who had already taken off, either from that base, or from another one nearby, or even from a distant base in the same region?

They might, of course, guess at the true reason: that an unprecedented accident had occurred. But even if that occurred to them at all, it would be competing with another explanation, which might seem much more likely under the circumstances. After all, why were they in the air at all with their bombs aboard? Was it an unprecedentedly realistic, no-warning drill, despite the risks? Or was it because a higher authority had perceived evidence of an imminent enemy attack, stronger than ever before, perhaps certain? And now this explosion! Whether it was nuclear or not might not be immediately clear, especially in the initial reporting or observation by the planes that had already taken off. The attack might appear to be taking place.

At this point a lot of communications would be taking place among the airborne planes and they would be attempting to communicate back to their base. But if there had been a partial nuclear explosion at that base, that would be impossible. The blast itself probably would have destroyed all transmitting points at the base, but beyond that the electronic effects of the explosion would have disrupted all high-frequency, long-distance communications in a considerable area.

That would mean that the last signal these planes would receive from their base, and perhaps, for quite a while, from any other bases in their vicinity, might be the sight of a mushroom cloud rising over the runway they had just left. They would then be out of communications locally: the explosion itself would black out radio transmissions. The later lack of an Execute or a Return order, or any other, would have an easy explanation: enemy attack. All this in the context of the fact that they had just received a launch order that was unprecedented, or nearly so—a circumstance that in itself would make some or all of them nearly certain that an attack had been imminent.

What this meant to me was that a false alarm deemed serious enough to trigger a launch command to alert tactical forces on any base in the Pacific—and probably anywhere in the world, at least where the weapons carried were such as to preclude frequent rehearsals of launch—was likely to generate the belief in the minds of some airborne pilots armed with thermonuclear weapons that, although they had not received an Execute order, general nuclear war was under way and that they had no ability to receive an Execute order because communications had been disrupted by the war.

Thus, a launch order might be followed closely by a large high explosive or even nuclear detonation on a U.S. base, accompanied by an outage of communications, precisely because it would have led to the actual launching of numbers of planes with nuclear weapons that were known to be less than maximally safe. In fact, these probabilities, individually low but not independent, could cascade even further.

If the false alarm leading to precautionary launch was widespread in the theater or even worldwide, the numbers of bases and planes involved would greatly increase the chance of an accidental explosion somewhere. But even if the initial takeoffs were at the initiative of a single base commander, a large explosion—especially with high explosive alone, which wouldn't knock out all communications—might lead to many precautionary launches elsewhere, likewise increasing the chances of a second explosion. And any of these might simultaneously disrupt communications.

My knowledge of military interpretation of orders and military dedication, based on my own experience in the Marines and, by now, on a lot of time talking with high-level Air Staff officers, convinced me that in such a situation many of the pilots would regard it as their duty to carry out their mission, the general war mission, in violation of the strict letter of their orders to await a positive authorization. Such authorization would likely not come, they would suddenly realize, if an enemy attack had intervened soon after their launch orders. Thus, without the commander realizing it, his command to initiate a precautionary launch might be tantamount to an Execute order after all.

When I tried out this line of reasoning to experienced staff officers at various command posts and bases in the Pacific, nothing I heard back was reassuring. They found it unfamiliar and immediately plausible. No one came up with some operational characteristic or practice I had left out that lowered the odds of the disastrous sequence I was projecting.

Finally I felt I needed to test out these thoughts at the lowest level of command. Looking at a map at a headquarters near Tokyo, I picked out a small U.S. airbase in South Korea: Kunsan. It was the northernmost base with nuclear-alert planes in Korea (that is, in the Pacific). In fact, its alert planes with nuclear weapons may have been closer to Communist territory than those on any other Pacific base. Individuals in our group could get rides on military planes, and we had "go anywhere, talk to anyone, see anything" clearance from Admiral Felt. On short notice, I decided to take a trip to Korea to talk to the officer in charge at Kunsan.

I landed in Seoul and secured a ride on a light plane over barren, unpopulated hills up to Kunsan. I found myself landing on a dusty airstrip in something like a little town in a frontier Western. The officer in charge of the base was an Air Force major. He was in command of twelve F-100s, each with an underslung Mark 28 thermonuclear weapon with a yield of 1.1 megatons. Each one of those bombs had the explosive equivalent of half the tonnage the United States dropped in all of World War II, in both Europe and the Pacific. That had been two million tons worldwide. The major in charge of this little collection of Quonset huts and planes in the hills controlled six and a half times World War II's worth of firepower.

As best I recall, as at Kadena, these weapons were not one-point safe at that time. In answer to my question, the major informed me that the pilots didn't practice taxiing or taking off in drills with weapons aboard. A portion of this squadron was on alert at all times. We were just minutes of flying time away from North Korea, but these planes were targeted on northeast Russia, perhaps an hour longer. I asked the major how long it would be, if they took off toward their rendezvous area, before they would be picked up on North Korean or Russian radar, and how long before they were out of line-of-sight communication with their base. He got edgy, said these were very sensitive questions, and refused to answer unless he "saw my authorization."

After he did this a couple of times, I got irritated and said, "Well, we'll just have to call Japan and let you talk to someone." We went into his command hut and he tried to get headquarters in Japan by radio. This brought out the interesting fact that he was out of communications with Japan, and had been for the past few hours. He couldn't get through to Japan via the main headquarters in Korea at Osan either. I asked him how often this happened, and he said that "about once a day" atmospheric troubles of different kinds put him out of touch with Japan.

I didn't think it was worth pursuing our discussion until he had talked to the operations desk in Japan about my access, so I waited for almost an hour, reading magazines in his hut. Osan had an alert strip too, where I'd had some discussions before I flew up to Kunsan. It occurred to me that if there were a nuclear explosion there for the reasons I was exploring, Kunsan could be cut off from communications with the rest of the world.

Finally he got through to Japan and got the word that he could tell me "anything." He asked me to run my questions by him again. I did, and he shook his head and said calmly that he didn't know the answers. That was somewhat amusing, after his expressed concern about security that had delayed us for the last hour. I asked myself if he was kidding me now, but he seemed sincere and I let it pass. From then on, he got quite communicative. He hadn't run into any researchers before at Kunsan and seemed to enjoy speculating about the issues I was raising.

Because this base was so close to Communist radar, I'd been told at Osan, the base commander at Kunsan didn't have the normal authority to launch his planes at his own initiative on positive control, even as a precaution against attack. He wasn't to launch them at all, under any circumstances, except on direct order from higher headquarters via Tokyo, possibly relayed through Osan. I wanted to hear him confirm that, then go on to test him on some hypothetical circumstances. It didn't end up happening that way.

I asked if there were any circumstances in which he would send his planes on alert into the air—for example, if he thought they were about to be attacked. The major said, "Well, you know when I'm supposed to do it, don't you?" He seemed to be testing me, what I knew.

I said, "Yes, only when you get an order from Japan or Osan."

He said, "That's right." Without any break he went on to say, "But let me tell you, I'm the commander of this base, and every commander has an inherent right to protect his forces. That is a fundamental law of war. It's the oldest principle of war that as a military commander I have the right and authority to protect my forces, and if I believed that they were endangered by anything, I would send them off."

I couldn't figure out why he was telling me this, why he seemed to want to put it on the record. We had just established that I was there investigating nuclear command and control for the Commander in Chief of Pacific Command, Admiral Felt, and he was telling me in the most matter-of-fact way that he felt empowered by fundamental principles of war to violate specific and explicit directives sent down by CINCPAC. It was hardly a surprise to me that a field commander might come to feel like that under some circumstances. That was the intuition that had brought me to Korea. But I didn't expect that he had already thought it through, or that he was so ready to tell me right out that he didn't feel bound by his orders from the headquarters I came from.

Those orders, after all, weren't just arbitrary. They were specific to Kunsan precisely because of the closeness to enemy territory and radar. A sudden squadron takeoff might be detected and interpreted by the Communists as a warning of imminent attack. (In fact, in view of what the major was about to tell me, the enemy wouldn't be foolish to think that.) So there was strong reason to keep his planes tightly under higher control, whether or not the major thought that violated principles of war.

But I didn't react. I wanted to explore what conditions might lead him to launch his planes. I asked him how he would interpret a sudden outage of communication that came during an intense crisis (like the Quemoy crisis just a year before). He said yes, that "might well" lead him to get his planes off the ground without orders from above.

Again, that wasn't a surprise in itself, or wouldn't have been on some other base, where it didn't imply any violation of their directives. This was so even in an era when an outage of communications from natural disturbances was a fairly frequent phenomenon. Atmospheric disturbances disrupting high-frequency communications occurred virtually every day all over the Pacific: about once a day at Kunsan itself, the major had told me. Even underwater cables to Japan had recently been cut accidentally by trawlers. During an actual crisis, all communications between NORAD and our Ballistic Missile Early Warning System had gone out at the same time, because, as I recall, a forest fire destroyed one set of landlines on one side of the continent and an earlier earthquake had destroyed the lines on the other.

Nevertheless, commanders and staff officers had told me that they would regard a sudden disruption of communications during a crisis as a very ominous sign, requiring at the least a high level of alert and perhaps a launch of some planes. So the major wasn't answering differently from other bases. He just wasn't acknowledging that his directives, which were different from theirs, were supposed to slow him down.

How about a report of a nuclear explosion, somewhere else in the western Pacific? Yes, he said, that would be more than sufficient. He wouldn't wait for an order.

Now the big question. I asked him what he thought would happen if he did order the planes off. He said, "Well, you know what the orders are. They go to a rendezvous area and fly around, waiting for further orders. They can do that for about an hour and still have enough fuel to get to their targets or to come back. If they don't get an Execute message, they're supposed to come back. Those are their orders."

They would be out of communications with the base at their rendezvous area, he'd told me earlier. If they were there as part of a theater-wide alert, there would be a coordinating plane with them at the rendezvous with stronger communications gear, sent from another base. But if he had sent them up himself, they would be circling up there by themselves, unable to send any messages out.

I asked, "How do you think that would work?"

The major said, "If they didn't get any Execute message? Oh, I think they'd come back." Pause. "Most of them."

The last three words didn't register with me right away because before they were out of his mouth, my head was exploding. I kept my face blank but a voice inside was screaming, "Think? You *think* they'd come back?!"

This was their commander, I thought, the one who gave them their orders, the man in charge of their training and discipline. As I reeled internally from that response, the next words, "most of them," got through to me.

He added, "Of course, if one of them were to break out of that circle and go for his target, I think the rest would follow." He paused again; then he added reflectively, "And they might as well. If one goes, they might as well all go. I tell them not to do it though."

I managed to keep a blank face. I had a few more questions to ask. Wasn't it true that there was a chance these Mark 28 weapons underneath the planes had some risk of a partial nuclear explosion if there was an accident on the runway? He nodded. I set the scene. What if the first five pilots to take off were to look back and see a mushroom cloud over the base, after the sixth plane fell over and exploded on the runway? What would they think, what would they do, after they felt the blast wave?

That was obviously a new question for him, and he seemed to find it interesting. His first response was indirect. "Well, of course it's not like Okinawa, where that would mean to the pilots that their families had just been destroyed." He meant, it turned out, that the likelihood that pilots would disobey their instructions and go on to target without explicit orders would turn on who had been killed in that explosion, as much as whether they thought it was an accident or an attack. "On Okinawa," where some of them had dependents stationed on the base, he said, "they'd go on, of course," if a blast wiped out their families. After all, they couldn't be sure it was an accident, and, he implied, they wouldn't feel they had much to live for anymore. On Kunsan, if the pilots in the air realized that they'd lost (only) the major and the base but they weren't sure it was an enemy attack, they might look for an alternate base and come back to it if they didn't get a go-ahead order.

After he had made this distinction, I reminded him that the premise of the question was that pilots had been launched on alert for the first time ever, whether by Tokyo or Osan, or by the major. With that in mind, and all the more if this had arisen out of a crisis, he agreed that a partial nuclear explosion on Kunsan, or for that matter a report of one on Osan or Kadena, would make his pilots certain that an attack was under way. Communications would be out, so they couldn't get an order to return. They would go on to their targets.

* * *

I returned to Camp Smith feeling that one of my questions had been pretty well answered: whether there were realistic circumstances in which even a disciplined officer—not a rogue or a madman—might disobey orders not to execute nuclear war plans without an explicit, authenticated order from superiors. But throughout my work on command and control, at RAND and in the Pacific Command (PACOM), I had also been asking another question as well. What if they did receive such an order; how certain was it that it truly came from the president or other high authority? Could one subordinate individual, on his own initiative, issue such an "authenticated" order?

In theory—meaning, by explicit command directives—the answer was no. But in my first month at RAND in 1958, I had come across a SAC manual describing the procedures for authenticating the Execute order for bombers. It had indicated to me another vulnerability in the fail-safe system that I described in my first item of classified research.

I posed the possibility in that memo that, perhaps on the basis of the circumstances described above, one pilot on alert *had* decided that "while it isn't certain that the war is on, the chances were good enough to justify going ahead." It would seem to make sense to him, I suggested, "to try to take some of his buddies with him, if he could, by sending them an apparently authentic 'go-ahead' signal. Whether or not these conditions seem likely," I wrote, "I find it interesting that it appears *he would be able to do this*." (emphasis in the original)

According to SAC procedures, the alert pilot had in his plane (or on his person) an envelope that had a group of code numbers—say, four—on the outside and another group of four in a card inside the sealed envelope. After receiving a radio signal with a group of eight numbers, the first four matching the numbers on the outside of his envelope, the pilot was to open the envelope and check the numbers on the card inside. If they matched the last four numbers in the signal, he has received an authenticated Execute code and should proceed to target.

Several RAND colleagues who were knowledgeable about SAC procedures supported my guess that the numbers in the code were the same for all planes in the SAC alert force. Only a single radio signal needed to be sent out. And their understanding was that the code was changed very seldom.

What I found in the land-based tactical forces in the Pacific was that the procedure, code-named Spark Plug, was essentially the same as in SAC. According to my notes from a directive, "Spark Plug procedures are the only method by which Quick Strike [alert] forces may initially be launched or initially directed to expend [nuclear weapons on targets].... Presidential authority to use atomic weapons is implicit in ... an authentic Spark Plug expend message."

Each alert plane or command post had a double envelope. When a Spark Plug message was received:

> Outside [of the outer envelope] tells the series.... If message gives the correct series, open the envelope. The face of the inner envelope gives first two phonetic code letters; if these correspond to first two letters in message, "Launch." If a message is received (then or later) containing four letters, first two of which correspond to those on the face of inner envelope, open inner envelope. If card inside has all four letters, "Expend" weapons on assigned target.
>
> Where feasible, and in order to reduce probability of an inadvertent or unauthorized act, the envelope should be opened while in the presence of at least one other person who is knowledgeable of Spark Plug procedures (this cannot be applied to airborne bomb commanders).

This two-man requirement applied only to command post procedures, either for launch or expend, since nearly all PACAF bombers, unlike SAC's, were single-pilot planes. "On receipt of message, facilities will transmit message in the clear [i.e., not encrypted] immediately at designated time intervals for one hour, unless directed to stop."

It turned out to be true for both SAC and the Pacific forces that the codes were the same for all planes and changed infrequently. In both SAC and PACAF, that meant that any pilot in the alert force, whether aloft or not, simply by opening his envelope—for PACAF, two envelopes—could learn the entire authentication code.

Since any pilot in the air receiving such a signal was directed to pass it along to other planes in his squadron by direct line-of-sight, ultra-high-frequency radio, a pilot who had been launched on warning and who wanted to take a group of alert bombers with him to Russia could, having ripped open his envelopes, radio other planes at the positive control line that he had received a very faint long-distance, high-frequency signal with the code in question. Especially under the circumstance such as I described above, that initiative would probably be effective.

Looking back at that first memo of mine on national security matters, I find that it both influenced the questions I investigated at various air bases throughout the Pacific Command the following year and foresaw the alarming responses I heard. No one I spoke with had earlier considered any of these issues, but none considered them unrealistic when I raised them.

For example, on the matter of the envelope authentication, when I posed the possibility that a conscientious (or unbalanced) pilot who felt impelled to go to target might try to convince others to go with him in the way my memo had speculated, the typical response was: "Well, he can't do that, because he doesn't know the whole authentication code."

I would pause at this point, waiting to hear a second thought expressed (which never occurred). Then I would say offhandedly: "Unless he opened the envelopes."

Even this hint often failed to turn a light on. I'd hear: "But that's against his orders. If he hasn't gotten the whole signal, he *can't* open it."

That answer usually hung in the air only a moment or so. The premise was, after all, that the officer in question had come to feel, on some basis or other (like General Jack D. Ripper in Kubrick's *Dr. Strangelove*, a few years later), that it was time to commence World War III. He was on his way to drop a thermonuclear bomb on Russia, and he wouldn't expect to come back. Everyone I encountered came to agree by this point in the discussion that there was a real problem here, however unlikely.

* * *

Moreover, I had by this time discovered that a comparable situation prevailed not only with alert pilots but also with duty officers at the level of bases, carriers, and the entire Pacific Command. And another pervasive phenomenon I found was the *non*-observance of the two-man rule in command posts throughout the Pacific.

To prevent unauthorized action by a single duty officer with access to Execute codes in any particular command post, there was a universal and supposedly ironclad rule that at least two such officers must be on duty at all times, day and night, and they must both be involved in, and agree on, the authentication of an order to execute nuclear war plans from a higher authority and on their decision to relay this order to subordinate commands.

Since physical conditions varied at different bases, each command post had, I found, devised its own procedures for assuring that this directive was obeyed. A typical procedure would be to have half the authentication code in each of two separate envelopes, with each of the two duty officers to be present at all times holding only one of the envelopes. Then, half the codes to be sent to lower commands for Execute orders and authentications would be filed in one of two separate safes.

Each of the two duty officers would hold one envelope and would possess the combination to only one of the safes. If a signal with an eight-number group, say, was received in the duty office, the officers would open their envelopes and see if the two respective cards inside, each with four numbers, corresponded to the whole group of numbers received. Then, each would open his safe and the two of them would agree (or not) to send the combined messages inside.

In other posts where the office had only one safe, each officer might have just half the combination to it. One way or another, each post purported to have arrangements so that one officer by himself could neither authenticate orders received nor send out authenticated Execute commands.

But in practice, not. As various duty officers explained to me, oftentimes only one man was on duty in the office. The personnel requirements for having two qualified officers sitting around in every such station at literally every moment of the night were just too stringent to be met. Duty rosters did provide for it, but not for backups when one officer "had" to be elsewhere—to get some food or for a medical emergency, his own or, on some bases, his wife's. Did that mean that all subordinate commands would be paralyzed, unable to receive authenticated Execute orders, if the one remaining duty officer received what appeared to be an order to commence nuclear operations during that interval?

That couldn't be permitted, in the eyes of the officers assigned to this duty, each of whom had faced up to the practical possibility of this situation. So each of them had provided for it "unofficially," in his own mind or usually by agreement with his fellow duty officers. Each, in reality, had the combinations to both safes, after all, or some arrangement for acquiring them. If there was only one safe, each officer would, in reality, know the full combination to it. One officer would hold both envelopes when the other had to be away. Where there were more elaborate safeguards, the officers had always spent some of their idle hours late at night figuring out how to circumvent them, "if necessary." They had always succeeded in doing so. I found this in every post I visited.

The officers would tell me this "off the record" but with some pride, partly to reassure me that they had conscientiously and sometimes ingeniously managed to assure that the system would work (to "Go") even if they or their partner didn't happen to be on hand at the crucial moment. But that meant that the two-man rule was only a facade throughout the Pacific. The system's ability to prevent one man alone from sending off Go commands to subordinate units was a false promise. And that was in addition to the fact that the two-man rule, even if both men were present, was obviously vulnerable to collusion between them or coercion (such as a gun in the hand of one of them), either of these especially plausible in a crisis. Some fifteen years later, when I described these early command and control discoveries, and this one in particular, to journalist Bob Woodward, he informed me that he himself had been a nuclear control officer on a command ship during his active duty in the Navy and could confirm my account. He recalled vividly the "precautions" he and his fellow duty officers had taken to assure that one man alone could "if necessary" send an Execute message to subordinate forces. There must be thousands of other former duty officers with memories of their own arrangements for circumventing the two-man rule (which to this day is trumpeted reassuringly in all official descriptions of the nuclear control system).

Later procedures for controlling the launch of silo-based land missiles became much more elaborate, physical, and, supposedly, reliable. But even these had their vulnerabilities.

John H. Rubel, former deputy director of defense research and engineering, writes that the operators of the Minuteman missiles had circumvented the design feature requiring that two different launch control centers, with two duty officers in each, agree within a limited short time to launch. In case one of them had already been destroyed, the system allowed a launch order from just one center to be executed if there had been no signal from the other within a certain predesignated time interval, X. In practice, Rubel found, X was often (perhaps always) set at zero, making it possible for one center alone to launch at any time.

Partly at Rubel's urging, Secretary of Defense McNamara later compelled the Minuteman developers, against great resistance, to install the equivalent of an electronic lock on the Minuteman, such that it couldn't be fired without the receipt of a coded message from higher headquarters. Decades later, long after McNamara's retirement, Bruce Blair, a former Minuteman launch control officer, informed the former secretary that the Air Force had ensured that the codes in the launch control centers were all set continuously at 00000000. According to Blair, McNamara responded, "I am shocked, absolutely shocked and outraged. Who the hell authorized that?" "What he had just learned from me," Blair continues,

> was that the locks had been installed, but everyone knew the combination. The Strategic Air Command (SAC) in Omaha quietly decided to set the "locks" to all zeros in order to circumvent this safeguard. During the early to mid-1970s, during my stint as a Minuteman launch officer, they still had not been changed. Our launch checklist in fact instructed us, the firing crew, to double-check the locking panel in our underground launch bunker to ensure that no digits other than zero had been inadvertently dialed into the panel. SAC remained far less concerned about unauthorized launches than about the potential of these safeguards to interfere with the implementation of wartime launch orders. And so the "secret unlock code" during the height of the nuclear crises of the Cold War remained constant at 00000000.

The reality, as I discovered over and over in the Pacific, was that in the minds of commanders and operators at every level up to CINCPAC Admiral Harry Felt himself, the first task assigned to our study group—assuring that every unit under his command would receive as promptly and reliably as possible a Go order for general nuclear war operations when Felt issued it—was regarded as incomparably more important than the seemingly parallel aim I had chosen to focus on: assuring that no forces would attack enemy targets when Felt or another higher authority had *not* issued such an order and did not desire it to be executed. As we'll see in what follows, these same priorities applied in all commands and at the highest national military and civilian levels during the fifties, and to a considerable degree later.

Throughout the Cold War such priorities reflected a command environment in which

—it was regarded as overwhelmingly more important to assure a Go response when required than to prevent a false alarm or an unauthorized action; and

—there was tremendous emphasis on a *fast*, immediate response to warnings of a nuclear attack and to a high-level Go command, for two reasons:

1. to destroy enemy weapons before they were launched; and
2. to get American weapons launched before they, or command posts and communications, were destroyed.

Effective safety catches, whether in the form of rules or physical safeguards, meant potential *delays* in response. And delays were anathema, dangerous to the mission—of disarming the enemy—and to the survival of the weapons, the command system, and the nation. For one thing, the military commanders were far more conscious than they tended to acknowledge to civilian superiors or staffers of the extreme vulnerability of command centers and communication links. In the face of an enemy believed to be Hitlerian in savagery and armed with a nuclear force believed (incorrectly) to be superior to our own, all these concerns and considerations of safety and high-level control gave way.

And there was a further reason—so I was given to understand by some officers—for the Joint Chiefs of Staff to tolerate the shortcomings of the control system, to put up fierce and prolonged resistance to measures that would tighten control of nuclear weapons up and down the line. That was their distrust, above all in a crisis, of the judgment of civilian commanders and their staff and advisors, especially their willingness to launch nuclear attacks when military commanders believed them to be urgently necessary. That distrust had emerged under Harry Truman during the Korean War (despite Hiroshima and Nagasaki) and intensified under Eisenhower, especially during the Taiwan Straits crisis of 1958. It was to become even more intense under JFK and McNamara.

This was reflected in what seemed to me a peculiar and startling omission, in the envelope authentication procedures of the Pacific Air Forces, which I came across early on in my research in 1959. It proved to be true as well of the strategic forces in SAC. There was only one card in the envelope (and only one envelope) with which to authenticate the last four digits in the eight-character signal. It was, in effect, a Go code to execute the general war plan.

There was no Stop or Return code in the envelope or otherwise in the possession of the plane crew. Once an authenticated Execute order had been received, there was—by design, it turned out—no way to authenticate an order to reverse course from the president or anyone else. And no such unauthenticated order was to be obeyed.

There was no officially authorized way for the president or the JCS or anyone else to stop planes that had received an Execute order—whether they had just taken off or had passed beyond their positive control line—from proceeding to the target and dropping their bombs. From that point on, the planes, whether tactical or strategic, could no more be called back by the president or any subordinate from their attack project than a ballistic missile. This despite the fact that for many SAC planes launching from the United States, the remaining time before they reached their assigned targets after receiving an Execute order might be twelve hours or more: time enough for world history and the framework of civilization to have altered decisively since the initial order, whether by nuclear explosions, coups in the Sino-Soviet bloc, or convincing offers of Soviet surrender, not to mention the discovery of a terrible error.

But that meant there would also be time enough after issuance of an Execute order—as several high-level staff officers told me their superiors worried about—for a presidential change of mind. Fear of that contingency was not the first explanation to be proposed by a control officer for the absence of a Stop or Return order from the authentication envelopes. A common one offered was that if there were two cards in the envelope, one with numbers corresponding to Stop and the other to Go, in the pressure of the crisis the crew member designated to open the envelope might look at the wrong card by mistake. That was pretty feeble as an explanation; if there had been no code received corresponding to a Go card, a Stop code would be unnecessary and meaningless.

The stronger reason given to me in 1960 was that "the Soviets might discover the Stop code and misdirect the whole force back." This is precisely the explanation given to the president in *Dr. Strangelove* for his lack of ability to send a Stop order to the planes that have been launched by the mad base commander General Jack D. Ripper.

I was dumbstruck by the realism of this point, among others, when I first saw the movie in 1964. Harry Rowen and I had gone into D.C. from the Pentagon during the workday to see it "for professional reasons." We came out into the afternoon sunlight, dazed by the light and the film, both agreeing that what we had just seen was, essentially, a documentary. (We didn't yet know—nor did SAC—that existing strategic operational plans, whether for first strike or retaliation, constituted a literal Doomsday Machine, as in the film.)

How, I wondered, had the filmmakers picked up such an esoteric, highly secret (and totally incredible) detail as the lack of a Stop code, and the alleged reason for it? Or, for that matter, the real lack of any physical restraint on the ability of a squadron commander, or even a bomber pilot, to execute an attack without presidential authorization? It turned out that Peter George, one of the screenwriters and the author of *Red Alert*, the novel on which the film was based, was a former Royal Air Force (RAF) Bomber Command flight officer. That suggests that Bomber Command's control system had the same peculiar characteristics as SAC's. And probably for the same underlying reasons.

The real concern, I was told privately by more than one credible staff officer—among others, by Lieutenant Colonel, later Major General, Bob Lukeman in the Air Force office for war plans—was that a civilian president or (if the president were unavailable or Washington was destroyed) some civilian deputy, on whatever basis, might have second thoughts about the attack under way after an Execute order had been sent, and try either to modify it midway or to cancel it. At best, he would be passing up the opportunity for a coordinated *surprise* attack, and at worst, leaving our forces totally disorganized and vulnerable—along with the country— to an enemy attack either already under way or launched as soon as the enemy had detected and figured out what had just happened on our side.

That's the exact argument of General Buck Turgidson, played by George C. Scott in *Dr. Strangelove*, against the president's attempting to recall all the planes that General Ripper had launched toward Russia. It represented fairly the view to be expected in such a situation from any number of Air Force officers, high or low. As the major in Kunsan had put it to me, "If one goes, they might as well all go."

Whether or not this distrust of high-level civilian readiness to initiate nuclear war—which I encountered over and over in my experience in the Pentagon—was a key motive for the absence of a card with a Stop code in the envelopes of the alert forces, it was a fact that the systems designed and operated by the military assured the practical inability of the president or any civilian to reliably stop any bombers from carrying out attacks once they had received authenticated Execute orders (from whomever).† Nor could the president then or now—by exclusive possession of the codes *necessary* to launch or detonate any nuclear weapons (no such exclusive codes have ever been held by any president)—physically or otherwise reliably prevent the Joint Chiefs of Staff or any theater military commander (or, as I've described, command post duty officer) from issuing such authenticated orders. That is, of course, contrary to the impression given to the public by every president up to the present. The impression is false, as I was to discover.

CHAPTER 3

Delegation

How Many Fingers on the Button?

In 1959 the nuclear control officer on the staff of CINCPAC Admiral Harry D. Felt told me that President Eisenhower had given Felt a secret letter, signed by himself, delegating to Felt the authority to execute his nuclear plans on his own initiative if he felt it necessary at a time when communications were out between Washington and his headquarters in Hawaii.

That meant Admiral Felt had this authority for part of every day. That was how often, on average, communications were out between Washington and Hawaii because of atmospheric disturbances to high-frequency radio transmissions.

I didn't ask him if he had actually seen the letter, but he seemed certain that it existed. What he was telling me, in great secrecy, contradicted the most frequently reiterated and emphatic dogma about the nuclear control system: that there were was no pre-delegation of authority, that only the president could legitimately make the decision whether or not to go to nuclear war, and that he must make that determination personally at the moment of decision.

That is what the American public has been told throughout the nuclear era. For decades that assurance, of exclusive presidential control of the decision to go to nuclear war and how it is to be conducted, has been symbolized—and more than symbolized, apparently embodied—by the iconic "football," the briefcase carried by a presidential military aide that is to accompany the president "at all times," containing codes and electronic equipment by which the president, on receiving warning of a nuclear attack, can convey to the military his choice of a response "option" to be executed. In a truly symbolic gesture that television cameras often capture during the inauguration of a new president, the aide carrying the football visibly shifts his gaze from the departing president to the new one at the moment of his swearing in. That shift signifies not only that the new president has acquired the full authority of his office but also that the existence of a civilian commander in chief of the nuclear forces of the United States—with, supposedly, exclusive control of these almost godlike powers of destruction—must not be and has not been interrupted for a single moment.

Now I was hearing that this impression and all the official statements that led to it were false. It was not only the president who could make the decision and issue the orders, and not even (as most people probably assumed, if they thought about it) the secretary of defense or the Joint Chiefs of Staff in the Pentagon, but commanders in the field thousands of miles from Washington who thought their forces might be about to be destroyed. Similar letters, the control officer told me, had gone out to all the unified commanders with nuclear forces and to the commander of the Strategic Air Command in Omaha.

I had come to the Pacific in the command and control study group believing what virtually all Americans believed, in or out of the government: that the president alone was authorized to decide when to launch nuclear attacks. That was why my investigations of how U.S.-initiated nuclear war might arise, as described in the preceding chapter, focused entirely on the possibility of *unauthorized* actions. Now I was hearing from a very credible source that I, along with everyone else, had been mistaken. The current president had, after all, delegated his authority to theater commanders, as well as the Commander in Chief of Strategic Arms Command (CINCSAC). In some circumstances, commanders of four-star rank could issue in their own name an *authorized* directive to undertake nuclear attack without the immediate prior involvement of the president.

Surprising as this was to hear, the practical logic of making such a delegation was clear enough. Without it, the Soviets could paralyze any retaliation to a nuclear attack on the United States simply by destroying Washington before the president had given an Execute order, or perhaps before there was any warning at all. That could not be allowed to happen.

A single nuclear warhead on the capital could kill not only the president but all of his legally designated successors in the cabinet and Congress (and the JCS along with the secretary of defense, the only civilian aside from the president in the military chain of command)—all of them who were in town at that moment. If nuclear deterrence were to have any substantial backing at all—if it were to be more than an empty bluff—it could not be the case that one such explosion would definitively block any authorized, coordinated nuclear response to that or any subsequent nuclear attack. That would be virtually an invitation to the Soviets in a crisis—when they had any reason to fear U.S. escalation to nuclear war—to forestall reliably either a U.S. first strike or even U.S. retaliation to a Soviet preemptive attack by delivering a single warhead on Washington, "decapitating" American political and military leadership.

In fact, if the Soviets were confident that a small, initial "decapitating" attack would thoroughly paralyze our strategic and tactical nuclear forces, a premeditated surprise attack would look not only feasible but also safe for them. Even the best American warning system couldn't reliably, if at all, alert authorities to the approach of just a single vehicle: in particular, a low-flying cruise missile or a short-time-of-flight medium-range ballistic from a submarine or ship, or even a "suitcase" bomb, perhaps smuggled into the capital long in advance.

It seemed obvious once I thought about it. The public's impression of exclusively presidential or even high-level military control, which I'd shared up until that moment, could not be valid. That applied all the more to the notion that only the president himself could "push the button." Could a single assassin's bullet, or a temporary separation of the "football" from the president (as has happened several times, including, later, following the shooting of President Reagan) open a window of total inability to respond to a nuclear attack?

Not really. The theatrical device represented by the president's moment-by-moment day-and-night access to the "football," with its supposedly unique authorization codes, has always been exactly that: theater—essentially a hoax. Whatever the public declarations to the contrary, there *has* to be delegation of authority and capability to launch retaliatory strikes, not only to officials outside the Oval Office but outside Washington too, or there would be no real basis for nuclear deterrence.

At that time, no system of Permissive Action Links (PALs) existed, in which a coded signal was necessary to permit the physical detonation of any nuclear weapon or the launching of a nuclear-armed missile. This would physically prevent launch or detonation without a coded "combination" from a higher authority. If such a system ever came into existence—as I, among others, hoped fervently to help bring about—the combination couldn't be held exclusively by the president or by any individual or group of officials in Washington, D.C., or the Pentagon in Arlington, Virginia. If it were, one large bomb or device exploding on that joint target would lock up and render impotent the entire retaliatory capability of the United States.

The most obviously necessary delegation would be to the headquarters of the Strategic Air Command at Offutt Air Force Base, in Omaha, Nebraska. But that was just as vulnerable to one large bomb as the capital, despite underground shelters in both. SAC had at that time, and throughout the Cold War, an airborne command post with a brigadier general aboard in flight at all times. That one-star Air Force officer would have to have (and, General Curtis LeMay later confirmed to me, he did have) the delegated authority to direct the execution of the SAC war plan. And what I was now being told was that delegation had extended as well to the tactical forces under theater command.

After all, without delegation to CINCPAC, carriers and bases all over the Pacific might be precluded from launching retaliatory strikes just by atmospheric conditions that prevented an Execute message from getting through from the Pentagon to Hawaii, even if Washington had not been hit. But the same logic applied to the problem of relaying an Execute order from CINCPAC headquarters on Oahu to CINCPAC's nuclear forces. Most of these were in "WestPac," the Western Pacific, with the Seventh Fleet carriers or on bases in Korea, Japan, Okinawa, Taiwan, or Guam. They were as far from Oahu as Hawaii was from the continental United States. And communications from Oahu were just as subject to storms over the Pacific and other disturbances as radio signals from Washington were. On average, our study group learned, commanders in Hawaii were cut off from communications from or to Washington *for some part of each day.* Exactly the same was true for communications between commanders in Hawaii and Westpac.

Therefore, the CINCPAC nuclear control officer told me, Admiral Felt had made a comparable delegation of authority to his next lower level of command, including the commander of the Seventh Fleet. Again, this was plausible, logical. And yet, like his first statement, it was startling to me. Was it really true that our practical, secret command arrangements were so sharply at odds with the policy declarations of the White House and secretary of defense? The control officer clearly believed what he was telling me in great confidence (as a member of a high-level consulting team reporting directly to Admiral Felt). But could he be right?

I had the chance to check this out later on our visit to the cruiser *St. Paul*, the command ship of the Seventh Fleet. As recorded in my notes of the January 26, 1960, meeting with Vice Admiral Frederick N. Kivette, commander of the Seventh Fleet, and Vice Admiral Clarence E. Ekstrom, commander of Naval Air Forces in the Pacific, both empha-sized the importance of the Navy doctrine that actual combat operations must be left to the engaged units acting with relative autonomy and with minimal attempt to control them by higher command. Even in limited war, Kivette said, "it wouldn't matter" if communications were out between Oahu and the Seventh Fleet, or even between the Seventh Fleet and the carrier task groups: "Operations would be decentralized, I wouldn't be interfering, unless I had some intelligence they didn't have."

Kivette believed that a limited war would remain centralized only so long as political maneuvering predominated, with no shooting, as in the earlier Lebanon and Taiwan crises in 1958. (Ekstrom had commanded the Sixth Fleet in the Mediterranean during the Lebanon-Iraq crisis.) The two admirals expected and approved extreme decentralization "as soon as shooting started." Thus, although they expected communica-tions to be disrupted frequently, especially in wartime but even for natural causes, they were both relaxed about the implications of this.

They both rejected notions that preplanning could solve problems. One couldn't plan for everything—surprises must be expected. But at the same time, they didn't foresee or desire centralized direction during hostilities. They preferred to rely, they both said, on the judgment of the carrier task group commanders, simply providing them with objectives. And, they stressed, the commander afloat must be given great latitude in interpreting and executing his orders. "You've just got to trust your commander at sea." This applied all the more, they said, to conditions of general nuclear war. They agreed that it would be "nice to know" what Air Force bases had been hit at the outset of a nuclear war or what carriers had been destroyed. But under the conditions of the CINCPAC plan for general nuclear war, "it probably wouldn't matter anyway."

By this point in the discussion, our team seemed to have established some rapport with the admirals. I hadn't indicated to them the unease that I was beginning to feel about their seeming indifference to the unreliability of communications in nuclear war, or in a non-nuclear war that could suddenly turn nuclear. So I ventured to raise the issue I'd been told about in great secrecy. I asked Admiral Kivette if he had heard of a letter from President Eisenhower to Admiral Felt delegating authority over nuclear operations if communications were out. He said, yes, he knew that Admiral Felt held such a letter.

I asked him how common it was for his own flagship to be out of communications with Admiral Felt in Hawaii. He said, "Virtually every day, part of the day."

I asked him, "What if your communications with Oahu were out and you thought, for other reasons, that nuclear war might have commenced, or might be about to? What would you do?"

To all our earlier questions, one or the other of the two admirals had responded immediately and at length. At this one, Admiral Kivette paused meaningfully, then said to me, "I stand mute."

It was the only question that he didn't answer explicitly, and he drew himself up in his chair rather formally as he said it. But he was smiling, indicating—it seemed to me—that he assumed I knew the answer to my question, but that this was all he was supposed to say, and that he knew that it was, in context, an answer. Evidently, he regarded, or he wanted us to know that he was supposed to regard, Admiral Felt's delegation of nuclear authority to him as a more sensitive matter than Eisenhower's delegation to Felt (about which I had already revealed I knew).

After a further pause he added, "Anyway, I just can't believe that we could be cut off from all communications; we could get through to someone, and he would know what was happening."

Admiral Ekstrom added to this, "It would depend on the whole picture. What had been happening up to that moment, how ready are we, are we fueled up, etc."

An hour later I raised the question with Admiral Kivette's nuclear control officer. This officer readily told me that, yes, Admiral Felt had delegated to Admiral Kivette the same authority that, he said, President Eisenhower had delegated in writing to Admiral Felt: to launch nuclear weapons at his own initiative during a crisis in case of communications outage.

If they were right about the letter from the president, this contravened and superseded the guidance I'd read in Top Secret war planning—including the Pacific Command's General Emergency Operations Plan (GEOP) for general nuclear war—that U.S. nuclear attacks could be initiated only by a presidential decision at the time of the attacks. The general public believed that as well, and believed further that the president would never delegate this authority under any circumstances. For once what the public had been told corresponded to the actual secret guidance written into war plans by the JCS. Yet if these officers were correct in what they were telling me, written authorizations by the president, the commander in chief, secretly contradicted this JCS guidance in the war plans. As did further sub-delegation by CINCPAC. It wasn't only one or half a dozen four-star admirals and generals who felt authorized to initiate nuclear operations in some realistic circumstances but their far-flung three-star subordinates as well. And who knew how many others?

I still didn't feel certain that the alleged letters from President Eisenhower actually existed; no one had offered to show them to me, or even claimed to have seen one himself. Yet the affirmation from the Seventh Fleet nuclear control officer that CINCPAC had on his own authority made such a delegation to the Seventh Fleet commander (and perhaps others) meant to me that the *belief* that Eisenhower had himself formally given such authorization to CINCPAC had consequences, whether or not that belief was true.

It was clear from both nuclear control officers' manner in speaking about this that they were telling me something of the highest sensitivity. I refrained from asking whether they were aware of even further delegations to officers still lower in the chain of command. In light of the broadly and firmly held understanding within the military (not only the public)—explicitly confirmed in secret war plans—that authority to initiate nuclear war rested exclusively with the president, such delegations would have looked questionable or even gravely illegal to the recipients if they had not shared a secret belief that the president himself had chosen to make such a delegation to theater commanders. But given that belief—and I found it widely held in the Pacific—it was clear that the same incentives that influenced the president existed for further delegations by lower commanders.

Each level of command had reason to worry that during a crisis, an outage of communications, whether due to atmospheric or technical difficulties or an enemy attack on that command headquarters, could paralyze the nuclear capabilities of subordinate units unless they'd been delegated authority to act under such conditions: as, the commanders apparently all believed, CINCPAC had been by the president. Indeed,

CINCPAC would logically infer that he could not reliably carry out the intention of the president with respect to the actions of his theater nuclear capability in the event that Washington was attacked or out of communication unless he provided explicitly for the possibility—actually, the likelihood—that he himself would also be attacked, or might be out of communications for other, quite ordinary reasons, with his subordinate commands.

He could provide for that only in the same way that President Eisenhower had: namely, by allowing lower commanders to exercise their own judgment in those circumstances. In any case, the two admirals found this sub-delegation totally compatible, even obligatory, in terms of naval traditions. But in this situation the logic that applied to the Navy and to CINCPAC applied as well to all the other unified and specified commanders to whom the president had allegedly delegated authority. These were the theater commanders in Europe, Alaska, the Mediterranean, the Atlantic, and the Strategic Air Command, as well as NORAD, the air defense command.

Unless the president forbade such further delegation explicitly (and perhaps even if he did), the example of his own delegation to CINCPAC and other theater commanders seemed likely to be imitated, not only in the Pacific but also in other theaters around the world. And it was implicit in what these officers told me that the president had *not* explicitly forbidden these theater commanders to delegate that authority any further in the manner that CINCPAC had sub-delegated to the Seventh Fleet.

Nevertheless, I found it hard to believe that the president would have wanted any further delegations, or that he even knew they existed. His own action of delegation—assuming these letters really existed—distributed the authority to just over half a dozen four-star generals and admirals. Further delegations multiplied the number of individuals with authority, under some conditions, to initiate nuclear war, and also drew into that circle officers of progressively lower rank, lesser experience and maturity, and narrower responsibilities and access to information.

At some point, as one moved down the chain of command, the advantages of providing further assurance of a retaliatory response would be outweighed—it appeared to me—by the increased risks of a wrong response. Not only were the risks progressively greater as lower units and levels of command became involved, but from the president's perspective, the need or incentive for subsequent delegations was progressively smaller, involving smaller portions of the overall retaliatory forces.

But to a commander at the lower level, whose mission understandably seemed to him to have transcendent importance if it involved any nuclear weapons at all, it wouldn't look that way. He would want to be sure that "his" weapons took part in the big war—the fight for national survival and victory. If you left the decision whether to delegate further to each successive layer of command, I suspected it would be likely to go down to the bottom. In the limit, every flight commander, if not every pilot with a weapon aboard, would feel *authorized*, under some circumstances, to initiate nuclear war with the Communist bloc. (He might even *be* authorized, orally or in writing, by an immediate superior, with or without the knowledge of higher levels of command.)

I accepted, as inescapable, the idea of Eisenhower's delegation of authority to execute war plans to a handful of four-star admirals and generals outside Washington. But I had growing unease, to put it mildly, at the prospect that this delegation reverberated downward in a widening circle that permitted *authorized* launch by more and more subordinate commanders, not to mention the physical possibility of *unauthorized* action by control officers or by crews of alert nuclear vehicles, whether planes or submarines.

That was already in my mind when I decided to take the trip to Kunsan described earlier. Disturbing as I found that base commander's expressed readiness for conscientious insubordination, it seemed more in sync with the looseness of nuclear control in the Pacific than I would have thought possible, had I not learned of the widespread practice of delegation.

Moreover, it occurred to me that arrangements made to allow an authorized initiation of nuclear attacks under emergency conditions, at a given level of command below Washington, could be exploited to permit an *unauthorized* initiative at that same level, either by an aberrant commander or perhaps by one of his subordinates, in the absence of a real emergency. (A few years later, that was the basic plot element in the film *Dr. Strangelove*.)

But what now seemed more likely was that one or another sane and conscientiously loyal commander might have reason to believe that he was *authorized* to start a nuclear war under not-uncommon circumstances: possibly on the basis of ambiguous or false tactical warning during a failure of communications with higher command. Moreover, indications of a possible imminent attack on his own forces would put great pressure on such a commander to take steps to protect them from destruction, as well as to preempt the enemy attack and limit damage to other U.S. forces and the population.

I felt that this sub-delegation was a situation that the president should know about. I suspected strongly that he didn't. I couldn't believe that he would have wanted or allowed authority to start World War III to be as widespread as it appeared to be. If so, then once informed, he might want to reconsider the initial delegation to theater commanders. Or more likely, since that seemed incompatible with the deterrence of a decapitating strike, he could take special pains to keep them from extending the authority to initiate nuclear war far down the command chain (and truly enforce measures to prevent unauthorized action, such as introducing Permissive Action Links).

In 1960 I didn't know what I could do about this problem. How, to whom, and through what channels I might raise it were delicate questions. It wouldn't serve anything if the main reaction to my reporting and recommendations was consternation that I knew and was conveying this sensitive information, along with an effort to track down and punish the people who had confided it to me. Since I was working for CINCPAC precisely on command and control of nuclear operations, the officers who had told me could argue that they felt I had a "need to know." But it was harder for me to make that case for telling someone outside the Pacific Command unless they were above CINCPAC in the chain of command. Who in Washington had the authority to investigate and perhaps change this situation?

Obviously, the president, but at this point I wasn't working for anyone in the White House on these matters, nor was anyone at RAND. It was hard to contemplate getting to the president or any staff person close to him without revealing what it was that needed urgent attention. The secretary of defense? Same problem. Yet to reveal it to anyone who didn't know it already (that is, to almost anyone) was to open myself to subsequent charges of extreme indiscretion, a major breach of security. That could quickly knock me, and RAND as well, out of the chance of remedying this or any other situation.

I wasn't sure how to manage it, but I was determined to find some way to bring this issue to the president's attention.

CHAPTER 4

Iwakuni

Nuclear Weapons off the Books

In my fieldwork for CINCPAC, I found yet another case where considerations of safety and even of alliances and rights to U.S. bases abroad yielded to a command's preference for fast action. In this case it represented a conflict with higher authority covered by secrecy and lies that amounted to insubordination and even to treaty violation. It was one more example of the surprising—and alarming—looseness of control of nuclear weapons in the Pacific Command.

In PACOM's GEOP, a number of the bases scheduled to deliver nuclear weapons in the event of general war were located in Japan. But U.S. plans for using these bases collided with a central Japanese policy, which renounced and forbade the development, possession, or *introduction* of nuclear weapons in Japan. A legacy of Hiroshima was what U.S. planners called Japan's nuclear "allergy." A major provision of Japan's mutual security treaty with the United States in 1960 was the explicit agreement that no nuclear weapons would be stationed in Japan. Any abrogation of this agreement could easily have cost us our major Asian ally and our most strategically important bases in the East.

In practice the United States acted as if there were one exception to this agreement. It was, I was told, known to some high officials in Japan, but it was never acknowledged publicly by either side. American warships that came into Japanese ports for R&R—rest and recuperation visits, which were very important to maintaining Navy morale in the Pacific, and thus reenlistment—virtually all had nuclear weapons aboard. This didn't apply only to the carriers, which were loaded with nuclear bombs for their planes. As Admiral Eugene LaRocque later testified, nearly every Navy ship that could carry a nuclear weapon of some kind did so, down to destroyers that had nuclear torpedoes and antisubmarine weapons. None of them ever offloaded these weapons before they came into a Japanese harbor.

The Department of Defense had and still has a policy that they will not acknowledge the presence or absence of nuclear weapons on any particular warship or base anywhere in the world. A major purpose of this policy is to avoid having either to lie explicitly or to admit having nuclear weapons aboard these ships in Japanese ports whenever the political opposition in Japan or antinuclear activists raised the question, which they did regularly. When high-ranking Japanese officials were asked this question, they said (falsely) they were confident no nuclear weapons were present on these ships, since they had not been notified otherwise by the United States, nor had there been the prior consultation required by the security treaty.

The United States could justify its failure to notify the Japanese otherwise on the grounds that Japanese officials didn't want to be told officially, thereby enabling them to continue giving this answer without demonstrably lying. And if the truth ever came out, the United States could say that its understanding of the agreement didn't require it to notify the Japanese of the presence of weapons that were not "stationed" in Japan but were merely in transit, on temporary visits.

Still, the fact that these weapons would be present in Japanese ports for days to weeks at a time on a given ship, and that at any given time there was usually one or more such ships somewhere at anchor in Japanese harbors, meant that Japanese coastal cities surely constituted high-priority targets in Soviet nuclear war planning, just as if they had had nuclear weapons permanently stationed there. And since these weapons were on ships, the chance of a collision or an accident detonating the high explosives on one of these weapons or otherwise releasing radioactive materials in the vicinity of a Japanese city was not zero, and it was higher than it would have been if the weapons had been stored ashore.

That possibility also applied to the nuclear reactors on nuclear-powered ships and submarines. Eventually, the Department of Defense hoped to be able to bring Polaris submarines into Japanese waters, with their additional risk of an accident involving a nuclear weapon, as was also true of the nuclear bombs on carriers or other ship-based weapons. A high-explosive detonation could conceivably lead to a partial or full nuclear explosion, but even without that unlikely result, the dispersion of radioactive material in a populated area would be a spectacularly bad way of announcing to the Japanese public the presence of U.S. nuclear weapons in their waters. But the risk, compared with the convenience of using Japanese ports, seemed small enough to be worth taking.

Apart from this arrangement, however, I was always told that we didn't violate the agreement to the extent of actually basing weapons ashore in any of our U.S. Air Force bases in Japan. Planes on these bases were assigned a very sizable number of nuclear targets in the Vladivostok area and China in the event of general war, but their weapons would have had to be delivered from Okinawa or Guam. There were KC-97 tankers on alert in Okinawa loaded with nuclear weapons for these Japanese bases. The operation involving them was code-named High Gear. If there was an order to execute war plans or a launch on warning, these planes would take off for Japan.

In principle, we were to get the approval of the Japanese government before any weapons could be landed in Japan or launched from Japanese bases. But the alert plans called for the transport planes, once launched from Okinawa on warning, to land on bases in Japan and deliver their weapons whether or not permission had yet been granted from the Japanese. There was no provision for them to return to their bases on Okinawa with bombs aboard if the warning turned out to be a false alarm, or if the Japanese failed to grant permission during the several-hour flight to Japan.

So a false warning, as well as a true one, could have resulted in U.S. nuclear bombs landing in Japan, in violation of the treaty. That was a possibility explicitly allowed in our planning, though it was kept secret from the Japanese. If that possibility had become known to the Japanese public, the effect might have been almost as bad as if they had become aware that the plan had been carried out. But it seemed unlikely that the Japanese would learn of this planning. The risk was regarded as acceptable. And if a false alarm did occur, the planes would be landing at U.S. bases, so the Japanese were unlikely to become aware of a temporary violation.

The sensitivity of these plans was a tribute to the fact that the treaty provision was actually taken with considerable seriousness. Everyone understood that a known violation of that provision was likely to lead to an abrogation of the security treaty, and probably to the fall of any pro-U.S. government in Japan and its replacement by a government that might entirely change its relationship with the United States and China. Almost certainly it would lead to the loss of U.S. bases both in Japan and Okinawa.

Given these stakes, there was apparently no pressure from the Air Force to have nuclear weapons stored on their bases in Japan, risking discovery by the Japanese of U.S. violation of the treaty. SAC already had nuclear forces stationed in Okinawa and Korea, so having marginally more forces in Japan didn't justify the danger of losing Japan as an ally.

However, in early 1960 I was told in great secrecy by a nuclear control officer in the Pacific that one small Marine air base at Iwakuni in Japan had a secret arrangement whereby its handful of planes with general war missions would get their nuclear weapons very quickly in the event of a general war alert. In contrast to all the other planes on Japanese bases, the Marines at Iwakuni would have nuclear weapons within minutes instead of hours. Because of the special relation of the Marines to the Navy, there was a flat-bottomed ship for landing tanks on a beach (LST, for Landing Ship, Tank), anchored just offshore Iwakuni with nuclear weapons aboard, loaded onto amphibious tractors, just for the small group of planes on this base.

This LST, the USS *San Joaquin County*, had a cover mission as an electronics repair ship. It was permanently stationed not just inside the three-mile limit of Japanese territorial waters but anchored a couple of hundred yards from the beach, in the tidal waters. By any standards it was stationed within the territory of Japan. And so were its nuclear weapons.

In a nuclear emergency, the *San Joaquin County* would operate as it was designed to do in an amphibious landing. It would haul anchor and come straight ashore. The front of the ship would open up like a clam-shell, and amphibious tractors loaded with nuclear weapons would come down a ramp into the water or directly onto the beach, then head on land straight to the airstrip where the weapons would be loaded onto the Marine planes.

Thus, this handful of planes would have nuclear weapons some six to ten hours in advance of the other hundreds of Air Force planes on bases in Japan. If they made use of this head start and launched their missions immediately, they would be among the first planes in the world, along with planes on Korea, to release bombs on Russian (or Chinese) targets. Since they were so few and their targets so peripheral, the main effect of this would be to alert Communist forces worldwide of the onset of general war, if they had not launched first. But presumably in most cases, the Marine planes would be held back to be launched with other forces, so that the effect of their having weapons sooner would be imperceptible.

However, the effect of the Japanese discovering the permanent presence of these weapons would be very perceptible indeed. It might well have blown the United States out of Japan. If the Japanese government had become aware of the situation, and more particularly if the political opposition had become aware of it, the United States would have been likely to lose all its bases in Japan. There could even have been a total rupture of diplomatic relations between the countries. Japan might possibly have shifted toward the Chinese.

For all these reasons, this was regarded, so I was told, as a super secret from the Japanese and was relatively little known even among U.S. Air Force and Navy planners. Yet the arrangement was apparently fairly well known at the base itself, and the LST was said to occasionally rehearse landing the tractors and bombs. What was known to the pilots, the tractor crews, and the LST crew at the base was potentially knowable to some fraction of their Japanese girlfriends in the region. In fact, the planners to whom I spoke about this, at Seventh Fleet in Japan and back in Hawaii, tended to assume that Communist spies must already know of the situation and were waiting for the right time and opportunity to reveal it to biggest effect.

RAND studies of the possibilities of sabotage suggested to me what that way could be. It would be no trick for Communist frogmen, Japanese or others, to swim out to that ship and plant limpet mines on its side. An explosion on what purported to be an electronics repair ship would at the least raise public questions about its nature and provoke an official investigation, which could quickly reveal its cargo of nuclear weapons. If the saboteurs were lucky and used a big enough mine, they might even detonate the high explosive on one or more of the nuclear weapons aboard, scattering radioactive material in the Iwakuni region (which happens to be not far from Hiroshima), or even conceivably cause a partial nuclear explosion. There would be no way of telling, in any of these cases, that the explosion had been caused by outsiders as opposed to an accidental explosion of American weapons stationed aboard the ship. The actual cause of the explosion that destroyed the battleship *Maine* in Havana harbor, propelling the United States into war more than a hundred years ago, was controversial for seventy-five years.

The stationing of these weapons in Japanese tidal waters, to no tangible military benefit whatever, was one of the most irresponsible actions imaginable. That's how it seemed to all the nuclear planners who were in on the secret. But they didn't know what to do about it, since they presumed it had been accepted by CINCPAC, a Navy admiral. Did any civilian authorities or military commands higher than CINCPAC know about it? These officers didn't know, and only at great risk to their own careers could they try to find out or alert higher levels bypassing the intermediate levels of command and CINCPAC.

That may be why one officer told me about it in the first place, and why others told me about their concerns. As a RAND consultant, someone not permanently wired into their chain of command, I could alert higher levels or other agencies without paying the same price they would have faced. And they could justify telling me because of the general instructions that they could tell me anything for purposes of my research.

Still, just as with the issue of sub-delegation in the last chapter, I wasn't sure what to do with the information, since I didn't then have contacts in the Office of Secretary of Defense, the State Department, or the White House. I told high officials at RAND about it, and they in turn, I was told, passed it on to a general in Air Force Plans. Richard Goldstein, a RAND vice president, brought the word back to me that Air Force officers agreed that this situation was extremely serious but that it wasn't easy for them to do anything about it because it was a Navy matter. For many years there had been a working alliance between the Navy and the Air Force to emphasize the strategic importance of nuclear weapons, a principle that worked to the budgetary disadvantage of the Army. It would be a delicate matter, threatening this alliance, for the Air Force to raise questions about where and how the Navy was storing its nuclear weapons.

For the same reasons as in the case of delegation, I had to proceed carefully.

CHAPTER 5

The Pacific Command

From the beginning of our study group's work in Hawaii, I had urged that we needed to know the nature of the war plans that an Execute order would set in motion. I was assigned this part of the study. To this end, I asked for and was granted access to the Top Secret "cage" in the Plans section of CINCPAC headquarters. This was literally a cage covered by heavy wire netting, guarded by a warrant officer and another guard who was also a librarian. Inside, the cage was the size of a small library room, with many shelves of documents and a filing system. My access was apparently unique for a civilian.

I spent days, nights, and weekends in the cage, poring over current nuclear plans. I soon learned the structure of the overall U.S. nuclear war plan, up and down the chain of command. These all flowed from the CINCPAC's GEOP, which outlined the broad objectives and princi-ples of U.S. nuclear capability in the Pacific and was the basis for the Army, Navy, and Air Force plans, which in turn formed the basis for the plans of fleets, divisions, squadrons, carriers, and even individual pilots down various branches of the chain of command.

In reading these plans, and later as I visited command centers, aircraft carriers, and airstrips throughout the Pacific, I began to notice what seemed to me a startling omission. I presumed without question that at the highest level of nuclear planning, provision was made for conflicts that involved only the Soviet Union: arising, for example, over access to West

Berlin or a Soviet attack on Europe or the United States. Yet, I soon discovered that in the plans of Pacific forces, from top to bottom, there was no provision at all for attacking only the Russian targets in their sphere. In every plan for war with the Soviet Union, Chinese targets (including every major city in China) were also struck.

As I gathered from talking with CINCPAC nuclear planners, there was a strong incentive for them to assume—and they did assume—that under any circumstances in which we were fighting Russia, we would also want to annihilate its Communist partners, the Chinese. Because of range limitations, almost no Russian targets lay within CINCPAC reach, except for a few in the area of Vladivostok and Siberia. Thus, if the president gave an order to attack only Soviet targets, CINCPAC forces, having destroyed Vladivostok and a few other minor targets in eastern Russia, would essentially have to sit out the war as observers—"on the sidelines," as they thought of it—during the big game.

That this thought was intolerable to officers in the Pacific at levels near the very highest was confirmed for our whole study group on the afternoon we made an official visit to the flagship of the Seventh Fleet, the *St. Paul*, steaming in western Pacific waters. After landing by helicopter from a carrier, we held a meeting with Vice Admirals Kivette and Ekstrom, Commander of Naval Air in the Pacific.

I have previously described their comments on the problem of delegation. However, by far the strongest reaction to any question we raised with the two admirals in our two-hour meeting came when I mentioned as a possibility a decision by the president to go to war against the Soviet Union alone, not against China. Both admirals drew back and seemed genuinely to go into shock. Admiral Kivette said, "I would hope that's out of the question!"

I repeated the question: "But suppose that an order did come from the JCS to execute war plans against the Soviet Union only. How would you respond to it, and how long would it take you?"

There was a long silence in which it appeared that Admiral Ekstrom was almost holding back an urge to vomit. Then he said, enunciating each phrase separately, almost gasping, as if in pained incredulity, "You have . . . to assume . . . some . . . modicum . . . of rationality . . . in higher authority . . . that they would not do something . . . so insane . . . as to go to war . . . against one Communist power . . . while letting the other one off . . . scot-free."

Faced with such a visceral response (the elisions are in my notes, handwritten just afterwards), I chose not to pursue that line of discussion, although it was already becoming evident in intelligence available at RAND that a split between the Chinese and the Soviets had developed. (It turned out to have arisen in particular out of the Russian refusal to provide nuclear weapons to the mainland Chinese during the Taiwan Strait crisis of 1958, and their subsequent withdrawal of Soviet nuclear technicians from China.)

I thought I was discovering a parochial bias in the Pacific Command that should be brought to the attention of planners and decision makers at the national level. I was wrong. It was the next year that I learned, in the Pentagon, that President Eisenhower and the Joint Chiefs of Staff shared the admirals' views entirely. They had no intention, under any circumstances, to shock Admiral Kivette with an order to spare the Chinese—even initially or provisionally—in any war with the Soviet Union.

But by the time I learned that, it had long been clear to me that if the highest authorities did give such an order—if they had changed their minds in a crisis and did, after all, wish operations to exclude China at least initially—it would be virtually impossible to implement that order quickly in the Pacific. That was true for technical as well as bureaucratic reasons. CINCPAC planners were working extremely hard, around the clock each year, just to produce one single plan for nuclear war against the Sino-Soviet bloc, and they simply didn't have the ability to produce a second plan for war with the Soviet Union alone.

Out of a list of tens of thousands of targets throughout the Sino-Soviet bloc that intelligence had identified as important, the Pentagon ordered lower levels to make plans to hit around a thousand of the most valuable of these in the case of general war with the Communist bloc. The major challenge lower-level planners faced was that many of these targets were co-located: that is, two targets to be hit by two different planes were close enough that the blast from one could knock the second plane out of the air, or, at a much greater distance, blind its pilots.

To avoid this problem—referred to as "interference"—the planners were doing extremely intricate calculations, mostly by hand, to devise routes into the target timed so that the planes wouldn't be blown out of the air by nearby explosions. (In this era, nuclear warheads were to be delivered primarily by planes. When, decades later, delivery systems mostly switched over to missiles, planners discovered the same problem: the blast from one missile would knock other missiles off course or destroy them.) They were dealing with thousands of targets with multiple weapons on most of them, so they had plans for the planes to weave through a virtual minefield of detonations, timing it perfectly to miss an explosion on this side of the plane, and then one on the other, on and on.

The key to all this was knowing exactly when each explosion was going to go off. Thus, everything had to be timed perfectly, based on how long it took for a crew to get off the ground after receiving an Execute order, how long it took to get up to altitude, the cruise speed of the plane once it reached altitude, and the distance to target. Plans specified that a particular explosion would go off at time-over-target, or TOT (for example, 117 minutes and 32 seconds after the Execute order), and then a nearby explosion would go off 2 minutes and 12 seconds later, and so forth. If everything went according to plan, no plane would be struck down by the explosion from a bomb dropped by another plane; no "fratricide" would occur.

As I read these plans and discussed them with the planners, I quickly noticed several glaring problems with this entire endeavor: obvious and predictable reasons why everything would *not* go according to plan.

To begin with, I read reports from launch drills all over the Pacific and saw that the difference in times, for different bases, was often *hours* between sending the Execute order and the actual launches on the various bases, in a plan in which *seconds* mattered for planes to miss nearby explosions. The problem was not with crews on alert; they practiced getting the planes off the ground a great deal, and could do it within ten minutes of receiving their orders. (Of course, that, too, varied in reality, but this element of the chain was comparatively dependable.) However, that was ten minutes from *receiving the order.*

The orders were supposed to get to the hundreds of different aircraft carriers and bases throughout the Pacific at the same time, and all the plans were based on the assumption that they would. Yet, as I read the reports of command post exercises—lists of when drill orders went out and when the bases actually received these orders during the exercises— I saw that the actual time when the various bases received their orders often varied by one, two, or as much as four hours. Some bases *never* received the orders. There were always problems in atmospheric disturbances or in messages getting misdirected or held up in some relay point.

Furthermore, the ability to meet the times in the plan depended very heavily on wind. If the planes were all coming from the same direction, then wind would have little effect; it would either slow all the planes down or speed all of them up at the same rate. However, the planes hitting each target came from different bases; this was deliberate cross-targeting (in case one base had been destroyed). The planes often came at the target from 90- or even 180-degree differences in angle. Thus, whatever the wind was doing, it would affect the two sets of planes totally differently—slowing one down and speeding the other up.

How did the planners deal with the fact that you wouldn't even know which way the wind would be blowing on the various paths to the targets at the actual time of the real Execute order? There was no way to make arrangements for each possible variation in wind direction and intensity, so their way of dealing with the problem was not to allow for wind at all. They simply assumed there was no wind. This made the plans worthless for avoiding interference.

I pointed these two problems out to a planner once. "Yes, I've thought of these problems before," he said.

"Well, doesn't that make you question the value of making all these calculations and plans?"

"These men are risking their lives flying out there. We've got to do what we can to save their lives."

"But it doesn't seem that this plan has any chance to save any lives at all. It would save lives only if the execution followed the plan down to the second, and there's not even the remotest possibility of that happening."

"Well, we're ordered to make these calculations, so that's what we do."

The complexity of the calculations involved in this (illusory) effort meant that the planners couldn't make many alternate plans. It took them all year to produce the single yearly-updated plan, and while they paid lip service to the need for flexibility, in practice they were extremely resistant to the idea of allowing for more than one plan: their plan, which included targets throughout China as well as Russia. The thought of even tinkering with their target list—let alone omitting a whole nation from it—sent shudders down planners' spines whenever I raised it.

Many operations and plan centers and command posts in Okinawa, Formosa, Guam, and Tokyo, and on several carriers and command ships in the Pacific that I visited, had a large map showing nuclear targets. It was their most secret map, usually covered by a screen or curtain when people who lacked authorization (unlike me) were being briefed in the room. These maps, typically, did not demarcate at all between China and Russia. The Sino-Soviet bloc appeared as one giant landmass, with arrows and pins indicating the various targets. You could not tell simply by inspecting the pins whether they were in China or Russia. On some maps, local planners had pinned a piece of colored string indicating roughly the boundary between Russia and China.

This meant that a high-level planner in that division, faced with orders to strike one country but not the other, could not, just by inspecting those targets, decide reliably which ones to pull. In fact, as I learned, doing so would be an extremely laborious process. The computer programs listed tail numbers (which was the way airplanes were designated) assigned to particular coordinates, but they did not list the countries along with the coordinates. Sorting out what coordinate was in which country could not be done in minutes or hours; it would take days or weeks.

Furthermore, on actual runways I visited in Guam, Okinawa, and Korea and on carriers, planes were targeted in a particular fashion on the alert runway—ready to take off on a ten-minute alert. One plane with a 1.1-megaton bomb slung under it was targeted for the Vladivostok area, while a plane next to it on the runway, which would be taking off at a few seconds' interval, was targeted and briefed and rehearsed for a target in China. Thus, planes within an alert section on a given runway would be entirely scrambled in terms of their national targets. They practiced their drills—which involved complex timing between the different takeoffs—to launch in the same routine sequence. There was no routine for only the China-targeted planes to launch, or only the Russia-targeted planes.

The pilots themselves generally did not know which country they were targeting; the targeting was handled by the crew of an IBM computer system, which did not identify whether the target would hit China or Russia, providing only coordinates instead. Thus, there was no way, either manually or in the computer programs, to quickly unscramble the targets and assure that, for example, only planes 7, 6, and 11, which were targeted for Russia, should take off from that alert force.

All these factors combined to create a situation in which, if we were under attack, it would be simply physically impossible to retaliate against Russian or Chinese targets alone, even if the president ordered his forces to do so.

High-level authorities, wishing to target Russia alone, could, in principle, cut out CINCPAC forces entirely, since all but a few of their bases were focused on China. But they would do that only if it occurred to them that there might be a problem. I never found anyone in Washington who had any idea that there was this kind of problem. No one, as far as I could tell, was aware of it. Few people had access to more than a couple of levels of nuclear war planning, and those who did didn't take the time to review far lower-level plans or to observe actual implementation provisions in the field. They left these tasks to lower-level commanders (who generally didn't have access to the higher-level plans).

But as I was to learn, the reason they hadn't confronted this as a possible problem was not due, as I'd come to imagine, to the idiosyncrasies of the PACOM commanders or their geographic position. It had come from above. As I came to see the highest-level planning in the Pentagon—not available at PACOM and not supposed to be seen by civilian officials—the president and CINCSAC were no more inclined than the Pacific Command to contemplate a war with Russia alone that spared the Chinese.

CHAPTER 6

The War Plan
Reading the JSCP

In the course of my work in the Pacific, I had several discussions with Dr. Ruth M. Davis, who was in charge of computer development for CINCPAC. She was one of the highest-ranking civilians working directly for the military anywhere. When I described some of the puzzles and startling characteristics of the plans I was reading, she told me, in great confidence, of a plan she said I should see if I wanted to understand the nature of U.S. nuclear war planning. It was called the JSCP (pronounced "J-SCAP"), for Joint Strategic Capabilities Plan, and it was on this that CINCPAC's GEOP was based. She said that the secretary of defense and the president did not know of the nature or even the existence of the JSCP, nor did any other civilian authority. That was confirmed for me by an officer in the war plans division of the Air Force, Lieutenant Colonel Bob Lukeman, who eventually lent me a copy to read in the Pentagon.

To understand how there could be a top-level nuclear war plan of which the secretary of defense had no awareness, it's necessary to know something of the history of the relationship between the secretary of defense and the military. Prior to 1947, when the National Military Establishment, renamed in 1949 the Department of Defense, was created—combining the Departments of War (Army) and Navy, with the Air Force emerging from the Army as an independent service—there was no secretary of defense. The responsibilities of the secretary of defense gradually evolved over the next decade. Before 1958, the secretary of defense and his assistant secretaries in the Office of the Secretary of Defense (OSD) were seen as functioning essentially in nonoperational areas such as procurement, research and development, personnel, and budget, and not as having responsibilities or command powers in direct areas of combat operations or planning.

Thus, a secretary of defense like Charles Wilson might or might not be in on high-level crisis discussions and decisions, such as the Quemoy crisis of 1954–55. The record of this early period shows that the secretaries of defense were sometimes present in crucial meetings and sometimes not. It depended on their personalities and their relationship with the president. During the whole early era of the institution of this office, the JCS had a basis for saying that the secretary and his subordinate staff had no "need to know" operational war plans, since he was not involved in the operational command.

In 1958, however, the Reorganization Act put the secretary of defense directly in the chain of command, second to the president as a link to the unified and specified commanders and their subordinate commands. (A unified commander was, essentially, a theater commander who, as in the Pacific or Europe, had elements from different services under his command. A specified commander—there was only one, the Strategic Air Command—had units from just one service.) This act cut the JCS out from the chain of command. It was President Eisenhower's specific intent to do that. He had no respect for the JCS as a body, having dealt with them as Army chief of staff and later as the supreme commander in Europe. He was particularly disillusioned with their postwar performance and wanted to abolish them entirely. However, they were preserved mainly by Congress, which wrote into the Reorganization Act that, without being in the chain of command, the JCS should serve as the "principal military advisors" to the president.

The secretary of defense at the time of the 1958 act was Neil McElroy, who had been CEO at Procter & Gamble. He was said to be a very intelligent man, but he had no background in military matters and he put in an unusually short workday because he tended to his sick wife. Thus, as I was later told by Air Staff officers, it was relatively easy for the JCS to manipulate him. They got McElroy to sign a Department of Defense directive that reinterpreted the legislated act: "The chain-of-command is from the President as Commander-in-Chief, to the Secretary of Defense, to the Unified and Specified Commanders, *through* the Joint Chiefs of Staff" (emphasis added). This implied that the Joint Chiefs would be, in some sense, a channel for his directives. They further got him to agree, as a practical matter, to delegate all operational responsibilities to them. In effect, the act and President Eisenhower's intentions were circumvented. Although it was still on the books, it resulted in no real change of operating responsibilities in 1958 or 1959.

Secretary Thomas Gates, who succeeded McElroy under Eisenhower, had much stronger instincts to exercise control. Yet, with respect to the Office of the Secretary of Defense—comprising the secretary and his staff but also all the deputy and assistant secretaries and their staffs— the JSCP was and remained what later secretary of defense Donald Rumsfeld would have called an "unknown unknown": something they didn't know they didn't know about.

In fact, I was to learn, the JCS had formally adopted, in writing, a set of practices designed to keep the secretary of defense from ever asking any questions directly about the general war plan. The first protective practice was to call the annual war plan the Joint Strategic Capabilities Plan, which did not betray to a layman that it had to do with current operations or, more specifically, with current nuclear war targeting. It was usually referred to by its initials JSCP, but the JCS had issued a directive in writing, which I read, that the words "Joint Strategic Capabilities Plan, or the capital letters JSCP, should never appear in correspondence between the JCS and any agency of the Office of the Secretary of Defense."

Any JCS staff papers to be referred to the secretary of defense or his office were to be retyped to eliminate any possible references to the JSCP. If there was an absolute need to refer to such plans in some oblique fashion, the directive continued, reference was to be made to "capabilities planning" (lowercase), which would, again, not suggest the existence of a specific plan or suggest that it was any kind of war plan at all.

That phrase—no less than the official title, Joint Strategic Capabilities Plan—was a euphemism, a cover. It was meant to obscure from the secretary—and more important, from his deputy and assistant secretaries and their civilian staffers—that there existed a single highest-level annual operational plan for the conduct of general and limited war, the authoritative guidance for all lower-level operational war plans.

All this was intended to preempt the JCS nightmare: that the secretary or a civilian working for him might see this acronym in a document, might ask what it meant, and then ask to see the plan. This could open the possibility of civilians working for the president actually reviewing the plan and demanding changes. A vague reference to "issues arising in capabilities planning," which the JCS directive prescribed, gave such officials no handle to ask for a specific document, or a hint that there was an overriding piece of paper that would be worth their while to read.

As a result, almost no civilian, including the secretary of defense, was aware that a piece of paper of the character of the JSCP existed. That, of course, extended to its critical "Annex C"—the SAC war plan, which laid out in some detail the nature of our general (nuclear) war operations. The JSCP stated, "In the event of general war, Annex C would be executed."

Reading that statement by itself, knowing what Annex C was, one might naturally infer that that provision virtually defined "general war," in operational terms. It was when the president would direct that the SAC war plan, attached, should be executed against our principal adversary, the Soviet Union. But when might he do that?

Obviously, such a fateful decision would depend on circumstances and the president's judgment, and could be left unspecified. At the same time, it would have seemed natural to give some sense of the various circumstances contemplated. Obviously, the arrival or unmistakable imminence of a Soviet surprise nuclear attack on the United States or its forces would be one such circumstance. This was the scenario that RAND strategic analysts focused on almost exclusively.

Those with knowledge of NATO planning and commitments (almost any planner working in the Pentagon) would know that a massive Soviet non-nuclear attack that threatened to overwhelm NATO forces and to occupy Western Europe would be a compelling occasion for the president to launch the SAC war plan. (Polls throughout the Cold War showed, surprisingly, that most Americans—in contrast to most citizens of Western Europe—were not aware that the United States had made such an official commitment to our NATO allies.) Were there any other circumstances that justified the deployment of SAC and other tactical nuclear forces?

In fact, an explicit definition of "general war" did appear in the JSCP. This was perhaps the most sensitive piece of information in the entire document, and the main reason for protecting it from the eyes of civilian authority. I'll never forget the moment when—thanks to Lieutenant Colonel Bob Lukeman of the Air Staff—I was given an opportunity in a basement room of the Pentagon to read this holy of holies, and I finally came upon the definition: "General War is defined as *armed conflict with the Soviet Union.*"

To properly understand the hair-raising import of this proposition, one had to read it in the context of two other key assertions in the JSCP: "In general war, Annex C will be executed"; and "in general war, a war in which the armed forces of the USSR and of the U.S. are overtly engaged, the basic military objective of the U.S. Armed Forces is the defeat of the *Sino-Soviet Bloc.*"

The meaning of "*armed conflict*," in this case the key trigger to unleashing the full fury of the SAC war plan against both the Soviet bloc and China, was subject to some narrow controversy in military circles. It was generally accepted that a platoon or company-level skirmish with Russian forces in the Berlin corridors or on the borders of East Germany—which might not represent a deliberate decision by any Soviet leader—was not to be regarded as "armed conflict" for the purposes of this definition in the JSCP. But what about a brigade-level conflict (two battalions) or a division or two (as could quickly erupt in a hot Berlin crisis)? That would undoubtedly meet the conditions for the definition, and what was directed to follow from it.

And the definition was not confined to Europe. It implied that any conflict pitting U.S. forces against any more than several battalions of Soviet troops anywhere in the world—Iran, Korea, the Middle East, Indochina—would lead to instant U.S. strategic attacks on every city and command center in the Soviet Union *and* China. It was hard to imagine that such a plan could actually be carried out. Yet according to what I had already come to discover in the Pacific, and what turned out to apply worldwide, *no alternative plans existed* for a war involving Soviet forces on a level beyond a division or two except for the general war plan. And that lack was by the directive of President Eisenhower, who had decreed that there should be no plans for "limited war" with the Soviet Union, whether nuclear or conventional, under any circumstances, anywhere in the world.

This reflected Eisenhower's military judgment that no war between any significant forces of the United States and the Soviet Union could remain limited more than momentarily. Therefore if such a conflict were pending, the United States should immediately go to an all-out nuclear first strike rather than allow the Soviets to do so.

But even if those military judgments were challenged—as they were, repeatedly, by Army Chief of Staff General Maxwell Taylor—Eisenhower believed that any alternative approach was unacceptable from a *fiscal* point of view. Under the influence of conservative economic advisors, he was convinced that preparation to fight even a limited number of Soviet divisions on the ground (as Taylor proposed), with or without the use of tactical nuclear weapons, would compel an increase in defense spending that would cause inflation, precipitating a depression and "national bankruptcy."

The budgetary battle between the services had come to be fought, oddly, over the definition of "general war." All the services accepted that "general war," in the nuclear era, implied all-out nuclear war with the Soviet Union, in which the Strategic Air Command would play a predominant role. The Navy, with its carrier aircraft and submarines, would be second in importance, with Army operations problematic and subordinate at best. For purposes of planning—the structure of forces, deployments, and operations—and, above all (from the services' point of view), determining the size and division of the budget, the vital question was *when*, among the wide range of possible circumstances in the world threatening to U.S. interests, such an apocalyptic response might be invoked.

Army leaders like Taylor, and initially those in the Navy as well, wanted to define "general war" as narrowly as possible, leaving a broad range of conflict situations to be planned for, budgeted for, and addressed if they arose, *without* necessarily involving an attack by SAC on the Soviet Union or China. They argued, with a good deal of plausibility, that since such an attack involved a high risk, if not a certainty, of devastating retaliation against the United States, it should be reserved for only the most extreme, exigent contingencies.

One definition they proposed was that "general war" was an armed conflict with the USSR and the United States as the principal protagonists "with the national survival of both deemed to be at issue." Air Force Intelligence countered, according to my notes, that USAF "does not accept implication that there could be armed conflict between the US and SU in which the national survival of both was *not* at issue." As early as 1956 Eisenhower sided with the Air Force on this, against Taylor, asserting that the qualifying phrase at the end should be omitted from the definition, which would simply be "armed conflict with the USSR."

The Army and Navy didn't give up, though they continued to be over-ruled. In my notes of the Army and Navy view as of October 30, 1959, general war should be defined as "governmentally directed overt armed conflict between nations with the objective of complete subjugation or destruction of the national entity of the enemy," with other forms of armed conflict, including between U.S. and Soviet forces, characterized by "limitations on locale, weapons, forces, participants, or objectives."

To the layperson, this might appear sensible enough. But what Eisenhower, the Air Force, and successive chairmen of the JCS detected behind these innocent-sounding definitions was a charter for the Army to go to their allies in Congress to seek capabilities for fighting even multiple Soviet divisions in a limited, non-nuclear, and non-general war. That was precisely what the budget-obsessed President Eisenhower and the Army's service rivals feared and wanted to avoid. My friend Colonel Ernie Cragg in Air Plans was pointing out in dueling memos with the Army as late as January 21, 1961 (the day after Kennedy's inauguration):

> Adoption of the "view" that limited wars between the US and the USSR are possible is an "invitation" to attack. It also could open Pandora's box with respect to forces for limited war at the expense of general war forces. . . . It would allow the Army and Navy to increase their "requirement" for forces for limited war to almost unlimited levels.

The latter point, frequently echoed by Eisenhower, seemed especially compelling since, for years, both American and NATO intelligence had produced enormously inflated estimates of Soviet ground strength. For example, they ignored that a Russian division was less than half the size of an American division. Moreover, the supposed number of Soviet divisions was grotesquely overstated. Most of the oft-quoted figure of "175 Soviet divisions" referred to units that existed only on paper, subject to wartime mobilization, or to units that were grossly undermanned and under-equipped, and many that consisted of nothing more than a headquarters staff. Still, matching even the twenty crack Soviet armored divisions deployed in East Germany would legitimize large budgetary Army requests. These, if granted, would come at the direct cost of Air Force and Navy budgets.

One major reason for the JCS to keep any dispute over numbers from the attention of the secretary of defense was a fear that he would decide them in a way that would unfavorably influence the budget for the Air Force, or for one or another service. Even though Secretary of Defense Gates increasingly insisted on having a say in operational matters, in practice he became aware of only those problems that the chiefs unanimously agreed to submit to him. This had to represent a definite judgment on each of their parts that they had more to gain by such a submission than they did by bargaining among themselves. So while many important problems were never brought to the defense secretary's attention, one matter that was, however, was the definition of "general war" to be used in "capabilities planning." In June 1960, by my notes, Secretary Gates confirmed the definition: "war with the USSR."

Since there was to be only one plan for fighting Russians anywhere in the world under any circumstances—including, along with SAC, Polaris submarines, and theater forces—Eisenhower endorsed in 1959 the coordination of a single strategic plan at SAC headquarters in Omaha. Annex C of the JSCP came to be, by December 1960, the Single Integrated Operational Plan (SIOP).

By 1960, the planners of the SIOP, the Joint Strategic Target Planning Staff, had gathered all the general-war target lists of the various commands, including SAC, NATO, and PACOM, into one coordinated target list to allocate weapons more efficiently to targets all over the world. A major argument for centering the targeting effort at SAC headquarters was the allegedly unique capabilities of SAC's computers. In reality, these were still at such a rudimentary state of development that much or most of the computation had still to be done by hand, with the aid of calculating machines.

Again, there was an intense concern for minimizing the "interference" or "fratricide" of vehicles aimed at targets in close proximity. There was also a desire by Eisenhower to reduce "duplication" of efforts by different commands. In the actual planning, both concerns were totally frustrated; the latter because each command and service was determined to cover important targets by its own forces. By some counts, over eighty weapons were dedicated to Moscow; other counts put this at a hundred and eighty. Meanwhile, the prevention of "interference," as in the Pacific, remained a delusional objective.

As with the CINCPAC plan I had read earlier, the coordination involved in this higher-level plan was so complex that there was room for only one real strategy. The price of bringing all the theater and component service plans into harmony with each other, into one plan, was the total elimination of any flexibility in carrying it out. So much planning was involved in producing this one scenario that there was simply no staff or computer time available to produce an alternative. As with the CINCPAC planners I met earlier, the SIOP planners themselves were appalled at the confusion and chaos that might ensue if any alternative was proposed.

Following the guidance of the JSCP, the planners at SAC headquarters set out to weld all the warheads in the U.S. arsenal into one hydra-headed monster that would arrive on its targets as near simultaneously as possible, preferably before any Soviet warheads had launched.

On strips like Kunsan or Kadena and on aircraft carriers surrounding the Sino-Soviet bloc (as it was still described in 1961, though China and the Soviets had actually split apart a couple of years before that), more than a thousand tactical fighter-bombers were armed with H-bombs in range of Russia and China. Each of them could devastate a city with one bomb. For a larger metropolitan area, it might take two. Yet until this time, SAC planners had regarded these tactical theater forces as so vulnerable, unreliable, and insignificant a factor in all-out nuclear war that they had not even bothered to include them in calculating the outcome of attacks in a general war.

In 1961 there were about seventeen hundred SAC bombers, including over six hundred B-52s and a thousand B-47s. In the bomb bays of the SAC planes were thermonuclear bombs much larger than those I had seen in Okinawa. Many were from five to twenty-five megatons in yield. Each twenty-five-megaton bomb—with 1,250 times the yield of the fission bomb that destroyed Nagasaki—was the equivalent of twenty-five million tons of TNT, or over twelve times the total bomb tonnage we dropped in World War II. Within the arsenal there were some five hundred bombs with an explosive power of twenty-five megatons. *Each* of these warheads had more firepower than all the bombs and shells exploded in all the wars of human history.

These intercontinental bombers and missiles had come to be stationed almost entirely in the continental United States, though they might be deployed to forward bases overseas in a crisis. A small force of B-52s was constantly airborne. Many of the rest were on alert. I had seen a classi-fied film of an incredible maneuver in which a column of B-58s—smaller than B-52s but still intercontinental heavy bombers—taxied down a runway and then took off simultaneously, rather than one at a time. The point—as at Kadena and elsewhere—was to get in the air and away from the field as fast as possible, on warning of an imminent attack, before an enemy missile might arrive. In the time it would normally have taken for a single plane to take off, a squadron of planes would be airborne, on their way to their pre-assigned targets.

In the film, these heavy bombers, each as big as an airliner, sped up in tandem as they raced down the airstrip, one behind the other so close that if one had slackened its pace for an instant, the plane behind, with its full fuel load and its multiple thermonuclear weapons, would have rammed into its tail. Then they lifted together, like a flock of birds startled by a gunshot. It was an astonishing sight: beautiful and terrible at once.

On carriers, smaller tactical bombers would be boosted on takeoff by a catapult, a kind of large slingshot. But since the general nuclear war plan, as I knew, called for takeoff around the world of as many U.S. planes and missiles as were ready at the time of the Execute order—as near simultaneously as possible—the preparations contemplated one overall, inflexible global attack, as if the entire destructive arsenal of the United States were launched by a single catapult—a slingshot made for Goliath.

The preplanned targets for the whole force included, along with military sites, *every city in the Soviet Union and China.* There was at least one warhead allocated for every city of 25,000 people or more in the Soviet Union. The "military" targets (many of them in or near cities, and many only tendentiously described as military) were by far the great majority, since all the cities could be totally destroyed by a small fraction of the attacking vehicles.

In 1960–61 it was in reality quite possible—though USAF and CIA "missile gap" estimates implied otherwise—that not a single nuclear warhead would land on U.S. territory after such an American first strike. Worldwide fallout in the stratosphere from our own strikes would certainly kill Americans, but over so long a time, with radioactivity decaying in the atmosphere on the way over and deaths from cancer long delayed, that the increase in mortality in any one year might not be statistically perceptible. But our Western European allies in NATO would be quickly annihilated twice over: first from the mobile Soviet medium-range missiles and tactical bombers targeted on them, which our first strike couldn't find and destroy reliably, and second from the close-in fallout from our own nuclear strikes on Soviet bloc territory.

John H. Rubel's brief memoir provides a vivid account of the first high-level presentation on the completed SIOP-62 by one of the handful of civilians who was present on that historic occasion. I quote his description at length, because I don't know of anything else like it in print from an insider. Rubel is the only person exposed to the SIOP who has recorded, in his comments toward the end, the same emotional reaction to it that I experienced a few months later in the White House when I saw the JCS estimate of the death toll from our own attacks.

> The meeting took place near mid-December 1960 at Strategic Air Command (SAC) headquarters at Offutt Air Force Base near Omaha, Nebraska, attended by Secretary Gates, Deputy Secretary Jim Douglas, myself, the Joint Chiefs of Staff, and a multitude of general officers representing every unified and specified Command from all over the world.
>
> The SIOP briefing was held on the floor of the command center at SAC headquarters. The viewers faced a high wall along which enormous panels bearing maps and charts ran on tracks the entire length of the room, perhaps a hundred feet or so. Behind and over one floor up was a glass-enclosed balcony. The generals would run SAC's part of the war from up there behind a long line of desks, glued to telephones, peering through the enclosing glass at the maps depicting the scene of wartime activity somewhere—indeed, anywhere and perhaps almost everywhere—in the world. . . .
>
> At a signal from General Power [the SAC commander] the briefer stepped on stage as it were, directly facing his audience, about fifteen or twenty feet in front of the first row. . . .
>
> After presenting a few charts he came to one defining the first wave of attacks to reach the Soviet Union. As I recall, these came from carrier-based fighter-bombers stationed near Okinawa. Having made this disclosure, he stepped aside.
>
> Thereupon two airmen appeared, one from each side of the long wall lined with maps, each carrying a tall stepladder. Each airman stopped at the edge of the large map which, we now observed, showed China and the Soviet Union and probably some other nearby features on a heroic scale. Each man climbed his tall ladder at the same brisk rate, reaching the top at the same instant as his counterpart. Each reached up toward a red ribbon which, we now noticed, encircled a large roll of clear plastic. With a single motion, each untied the bowknot securing the

ribbon at his end of the roll, whereupon the plastic sheet unrolled with a *whoosh!*, flapped a bit and then dangled limply in front of the map. A bunch of little marks appeared, most of them over Moscow, representing nuclear explosions. The men descended the ladders, folded them, carried them off, and disappeared.

The briefer repeated this performance several times as successive waves from B-52s already aloft on Headstart [airborne alert] missions and fighter-bombers from carriers in the Mediterranean and from U.S. bases in Germany and others from carriers and bases around Japan and B-47s and B-52s launched from bases in the United States and some from bases in Europe and a few ballistic missiles (many more would become part of the plan during the next few years) dropped their lethal loads over the USSR.

Each time the briefer described an attack wave the ballet of the ladder masters would be re-enacted. They would untie another pair of red ribbons, a plastic roll would come whooshing down and Moscow would be even further obliterated beneath the little marks on those layers of plastic sheets. There were little marks in other places, too, but somebody noted that a third of Soviet industrial-military strength was concentrated in the greater Moscow area, hence the concentration of bombs dropped on that region. I recall that the plan called for a total of forty megatons—*megatons*—on Moscow, about four thousand times more than the bomb over Hiroshima and perhaps twenty to thirty times more than all the non-nuclear bombs dropped by the Allies in both theaters during more than four years of WWII . . .

At the point in the briefing where some bombers were described flying northeast from the Mediterranean on their way to Moscow, General Power waved at the speaker, saying: "Just a minute. Just a minute." He then turned in his front row chair to stare into the obscurity of uniforms and dusk stretching behind me and said, "I just hope none of you have any relatives in Albania, because they have a radar station there that is right on our flight path, and we take it out." With that, to which the response was utter silence, Power turned to the speaker and with another wave of the hand, told him to "Go ahead."

A subsequent chart shown by the briefer displayed deaths on the vertical axis and time in hours, extending out to weeks, along the horizontal axis. He announced that there were about 175 million people in the USSR. This chart depicted the deaths from fallout alone—not from the direct effects of blast or radiation from a bomb going off, just from fallout subsequent to the attacks when radioactive dust propelled to high altitudes by the initial blast begins to fall back to earth. The curve of deaths, rising as time went by, leveled off at about 100 million, showing that more than half the population of the Soviet Union would be killed from radioactive fallout alone. . . .

The briefing was soon concluded, to be followed by an identical one covering the attack on China given by a different speaker. Eventually, he too arrived at a chart showing deaths from fallout alone. "There are about 600 million Chinese in China," he said. His chart went up to half that number, 300 million, on the vertical axis. It showed that deaths from fallout as time passed after the attack leveled out at that number, 300 million, half the population of China.

A voice out of the gloom from somewhere behind me interrupted, saying, "May I ask a question?" General Power turned again in his front-row seat, stared into the darkness and said, "Yeah, what is it?" in a tone not likely to encourage the timid. "What if this isn't China's war?" the voice asked. "What if this is just a war with the Soviets? Can you change the plan?"

"Well, yeah," said General Power resignedly, "we can, but I hope nobody thinks of it, because it would really screw up the plan."

Rubel comments:

That exchange did it. Already oppressed by the briefings up to that point, I shrank within, horrified. I thought of the Wannsee Conference in January 1942, when an assemblage of German bureaucrats swiftly agreed on a program to exterminate every last Jew they could find anywhere in Europe, using methods of mass extermination more technologically efficient than the vans filled with exhaust gases, the mass shootings, or incineration in barns and synagogues used until then. I felt as if I were witnessing a comparable descent into the deep heart of darkness, a twilight underworld governed by disciplined, meticulous and energetically mindless groupthink aimed at wiping out half the people living on nearly one third of the earth's surface. Those feelings have not entirely abated, even though more than forty years have passed since that dark moment.

The next morning, as Rubel relates, Secretary of Defense Gates called a meeting "to discuss the proceedings of the previous evening. The Chiefs were there, I was there, and the Secretaries of the Army, Navy and Air Force joined the group." Starting with the chairman of the JCS, General Lyman Lemnitzer, each of these discussants said much the same thing: "The men had done a very fine job, a very difficult job, and that they should be commended for their work."

> Gates, thank Heaven, never turned to me. I had no idea what I would say if he did. I should have, but fear I would not have had the courage to say that this was the most barbaric, unthinkable, crazy so-called "plan" I had ever heard and could never have imagined.

One person, alone, at the second session raised objections. It was the commandant of the Marine Corps, David M. Shoup, who had earned the Congressional Medal of Honor for commanding from the beach the Marines who landed at Tarawa. Five years before this briefing I had heard him address my graduating class in the Infantry Basic School in the Marine Corps at Quantico. (From 1961 to the end of the war, he opposed vigorously our intervention in Vietnam.)

> "All I can say is," [Shoup] said in a level voice, "any plan that murders three hundred million Chinese when it might not even be their war is not a good plan. That is not the American way."

It was, however, the American plan. Though President Eisenhower was distressed when his science advisor George Kistiakowsky reported to him the tremendous amount of "overkill" in the plan, Eisenhower endorsed the plan and passed it on without any modification to John F. Kennedy a month later. It was my passion to change it.

CHAPTER 7

Briefing Bundy

It wasn't only the handful of civilians exposed to the Single Integrated Operational Plan (I actually knew no others at the time, such as Rubel) who felt that this insane plan must be radically changed. Through my contact with Air Force staff, I become aware that a number of Air Force planning officers were concerned about the madness of the planning process and current plans. But insofar as these plans were determined by their higher-level superiors, these men were unable to influence the plan through ordinary command channels.

In principle, the same was true for me and for RAND. During this period, RAND did not work for the secretary of defense, but rather for the Air Force. Thus, only by going out of channels in a way that would directly threaten the budget and existence of their institution could RAND researchers and officers have made the secretary of defense aware of the situation.

Yet, I came increasingly to feel it was essential that the president and the secretary of defense be made aware of the nature of the general war-planning system, with all its attendant risks of increasing the likelihood of war, and the likelihood that any sizable war involving Russian troops would trigger multi-genocidal effects on an almost unimaginable scale throughout the world. It seemed essential to me that the president himself have before his eyes, for the first time, the actual Joint Strategic Capabilities Plan, so that he could read it in context with the SIOP and become aware of the extreme simplicity, not to mention rigidity, stupidity, and incredible bloody-mindedness of these plans. The extremity of these qualities, I felt, was impossible to convey without examining the written plans.

For several years one of my highest objectives for my own personal influence on national defense was moving a few pieces of paper from one level of authority to a higher one, from a military to a civilian level. In particular, I wanted to move one document, the JSCP with its Annex C, from the offices of the Joint Staff or Air Staff to the Office of the Secretary of Defense and to the Oval Office, so that civilian authority could become aware of and then act to control and change the nature of our general war plans. (A decade later, my personal objective was very similar, with a different level of civilian authority in mind: I wanted to move seven thousand Top Secret pages—the Pentagon Papers—from the Pentagon and RAND to the Senate and the American public.) I also wanted to make civilian authority aware of the extreme degree of reliance on delegation, as well as all the other risks of unauthorized action I had discovered. Unfortunately, I had no direct line of access to Secretary Gates.

In 1960, after returning from the Pacific command and control study, I came into contact with two people who were widely rumored to be future officials in the Kennedy administration. One was Paul Nitze, who took part in a RAND-sponsored conference on alternative military strategy at Asilomar in Monterey. During a break in the conference, I spent a long drive to and from visiting Big Sur in the backseat of a car with Nitze. He had been the drafter of the famous National Security Council Paper NSC-68, which had been the planning basis for our armament buildup in 1950. He was now head of the committee on foreign policy of the Democratic Advisory Council (DAC), the main Democratic figure on military-political planning. He was expected to become a high official.

I spent the time in the car explaining to him how important it was that the president personally come to read, take an interest in, and insist on monitoring and supervising the general war plans, though I didn't describe them to him in detail. He had Top Secret clearance—he had briefly served as assistant secretary of defense for international security affairs under Eisenhower, and he remained a consultant. Nevertheless, according to the rules of the game, at that moment he had no "need to know" this sensitive information. Nor did I, technically speaking. The fact that some staff colonels had thought otherwise didn't mean that I could go around telling others who weren't officials. For the same reason, I hadn't informed any of my RAND colleagues on these matters. To Nitze I simply emphasized at length the urgency of the problem, and that if he should become an official in the new administration, he should see to it that the president immediately inform himself on these matters.

I gave the same message to Walt Rostow, who, like Nitze, was a member of the DAC committee on foreign policy and was also expected to be a national security official if Kennedy won the election. I met Rostow during the Kennedy campaign at a meeting of advisors on policy speeches convened at the Harvard Law School by Archibald Cox, a professor at the school. During a long break I spoke to Rostow in the law school's parking lot, repeating what I had told Nitze. I urged that if Rostow were ever close to the future president (in 1961 he did become an aide to McGeorge Bundy in the White House), he must ensure that the president ask to see the JSCP and its Annex C.

In January 1961, as a result of my help in arranging for RAND researchers to give input on speechwriting for Kennedy during the campaign, I was invited to the inaugural ball in Washington. On the Monday after the inauguration, I went to see Paul Nitze in his new office as (again) assistant secretary of defense for international security affairs (ISA).

I reminded him of our conversation the previous fall in Monterey. "Now that you're in office, I can tell you the details of these plans," I said. The ISA assistant secretary was in charge of policy planning in the Defense Department, and he was the natural official to deal with any kinds of plans, although in practice the office had never dealt with operational military plans before.

As a result of this conversation, Nitze asked to see the JSCP, through Harry Rowen, my close friend and former RAND colleague, who was now Nitze's deputy assistant secretary for planning and policy. Harry passed the mission to me, as an ISA consultant from RAND.

I went to see a military officer in charge of plans under Rowen, an Army general who had been in that office for some time in the previous administration. I asked him to get me the JSCP, for Rowen and Nitze. He curtly refused. He said bluntly, "You have no need to know." More challengingly, when I reiterated that this was at the request of his boss, the assistant secretary, he said, "He has no need to know either." I asked him if he himself had ever seen it, and he said that he had, but as an

Army general, not in his capacity as an official within ISA. I reported this to Harry, his immediate superior. Nitze didn't get the JSCP.

Later that first month, Rowen arranged for me to see McGeorge Bundy, assistant to the president for national security, to brief him on the war plans and on the command and control problems I had discovered in the Pacific. I was ushered into Bundy's office by Bob Komer, his deputy. I had never met Bundy, who had been dean of faculty at Harvard while I was a graduate student in the Society of Fellows (of which he had been a member a decade earlier). I had met Komer several times before when he had visited RAND.

I had an hour scheduled with Bundy. As I walked in, I started to worry that he was likely to be skeptical or suspicious of the fact that, as a civilian, I seemed to know so much about war plans. I felt that I ought to begin by giving him some hints as to how I had acquired this information. I began to talk of my participation in the CINCPAC command and control project and my work with the Joint Staff. After two or three minutes of this, he interrupted me in a dry, frosty tone with the question: "Is this a briefing or a confessional?" He was famous for his arrogance with intellectual inferiors (most people) and for curtly cutting off subordinates who weren't giving him information "crisply" enough.

I thought to myself, "All right, wise guy, you asked for it." I told him crisply that there was a lot about the war plans and nuclear operations that he probably didn't know. I proceeded to tick off the characteristics of the JSCP—including its nature as a first-strike plan and its city-busting targeting of the Sino-Soviet bloc under all circumstances—and the defects in the control system. I had the satisfaction, within a few minutes, of seeing his mouth drop open. He began to take furious notes, shaking his head and exclaiming under his breath.

Throughout and at the end of my briefing—he kept me there nearly another hour—I gave him recommendations, all of which he noted down. The first was that he should assert his authority to get hold of the JSCP, then read it, familiarize himself with it, and begin to work on it with the help of military aides who could explain the underlying controversies and the operational implications.

I told him of the LST with nuclear weapons at Iwakuni, the general violations of the two-man rule, and the universal lack of physical controls—any form of locks—on nuclear weapons. In particular, as a matter for urgent White House concern, I described the widespread belief—contrary not only to public declarations but also to assertions in Top Secret planning—that President Eisenhower had delegated authority to initiate nuclear attacks in a variety of circumstances. Bundy, who had been in office only a couple of weeks at this point, showed every sign of surprise and shock at this news, though not disbelief.

I told him of the purported letters from President Eisenhower to the unified and specified commanders. I said I hadn't seen them myself, but that I did know that important officers in the Pacific *believed* they existed, and that their belief had dangerous consequences. It had led to sub-delegation far below the level of the theater commanders, probably—I presumed—far more widely than President Eisenhower was aware or had intended.

Some forty years later, I was to learn from newly declassified documents from the late 1950s that I had been mistaken about this. To my great surprise, it turned out that Eisenhower had actually foreseen and authorized this sub-delegation, dangerous as this seemed to me. But if I had known this at the time, it wouldn't have changed my recommendations to Bundy. The risks of having so many subordinate commanders with both the ability and the presumed right to take nuclear initiatives in crisis conditions seemed so great that it was urgent for President Kennedy to bring his own judgment to bear and take steps to reestablish his control of the system.

*   *   *

A few days after my briefing to Bundy, Harry Rowen told me that he and Bundy had agreed that the question of delegation was an important subject to investigate. Bundy could see nothing in the files available to him that supported what I had described, but he already knew that was not conclusive, since Eisenhower had taken most of his White House files with him. At an NSC staff meeting, Bundy announced that a joint White House–DOD committee of one—namely, Daniel Ellsberg—was being formed to investigate the problem of presidential authorization of the use of nuclear weapons. My task, Rowen told me, was to find out whether the letters I had heard about actually existed. I would have full authority, which would be confirmed by the White House, to "go anywhere, ask anything, see anything" bearing on this effort.

My first visit was to Commander Tazewell Shepard Jr., President Kennedy's naval aide in charge of the nuclear alert procedures and the one who carried the nuclear "football." I told him what I had heard in the Pacific. He said it was news to him and seemed genuinely convinced that it was baseless. He confirmed that, as the president's liaison with the nuclear command and control system, he was the one who ought to know if such letters existed. He swore that he had never heard of them. Moreover, he said, he had no knowledge of any authorization having been given in any form to any of the unified or specified commanders for executing their war plans in the absence of an express presidential order. He felt that if such an authorization existed, he would have known about it.

By that time I was experienced enough to know that an officer in his position could and would lie convincingly about such matters in the interests of secrecy. But my best judgment in this circumstance was that he was trying to be helpful, and that he was being honest with me. He knew that my authority to ask questions and get straight answers came from Bundy, and it didn't make sense that he would want to deceive the president's assistant.

Shepard undertook to ask others working at the presidential command post in the White House about the issues I raised. Everyone he asked denied knowledge of any of these issues. He then arranged for me to visit the underground command posts involved in disseminating nuclear directives in the event of nuclear war. One of these was the Alternate Joint Communication Center, which served as an alternate command center for the JCS inside Raven Rock mountain, forty miles from Washington. Others were High Point under another mountain, supposed to house the civilian leaders of the government during a nuclear emergency, and Camp David, the presidential retreat in Maryland.

Shepard asked me to let him know whatever I found out. But the officers in those centers claimed to be just as ignorant as he was of any such delegation. Nor did they seem to be aware of the widespread assumption in the Pacific that such an authorization existed.

In addition, I talked to officers in charge at the White House Situation Room. They all felt that they ought to know if someone other than the president was authorized to start a nuclear war—they felt sure that they would know if that were the case—but they said they didn't know. Again, none of them was aware that this was widely believed in the Pacific. Meanwhile Shepard reported back to me that his own further investigation had failed to disclose any evidence of pre-delegation.

I concluded, tentatively, that the belief in the Pacific was based on a myth, a myth that was clearly important to dispel. Of course, I couldn't be definitive about such a negative finding. It was a matter of my judgment that Shepard and the other officers were not deceiving me, and that such an authorization, still less actual letters, probably could not have been passed to the commanders before Shepard's arrival without Shepard being able to find any hint of it and without any of the others knowing about it.

I reported this to McGeorge Bundy's new deputy, Carl Kaysen. (Kaysen, a professor of economics at Harvard and a former junior fellow himself, had read my honors thesis at Harvard and recommended me for the Society of Fellows.) I explained my puzzlement at the situation. I had failed to find anyone in the Washington area, where the supposed delegation had been made and where highest-level command was exercised, who had even heard that anyone anywhere believed that someone outside Washington was authorized to launch nuclear attacks on his own. Yet there seemed no reason to doubt either that officers in the Pacific believed that such a delegation had been made, or that lower-level sub-delegation had actually occurred.

There were several possibilities to explain this discrepancy. I told Kaysen that my best judgment was that the officers in the Pacific were misled. The supposed letters from Eisenhower probably did not exist. But I felt quite sure that the belief in the letters was real and that it had real consequences, dangerous ones, which needed correcting. It provided a false precedent for the lower-level delegations that CINCPAC and perhaps others were reported to have made, which I was quite sure did exist. (If the Eisenhower letters did exist, after all, the precedent was not false, but just as dangerous in its effects.) Either way, a dangerous situation remained that Kennedy needed to address.

About a month later, in late June or early July 1961, I was in Kaysen's office in the Executive Office Building when he mentioned to me, "By the way, we found your black notebook."

"What notebook?" I hadn't heard of a notebook, and I hadn't mentioned one to him.

"The one with the letters from Eisenhower." He pointed to a loose-leaf notebook on a table by his window. He told me there were copies in it of letters signed by Eisenhower to each of the theater commanders along with SAC and NORAD who controlled nuclear weapons, specifying circumstances under which they were authorized to use nuclear weapons without immediate presidential authorization.

He said the circumstances included the need, in their judgment, for fast action at a time when communications were out with Washington. But they weren't limited entirely to that. They also provided for situations when the president was physically incapacitated, as during Eisenhower's stroke. (That didn't seem to allow for command to be reserved for the secretary of defense, who was second in the chain of command by the National Security Act of 1958. But these letters were originally sent in 1957.)

I should have asked to read the actual letters, but I didn't. Nor did I press for details when I asked him how he had found them. He just told me he hadn't been entirely satisfied by my conclusions and had kept probing, and the notebook had finally turned up. I asked, "What has the president decided to do?"

"Nothing. He's not doing anything. He's letting them stand."

This wasn't what I wanted to hear. I asked, "Why is he doing that?"

Kaysen said, "This is not the time for Lieutenant Kennedy to reverse the decision of the Great General."

"Lieutenant" was Kennedy's naval rank in World War II. In all his campaigns he had run as a war hero, but that status had been earned after he had allowed his PT boat to be cut in two by a Japanese destroyer. Kennedy might now be commander in chief, but he had never been supreme commander of Allied forces in Europe, and it wasn't the time, Kaysen was saying, for him to be disagreeing with the prior judgment of the general who had been.

It was "not the time" for it. I could understand the politics of this, both bureaucratic and diplomatic—it was just after the debacle of the Bay of Pigs and reports of JFK's weak performance at the Vienna Summit with Khrushchev—but it still jarred me. It meant that Kennedy and the NSC were not going to look into or do anything about the problem that seemed to me the greatest danger, the sub-delegations and the general looseness of control below the level of the four-star admiral or general. If I'd been asked, I would have urged Kaysen and Bundy to make sure that this time the letters ruled out—or, at the least, limited—*further* delegation.

But that would have meant a confrontation with the military over the issue of sub-delegation just as sharp as the one to be expected if Kennedy had tried to withdraw Ike's delegation to CINCPAC, CINCSAC, and the other unified and specified commanders. General Lauris Norstad at NATO and others would have leaked to Republicans in Congress to raise in closed hearings—which would in turn have leaked to the public—that Kennedy was not only contradicting their own judgment of the requirements of national security, but was also reversing the decision of the Great General.

Precisely to compensate for an impression of inexperience after the events of the last few months, Kennedy just then named as chief of staff of the Air Force General Curtis LeMay, the man with the toughest militarist image in the armed services. This despite the fact that a number of observers, including Robert Kennedy, would report incidents when certain military men—LeMay above all—would give Kennedy the impression that they were essentially insane, madly reckless, or out of touch with reality. (These included, the next year, LeMay's strongly worded advice on the Sunday morning in 1962 when Khrushchev announced he was dismantling his missiles in Cuba that the president should go ahead and attack Cuba anyway.) Yet it was Kennedy who had named LeMay as chief of staff of the Air Force on June 30, 1961, and kept him there.

In the fall of 1961, as part of my work for General Earle E. Partridge's Working Group on Presidential Command and Control, I made an appointment to interview the Air Force chief of staff. I had mentioned the upcoming interview to Kaysen and he asked if he might accompany me, having never met the legendary LeMay.

In the course of our talk, I asked LeMay how concerned he had been, as commander of SAC, about the possibility of a surprise attack by a Soviet submarine on Washington. He said calmly that he had "felt satisfied" with his authority as CINCSAC to carry out his plans in that event, which was clearly a reference to the Eisenhower delegation that I had reported on at the start of the year and which Kaysen had confirmed.

But before I could pursue that—the first face-to-face reference to delegated authority from a military officer I had heard outside the Pacific Command—LeMay took the discussion into territory I had never explored before. Suppose that Washington had *not* been hit, he said, when warning of an enemy attack came in. Should the president be part of the decision process at all, he asked us, even if he were alive and in communication?

Neither Kaysen nor I had ever heard that question raised before. We waited for him to continue, which he seemed to have expected. He rolled his cigar at the corner of his mouth in a way I'd seen imitated by some of his staff officers. (His ever-present half-smoked cigar gave him a tough look, befitting his reputation. I learned later that he used it to disguise a touch of Bell's palsy.) Speaking gruffly, he asked rhetorically, "After all, who is more qualified to make that decision [of whether to go to nuclear war on the basis of warning]: some *politician* who may have been in office for only a couple of months . . . or a man who has been preparing all his adult life to make it?" Both his lips and his voice curled contemptuously around the words "some *politician*." The "p" was an explosive puff. And the personal reference seemed pointed. This was the first year of the current politician's presidential term, in which "Lieutenant Kennedy" had held back air support from his beleaguered invasion force at the Bay of Pigs. (And, as I learned later, the year he had refrained from knocking down the new Berlin Wall and then refused to send combat troops to Vietnam, having earlier rejected sending them to Laos.) The general making the comment, for years the commander of the Strategic Air Command, was the man who had planned and directed the immolation of a hundred thousand Japanese civilians in the firebombing of Tokyo on March 9–10, 1945, and five months after that had commanded the atomic-bomb strikes on Hiroshima and Nagasaki.*

I never found out why I had been unable to confirm the existence of the letters myself earlier. When I raised the issue much later with Tazewell Shepard—by then a Navy captain—after Kaysen had turned up the notebook, he assured me convincingly that he hadn't been kidding me; he really hadn't known of their existence when I asked. If I hadn't run across the issue in the Pacific and raised it with Bundy when I did, it's possible that no one in the White House would have known of it for a long time.

*   *   *

---

*Long after drafting this account, I read John Rubel's memoir *Reflections on Fame and Some Famous Men* (New Mexico, 2009), in which he confirms my memory of General LeMay's locution in discussing presidential command authority. "The matter came up as I stood facing the general as he stood across from me at his desk. Somehow . . . I must have uttered the term, 'command and control.'

"LeMay expostulated contemptuously, 'Command and control! Command and control! What's that? It's telling the fighting man what to do, that's what it is. And that's a job for the professional soldier. They talk about the president exercising command and control. What is the president?' He spit out the 'p' in 'president.' 'A politician.' 'What does a politician know about war?' He dwelled on w-a-a-h-r. 'Who needs the president if there's a w-a-a-h-r? Nobody! All we need him for is to tell us that there's a war. [Not that Curtis LeMay needed a president for that.] We are professional soldiers. We'll take care of the rest.'" (pp. 65–66)

Meanwhile, my new access to the White House made it possible to tie up another loose end. In April 1961 I told Harry Rowen about the situation in Iwakuni. His boss, Paul Nitze, was in charge of military liaison with foreign countries, including base rights. He had the civilian authority, under Secretary McNamara, for dealing with our relations with Japan and the question of possible treaty violation at Iwakuni that I'd been told about. Harry asked me to describe the problem in writing for Nitze and to do the typing myself for special security within the office. Thus, I typed out a memo and stamped it "Top Secret—Eyes Only for Paul Nitze."

"Eyes Only" was not a classification but a handling designation indicating that this was not for routine distribution within an agency or office and was not to be copied or shown to anyone other than the specific addressees listed in the heading. It was "for their eyes only." The need for special handling within the office was that ISA was staffed largely with active-duty military officers from various services. In theory, their immediate current loyalty was to ISA and its boss, but in practice, their careers depended on their relations with past and future superiors in their home service. They tended to keep those channels open and inform their service headquarters privately of anything that might concern them. In this case, where the Navy or Marines might take strong objection to a decision by Nitze to change their practices, it was important to delay their finding out what might be coming from the assistant secretary.

I wrote in detail all that I knew about the nuclear weapons on the USS *San Joaquin County* and how I had come to know it. I also provided an exhaustive analysis of the pros and cons, since anyone first hearing of such an anomaly would tend to assume there must be some highly technical reason justifying it. I reported that, to the officers aware of it in the theater, there was evidently no strategic or technical rationale at all for the arrangement, no tangible military advantage counterbalancing what they saw as obvious diplomatic risks.

The reason the Marine planes on Iwakuni were provided such ready access to nuclear weapons was simply that their landing strip was near the beach, the Marines were part of the Navy and practiced in amphibious operations, and the Navy was able and willing to provide them secretly with a nearby LST (landing ship, tank). Presumably the Air Force wasn't tempted to do something similar for its own planes, because it wasn't practical to keep, say, a KC-97 tanker loaded with nuclear weapons flying continuously above an Air Force base in Japan. It wasn't even as though a large number of Navy bases were benefited by this arrangement.

This violation of the treaty affected only a handful of weapons at one base. Yet the political risk was virtually the same as if it had been a lot of bases.

Nitze had my memo "staffed out." He assigned his assistant Timothy Stanley to investigate the problem, and Stanley had me rewrite my report for other staffers. Eventually I was shown various reports that came out of this. All the facts that I had presented were confirmed. The foreign affairs specialists within ISA also corroborated that the situation was a clear-cut violation of both the letter and the spirit of our security treaty with Japan.

In these responses, Iwakuni was contrasted with marginal cases like the carrier visits and even the possibility of our emergency alert plans being executed. The *San Joaquin County* was a permanent arrangement. It couldn't even be said to be "in the waters, not on the territory," since the ship was so close to shore that it would be regarded by every legal test as being on the territory of Japan. The answers also corroborated the extreme diplomatic risks this situation involved and concluded that it was highly urgent to correct this situation immediately.

But a new piece of information came in as well. One of the staffers reported that, on first investigating the situation, he went to the special assistant to the secretary of defense for atomic weapons and atomic energy, Gerald W. Johnson, who was responsible for knowing the current where-abouts of every individual nuclear weapon in the world, including test devices and weapons under production. The special assistant possessed an enormous loose-leaf notebook that contained the reported current location of every operational weapon in the world. No weapons were listed in Japan. No ship carrying weapons was listed as stationed there. In fact, the book contained no indication that a situation such as I described existed.

When Nitze's investigator pressed the point, Johnson, whose job as a direct representative of the secretary of defense afforded him very high status, picked up the phone and called his Navy counterpart to check on it. He was told that there was no such situation, that my story had no basis.

However, in pursuing the name I had supplied for the LST, Nitze's man soon discovered that the *San Joaquin County* was listed in Navy records as homeported in Okinawa. By further interviews, he discovered that it was being carried that way in Navy reporting precisely as a cover to deceive the special assistant and his boss about the fact that it was permanently based in Iwakuni, except for a few months every three years when it was in Okinawa for repairs and overhaul. By coincidence, at the very time of this investigation it was back in Okinawa undergoing its triennial refitting, which would take another month or so.

Deceiving the secretary of defense on the whereabouts of a nuclear weapon was the highest imaginable offense within the bureaucracy. No one reading this report could miss that point. It was not within the rules of the bureaucratic game, in the remotest sense. But there was an obvious bureaucratic solution. All that had to be done was to keep the LST home in Okinawa. Nitze's staff recommended that he take this up immediately with McNamara. A directive was drafted for him to give to McNamara, ordering the ship not to return to Japan. McNamara signed and sent it to the chief of naval operations (CNO, the Navy chief of staff), Admiral Arleigh Burke.

Harry Rowen told me what happened next. Soon after the directive went out from McNamara, Nitze happened to be at a meeting in McNamara's office on another matter, along with Admiral Burke. At the end of the meeting, Burke asked Nitze to return with him to Burke's office, in a different part of the Pentagon. When they arrived at the office, Burke sat down at his desk. Nitze saw immediately that he had in front of him a "burn copy" (the predecessor to the Xerox copy—a somewhat fuzzy duplicate on tan, flimsy paper) of my "Top Secret—Eyes Only" memo, which was intended for Nitze alone and wasn't supposed to be copied.

It was obvious that some commander or captain or rear admiral working for Nitze had seen my memo, "burned" it, and delivered the copy to Admiral Burke. He also had on the desk a copy of the ISA investigative report, along with McNamara's directive to him.

Burke started discussing my memo and the report, not bothering to explain what they were doing on his desk. "Burke was furious," Nitze told Harry. Burke was famously given to rages, but this one, in front of an assistant secretary of defense, was surprising to Nitze. Burke made no attempt to deny the facts of the reports or to justify anything. The only thing he had to say, in a fury, was "What did you think you were doing, as a civilian, interfering with the operations of ships of the U.S. Navy?"

The fact that this ship was in violation of one of our most important security treaties and was posing enormous diplomatic risks, that it was carrying nuclear weapons in violation of regulations on their whereabouts and in deliberate deception of the secretary of defense, that the special assistant to the secretary had been lied to by the Navy—none of these points was addressed by Burke, nor was he willing to hear about them. He maintained that it was absolutely unacceptable that the secretary of defense should presume to tell the Navy where to put its ships.

Rowen got the impression that Nitze left the office quite shaken by Burke's willingness to confront him in this way but determined to have the Navy brought into line. He himself wasn't in a clear-cut command position with respect to Burke, except as he was accepted as a direct representative of the secretary. So everything depended on McNamara's standing by his directive and backing Nitze on this issue. Rowen told me that Nitze went to McNamara and told him that this was of the highest urgency and that he should order Burke to comply with his directive and with the treaty.

I asked Harry, "So, what's happened?"

"McNamara decided to withdraw the directive. He backed off. With all the fights he's having with the services, he didn't want to add this one."

I asked, "Does McNamara know he was lied to by the Navy?"

"Yes." Harry said, "That's what made him furious in the first place. It's what got him to send the directive."

But faced with Nitze's account of Burke's own rage, McNamara had to pick his fights, which included a struggle over the number of nuclear-powered carriers. In this case, I could guess, he would face the likelihood that the Navy would leak the dispute to a friendly committee in Congress, in distorted fashion, and make him defend himself from the charge he was unduly entering into operations by ordering around individual ships.

I myself was faced with questions from the vice president of RAND, Richard Goldstein, when I returned to California. General LeMay had recently sat in on a meeting of the Air Force Advisory Board, which controlled the RAND budget. Goldstein called me into his office and said, "Dan, this is hard to believe, but we have a charge here from General LeMay—he's been told by Admiral Burke—that you have been giving the Navy orders on how to operate a destroyer squadron. Is this possible?"

I said, "*What*?!" It was true that most of the things I was doing in Washington would look madly presumptuous to most military officers, but I told him I had never done anything remotely like that. It took a second or two to guess what it must be referring to. The mention of Burke was the tip-off. I told Goldstein the whole story, and he passed it on. No one reprimanded me, though I learned that Burke had asked LeMay to have me fired from RAND.

The *San Joaquin County* went back to Iwakuni from Okinawa, with its cargo of nuclear weapons. A couple of years later Nitze made another abortive attempt to move it, but it stayed until 1966, when Edwin Reischauer, our ambassador to Japan, learned of its presence—through a leak to his office—and demanded that it be removed. He threatened to resign if it wasn't. In 1967 it finally moved back to Okinawa.

CHAPTER 8

"My" War Plan

Meanwhile, throughout the spring of 1961 I was working on a project that Harry Rowen had passed on to me. He had been asked by his boss, Paul Nitze, to draft the new basic national security policy (BNSP) for the Department of Defense. President Eisenhower had initiated this series of annual Top Secret policy documents to serve as the civilian authority's statement on the objectives and guidelines for all war planning within the Department of Defense.

Under Eisenhower each BNSP, usually no more than three or four pages, had embodied the "New Look" and "massive retaliation" doctrines of John Foster Dulles and chairman of the JCS Arthur W. Radford. These emphasized "main but not sole reliance" on nuclear weapons, as opposed to conventional, or non-nuclear, weapons. In fact, this emphasis was expressed in a trend by Eisenhower officials of describing nuclear weapons themselves as "conventional." For some years as a senator, John Kennedy had been associated with a critique of massive retaliation and an espousal of what General Maxwell Taylor, chairman of the JCS, called a "strategy of flexible response." Thus, following JFK's election as president, it was understood in the Pentagon that a significant change in the policy directives guiding war planning was in order. It was assumed that this would take the form of a radically revised basic national security policy.

Already in February, Bill Kaufmann of the RAND social science department had briefed Secretary of Defense McNamara on some proposals within the Air Staff aimed at moving away from what our RAND colleague Herman Kahn labeled a "spasm" concept of general war (or, as he often put it, referring to its all-out, nothing-held-back character, "a wargasm"). Kaufmann had pressed instead for developing a capability for sustained and controlled "war fighting," focused mainly on military targets, with cities witheld from initial attack.

In the eyes of advocates in the Air Force (which did not include LeMay), this was a strategy aimed as much at their service rivals in the Navy as it was at the Soviet Union. The sub-launched missiles on Polaris submarines, after all, were smaller than those on Air Force land-based ICBMs and much smaller than those on bombers. They were also, in the days before GPS systems, much less accurate than either of those vehicles. While the relatively invulnerable Polaris missiles were well suited to a deterrent policy aimed at targeting cities, they were less effective against hardened military targets like silo-based ICBMs (of which the Soviets had none in 1961, but were expected shortly to have hundreds to thousands). For that strategy, the Air Force bombers and missiles had an advantage. In fact the only role in which they had a relative advantage was as counterforce weapons—limiting damage to the United States in an all-out first strike by destroying Soviet land-based missiles before they were launched. Naturally, this was the preferred Air Force position, and after hearing Kaufmann's briefing on the arguments, McNamara had seemed sympathetic.

It would have been natural then for Harry to assign Kaufmann—who was also, like me, working as an ISA consultant in Washington at this time—to draft the general war section of the new BNSP. But somewhat to my surprise, Rowen asked me to draft that section, and instead assigned Kaufmann the task of drafting a section on limited nuclear war. I knew that my own views as to what the policy should be were closer to Rowen's attitudes than Kaufmann's on the importance of counterforce, and I presumed that was why I was given the job. This encouraged me to undertake the drafting as a process of refining my own views and making them as specific as possible, with the expectation that the end result would probably be acceptable to Rowen. That must have been his expectation too, because the only directive he had given me was, "Write what you think the guidance should be." That's what I proceeded to do.

The Air Force concept of "war fighting" or "damage limiting" (limiting damage to the United States from Soviet offensive nuclear forces) involved prolonged and controlled counterforce attacks on a military target system in the Soviet Union and its satellites in Eastern Europe. That included precise attacks against hardened missile sites and command and control centers. Along with our land-based ICBMs, this concept called for increased numbers of high-performance bombers capable of penetrating Russian defenses—by either flying underneath the radar or higher than the range of air defense missiles—to deliver high-yield payloads more precisely than missiles could do. Thus it gave support to the Air Force proposals for the B-70 bomber program (later called the B-1).

General Curtis LeMay, the former head of SAC, was by instinct hostile to ideas that downplayed attacks on cities. But he wanted the Air Force to have big, high-flying, fast bombers that could carry a heavy payload, and he was passionately devoted to the B-70 program. My friend Lieutenant Colonel Bob Lukeman said to me that he had heard a civilian in the Pentagon, on being told by a general officer that the first priority of the Air Force in 1961 was to get the B-70, ask what its second priority was. He was told, "There is no second priority." Lukeman explained to me, "The Air Force has one priority at a time."

The counterforce strategy also implied a crash effort to improve the accuracy of our missiles. That was another objective then thought to disfavor the Navy's mobile missile, the Polaris, in favor of land-based missiles controlled by the Air Force. Meanwhile, it called for large numbers of the land-based missiles to compensate for their current inaccuracy against small and hardened military targets. Before the year was out, LeMay and General Thomas Power, who had earlier replaced LeMay as the head of SAC, were calling for ten thousand of the prospective Minuteman land-based ICBMs.

In making this pitch to McNamara, Kaufmann certainly gave him what our RAND USAF sponsors wanted in the way of a rationale for the B-70 and for land-based missiles controlled by the Air Force. Whether he truly believed in the pitch for the Air Force's counterforce mission I never knew for sure. Others at RAND were unconvinced by the Kaufmann-USAF strategy. Yet it was not unwelcome to RAND management and analysts to find that Kaufmann's briefing was met with enthusiasm both by Air Force high command (some of whose subordinates had actually inspired it) and by the new secretary of defense.

I was one of the doubters, and so was Harry Rowen. On the basis of the calculations I'd seen at RAND, the merits of counterforce attacks in limiting damage either to the target area or to the United States did not impress me. Assuming as we did in the spring of 1961 that the Soviets had sizable numbers of ICBMs, before long to be hardened and accompanied by sub-launched missiles, it seemed obvious to me that once a process of general nuclear war was under way, *nothing* could be relied on very much to limit damage to less than catastrophic levels. Thus, there was an incalculably vast premium for all nuclear powers on deterring, preventing, and avoiding a general nuclear war under any circumstances.

However, the question remained: What did we do if deterrence failed? Like Kaufmann, I accepted the notion that if a general nuclear war did commence, our land-based missiles should be aimed at military targets, primarily Soviet missiles and air bases, for whatever prospect of limiting damage that might offer. But what seemed to me to offer relatively more promise than simply the "damage-limiting by controlled counterforce attacks" that Kaufmann was expounding were the *other* parts of the "coercive," "no cities" strategy he had presented to McNamara, aimed at terminating the war as quickly as possible, before all weapons on both sides had been employed, and particularly before any, many, or all had been employed against urban targets. (It was a long time before I recognized the fatal contradictions between these two components of what was supposedly the same strategy, along with the effective infeasibility of either of them.)

This latter goal required both deterring—if possible—an opponent from launching strikes against the cities of the United States and its allies, even if nuclear war was initiated by one side or the other, and at the same time inducing the opponent's command authority to stop operations short of expending all his weapons.

Both of these sub-goals called for three characteristics in our own planning and operations. First, it meant avoiding enemy cities altogether in our own initial strikes: what came to be known as a "no cities" approach. We would have to announce that intention long before hostilities began. Right away, this would be a marked departure from a policy of indicating beforehand and then carrying out our intent to destroy cities in all circumstances, a policy that removed any restraint on the enemy from targeting our own cities.

Second, it required maintaining protected and controlled U.S. reserve forces under virtually all circumstances, thus preserving a threat capability in order to terminate the war. That might also deter enemy preparations to destroy our cities as an inevitable and automatic wartime strategy.

Third, it called for preserving on *both* sides a command and control system capable of both controlling reserve forces and terminating operations. We would need a survivable command system capable of more than a simple "Go" decision; and *we could not afford to deprive the Soviets of the same capability.*[†]

The first two of these points were part of Kaufmann's briefing to McNamara in early 1961. They were rooted in RAND discussions and studies going back years before I arrived there, starting with Bernard Brodie, Andrew Marshall, Jim Digby, Charlie Hitch, and others, as Fred Kaplan has ably shown. Both notions appealed to me from my own background as soon as I encountered them at RAND: "no cities" from my earliest aversion to bombing civilians; the notion of inducing the Soviets, possibly, to do the same, and to end the war, by holding their own cities hostage to our reserve forces, was in line with my more recent analysis of coercion. That focus led me to emphasize, more than others did, the key importance of preserving command and control on both sides, not only our own. (That turned out to be an insuperable disability of the approach in the eyes of military planners on both sides.)

Neither I nor Harry Rowen had at that time the illusion that any such planned measures had a great likelihood of achieving the desired effects either on enemy planning or on the course of hostilities. Still, the possibility of having *some* desirable effect—saving some, perhaps many cities on both sides, and ending a war, once started, short of mutual annihilation—seemed greater than with the Air Staff strategy, which focused exclusively on counterforce tactics and failed to provide any mechanism for either terminating the war or significantly limiting damage.

This combination of damage-limiting and war-terminating goals implied that there were some choices to be made by the highest surviving U.S. authority even after general war hostilities had begun. Given the nature and urgency of such decisions—which might mean life or death for our entire society—it was obviously desirable that the president himself, or at least someone having his full confidence, be physically capable of making such decisions after general war had begun. (Eisenhower's wholly preplanned, truly "single" integrated operational plan didn't really require this.) That required preserving the president or his representative physically as well as preserving reliable communication capabilities.

At the same time, I saw a second, more important, advantage in demanding that a highest civilian authority be able to choose among options even in the midst of war.

It provided a rationale—a "need to know"—for the president to inform himself and his civilian advisors *before* the war of the detailed nature of the proposed war planning.

And there was a third advantage to my plan: Once it was acknowledged that the capability of highest-level authority (civilian or military) to command should be preserved during war, and once physical measures had been taken to achieve that with high reliability, there could no longer be compelling military objections against implementing lower-level *physical* controls over nuclear weapons—Permissive Action Links (PALs)—that would make it impossible for lower commanders to mistakenly or insubordinately initiate the use of nuclear weapons on their own.

Finally, focusing critical attention on the existing, current plans, which called for the prompt destruction of Soviet and Chinese urban targets under all circumstances of general war, opened up the possibility of a strategic and moral critique of such plans. Up until now these plans had been regarded as beyond question—especially by civilians—because there was supposedly no alternative to them for purposes of deterrence or wartime operations.

My personal hope was that higher-level, civilian scrutiny of these plans could eliminate or at least greatly reduce the probability of the particular insanities that involved targeting China in all circumstances of war with the Soviet Union, and of automatically targeting cities en masse either in China or the USSR. By emphasizing the importance of withholding reserve forces (which meant mainly city-busting Polaris missiles) and withholding initial attacks on cities, I privately hoped to avert or minimize attacks on cities altogether, whether we struck preemptively or in retaliation.

Such an approach called for drastic changes in both plans and preparations from the posture that had developed since 1953, culminating in 1960. For that reason it seemed clear that the new BNSP should be drafted in considerable concrete detail, rather than being the brief and vague document which the military had come to expect in the years when it simply reaffirmed the existing New Look doctrine, which emphasized reliance on nuclear weapons, both strategic and tactical, largely for long-haul budgetary reasons. Moreover, although in principle the BNSP directive officially defined national policy, rather than arguing for it, some of these notions were so unfamiliar in classified strategic dialogue that it seemed desirable to smuggle in as much rationale as possible, both to undermine resistance and to introduce the planners to considerations that had not recently appeared in military writing.

For example, even a high civilian planner in the Defense Department—having been kept unfamiliar with the details of these plans and preparations by military bureaucratic secrecy—could have been expected to wonder why it was necessary to specify in the highest-level policy document something as obvious as the need for maintaining reserve forces. The answer, remarkably, was that the highest-level war plans for the United States at that time called for the immediate expenditure of all weapons as soon as they could be made operationally ready, under all circumstances of initiation of general war ("armed conflict with the Soviet Union"). In other words, these plans, and all supporting training and preparation, not only failed to provide for the maintaining and subsequent commitment of any tactical or strategic reserves—the core consideration in classical military planning—but they positively required that there should be no meaningful reserves.

Moreover, to avoid the previous ambiguity of the meaning of "general war," Kaufmann and I agreed in our drafts to use the term "central war" (a RAND term), as distinguished from "local war" (instead of "limited war"). "Central war" was defined in my draft (later signed by McNamara) as "war involving deliberate nuclear attacks, instituted by government authority, upon the homelands of one or both of the two major powers, the United States and the Soviet Union." That was in the spirit of the narrow definition of "general war" proposed by the Army and Navy in earlier disputes, rejected by the Air Force, Secretary of Defense Gates, and President Eisenhower. There was no longer in our guidance a concept of "general war" defined simply as "armed conflict with the Soviet Union."

"Local war" was defined in our drafts as "any other armed conflict." The previous JSCP concept of "limited war"—as distinct from war with the Soviet Union—was discarded because we proposed to aim at limiting, if possible, even hostilities with the Soviet Union, even in central war.

In the late afternoon of April 7, 1961, with a good deal of satisfaction, I wrote the last line of my first draft of the general war section of the BNSP. I remember looking up at the clock on the wall in the outer ISA office where I was typing and noticing that it was five P.M. For the first time that day, it occurred to me that it was my birthday. I was thirty. I remember thinking: for the rest of my life, I won't have done anything more important than this. I told Harry that it was my birthday and I had finished a first draft. He said we should knock off (early!) and celebrate; he took me out to dinner.

Some days later I had a finished product. This took the form of a twelve-page discussion of goals, contingencies, and requirements, intended to make both the desired changes and the reasoning for them fully explicit to the military planners working on the JSCP and the subordinate plans.

To an uninformed reader—nearly everyone outside the actual nuclear planning process, including the secretary of defense and the president—these proposed policies would probably appear commonsensical. And so they were, except for the fact that almost every sentence constituted a radical challenge to and departure from some fundamental character-istic of the then-existing plans and preparations. For instance:

- My proposal to retain a strategic reserve (particularly of the city-busting Polaris missiles) ran completely counter to the previous plan, in which all ready vehicles, including the Polaris missiles, were committed to preplanned targets as soon as possible.
- My insistence on the importance of maintaining reliable command and control ran against the notion that unauthorized "initiative" might be necessary, either at high military levels of command or at low, an attitude that increased the possibility of unauthorized "initiative" in a time of crisis, under the stress of ambiguous indi-cations or an outage of communications with higher command.
- While there existed physical safeguards against accidents, there had been almost none against unauthorized action, either in connection with individual vehicles or in command post opera-tions. I proposed that such safeguards could take the form of a combination lock on weapons, requiring a code sent by higher authority to unsafe or release the weapon (some form of PALs).
- The rigid SIOP provided for no distinction between the USSR and China; it allowed for no avoidance or postponement of attacks on cities; it allowed for no option to minimize nonmilitary casu-alties; it offered no option for preserving enemy command and control capability. In contrast, I called for flexible contingency planning that allowed for all these options.
- Existing planning allowed for no Stop order once an authenti-cated Execute order was received by SAC forces. Since this unleashed attacks on all major Sino-Soviet urban-industrial centers and governmental and military control centers, this policy

maintained no plausible basis for inducing any Soviet commanders or units to *terminate* operations prior to expending all their weapons upon U.S. and allied cities. I proposed that a secure system of command and control was necessary to allow the option of limiting or terminating a conflict before all our forces were deployed, with reliable "stop" or "recall" orders.

All this was laid out in a memo for Harry Rowen, Paul Nitze, and Secretary of Defense McNamara, listing some of the limitations of the current plans that I intended to redress.

A second memo listed some of the changes my draft guidance called for:

- elimination of the SIOP as a single, automatic response in central war;
- elimination of the automatic inclusion of China and Soviet satellite states;
- plans to withhold some survivable forces, and an initial avoidance of enemy cities and governmental and military controls;
- the requirement of a survivable, flexible command and control system, headed by the president or as high an authoritative figure as possible;
- an effort to induce the enemy to terminate war by not destroying all major urban-industrial areas at the outset;
- plans and preparations to use conventional weapons in local conflict, up to large-scale conflict (in addition to plans to use nuclear weapons);
- rejection of any single, inflexible plan to be adopted for use in a wide range of circumstances of central war (let alone the SIOP), or that any given set of targets should be marked for immediate, automatic destruction under all conditions of central war; and
- rejection of the inevitability of central war in war with the Soviet Union.

On the basis of these memos, as well as an additional one that laid out steps that could be implemented in the short run, I got word from McNamara's office that I should prepare a draft for the secretary to send to the JCS directing CINCSAC, as director of strategic target planning, to explore and make concrete recommendations for introducing command flexibility and alternative options to the war plans in the relatively short run. I had spent an afternoon with Alain Enthoven in his office of Systems Analysis roughing out "options" in line with my guidance, which were refined in specifics by his RAND consultants Frank Trinkl and Dave McGarvey (on whom both Alain and Bill Kaufmann had long relied for crucial calculations).

When I showed my first draft to Colonel Lukeman on the Joint Staff, he warned me that it wasn't tactful enough to get a helpful response from General Power. In particular, Power would be offended by the implication that there weren't any real alternative options in the current plan. They had, after all, what they called "options" in the plan (although they all involved attack by all ready forces—and eventually all forces, with none in reserve—against the same target list). He edited my draft to make it less provocative to SAC, posing "questions," and adding a sentence beginning, "Recognizing that these plans already permit a variety of options keyed to duration of warning, geographic discretion, constraints, and specifics of weather and visibility . . ."

The final version, redrafted for Deputy Secretary of Defense Roswell Gilpatric's signature, was sent to the JCS chairman on May 5, 1961, with the heading "Policy Guidance on Plans for Central War," along with my draft portion of the proposed BNSP.[†] (For texts of all these memos and drafts, see ellsberg.net/BNSP.)

"My" revised guidance became the basis for the operational war plans under Kennedy—reviewed by me for Deputy Secretary Gilpatric in 1962, 1963, and again in the Johnson administration in 1964. It has been reported by insiders and scholars to have been a critical influence on U.S. strategic war planning ever since.[†]

Years later, when I mentioned to a friend that I had finished my first draft of the Top Secret guidance to planning for general nuclear war on my thirtieth birthday, his uncharitable reaction was, "That's frightening." I said, "True. But you should have seen the plan I was replacing." In years to come, the memory of this accomplishment did not bring me the same satisfaction it brought when I was thirty.

CHAPTER 9

Questions for the Joint Chiefs
How Many Will Die?

In the spring of 1961, Harry Rowen told me that after my briefing to McGeorge Bundy in January, Bundy had called the director of the Joint Staff of the JCS and asked him to "send over a copy of the JSCP."

The director told him, "Oh, we can't release that."

Bundy said, "The president wants to read it."

The director said, "But we've never released that. I can't."

Bundy told him, "You don't seem to be hearing me. It's the *president* who wants it."

"We'll brief him on it."

Bundy said, "The president is a great reader. He wants to read it."

It was finally agreed, Harry told me, that the president would get the JSCP *and* a briefing by a member of the Joint Staff.

Soon after I had finished drafting the basic national security policy, Rowen and I were talking to Deputy Secretary of Defense Roswell Gilpatric in his office in the Pentagon, and Gilpatric remarked to me, "By the way, we finally got the JSCP." He said that instead of sending it over to the White House, the Joint Staff had finally negotiated that they would give a briefing on it in Gilpatric's office. McNamara had attended, and McGeorge Bundy came over from the White House.

I asked him if they had seen an actual copy of the plan after all. He said yes, the briefer had left the plan with him. I asked if I could see it. Gilpatric led us into his safe. Instead of a safe with drawers, he had a long closet that had been converted into a bank-like vault with a heavy steel door. It had a tall ceiling and reinforced walls lined with library shelves filled with documents stamped "Top Secret" and higher. He found a document lying on one of the shelves near the front and handed it to me.

At a glance, it didn't look to me like the JSCP, because it was typed on regular eight-by-ten-inch paper, not the heavier eleven-by-fourteen-inch legal-size pages of a finished JCS document. Well, I thought, they might have just retyped it on regular-size paper for the deputy secretary. I looked immediately for the key section that appeared nowhere else but in the JSCP, the part the JCS had taken such care to withhold from civilians, the definition of "general war."

It wasn't there. There was no definition section, no definition of "general war" or "limited war." I looked back to the first page and read the heading. It didn't say "Joint Strategic Capabilities Plan." It said, "Briefing on the JSCP." Even that went beyond the terms of the earlier JCS directive I had seen, which told the Joint Staff that "neither the title Joint Strategic Capabilities Plan nor the initials JSCP are to be used in correspondence with the Office of Secretary of Defense." This heading broke that rule by using the forbidden initials "JSCP," apparently because Bundy's call to the director had revealed that that cat was out of the bag. Someone had leaked the acronym at least. But it wasn't yet clear to the Joint Staff that the White House or the Office of the Secretary of Defense knew more than the acronym—knew the contents of the plan and their implications—and the JCS hadn't yet given that up.

I told Gilpatric, "This isn't the JSCP. Is this all they gave you?"

He looked taken aback, for once confused. He said, "Yes, it is. But I'm certain they told me it was the JSCP—they were leaving me a copy of the JSCP. Are you sure it isn't?"

I showed him the title. "It's not the JSCP. It's a copy of the briefing they gave you." I remarked on the size of the paper and told him about the crucial part that was missing. Evidently, they had left that out of the briefing. There might be more they had omitted.

Gilpatric seemed more embarrassed than angry. He said, "They told me they'd be glad to answer any questions we might have from the briefing and the paper. Would you take this and write out some questions for me to send to them?"

I took the briefing paper back to the room where I was working in Rowen's suite of offices and put it in the safe. Then I walked down to an office in the Air Staff and asked Lieutenant Colonel Bob Lukeman, who had originally shown me the JSCP, if I could borrow a copy again. I didn't tell him what it was for, and he gave it to me without any questions.

Within minutes I was back in my office with the paper that Bundy—speaking for the president—and the secretary of defense had been unable to get. There were, as before, some advantages to being from RAND. The Air Staff thought of us as one of them. That was why I'd been shown the JSCP the year before. But by this time, in 1961, Lukeman knew that I was a consultant to the secretary of defense, which would normally have meant (and did mean for the Air Force chief of staff) that I was working for "the enemy," as formidable an adversary as the Navy or Congress.

He had to have gotten in advance the approval of his immediate boss, Brigadier General Glenn Kent, for him to be showing me anything. I gathered that what was true for my friend the colonel must also be true for his boss. They disagreed with the policy embraced by the highest levels of the Air Force, wanted to see it changed, and were using me as a channel to the civilian authorities to make an end run around their own superiors.

I put the JSCP on a table next to the copy of the briefing paper from Gilpatric and began to compare them line by line. I made a list of the discrepancies and then began to lay out issues to be put to the JCS. I have my rough notes on questions for them. It took me a week of long days to finish them.

Some of these probed for the rationale of attacking cities and population en masse, immediately (or ever) under all—or for that matter, any—circumstances of war initiation. That was an aspect of the "optimum mix" concept that was embodied in the SIOP. I asked:

- Why are major urban-industrial centers, or government controls, to be attacked *concurrently* with nuclear delivery capabilities?
- What national objectives require that urban-industrial centers be on the "minimum essential list" for initial attack? By what reasoning are these "essential"? What would be the costs, in terms of U.S. objectives, to omitting attack on these targets, relying upon residual strength to achieve objectives listed above?
- What is the distribution, by type, of targets in the satellite states? What contribution do they make to immediate Sino-Soviet bloc offensive capabilities?

- What is the total megatonnage dropped in the alert case? In the strategic warning case [full force]? What is the total of fission products? How much is air-burst, how much ground-burst? What would worldwide fallout be? What worldwide casualties?
- To what extent, and in what precise ways, does the planned attack upon urban-industrial centers and bonus targets differ from an attack intended to maximize population loss in the Soviet Union?[†] In Communist China? In what ways will the execution of such attacks, under the several conditions of war initiation, contribute to U.S. wartime or postwar objectives?
- Does the plan proceed on the assumption that it is national policy to hold the population of the USSR and Communist China responsible for acts of their governments? Are Communist Chinese people held responsible for acts of the Soviet government?

Other questions pointed to the lack of flexibility in the planning, another aspect of the SIOP ("Annex C" of the JSCP, guidance for the operational plans of SAC and Polaris, not mentioned as such in the briefing):

- The plan provides for "optimum employment . . . under the several conditions under which hostilities may be initiated." What are examples of those several conditions, other than Soviet surprise [nuclear] attack? How does the planned response differ for the different conditions? Is a single, uniform response optimal for all?
- Why do all options provide for total expenditure of the force? Why is no provision made for a strategic reserve?
- What is the ability of the JCS to accept the surrender of the enemy forces during the execution of the SIOP? What preparations have been made for this event? Have acceptable surrender terms been drafted? How reliable is the capability to STOP remaining attacks after Execute orders have been transmitted? Have preparations been made to monitor conformity to surrender terms?

Some of my questions couldn't possibly have occurred to anyone simply from reading the briefing. I threw them in to warn the recipients that someone working for Gilpatric was already familiar with the problems of the operational planning:

- Does planned coordination assume that all offensive vehicles will get the Execute message simultaneously? If so, what is the estimated validity of this assumption? What will effects on coordination be of estimated lags in receipt of message? Or of different wind direction and strength affecting different parts of the attacking forces, in planning to avert interference?

Since these questions were supposedly coming from Gilpatric, who hadn't been given the JSCP, I had to find a way to draft them so that they would purport to be based only on the briefing paper that the JCS had given to him. But anyone who knew the actual plans would know that the person writing those questions was not Gilpatric. It had to be someone who was intimately familiar with the JSCP itself and all the controversies that lay behind it, who probably had a copy of it sitting in front of him. In other words, the Joint Staff and their bosses, the JCS, would know immediately that a copy of the JSCP had finally found its way to the Office of the Secretary of Defense. Moreover, they would know that someone who was either a military planner himself (a mole) or who had been very well educated by such planners was advising the deputy secretary.

The questions were the message. They were intended to *leak into* the JCS the news that their processes, their conflicts, compromises, and maneuvers, had become transparent to the Office of the Secretary of Defense. I hoped they would figure the game was up; they had to come clean and give straight answers. They had to fear that any efforts to lie or evade would be quickly spotted by whoever wrote these questions. (He might actually know, through some direct channel, their inner discussions of how to deal with the problem of responding to Gilpatric.)

Each question, still more the whole set, was designed to convey that someone working for Gilpatric knew, as military staffers used to say, "where all the bodies were buried." It would be clear not only that "he knows the JSCP, and he's got a copy," but also that he knew, somehow, why it was written the way it was, where the controversies were, how they had been papered over, and all the other things that it would be hard or impossible for the JCS to explain or justify.

I don't have the final memo that I submitted to Gilpatric, in which the questions were more elegantly phrased than above. To keep up the pretense (however transparent to the recipients) that the questions were based on the briefing to Gilpatric rather than on the JSCP itself, most of my thirty or so queries started with a reference to a statement in the briefing paper and then presented a list of sub-questions purporting to relate to it. I happen to recall verbatim the wording of the first question:

> You say, on page 1, that each operational plan is submitted for review and approval to the next higher level of command.
>
> a) Was the JSCP submitted to Secretary of Defense Gates for his review and approval?
>
> b) When in the annual planning cycle, is it customary to submit the JSCP to the Secretary of Defense for his review and approval?

True answers would have been (a) No; and (b) Never. It was obvious that the drafter of the questions knew that. It was not obvious what a satisfactory explanation of those answers would be. Or those for the rest of the questions, which tended to get tougher from there.

When I handed the list to Gilpatric, he glanced through it, nodded his head, and said appreciatively, "These are very . . . *penetrating* questions." He read it over more carefully, shook his head several times, thanked me warmly, and sent it off to the Joint Staff with a cover letter and without any changes.

There was no good way for the JCS or its staff to respond to these questions. If they lied or evaded, it was clear they would be found out. But if they answered truthfully, it would have seemed appropriate to send at the same time their letters of resignation. Bob Komer, McGeorge Bundy's deputy at the NSC, put that more strongly. After he read the draft I showed him in his office next door to the White House, he said to me, "If these were Japanese generals, they would have to commit suicide after reading these questions."

The generals and admirals who got the questions were not Japanese. They did not commit suicide, but they did get the message. Within hours of the questions being sent, the director of the Joint Staff was on the phone to Harry Rowen. As Harry told me, he asked very intensely: "Do you know anything about a set of questions we just received from Gilpatric?"

Harry said, "I might."

There was a long pause. Then a curt "Who wrote them?"

Harry declined to say. End of conversation.

In a season when military staffs were working night and day to meet without fail or delay the secretary's short deadlines on numerous studies, this was *the one* set of questions that was simply never answered at all. As the first deadline approached, the director asked for an extension, and when time ran out on that, he asked for another, then a third. When I asked Gilpatric about it, in a later meeting, they still had not made a formal reply. They never did.

"That's perfect," Gilpatric told me. "We'll just leave them hanging there. Then if they fight us on the new plans, we'll just say, 'Well, then, let's go back to a discussion of your old plans.' And we'll start with those questions again."

Meanwhile, my revised guidelines on basic national security policy were signed by the secretary of defense, sent to the JCS as Secretary of Defense Guidance on War Planning, and eventually became the new policy. (President Kennedy had decided not to issue a new BNSP in his own name.)

*   *   *

As it turned out, *one* of the questions I had drafted for Gilpatric got a different treatment. As part of the list he sent to the Joint Staff, it got no more response than the rest. But it was picked out of my list by Bob Komer at the White House and sent to the JCS as a presidential query. And this question, to my surprise, got a quick, specific, and apparently accurate answer.

As recounted in the prologue, this question was the following: "If existing general war plans were carried out as planned, how many people would be killed in the Soviet Union and China alone?"

In posing that question originally, my tentative understanding from Lukeman and his Air Staff colleagues was that the JCS had never calculated an up-to-date answer to it for the current operational plans, which called for the quick and reliable destruction of a target system that included every major city in the Soviet Union and China. That might seem a peculiar supposition, but I had a basis for it. Despite my knowledge of the war-planning process and the plans themselves, which was extensive and virtually unique for a civilian, I had never seen such an estimate. Colonels Lukeman, Cragg, and others had told me they had never seen one either, and they believed it did not exist. And it was easy for someone familiar with the military bureaucracy to imagine bureaucratic considerations that would have blocked it from ever being investigated, having to do with a fear of leaks to the public, but also with the use that internal military critics of the plans could make of realistically horrific figures.

So I thought that the JCS would probably have to admit that they didn't know. Or they would have to ask for more time to calculate an answer. Either response would put them off balance in defending their current plans against our proposed alternatives. "What, you don't even know the consequences of your own plans for human fatalities?" It was to make that as embarrassing as possible that I drafted the question to cover the Soviet Union and China alone, so that they couldn't pretend they needed extra time merely to calculate answers for fatalities in Albania.

I thought it was also possible that they would turn out a hasty answer, which could probably be shown to be absurdly low. The only estimates I had ever seen in war plans had that character. They were from the early 1950s and ranged from about one million dead in the Soviet Union at the beginning of the decade to up to ten million or fifteen million dead in plans a few years later. I had read those as ridiculously low even for the era of A-bombs (which were already, by that time, much larger than the Hiroshima and Nagasaki weapons). If they came back with any estimate at all, I expected that it would be comparably unrealistic in the era of thermonuclear weapons, H-bombs. New underestimates would serve the same purposes in the inner bureaucratic bargaining over the plans as no estimates at all. The possibility that the JCS would come up quickly with a realistic estimate was one I barely considered.

I was mistaken. So were the usually knowledgeable colonels I had consulted. Not only did some section of the Joint Staff have a plausible computer model for calculating such effects, but they supplied the White House with an answer within a day or two. As I've described earlier, it was classified "Top Secret—For the President's Eyes Only," but since I had drafted the question, Komer called me over to the NSC offices to look at it.

The answer was in the form of the graph depicted in the prologue (page 2) that showed 275 million would die in the first few hours of our attacks and 325 million would be dead within six months. (I had only asked for fatalities, not for casualties, which would have included wounded and sick.) While this was for the Soviet Union and China alone, the speed of their response suggested that they had an existing computer model and probably had estimates on hand for other areas as well. So it proved. I drafted for Komer a follow-up question covering areas contiguous to the Sino-Soviet bloc, and the Joint Staff provided comprehensive estimates with equal dispatch. These were listed in a table.

Another hundred million or so would die in the Eastern European satellite countries from the attacks contemplated in our war plans, many of which were on air defenses and military installations in those countries, most of them near cities (even though Eastern Europe cities were not targeted as such). To open "air corridors" for subsequent bombers advancing toward the Soviet Union through Warsaw Pact territories, the first wave of bombers would "bomb as they go," dropping megaton weapons on radar stations, antiaircraft installations, and surface-to-air missile sites as they came to them in Eastern Europe. (Recall General Power's remark, at the SIOP briefing attended by John Rubel, on the unhappy fate of Albania, site of a radar station en route to Russia.) Although population destruction was not regarded as a "bonus" in the "captive nations"—as it was in the Soviet Union and China, where it was deliberately maximized—most warheads in Eastern Europe, as elsewhere, were ground-burst, maximizing fallout.

Fallout from our surface explosions in the Soviet Union, its satellites, and China would decimate the populations in the Sino-Soviet bloc as well as in all the neutral nations bordering these countries—Finland, Sweden, Austria, and Afghanistan, for example—as well as Japan and Pakistan. Given prevailing wind patterns, the Finns would be virtually exterminated by the fallout from surface bursts on Soviet submarine pens near their borders. These fatalities from U.S. attacks, up to *another* hundred million, would occur without a single U.S. warhead landing on the territories of these countries outside the NATO and Warsaw Pacts.

Fallout fatalities inside our Western European NATO allies from U.S. attacks against the Warsaw Pact would depend on climate and wind conditions. As a general testifying before Congress put it, these could be up to a hundred million European allied deaths from our attacks, "depending on which way the wind blows."

As I had intended, the JCS had clearly interpreted the phrase "if your plans were implemented as planned," to mean "if U.S. strategic forces struck first, and executed their planned missions without disruption from a Soviet preemptive strike." These figures clearly presumed that all or most U.S. forces had gotten off the ground with their weapons without having been attacked first. That is, it was implicit in these calculations—as in the greater part of our planning—that the United States would be initiating all-out nuclear war: either as escalation of a limited regional conflict that had come to involve Soviet troops or in preemption of a Soviet nuclear attack of which we had tactical warning. (The warning, it was understood, could be a false alarm. Or if it were not, the Soviet attack under way might be in response to a Soviet false alarm of a U.S. attack.)

The phrase "implemented as planned" referred to the assumption on which nearly all our planning was based: that in the whole range of circumstances in which nuclear war was likely to occur, we would "take the initiative." Before enemy warheads had arrived or, perhaps, had been directed to launch, we would be striking first.

Thus, the fatalities the JCS were reporting to the White House were the estimated results of a U.S. first strike. The total death count from our own attacks, in the estimates supplied by the Joint Staff, was in the neighborhood of six hundred million dead, almost entirely civilians. The greater part inflicted in a day or two, the rest over six months.

And these were solely the effects of U.S. warheads, not including any effects from Soviet retaliatory attacks on the United States or U.S. and Allied forces in Europe or elsewhere. The CIA intelligence estimate in June 1961 credited the Soviets with well over a hundred ICBMs at that time, of which they claimed to be able to locate, and thus to target, only a small fraction. Estimates of U.S. fatalities from Soviet retaliation consistent with those estimates would have added scores of millions of U.S. dead to the total, even after a very effective U.S. first strike.

Army and Navy estimates of Soviet ICBMs threatening America were "a few." But by all estimates, several hundred intermediate and medium-range missiles were aimed at Western Europe, Germany in particular, along with hundreds of medium-range bombers. Even after the most successful U.S. and NATO first strike, Soviet retaliation against Europe could have added a hundred million to the Western European death count from blast, fire, and immediate exposure to radiation even before the fallout from our own attacks had arrived from the east, borne on the wind.

Holding the graph in my hand—the answer to my initial query, covering only fatalities from the Soviet Union and China—looking at it in an office of the White House Annex on a spring day in 1961, I realized, "So they knew." As I said in the prologue, the graph seemed to me the depiction of pure evil. It should not exist; there should be nothing real on earth that it referred to.

But what it dealt with was all too real. I had seen some of the smaller bombs myself, H-bombs with an explosive yield of 1.1 megatons each—equivalent to 1.1 million tons of high explosive, each bomb half the total explosive power of all the bombs of World War II combined. I saw them slung under single-pilot F-100 fighter-bombers on alert at Kadena Air Base on Okinawa, ready to take off on ten minutes' notice. On one occasion I had laid my hand on one of these, not yet loaded on a plane. On a cool day, the smooth metallic surface of the bomb was warm from the radiation within: a bodylike warmth.

Three thousand warheads like these—most of them much larger in yield, up to twenty times as great—would be delivered on the Soviet bloc and China in the first stage of execution of the SIOP. Most of them, I knew, would be ground-burst, with fallout that would annihilate the population not only of the Sino-Soviet bloc but of its neighbors, including allies and neutrals.

It was not only the size of the numerical estimate of deaths that threw me into a state of shock, though I was not at all used to seeing estimates like that in classified studies. At RAND I'd read almost exclusively estimates of the population damage the United States could reliably threaten to produce in a retaliatory *second* strike, for purposes of deterring a Soviet first strike. In the context of Albert Wohlstetter's and RAND's concern that a well-designed Soviet Pearl Harbor–like attack might totally eliminate SAC's currently deployed retaliatory forces, the focus in those studies was how to assure that Soviet casualties from U.S. retaliation could be as high as, say, the Soviets had suffered in World War II: in the neighborhood of twenty million. Nothing less, Wohlstetter argued, and his acolytes (like me) accepted, would reliably deter cold-blooded Bolshevik leaders in an intense crisis. I'm not sure that I'd ever seen in a RAND study an estimate of the human consequences of a U.S. first strike by an undamaged force, a possibility that was scarcely considered at RAND except by Herman Kahn.

But since I'd seen actual war plans in the Pacific and the Pentagon, I'd become aware that they focused preeminently on just such a case: a U.S. first strike, either preemptively or in escalation from a regional conflict. And not, in either case, what RAND analysts would have considered a well-designed first strike—that exclusively focused on Soviet military targets—but one that explicitly attacked all Soviet (and Chinese) cities in the early waves. So I'd long been aware that the destruction wrought by executing such a plan (unimagined by RAND, for the United States) would be "huge," "horrible," beyond the RAND calculations I'd seen, but I'd never formulated a specific measure of it in my own mind, and I'd never seen one. This one seemed realistic.

To see it in print was startling, despite the fact that I had long privately thought, while reading war plans during the previous two years, that I was looking at the way the civilized world might end. These were plans for destroying the world of cities, plans that someday might be carried out. But I had thought that none of the others reading or writing them had faced up to that.

The shock, for me, was to realize that the Joint Chiefs were, after all, aware of it. Their planning process was not so mindless of overall consequences as I had come to suppose. It was worse. What was beyond surprising—it was unfathomable—was that they felt they could afford to be so candid about this particular answer, so prompt, responsive, realistic, while they stalled on all the others.

Far from being accompanied by any offers to resign, there was no evident embarrassment, no shame, apology, or evasion: no apparent awareness of any need for an explanation of this answer to the new president. I thought: this was what the United States had come to, sixteen years after Hiroshima. Plans and preparations, awaiting only presidential order to execute (and, I'd discovered, not requiring even that in some circumstances), for whose foreseen consequences the term "genocidal" was totally inadequate.

I myself at that time was not a critic of the explicit logic of deterrence or its legitimacy. On the contrary, I had been urgently working with my colleagues at RAND and in the Pentagon to assure a survivable U.S. capability to threaten clearly unacceptable damage to the Soviet Union in response to the most successful Soviet nuclear attack on the United States. But the planned slaughter of hundreds of millions of Soviets (and Chinese), twenty times the staggering deaths of Soviet citizens in World War II, along with an equal number of our allies and citizens of neutral countries! That expected outcome exposed a dizzying irrationality, madness, insanity, at the heart and soul of our nuclear planning and apparatus.

The fact is that the estimate of fatalities, in terms of what was calculable at that time—even before the discovery of nuclear winter—was a fantastic underestimate. More than forty years later, Dr. Lynn Eden, a scholar at Stanford's Center for International Security and Cooperation, revealed in *Whole World on Fire* the bizarre fact that the war planners of SAC and the Joint Chiefs—throughout the nuclear era *to the present day*—have deliberately omitted entirely from their estimates of the destructive effects of U.S. or Russian nuclear attacks the effects of *fire*.

They have done so on the questionable grounds that these effects are harder to predict than the effects of blast or fallout, on which their estimates of fatalities are exclusively based, even though, as Eden found, experts including Hal Brode have disputed such conclusions for decades. (A better hypothesis for the tenacious lack of interest is that accounting for fire would reduce the number of USAF warheads and vehicles required to achieve the designated damage levels: which were themselves set high enough to preclude coverage by available Navy submarine-launched missiles.)

Yet even in the sixties the firestorms caused by thermonuclear weapons were known to be predictably the *largest* producers of fatalities in a nuclear war. Given that for almost all strategic nuclear weapons, the damage radius of firestorms would be two to five times the radius destroyed by the blast, a more realistic estimate of the fatalities caused *directly* by the planned U.S. attacks on the Sino-Soviet bloc, even in 1961, would surely have been double the summary in the graph I held in my hand, for a total death toll of a billion or more: a third of the earth's population, then three billion.

Moreover, what no one would recognize for another twenty-two years were the indirect effects of our planned first strike that gravely threatened the other two thirds of humanity. These effects arose from another neglected consequence of our attacks on cities: smoke. In effect, in ignoring fire the Chiefs and their planners ignored that where there's fire there's smoke. But what is dangerous to our survival is not the smoke from ordinary fires, even very large ones—smoke that remained in the lower atmosphere and would soon be rained out—but smoke propelled into the upper atmosphere from the *firestorms* that our nuclear weapons were sure to create in the cities we targeted. (See chapter 16.)

Ferocious updrafts from these multiple firestorms would loft millions of tons of smoke and soot into the stratosphere, where it would not be rained out and would quickly encircle the globe, forming a blanket blocking most sunlight around the earth for a decade or more. This would reduce sunlight and lower temperatures worldwide to a point that would eliminate all harvests and starve to death—not all but nearly all—humans (and other animals that depend on vegetation for food).

The population of the southern hemisphere—spared nearly all direct effects from nuclear explosions, even from fallout—would be nearly annihilated, as would that of Eurasia (which the Joint Chiefs already foresaw, from direct effects), Africa, and North America.

In a sense the Chiefs can't be blamed for their failure to foresee that the firestorms caused by their planned attacks would actually have led to the death by global famine of nearly all humanity—whether that was three billion as in 1960 or the seven billion that exist today; after all, the phenomenon of nuclear winter wasn't predicted by environmental scientists until decades after the Cuban missile crisis.

Still, one can ask why they didn't explore more vigorously the possible environmental consequences of this unprecedented ecological experiment—an all-out thermonuclear war—for which they were preparing. Or why, more than thirty years since scientists first posited these dangers, and more than ten years since scientific uncertainties about their calculations have been put to rest, our plans have *continued* to include "options" for detonating hundreds of nuclear explosions near cities, which would loft enough soot and smoke into the upper stratosphere to lead to death by starvation of nearly everyone on earth, including, after all, ourselves.

Yet even if I had known all this in 1961, it would scarcely have affected my reaction to the graph I held in my hand that spring morning. Moreover, that unabashed calculation by the JCS said to me then that any confidence—worse, it seemed, any realistic hope—that the alert forces on either side might never be used was ill-founded. Americans had built this machine, knowing, it turned out, that it would kill more than half a billion people if it were turned on (and they were unhesitant in reporting this to the president). Humans like that would not fail to pull the switch if ordered by a president—or, as I've discussed earlier, possibly on the order of a superior other than the president.

And the presidents themselves? A few months prior, Dwight Eisenhower had secretly endorsed the blueprints of this multi-genocide machine. He had furthermore demanded, largely for budgetary reasons, that there be no other plan for fighting the Russians. He had approved this single strategic operational plan despite reportedly being, for reasons I now understood, privately appalled by its implications. And when the Joint Chiefs responded so promptly to the new president's question about the human impact of our attacks, they clearly assumed that Kennedy would not, in response, order them to resign or be dishonorably discharged, nor order the machine to be dismantled. (In that, it turned out, they were right.)

Surely neither of these presidents actually desired ever to order the execution of these plans, nor would any likely successor. But they all must have been aware, or should have been, of the dangers of allowing such a system to exist. They should have reflected on, and trembled before, the array of contingencies—accidents, false alarms, outage of communications, Soviet actions misinterpreted by lower commanders, unauthorized action, foolish Soviet initiatives or failure to comply with U.S. threats, escalation stemming from popular uprisings in East Germany or elsewhere in Eastern Europe—that might release these pent-up forces beyond their control or that, in ways they had not foreseen, could lead them personally to escalate or to initiate a preemptive attack.

Eisenhower had chosen to accept these risks, to impose them on humanity and all other forms of life. Kennedy—and later, Johnson and Nixon to my direct knowledge—did likewise. There is much evidence that such catastrophic "major attack options" were among the choices offered to presidents Carter, Reagan, and George H. W. Bush, i.e., until the end of the Cold War. There is little known publicly about the range of options since then, although four hundred Minuteman missiles remain on high alert, along with a comparable number of Trident sub-launched missiles, each alert force more than enough to cause nuclear winter.

Moreover, I felt sure in 1961 that the existent potential for moral and physical catastrophe—our government's readiness to commit multi-genocidal extermination on a hemispheric scale by nuclear blast and fallout—was not only a product of aberrant Americans or a peculiarly American phenomenon. I was right. A few years later, after the humiliation of the Cuban missile crisis and the ouster of Khrushchev, the Russians set out to imitate our destructive capacity in every detail and surpass it where possible. By the end of the decade, they had succeeded. Ever since then, there have existed *two* Doomsday Machines, each on high alert and subject to possible false alarms and the temptation to preemption, a situation much more than twice as dangerous as existed in the early sixties.

To be sure, Americans, and American Air Force planners in particular, were the only people in the world who believed that they had won a war by bombing, and, particularly in Japan, by bombing civilians. But the nuclear era eventually put that demonic temptation—to deter, defeat, or punish an adversary by an operational capability to annihilate most of its civilian population—within the reach of many nations. By the spring of 1961, four states (soon to be five, now nine) had, at great expense, bought themselves that capability. Humans just like these American planners—and presidents—were surely at work in every nuclear weapons state, producing plans like these for nuclear attacks on cities.

I personally knew many of the American planners, though apparently—from this fatality chart—not quite as well as I had thought. They were not evil, in any ordinary, or extraordinary, sense. They were normal Americans, capable and patriotic. I was sure they were not different, surely not worse, than the people in Russia doing the same work, or the people who would sit at similar desks in later U.S. administrations or other nuclear weapons states.

I liked most of the planners and analysts I knew: not only the physicists at RAND who designed bombs and the economists who speculated on strategy (like me), but also the colonels who worked on these very plans, whom I consulted with during the workday and drank beer with in the evening. What I was looking at was not simply an American problem or a superpower problem. With the age of warring nation-states persisting into the thermonuclear era, it was a species problem.

A few years after leaving the White House, McGeorge Bundy wrote in *Foreign Affairs*, "In the real world of real political leaders—whether here or in the Soviet Union—a decision that would bring even one hydrogen bomb on one city of one's own country would be recognized as a catastrophic blunder; ten bombs on ten cities would be a disaster beyond human history; and a hundred bombs on a hundred cities are unthinkable."

In the last year of the Cold War, Herbert York cited Bundy's statement in a talk at Lawrence Livermore National Laboratory (of which he had been the first director), where, along with Los Alamos, all U.S. nuclear weapons had been designed. York posed the question, how many nuclear weapons are needed to deter an adversary rational enough to be deterred? Concurring with Bundy's judgment—as who would not?—he answered his question, "somewhere in the range of 1, 10, or 100 . . . closer to 1 than it is to 100."

In 1986, the U.S. had 23,317 nuclear warheads and Russia had 40,159, for a total of 63,836 weapons.

CHAPTER 10

Berlin and the Missile Gap

In early June 1961, just one month after Gilpatric had sent my proposed changes to the existing JCS-SAC war plan to the Joint Chiefs, the possibility that their horrific plan might soon be set in motion loomed abruptly. At the Vienna summit between Khrushchev and Kennedy on June 3–4, Khrushchev renewed an ultimatum he had earlier made to President Eisenhower in 1958 (after Sputnik) and then withdrawn from in the face of Eisenhower's intransigence. Now he again warned that he would turn over all control of access to Berlin to the East Germans by the end of the current year, in connection with signing a peace treaty with East Germany.

That would mean, presumably, that the East Germans would block our access unless we negotiated terms, including their rights of inspection of cargo. That would amount to recognizing the German Democratic Republic as a separate sovereign state rather than a Soviet puppet—something totally unacceptable to our close ally Konrad Adenauer, West German chancellor of the Federal Republic of Germany, who claimed exclusive legitimacy to represent the German nation.

If an American military convoy—rather than either meeting East German demands or returning to West Germany—attempted to force its way through, it would be confronting East German troops that would shortly be backed up by the full power of Soviet divisions. Such a confrontation would open the door to general war, a state of affairs for which the

United States still had one plan only. Khrushchev was confident that President Kennedy would not let things come to that pass.

The Berlin threat came at the end of the meeting in Vienna, after Kennedy had made an assertion to Khrushchev that many military officers in the Pentagon regarded as disastrously inappropriate. Kennedy said that for purposes of discussion, the nuclear forces of the two nations could be regarded as "equal." Khrushchev, indeed, seized eagerly on this acknowledgment, though remarking that in reality his generals told him that Russia was stronger.

The Air Force itself was still, in the spring of 1961, projecting Russian capabilities in a way that appeared to validate Khrushchev's statement, not Kennedy's. However, they were intensely dismayed that he should express openly to Khrushchev that U.S. strategic forces (which they were estimating to be greatly inferior in numbers) were "equal" to Russians rather than superior, since this "admission" obviously strengthened Khrushchev's hand in bargaining. They felt that this showed a combination of naïveté, with respect to bargaining procedure, and character weakness on the part of Kennedy. Like the rest of the military, the Air Force wanted the president to take a tough line in a Cold War crisis like this one.

Nevertheless, they could not bring themselves to stiffen his spine in the manner they thought necessary by assuring him that his understanding of the strategic balance was in fact mistaken, and that we were superior. After all, major decisions on the size of the U.S. missile force, which were based on the dimensions of the supposed Soviet threat, had yet to be made. It had actually been leaks from the Air Force about the alleged Soviet superiority in ICBMs that had encouraged Kennedy to campaign for the presidency on a promise to eliminate the "missile gap" by accelerating our own missile program. For the Air Force even to entertain what Army and Navy intelligence had been saying secretly for several years—that the Soviets were actually greatly inferior to the United States in strategic capability and numbers and that they showed no signs of attempting to change that situation—might have undermined the perceived necessity for an increased missile force, and perhaps radically lowered the size of the force that the Kennedy administration would procure.

This dilemma grew more intense for the Air Force as the crisis atmosphere deepened during the summer. Within the administration, former secretary of state Dean Acheson, acting as a high-level advisor leading a planning group with respect to Berlin, was urging strongly the necessity of standing fast in Berlin, conceding no change in our rights of access. Acheson stressed the desirability of being able to defend those rights militarily, if necessary, initially without using nuclear weapons. However, he emphasized equally strongly that in the face of superior Russian conventional force, the access could ultimately be guaranteed only if the president were willing to threaten the use of nuclear weapons. These threats, furthermore, could not be sufficiently credible, he argued, unless the president was in fact committed in his own mind to the decision to use them if and when necessary.

When JFK asked Acheson privately during the summer, with only Bundy present, at what point he should use nuclear weapons, Acheson replied that the president himself should give that question careful and private consideration well before the time when the choice might present itself, that "he should reach his own clear conclusion in advance as to what he would do, and that he should tell no one at all what that conclusion was." Evidently, Acheson feared that JFK's private conclusion, if leaked, would not be such as to deter Khrushchev. Bundy believed, in retrospect, that Acheson's own answer to the president's question would have been that "the right final choice might be to accept defeat, and the loss of West Berlin, if the only remaining alternative were to start a nuclear war."

I would have agreed with that wholeheartedly. I felt, like Acheson did, that it *was* highly important to maintain our position in Berlin, if possible. But I would never have believed nuclear war in Europe or elsewhere was justified in this effort. And consciously, I recoiled from the policy of relying on a threat that I thought must never be carried out. Along with several of my RAND colleagues, including Harry Rowen and Morton Halperin, a young RAND consultant on arms control, I believed that for the United States to initiate limited or general nuclear war under any circumstances would be catastrophic. We felt very strongly about this, though it was a position that opposed explicit U.S. defense policy and strategy in NATO, which rested centrally on U.S. readiness to carry out its threat and preparations for nuclear first use against a large Soviet conventional attack. And I had been given almost exclusive reason to believe that Robert McNamara secretly agreed with us on this.

In early July, Alain Enthoven had arranged for me to have a brief luncheon with McNamara, to discuss my work on the guidance to the JCS on the war plan, which he had already approved and sent to the

Chiefs. We ate at his desk, in his office. It was scheduled to last only half an hour, but it went on nearly an hour longer. I told him about the astonishing answers the JCS had given to the questions I had drafted in the name of the president, in particular about the effects they anticipated on our own European allies from their planned attacks on the Sino-Soviet bloc. I'd had no prior intention to bring up my own strongly heretical view on first use, but midway through our talk, he raised the issue himself.

There was no such thing as limited nuclear war in Europe, he said. "It would be total war, total annihilation, for the Europeans!" He said this with great passion, belying his reputation as a cold, computer-like efficiency expert. Moreover, he thought it was absurd to suppose that a supposedly "limited use" would remain limited to Europe, that it would not quickly trigger general nuclear war between the United States and Soviet Union, to disastrous effect.

I've never had a stronger sense in another person of a kindred awareness of this situation and intensity of his concern to change it. Thirty years later, McNamara revealed in his memoir *In Retrospect* that he had secretly advised President Kennedy, and after him President Johnson, that under no circumstances whatever should they ever initiate nuclear war.[†] He didn't tell me that, but it was implicit in everything he had said at this lunch. There is no doubt in my mind that he did give that advice, and that it was the right advice. Yet it directly contradicted the mad "assurances" on U.S. readiness for first use he felt compelled to give repeatedly to NATO officials (including speeches I drafted for him) throughout his years in office, as the very basis for our leadership in the alliance.

McNamara's assistant, Adam Yarmolinsky, had joined us for the last part of the lunch, without saying anything. When we left McNamara's office Adam took me into his small, adjoining room and said that he had never seen McNamara prolong a lunch that way. He had talked more frankly with me than Yarmolinsky had ever heard him talk with anyone else. The point of Adam's telling me this, and of my repeating it now, was to give weight to what he said next. "You must tell *no one* outside of this suite what Secretary McNamara has told you."

I asked if he was referring to fears of the reaction from Congress and the JCS (I could have added, "NATO"). He said, "Exactly. This could lead to his impeachment." I told him that I understood. But he went on to make that more explicit. "By no one," he said, "I mean, not Harry

Rowen, not anybody." Now, *that* I understood. Evidently he knew that Harry was my closest friend and confidant, a cleared colleague with whom I normally would have shared even such sensitive information—though I'd been told not to tell anyone—unless I was specifically told not to. I never did tell anyone, not even Harry, what McNamara had said, though he would have found it as heartening as I did. But I did ask Adam one question: "As far as you know, is President Kennedy's thinking on these subjects different from the secretary's?"

Adam held up his thumb and forefinger pressed together, no space between them, and said, "Not an iota."

I left the secretary's suite thinking that here, in Robert McNamara, was someone whose judgment was worthy of my greatest trust. He had, as I saw it, the right perspective on the greatest dangers in the world, and the power and determination to reduce them. And he and his assistant had the street-savvy to know that if he wanted to achieve that, he had to keep his cards very close to his chest.

*   *   *

On July 25, 1961, President Kennedy issued a tough speech in connection with the Berlin crisis, calling up reserves for a possible confrontation over Berlin, warning the public that nuclear war was a real possibility, and calling for a national fallout-shelter program. Herman Kahn had argued that to make a credible first-strike threat, we had to be prepared to show that we would survive a retaliatory strike with our fallout shelters, or at least believe that we would. To do that you had to act as if you believed—as Kahn did—that shelters would make all the difference, and you had to encourage people to build them. I remember hearing at the time that McGeorge Bundy had said, "We're going to do this not for the Herman Kahn reasons," by which he meant that we weren't making a first-strike threat or counting on the shelters to work; we were just . . . what else? Making a prudent effort that might help if a nuclear war happened to come about, I suppose.

But in fact there was no other reason than Kahn's for the president to be talking about fallout shelters at that time. If a nuclear war had come about that year, it would have been only because our efforts to maintain access to Berlin had led *us*, the United States, to initiate the use of nuclear weapons, which almost surely meant a resort to general war. To be sure, the Kennedy administration didn't make it explicit to the American public that the nuclear risks of his policy involved a U.S. first use or first strike, as Kahn might have done if he were writing the speech.

Nevertheless, the speech did set off a frenzy of concern about fallout shelters—and a great commercial interest in selling them for private homes. Charlie Hitch, the head of the economics department at RAND and the man who had hired me, actually built a fallout shelter in his backyard. (As I recall, it was eventually used for wine storage.) So did Willard Libby of the Atomic Energy Commission. His shelter, as it turned out, burned down in the midst of the Cuban missile crisis the next year, leading Leo Szilard to comment that this proved not only that there was a God but that He had a sense of humor. There were discussions in *Life* magazine of the ethics of equipping your shelter with a machine gun to repel neighbors without the foresight to have built one of their own from attempting to muscle into your fallout shelter. Some Catholic and Protestant theologians concluded that, yes, it was within Christian ethics to protect your family in that way.

Khrushchev's response to Kennedy's tough stand was to begin construction of the Wall around East Berlin on August 13. That stopped the hemorrhaging of skilled workers and their families from East Germany to the West, which had been the most urgent pressure on the Soviet regime to change the status of West Berlin. But Khrushchev didn't withdraw his year-end deadline for turning over control of access to Berlin to the East Germans, a development, we believed, that inevitably would lead to war.

*   *   *

In late August 1961, I visited Strategic Air Command headquarters in Omaha to find out the SAC reaction to the cable I had drafted, with Colonel Lukeman's help, for McNamara to send to General Thomas Power, commander in chief of SAC. The cable urged Power to find ways to adapt current planning and operations as soon as possible to the war-plan guidance to the JCS I had drafted, which wasn't scheduled for full implementation until the next year.

I talked to Colonel Dave Liebman, now chief of war plans for SAC, whom I had known and worked with earlier when he frequented the offices in the Air Force Plans Division along with Lukeman. Liebman said that, after some initial reservations, my guidance had been received with approval. He said the attitude in Omaha, radiating from General

Power, was "we can work with this." That was good news to my ears; I wouldn't have bet on it before the visit. (Looking back, I should have been uneasy, at best, that my guidance had gone down so well with Power.)

In the course of the conversation, he remarked how unhappy he and most of his colleagues at SAC were with President Kennedy's lack of resolve and toughness with respect to Berlin. He mentioned that the president was perceived as being scared of the prospect of nuclear war, even though, he remarked, at the urging of his boss General Power, the JCS had assured the president that "if worst came to worst" and it was necessary to go to general war over Berlin, "a preemptive attack on the Soviet Union would result in less than ten million deaths in the U.S."

The words "less than ten million deaths," as a reassurance, came more easily from the lips of a SAC officer than from most other humans aside from Herman Kahn, but even so I was startled to hear an estimate that low. I said, "Ten million? That's the population of metropolitan New York! One large warhead, or a couple of them, on New York or L.A. could give you that. How could Power say it would be that low?"

"Well, that's what he believes, and that's what the JCS told the president," Liebman said. "They told the president that he should understand, in going into his bargaining with the Russians, that he had the capability to back up his threats to that extent if worst came to worst."

Obviously, they weren't including Allied casualties in Western Europe, although the Soviets had hundreds of medium- and intermediate-range missiles within range of Europe, along with medium-range bombers—more, in fact, than we had ever predicted. (It later became clear that the U.S. intelligence community had *under*estimated Soviet nuclear forces targeted on Europe and England by as much as they had *over*estimated Soviet capabilities against the United States. In particular, the Soviets had bought themselves a medium-range missile force capable of making one deep smoking hole of West Germany: a final solution to their German problem.) What is more, they had also produced and deployed missiles and bombers that could cover all our overseas bases, which were scattered throughout Western Europe, North Africa, the U.K., and Japan. Soviet attacks on these targets, which couldn't remotely be eliminated by our forces striking preemptively, would effectively annihilate the populations of all these areas.

Moreover, as the JCS had informed the president earlier, merely the fallout from our own attacks on the Soviet bloc would result in a hundred million dead in Western Europe, along with another hundred million deaths in other areas contiguous to the Soviet Union and China. But the JCS evidently presumed the president would be so much less concerned with allies and neutral civilian deaths resulting from U.S. preemptive escalation and Soviet retaliation that they didn't need to mention any of this.

From the documentary record, they could have been right about that. It was typical of U.S. strategists, then and later, to leave European, North African, and Asian casualties entirely out of account in weighing the deterrent balance. And I don't know of any instance of a president or any civilian official raising this point. In retrospect, that's a startling commentary.

Later in the conversation in Liebman's office, we were discussing the CIA's latest estimate of current Soviet missiles, issued in June: 50 to 100 ICBMs as of mid-1961. The USAF assistant chief of staff for intelligence did not concur; he believed there were "at least" 120 ICBMs, maybe more, with 300 expected by mid-1962. Likewise, the director of intelligence in the State Department thought there were 75 to 125 missiles at present, but "possibly" 200, with 150 to 300 in a year.

There was also a dissenting footnote from the intelligence branches of the Army and Navy maintaining that the Soviets had deployed only "a few" missiles from mid-1960 to mid-1961. When I read the June 7 National Intelligence Estimate (NIE) in the Pentagon, it was the first time I'd seen this outlier estimate in print (along with a page of arguments justifying it). By the decision of the Eisenhower administration, contractor corporations like RAND had been cut off from receiving NIEs in 1958. From that time on, RAND employees had been exposed only to Air Force intelligence estimates for Soviet offensive forces. We knew these tended to be higher than CIA estimates. I'd heard bitter rumors about Army and Navy heresy on the missile gap from Air Force officers, who regarded it as virtually treasonous. They saw the Army and Navy as willing to jeopardize national security by espousing fairy tales, with no other reason than to minimize the Air Force budget requests for missiles. This was the first time I'd actually seen in official writing what they were talking about.

Aside from the presumptively service-biased Army and Navy branches, then the intelligence community put the *lowest* estimate of Soviet ICBMs in June as slightly higher than the forty U.S. Atlas and Titan missiles operational at the time, or perhaps twice that, but possibly ranging upwards of three to five times as many as ours. The key projection was when the Soviets would or might have 300 or more. That was generally agreed to be the number that would allow coverage by missiles alone of all SAC bases in the United States and abroad as well as our soft ICBM sites. General Thomas Power had testified to Congress that the Soviets might have had that critical, dangerous arsenal in 1960, as Herman Kahn had been predicting. The CIA, as of June, put that as an upper level in mid-1963. The State Department had it as an upper level in mid-1962, and the Air Force definitely estimated about 300 by mid-1962, with about 550 in mid-1963 and over 1,000 in 1965.

Those latter estimates underlay the Air Force pressure for huge increases in force size. McNamara was just then confronting the question of the prospective scale of a force of Minuteman ICBMs, solid-fuel (quickly launched) missiles in hardened silos, a kind of deployment that didn't exist yet on either side. McNamara couldn't admit inside the Pentagon that he was even considering a number as low as one thousand, which was his private target. General Power, with LeMay's support, was asking for ten thousand. McNamara told the president that we really didn't need more than four hundred, but that a thousand was the lowest figure he could get through Congress and "not get murdered."

The last year in which U.S. retaliation to a Soviet first strike would depend entirely on "soft" air bases and missile sites, subject to destruction by two hundred to three hundred Soviet ICBMs, was 1962. After that, thousands of Soviet ICBMs would be needed for high assurance of destroying in a first strike the large number of hardened ICBM silos the United States was programming (aside from U.S. submarine-launched Polaris missiles). In other words, 1962 was the last year the Soviets could hope to achieve a disarming first-strike capability with moderate to high confidence.

However, when I asked Liebman why the Air Force was continuing to contradict the lower CIA estimate, he gave a more concrete reason. "We just don't believe it. There is too much evidence that they have more than that." Then he said, "Do you know what the old man [General Power, his boss at SAC] thinks they have?"

I waited to be told.

"One thousand. He's sure they have a thousand. Right now."

I thought for a moment, then asked, "How many missiles does he think he knows the exact location of?" I was asking how many ICBMs SAC thought it could target now, out of the thousand that Power believed they had.

"About two hundred."

"Two hundred," I repeated. I remember pausing for a moment before saying, "So that leaves about eight hundred ICBMs whose location we don't know well enough to target?"

He nodded.

I said, "How does that fit with the estimate that we would have less than ten million casualties following a U.S. first strike?"

There was a long pause. Liebman narrowed his eyes and scrunched his mouth. Then he said, "You know, that's a very interesting question. I don't think I've ever heard it raised before." He thought for a while more, then said, "There's someone I'd like to hear you put that question to."

He took me down into the underground bowels of SAC headquarters and introduced me to the chief of the Air Estimates Division in SAC Intelligence, Colonel George J. Keegan Jr. Liebman described him to me as a "real intellectual," and I'd already heard of him in the Pentagon as the "father of the missile gap." (He was one of several rivals for that honor. In the late 1970s he was a fervid proponent of a "death-beam gap": a race for a "directed energy, charged particle beam" in which he claimed the Soviets were ahead.)

Liebman told Keegan, who was accompanied in his dimly lit office underground by a couple of other colonels, that I had just raised an interesting question, which he asked me to repeat. I did. Keegan didn't answer it. Instead he reacted almost exactly the way Liebman had. He looked at me expressionlessly and said, "That is an interesting question. Hmmm..."

After a short silence I said, "You know, if you're trying to encourage the president to take a strong stand with the Russians over Berlin, it might not serve your purpose to tell him he's facing a thousand Soviet missiles."

Keegan sat up sharply at this and seemed shocked and incredulous. "You're not suggesting, are you, that we should *fudge* our estimates?"

He looked piercingly at me, and I looked piercingly back at him, searching his face for irony and not finding any. He seemed totally unselfconscious of the widespread reputation of Air Force estimators—SAC's above all—for inflating their numbers. But this was not, it seemed, the moment to share a smile about this.

I said, "Certainly not. Of course not." (*Fudge*? I wanted to say, "Heavens, no!")

"But ..." I went on carefully, "if there should be a range of uncertainty, it might not be best from every point of view to emphasize only the upper end of that range."

Shortly, Liebman led me away.

*   *   *

In September there was a political-military simulation game on Berlin run by Tom Schelling, my former Harvard mentor on bargaining theory, who was now running a number of such games for the Pentagon. This one involved quite high-level participants, some of them current officials and some retired officials, both military and civilian. It had participants as high ranking as General Maxwell Taylor, for example, who was shortly to be the chairman of the Joint Chiefs, and later ambassador to Vietnam. At this time he was still a top-level military advisor to Kennedy in the White House.

The game was run as a command post sort of exercise where we would sit around a table and we would get simulated cables—sent by the game controller, Schelling—as if we were getting them in the war room from Germany and from various military posts, a flow of messages supposedly in real time. One of them, I remember, was that students were demonstrating at the Free University in Berlin against our military moves. (Just over a year later, Walt Rostow and I would be reading a real cable with the same substance in an actual crisis over missiles in Cuba; see chapter 12.)

The 1961 game went through various phases of probes to Berlin by us and Soviet repulses of various kinds. I remember very little of it except that, as usual in these games, it was quite hard to get the Blue Team, the U.S. side—on which I was—to decide to use nuclear weapons, though that was the basis of our actual planning. That was so obviously fraught with total disaster that it didn't look as though anybody on our side could imagine doing that very quickly. That wasn't, it seemed to me, because it was "only a game." As in other simulations Schelling had designed, the participants got very caught up in it, and there was a realistic sense of urgency and tension.

Well, fine. You wouldn't want to discover that you were working alongside a lot of officials who thought nothing of starting a nuclear war. Only, that implied that our actual contingency plans for forcing access to Berlin had a large element of unreality. Or to put it another way, it meant that they were bluffs. Or that they should be bluffs: because the reluctance of the gamers to initiate nuclear war—as the plans called for if the Soviets used anything like their full available forces in East Germany to block access—seemed sane, far saner than carrying out the plans. But there was also the possibility—all too likely—that they would turn out *not* to be bluffs because some U.S. units, outnumbered in the field, would use their nuclear weapons without orders, to defend or avenge themselves, against the wishes of U.S. and NATO high command. There were no locks on those tactical weapons (any more than on SAC's strategic weapons) to prevent them from doing so.

The clearest memory I have of the game is that, when it ended, I was walking out of the building with Abe Chayes, the former Harvard law professor who was legal counsel of the State Department, when he turned to me in the dusk and said, "We've got to get out of Berlin."

I looked at him and didn't say anything. He said, "You know, our position there is totally untenable. This game shows it. There's no way we can defend that place." In national security circles, that was the greatest heresy imaginable. I never heard anyone else say it, before or after. Yet in conventional military terms, there was no question: West Berlin was indefensible by NATO. It was not only in the middle of East Germany, surrounded by Soviet forces, but also the forces that surrounded it were the best in the Soviet Army. There were twenty-two Soviet divisions in the vicinity, mostly tank divisions with their latest model tanks, tremendously surpassing anything we could throw in there. And if it came to theater nuclear warfare, the Soviets had as many or more tactical nuclear weapons. There was no possibility of militarily confronting them effectively.

If we had any plan at all for responding if the Soviets simply walked a division into West Berlin—in effect, arresting our small military garrison there, or capturing the remnants if they put up any fight—I never heard of it. When it came to that contingency, I believe we didn't even want to think about it. The only challenge we envisioned was their repeating what they had done in 1948, blockading, using East Germans, in the first instance, to cut off all access to the city, but this time also blocking air access as well. The only way you could prevent them militarily from doing that with total effectiveness relied on the threat of initiating nuclear war.

Of course there would be a series of steps leading up to that. Paul Nitze was in charge in the Pentagon of contingency planning for a

Berlin crisis. The plans anticipated sending a small American unit to test the blockage at first, very small to begin with, a couple of platoons or a company along the access road. And if they were stopped, we'd send a battalion. If that was outnumbered by a blocking force, we might send a brigade or a regiment. But the proposals I'd seen all stopped there.

At that point, we would be facing Eisenhower's definition of "general war." In mid-1961, the only plan the Pentagon actually had for a large conflict with Soviet forces, left over from Eisenhower, was an all-out nuclear attack on the Soviet Union. Roswell Gilpatric had told me that it was the intent of McNamara and himself, if it came to a crisis like that, to throw out the old plans and create new ones. But really, what was there to do? NATO planning simply wasn't designed—by the nature of the alliance, and by the realities of the situation—for offensive operations into the Warsaw Pact territory.

Kennedy and McNamara did, over time, introduce to NATO the notion of a "flexible response" starting with conventional *defense* against a large-scale Soviet offensive into West Germany. That might even include "demonstration" nuclear shots, one or two warheads against carefully selected targets, to warn the Soviets of the cataclysm that threatened just ahead and get them to back off. McNamara had indicated to me in the luncheon in his office that he would never recommend any such thing. And as I've said, much later he revealed that in fact he had advised both Presidents Kennedy and Johnson never, under any circumstances, to initiate the use of nuclear weapons. He said that they had agreed with him. So that was, privately, a bluff. But the recklessness of such a crazy "demonstration," the likelihood of its simply triggering heavy nuclear attacks from both sides, seemed obvious to me. I could only hope the same was true for our allies.

So there was no way for me to answer Chayes about the indefensibility of West Berlin without sounding to myself wildly reckless: as wild as our actual strategy appeared to be. There *was*, after all, just one way to hold on to West Berlin (without negotiating an agreement with the Soviets and East Germans!). It was what we had relied on since Khrushchev's first ultimatum in 1958, and continued to do for the next generation. It was to *threaten* to carry out our actual Berlin planning. The planning we were threatening to carry out was best described by a skeptical Pentagon colleague: "We send in a series of increasingly larger probes. If they're all stopped, we fire a [nuclear] warning shot. If that doesn't work, we blow up the world."

That's what we were doing. Chayes was saying, in effect, that this was not a good plan: not even, he implied, as a bluff. It was not sufficiently credible or reliable as a threat, and catastrophic if carried out. Holding on to West Berlin was not worth it. I wasn't inclined to argue with that. Yet I wasn't ready to come out and say that I agreed with what he had just said, even to myself. My memories of the Berlin blockade when I was seventeen, reinforced by my years in the Marine Corps in my twenties and my Cold War beliefs, were still too strong for that.

At the same time, the idea of actually carrying out the threats we were relying on was total anathema to me. And incredibly, in August 1961, we were making those threats at a time when, according to our official estimates, we were inferior in power to the Soviet Union in strategic nuclear weapons. I couldn't believe that anyone in the Pentagon or the administration could take the idea of actually launching a U.S. first strike seriously in face of that opposing reality.

Yes, Andy Marshall had told me the year before—with no explanation—that "there isn't going to be a missile gap," and McNamara had said in February that there was no gap, in a backgrounder press briefing that he had thought was not for attribution. When his statement was published, he had offered to resign for embarrassing the president, who had just campaigned to eliminate a missile gap; Kennedy had brushed off the gaffe. But McNamara might have been wrong. (He had been persuaded of his judgment by Eisenhower's departing secretary of defense, Thomas Gates.)

It was true that the lowest estimate, aside from the purportedly aberrant one by the Army and Navy, showed no significant gap—fifty Soviet ICBMs to our forty—but the majority opinion in the intelligence community was estimating a missile gap in favor of the Soviets as late as the June 7 NIE, a few days after the Vienna summit.

*   *   *

In the last week of September 1961, Alain Enthoven, now the assistant secretary of defense for systems analysis, and Harry Rowen in ISA informed me of a new national intelligence estimate. It was astonishing. It essentially confirmed what the Army and Navy estimators had been saying for two years in their footnote dissents to the NIEs: that the Soviets had "only a few" ICBMs. The number observed was actually *four*.

"Observed"—that was the big secret. Neither Alain nor Harry told me, initially, just what type of information the new intelligence report reflected, but within days, discussions in the Pentagon had revealed it to me inadvertently. This was not just an "estimate," based on inferences about production capabilities, or Soviet "requirements," or ambiguous electronic intelligence. Four missiles had actually been seen, and photographed, at one site at Plesetsk by our most highly secret intelligence system at the time, the Corona satellite program. (The cover name for the program was Discoverer. It had replaced the U-2 spy plane program, which had been equally secret until the Soviets shot down a CIA U-2 over Russia and captured its pilot Gary Powers in 1960.) No other missile launchers had been seen elsewhere in the Soviet Union—except for a couple of prototype launch sites at the missile-test complex at Tyuratam—after what was finally nearly complete coverage of possible missile sites.

The fact that this was "hard" intelligence based on actual photos was what is now called sensitive compartmented information (SCI), higher than Top Secret. Access to it required a Keyhole (K) clearance, higher than Top Secret, which I didn't have at the time. The existence of clearances higher than Top Secret was in those years itself a well-kept secret, along with the nature of the information each of them covered and the actual information itself. It was extremely unusual for anyone holding such a clearance to give any hint of these secrets to someone who didn't have the special clearance.

The penalty for a security breach of that nature was to be dropped immediately, within minutes of the discovery of the indiscretion, from the computer listings of those with access to the special clearances. That meant exclusion from the list of those who counted in national security discussions within the government—those who had access to this information and could talk freely among themselves. That sanction helped keep those secrets very, very well. Leaks to the press were nonexistent, either about the clearances, the intelligence means, or the contents of the information. Breaches of discipline, either deliberate or inadvertent, even to close colleagues who hadn't been specially cleared, simply didn't occur, with few exceptions.

I happened to benefit from several such exceptional breaches. Talking with Colonel Ernie Cragg, of the plans division of the Air Staff, one late night in the Pentagon cafeteria, I asked him something about the basis for the new missile estimates. He started to answer, then broke off, looked at me, and asked, "Are you cleared for T and K?"

I said no, and Cragg clammed up, evidently realizing he'd already said more than he should have.

Cragg's question was breach number one. As I was briefed later, when I did get such clearances, if he were in doubt as to whether he was dealing with someone who was entitled to this information, he should never have mentioned to that person the code letters revealing the existence of these clearances. If he really wanted to discuss these matters, he should have excused himself, gone to a Pentagon phone to call a special number, identified himself by a code, and asked the officer at the other end, "Is Daniel Ellsberg cleared for T or K?" If the answer, based on a computer search in the control office he was calling, was no, he would come back and change the subject.

If the answer was yes, he would come back and tell me that I had checked out and invite me to go to a phone to check his clearance out using the same process. For a uniformed colonel in Air Force Plans that I knew personally, that might not have seemed necessary. But in theory, he could have been bluffing, having heard the initials "T" and "K" or perhaps even having found out their nature, tricking me into a discussion to which he was not entitled.

That possibility was the basic need for this rigmarole, and why only the first letters of the code words "Talent" (for U-2 photography) and "Keyhole" (for the reconnaissance satellite program and photos) were to be mentioned in a public place, where they might be overheard. Elaborate as it sounds, this two-phone-call routine was something I practiced many times in later years before talking with someone whose access was not known to me. Procedures like this—and the sanction of being summarily cut off from access, involvement, and advancement by violating them—kept a vast amount of information relevant to government decision-making ("higher than Top Secret," SCI) secret from the public, Congress, and most of the government, along with foreigners and enemies, for long periods of time; they were proof against leaks for decades and generations, even when information was known to hundreds or thousands of individuals cleared for it.

The cliché that "everything leaks; it all comes out in the *New York Times* eventually" is emphatically not true, above all for sensitive compartmented information. It's a cover story, designed both to hide and sustain the effectiveness of the overall secrecy system. (Edward Snowden was the first ever to expose a large amount of SCI, including massively unconstitutional and criminal dragnet surveillance of American citizens and others in the world without probable cause for suspicion. Many thousands of NSA employees had known for a decade of that mass surveillance and its criminality. Not one other had disclosed it. Snowden is currently in exile, probably for life.)

Ironically, the second breach was by an unlikely person, a normally very tight-lipped colleague who had long been known at RAND to have "intelligence clearances," whatever that meant. After Cragg's slip, I asked my friend, who was in D.C. consulting, the meaning of "T" and "K," and he actually told me.

In retrospect, it's amazing, even perplexing, that he did so, which was not only against rules that were almost never violated but was highly out of character for him. Moreover, he said that I should make an effort to get those clearances, along with SI clearance (for special intelligence, a cover term for signals intelligence, comprising communications intercepts and other electronic signals). The three together gave one what was called "all-source access," the *output* of communications and reconnaissance intelligence.

Those who had (only) SI, T, and K in addition to Top Secret clearance were told, and almost all believed, that with their "all-source access" they had all the existing clearances. That was another cover story. There were in fact many clearances higher than these.

The existence of special access programs (SAPs) known as "operational" clearances about special programs—including, say, the actual operations and decision-making process concerning the U-2 or its successors or the family of reconnaissance satellites or covert operations—was unknown to those who had "only" all-source intelligence. I got a dozen of these clearances when I was special assistant to the assistant secretary in 1964–65. For example, Ideal (I) was clearance for information about the operations of the U-2 program and the decision-making in connection with its uses and priorities. The existence of this clearance, and what it covered, would be unknown to the much larger number of people who had only Talent clearance to view the U-2 photography.

The final critical clue I got about how much to trust the new estimate of Soviet missile capabilities was that Harry Rowen (who now, like Alain Enthoven, had all-source clearances plus many more in his position in the Pentagon, as I later learned) described to me a conversation he'd had in Carl Kaysen's White House office with Carl, Alain, and some CIA officials. They had been passing around, Harry said, actual photographs from the Corona satellite of the four Soviet ICBMs and the nonexistence of such missiles at other suspected sites. One of them had said, Harry told me, laughing, "These pictures are worth a billion dollars." And someone else had answered, "That's about what they cost."

Harry's telling me that there were now photographs of all the suspected sites, and the one real one, was the third breach. It was the big secret that I wasn't cleared to know. Along with Cragg's question to me about T and K and my friends's explanation of the clearances to me, that clicked. The version of the new NIE I'd seen was only Top Secret. It didn't tell, or even hint, what the new evidence was that led to the new *assurance* of the astonishing pronouncement on the Soviet ICBM force, or the lack of one. The new NIE would not be available to my colleagues back in Santa Monica. But even if they'd read it, as I now had, they wouldn't have known enough of the evidence on which it was based to know whether to believe it. Now I did.

I've gone into all this to emphasize that the *credibility* of this new esti-mate—fantastic, inherently incredible to anyone who had been relying on Air Force estimates or even CIA estimates (anything but Army and Navy estimates)—depended on knowledge of a kind of information that most people in the national security field, inside and outside the govern-ment, had no inkling existed. From the internal leaks—"unauthorized disclosures"—to me within the bureaucracy, I did believe it, even though it totally contradicted the fundamental basis for my concerns and work for the past several years.

It wasn't just a matter of numbers, though that alone invalidated virtually all the classified analyses and studies I'd read and participated in for years. Since it seemed clear that the Soviets *could* have produced and deployed many, many more missiles in the three years since their first ICBM test, it put in question—it virtually demolished—the fundamental premise that the Soviets were pursuing a program of world conquest like Hitler's.

As the Air Force chief of intelligence had put it in his dissent to the low figures in the June estimate, that pursuit of world domination would have given them an enormous incentive to acquire at the earliest possible moment the capability to disarm their chief obstacle to this aim, the United States and its SAC. His assumption of Soviet aims was shared, as far as I knew, by all my RAND colleagues and with everyone I'd encoun-tered in the Pentagon:

The Assistant Chief of Staff, Intelligence, USAF, believes that Soviet determination to achieve world domination has fostered recognition of the fact that the ultimate elimination of the US, as the chief obstacle to the achievement of their objective, cannot be accomplished without a clear preponderance of military capability.

If that was their intention, they really would have had to seek this capability before 1963. The 1959–62 period was their *only* opportunity to have such a disarming capability with missiles, either for blackmail purposes or an actual attack. After that, we were programmed to have increasing numbers of Atlas and Minuteman missiles in hard silos and Polaris sub-launched missiles. Even moderate confidence of disarming us so thoroughly as to escape catastrophic damage from our response would elude them indefinitely.

Four missiles in 1960–61 was strategically equivalent to zero, in terms of such an aim. They could have hit Washington and SAC headquarters, but that would neither have disarmed nor paralyzed SAC's ability to annihilate them in response. The Soviets could hit a city or two, striking first. Suicidally. They had no second-strike missile capability at all against the continental United States.

Their four operational missiles, at one fixed site aboveground, were thin-skinned and liquid-fueled, with highly volatile fuel that couldn't be stored and that would take hours to load. A single U.S. missile warhead, landing several miles away, would destroy all four with near certainty. In 1961, at the high point of the Berlin crisis, in terms of actual survivable missile capability against the United States, the Soviets had no deterrent at all.

Khrushchev had been totally bluffing about his missile production rates. He had said he was turning them out "like sausages." That was realistic about his medium- and intermediate-range missiles within range of Europe and our overseas bases. But about ICBMs it was a flagrant lie. Moreover, it meant that he had consciously forsworn the crash effort needed to give him a credible first-strike capability in the only period when that might have been feasible.

Our assumptions about his aims and his sense of their requirements were now put entirely in question. Or they should have been.

My first reaction was that this startling turn of events must be made known to my colleagues at RAND as soon as possible, even though they weren't officially authorized to see the new estimate. I flew back to Santa Monica and scheduled something that was unusual at RAND and a first for me: a Top Secret briefing. Nearly all the work at RAND except for key reports was at the Secret level. Though everyone in the building, including secretaries and maintenance staff, had to have Top Secret clearance, many employees never had occasion to use it.

At RAND they took the regulations about classified procedures very seriously. That was never done to the same degree in the offices I frequented in Washington, where most of the documents being carried around (even in one's briefcase going from the Pentagon to the State Department or the White House) were Top Secret. A Top Secret briefing at RAND was by invitation only, in a room with a RAND security guard at the door, checking off attendees by name on a list on a clipboard. That was something I never experienced in Washington.

"Briefings" were the major form of oral communication of studies and results to RAND colleagues or to Air Force audiences. They were almost always accompanied by charts on a chart stand or projected on slides, with graphs or bullet points. I'd given many briefings at RAND, but never with charts. It wasn't my style. I didn't use the blackboards that everyone had in their offices either; I can't think well on a vertical surface.

But this time, when everyone had been checked off and had settled down, I started by saying, "Herman [Kahn] says you should always have charts, so for once I've made some." They were on a chart stand. I'd lettered them myself, in red ink, with "Top Secret" at the top and bottom of each chart, as appropriate.

The first chart said, "Yes, Virginia, there is a missile gap."

I flipped to the next one: "It is currently running about 10 x 1."

Then the third: "In our favor."

There was no response at all from the audience of about fifty department heads, top management, and key researchers filling one of our larger conference rooms at one end of the building. With puzzled looks, they waited. I explained: The latest intelligence estimate was that the Soviets had exactly four ICBMs, soft, liquid-fueled missiles at one site, Plesetsk. Currently we had about forty operational Atlas and Titan ICBMs. This was not including the intermediate-range ballistic missiles (IRBMs) we had within range of the Soviet Union, programmed to be about 120 within a year; or the Polaris sub-launched missiles that could be within range of the Soviets, almost 60 within a year. Hence, in terms just of ICBMs alone, the numbers were ten to one in our favor.

To sum up the heated discussion that followed: no one believed me. *No one.* "How would they know that?" was the theme. I couldn't tell them. They had belatedly learned, only the previous year, about the U-2 program, and then only because Khrushchev had shot down Gary Powers. Before he was captured, only a handful of RAND employees had been cleared for Talent, and those few had meticulously followed the rules and given no hint of the program to any others at RAND.

Likewise, half a dozen or so RAND engineers had Keyhole clearance (as I learned later, when I had it). They had actually been critical to catalyzing most of the national overhead reconnaissance programs, first with planes, then balloons, the U-2, then satellites. Even if they hadn't heard the latest results—which reflected the fact that the latest Corona passes had completed adequate coverage of all the suspected missile sites in the Soviet Union—they would have guessed immediately what the new estimate was based on. But if any of them were in my audience that day, they said nothing.

"Why would the CIA even think we should believe this?" I wasn't supposed to know the answer to that question myself. I knew better than to jeopardize my chance of getting the clearances (as I would later do, toward the end of the year) by revealing the basis for the intelligence estimates. At least one in the audience, Amron Katz, was a reconnaissance expert who had known about the U-2 program and knew that it hadn't discovered any ICBMs. But he had written a number of RAND memoranda conjecturing the possibilities for the Soviets to confound our reconnaissance by camouflage and concealment and distraction. He was not inclined to believe these findings without having studied the evidence in detail (even though, unknown to me and most of the rest of us except for top management, he had played an important role in the Corona program). The others of us had all spent the last several years in anxiety of a possibly imminent Soviet threat of attack with bombers and a sizable number of missiles.

Few, probably, took seriously the Air Force estimates—all that were officially available to RAND—of hundreds to thousands of Soviet missiles in the near future. But to the extent they had heard of the more moderate CIA estimates, they regarded those as quite possibly too low. (The rumored Army and Navy "estimates" were beneath contempt.) We had all read of McNamara's assertion that "there was no missile gap," but hardly anyone at RAND paid any attention to that. And at most it implied that the Soviets might not have much more than the forty ICBMs we deployed in 1961. That, in combination with bomber and submarine-launched attacks, was quite enough, according to our analyses, to paralyze SAC.

Only a few who had seen the actual NIEs in Washington—no longer available at RAND—were even aware of the official dissenting footnotes by the Army and Navy that predicted "only a few" Soviet ICBMs in 1959, 1960, and 1961. If they had seen those, they would surely have reacted the same way my Air Force colleagues in the Pentagon did, believing that the Army and Navy were taking service bias to wild, almost treacherous extremes.

Two of the top Soviet experts at RAND were Arnold Horelick—later head of Soviet estimates at the CIA—and Myron Rush. (Rush's claim to fame was that he had, almost alone, predicted the rise of Khrushchev to top power from studying the sequence of photographs of Kremlin officials gathered together for parades in Red Square or other formal occasions. It was an esoteric form of intelligence that gave rise to the term "Kremlinologist.") In 1959 they had co-authored a Top Secret memorandum—uncommon, as I've said, at RAND—that warned with unusual urgency that the Soviets were probably conducting a crash program on ICBMs that would give them a significant first-strike capability as early as 1959 (i.e., right then). Their main basis for this was a close analysis of all Khrushchev's statements on the subject. Their premise was that Bolsheviks did not bluff. On that assumption, the sequence of his allusions to rockets and sausage making told them that he had already arrived at the capability he had earlier predicted and now claimed.

They were wrong. Khrushchev had been bluffing. That was what the new estimate was saying. It was correct, as Horelick and Rush themselves acknowledged, not much later, in a Top Secret report that was subsequently published. But many at RAND had believed their earlier memorandum, and my briefing was not enough to change that inclination.

More important, the estimate contradicted and essentially invalidated the key RAND studies on SAC vulnerability since 1956. Those studies had explicitly assumed a range of uncertainty about the size of the Soviet ICBM force that might play a crucial role in combination with bomber attacks. Ever since the term "missile gap" had come into widespread use after 1957, Albert Wohlstetter had deprecated that description of his key findings. He emphasized that those were premised on the possibility of clever Soviet bomber and sub-launched attacks in combination with missiles or, earlier, even without them. He preferred the term "deterrent gap." But there was no deterrent gap either. Never had been, never would be.

To recognize that was to face the conclusion that RAND had, in all good faith, been working obsessively and with a sense of frantic urgency on a wrong set of problems, an irrelevant pursuit in respect to national security. That is not a recognition that most humans in an institution are quick to accept. It was to take months, if not years, for RAND to accept it, if it ever did in those terms. To some degree, it's my impression that it never recovered its former prestige or sense of mission, though both its building and its budget eventually became much larger. For some time most of my former colleagues continued their focus on the vulnerability of SAC, much the same as before, while questioning the reliability of the new estimate and its relevance to the years ahead.

Likewise, the Air Force, and especially SAC, was reluctant and slow to accept the new figures, despite the fact that they seemed to support what SAC and the JCS thought was a desirably tough U.S. position on the Berlin crisis. Both RAND and the Air Force expected the Soviets to build up their missile force. But that buildup, which did begin in 1963–64 (particularly after Khrushchev was replaced by Brezhnev), could never promise the Soviets the strategic advantages it might have offered in 1958–62.

Meanwhile the Berlin crisis itself still appeared very serious. The president's attempt to mobilize public opinion for a confrontation precisely by raising the serious possibility of nuclear war had backfired. His decision to encourage a major private fallout-shelter program was a misjudgment, mobilizing instead great controversy. The Russians continued to affirm their determination to sign a peace treaty and turn over access control of Berlin to the East Germans.

Flying back to Washington in late September following my abortive attempt to reorient thinking at RAND, and with the Berlin game and Abe Chayes's conclusion still fresh in my mind, I had one immediate concern: how could this new estimate be used to change our prospects in Berlin?

West Berlin remained deep within Soviet-controlled territory. The erection of the Berlin Wall had commenced, with Kennedy's acceptance (even relief). From Khrushchev's point of view, that was a solution to his immediate problem: the exodus of emigrants from East Germany through Berlin. It even turned out to be an adequate solution to his longer-term problem of stabilizing the regime in East Germany, and thus strengthening the Soviets' position in Eastern Europe. But that wasn't immediately seen or accepted by Khrushchev, and still less by the West. Khrushchev's ultimatum about giving control of access to the East Germans by the end of the year was still standing, as were his warnings against our trying to maintain our access by any military means.

Now suddenly both these threats appeared to have been based on an immense, years-long bluff about his strategic "parity" with the United States. Recently discovered documents from the Soviet archives show that he was at this time bluffing his own Warsaw Pact allies—as well as ours, in NATO—about this parity to reassure them about his management of the crisis and the risks of his apparently provocative diplomacy.

So why not let him know, privately, that his bluff had been discovered and that he should withdraw his ultimatum and his threats? I set out to draft proposals along those lines.

CHAPTER 11

A Tale of Two Speeches

For years the specter of a "missile gap" had been haunting my colleagues at RAND and in the Defense Department. The revelation that this had been illusory cast a new perspective on everything. It might have occasioned a complete reassessment of our own plans for a massive buildup of strategic weapons, thus averting an otherwise inevitable and disastrous arms race. It did not; no one known to me considered that for a moment. But in the short run, it offered other opportunities, particularly regarding the problem of Berlin.

My first thought was for President Kennedy to convey this new understanding of the situation directly to Premier Khrushchev. He could do this through private secret channels to minimize Khrushchev's humiliation and reluctance to back down. I wrote two memos, basically for Kennedy's eyes. To get them to Kennedy, I gave them to Carl Kaysen, who was working for McGeorge Bundy on nuclear issues and whom I'd dealt with on the delegation problem earlier in the spring.

One of the memos I gave him, dated October 9, was a recommended set of talking points for Kennedy to address to Khrushchev or to some representative of his. The other memo, "A Proposal for Educating Khrushchev," was to explain the first to the president—to make the purpose of the message to Khrushchev explicit.

The idea was to make it clear to Khrushchev that we knew exactly what he had, and I proposed to tell him not only the number—four

ICBMs—but also the precise coordinates of the base at Plesetsk. For completeness we could include the coordinates of the Tyuratam test site, where they had a couple of test missiles. The implied message was: "You can drop all this bullshit you've been putting out about 'parity' and 'superiority.' We know what you've got and where it is. You've got hardly anything, and what little you have is vulnerable. So stop talking about giving us trouble on Berlin. You know, and we know, you are in no position to do that." Those were not the words, but that was the meaning I wanted to convey.

Kaysen read these and offered to discuss them with me. He was driving from the White House over to a meeting elsewhere in Washington and asked me to come with him in the car. He said, "Look, Dan. You've got to take into account the nature of the channel here," using information-theory terms about the president, his boss. "Kennedy will simply never . . . he will not talk like this." It wasn't clear to me whether he was saying this critically about Kennedy or whether he agreed with the president's style. He just repeated, "It's unthinkable. Kennedy would not talk this way to Khrushchev."

It still seemed important to me, though, to get it through to the Soviets somehow that they should not commit themselves on this issue, as if they thought we believed their claims of strategic superiority or even equality. "We know these claims are not true, so don't dig yourself in on threats that you are not going to be ready to carry out." That was the minimum message I wanted Khrushchev to hear. "Commitments to threats like these carry real risks, and things can get out of hand." But I got it from Kaysen that Kennedy wouldn't say that directly to Khrushchev, either face-to-face with his representative or in a private message.

A day or two after that, I was back at the Pentagon in the office of Adam Yarmolinsky, the assistant to the secretary of defense. I was still a RAND consultant, paid by RAND on an open-ended Air Force contract, but I was spending more than half the year in Washington working on papers and staff work in the Pentagon and State Department. Adam told me that he was working on a draft speech for Kennedy to give at a war college. Several agencies had been asked to send proposed drafts to the White House, and he was drafting one for McNamara to send. He asked me to look at it and add anything I thought should be included. So here was another chance to get the president to send my message—this way publicly.

I put in many of the same themes I had included my memos, adjusting the tone to a public speech, not addressed personally to Khrushchev. I wrote them out longhand on notepad paper and gave them to Adam, who exclaimed, "This is good!" He put them all into his draft for McNamara. A little later he told me, "McNamara likes it. He's sent it to the White House."

Days later I read the speech Kennedy made, which confirmed what Kaysen had said to me about Kennedy's more conciliatory style. He hadn't used anything I said. So I gave up on Kennedy as the channel for my message.

But then I dropped in on my friend Timothy Stanley, Paul Nitze's special assistant in ISA—where I hung out most of the time in Washington—for whom I'd worked on the war plans earlier in the year and who had checked out my memo on the LST at Iwakuni. Stanley had a little cubbyhole office across from the entry to the assistant secretary of defense's office. (Three years later, I would inhabit this same office when I became special assistant to Nitze's successor, John McNaughton.) Stanley said that he was drafting a speech for Roswell Gilpatric.

I gave Tim my original handwritten notes and said, "Look, I wrote this for Kennedy and he didn't use it. You can use it if you want for *your* speech." He read what I'd written. It wasn't a whole speech, just several pages of key points, including this statement: "Our forces are so deployed and protected that a sneak attack could not effectively disarm us." Right after reading that, Tim looked up and read the next paragraph aloud:

> The destructive power which the United States could bring to bear even after a Soviet surprise attack upon our forces would be as great as—perhaps greater than—the total undamaged force which the enemy can threaten to launch against the United States in a first strike. In short, we have a second-strike capability which is at least as extensive as what the Soviets can deliver by striking first. Therefore we are confident that the Soviets will not provoke a major nuclear conflict.

He asked with surprise, "Is that true?" I said, "Trust me, Tim, it's true. That's the way it is." This particular calculation was pretty simple on the basis of what I'd just learned about the Soviet arsenal. Four ICBMs! One hundred and fifty-odd strategic bombers!

Although the new NIE had not made any comparison of U.S. and Soviet forces, before or after an attack by either, it was easy for me to be confident of my "net assessment" of a "nuclear exchange" (in Pentagon language), startling as it was to anyone who had spent years hearing about the missile gap or reading RAND classified reports on SAC vulnerability. I was sure it would stand up in the course of bureaucratic reviews of the speech.

The question was, would Gilpatric be allowed to say it—to make such a revelation—given that the administration had not chosen so far to do so? Tim had been given no assignment to make such a revelation, and his draft when I first saw it was the standard Pentagon boilerplate that every official in the Defense Department put in almost every speech— about our military buildup and how much we had added to the reserves and our offensive forces, plus some talk about Berlin. In adding, as he did, nearly all my points, he totally changed the tone and bearing of his draft. Some of my language didn't get in, but this did:

> Our confidence in our ability to deter Communist action, or resist Communist blackmail, is based upon a sober appreciation of the relative military power of the two sides. We doubt that the Soviet leadership has, in fact, any less realistic views, although this may not always be apparent from their extravagant claims. While the Soviets use rigid security as a military weapon, their Iron Curtain is not so impenetrable as to force us to accept at face value the Kremlin's boasts.
>
> The fact is that this nation has a nuclear retaliatory force of such lethal power that an enemy move which brought it into play would be an act of self-destruction on his part.

That was the key point. My intended message was, for informed ears in the Kremlin and NATO, "We've discovered they are bluffing!" And for the American and European public: "We're staying in Berlin, and there's going to be no war." I thought of it as calling Khrushchev's bluff. I even rammed it home:

> The Soviet's bluster and threats of rocket attacks against the free world—aimed particularly at the European members of the NATO alliance—must be evaluated against the hard facts of United States nuclear superiority which I discussed earlier.

And with my new confidence that U.S. patrols along the Berlin corridors would not be obstructed, I felt free to underline our commitment in the final paragraph:

> The United States does not seek to resolve disputes by violence. But if forceful interference with our rights and obligations should lead to violent conflict—as it well might [though I no longer believed this]—the United States does not intend to be defeated.

Gilpatric gave the speech on October 21, 1961, including these passages and others written by me, which were then quoted by the *New York Times* report of the speech. In fact, all the passages quoted there and in virtually every other journalistic or scholarly account since then were among those above, proposed and written by me.

In line with the subtitle to this book, a confession is in order here. For decades after my work in the sixties on nuclear planning, I would have said that I had never proposed or been party to a threat of a nuclear first strike or first use in a crisis. I'm confident I could have passed a lie detector test on that assertion. Yet that would have been false. What else was I saying in my draft passages for the Gilpatric speech but that if the Soviets blocked our enlarged patrols along the Berlin corridors with some of their armored divisions in the neighborhood, they would have been taking an unacceptable risk of U.S. first use of nuclear weapons against those forces. Moreover, I was implying that we could do so in confidence that the Soviets would not respond with their own plentiful short-range nuclear weapons, because we would then exploit our "nuclear superiority" in strategic weapons to disarm and destroy the Soviet Union itself.

How could I have failed to notice or recall, over the years, these implications of my own speech-drafting in the fall of 1961? Well, I have to conclude, the same way most humans manage not to recognize or remember discordant or unpleasant aspects or consequences of their own behavior. Like everyone I worked with (with the possible exception of Abe Chayes), I wanted to hold on to West Berlin. At the same time, like my closest colleagues, I would have been appalled to achieve this goal by initiating nuclear war on any scale. Yet—without making a deal with Khrushchev to recognize East Germany, something not within my ken— there was *never* any way to safeguard Berlin from Soviet conventional and nuclear-armed forces in East Germany except to *threaten* nuclear weapons and express a readiness to escalate to a nuclear first strike.

So far as I was concerned, that ought to have been a total bluff. But in the giddy euphoria of the new intelligence, it seemed to me a bluff that was sure to work. That made it easy for me not to notice, or to forget, that it was, after all, a first-use and first-strike nuclear threat.

That did not go unnoticed in the Soviet Union. The day after Gilpatric's speech, Minister of Defense Rodion Malinovsky told the Twenty-Second Congress of the Communist Party in Moscow that

> [Gilpatric had] addressed a meeting of the Business Council in Virginia, presumably not without President Kennedy's knowledge, and, brandishing the might of the United States, threatened us with force. What is there to say to this latest threat, to this petty speech? Only one thing: *the threat does not frighten us*!
>
> They are threatening to reply with force to our just proposals for a Germany peace treaty and the ending of the abnormal situation in West Berlin. . . . A realistic assessment of the picture would lead one to believe that what the imperialists are planning is a surprise nuclear attack on the U.S.S.R. and the socialist countries.

I was gratified to see the Soviet defense minister responding so promptly and directly to my words, and so defensively, as it seemed to me. His claimed interpretation of what I had written went right past me, as Soviet hyperbole. After all, I knew, and I supposed he knew, that we had no intention or plans for a "surprise nuclear attack." The speech said nothing explicitly about U.S. first-strike capabilities or conceivable intentions. And I, the drafter of the offending comments, had no desire to see nuclear war under any circumstances at all.

What was the "threat" Malinovsky was complaining about? In his words, it was merely a threat of force, not nuclear attack of any kind. More precisely, it was a warning that we would force our way, with conventionally armed patrols, past an attempt by East Germans to block our access to West Berlin. As I thought of it, then and later, we were simply puncturing their baseless claims of nuclear superiority and *their* threats of cutting us off from Berlin on the basis of their genuine conventional superiority in the area. Still, as I've just now acknowledged, there was more to what he was claiming about what I'd written than I admitted to myself.

What of the relation of President Kennedy himself to these threats? Most accounts of the origins of the speech attribute the substance of the passages I wrote to presidential initiative. As the historian Michael Beschloss puts it:

> The President, Bundy, Rusk, and McNamara collaborated with Gilpatric on a text for his Business Council speech. . . . Drafting of the speech was assigned to Daniel Ellsberg.

Not so. All those officials undoubtedly signed off on the finished speech before it was delivered, and some or all may have earlier encouraged a strong statement about our military buildup and relative superiority, which Tim Stanley was drafting when I approached him. Probably none of them, starting with Gilpatric, knew of my role at all; none communicated with me before or after; I had no assignment. I've described above the actual sequence of events. Beschloss goes on to correctly recount my earlier exchange with Kaysen, including my suggestion that we give Khrushchev the exact coordinates of his four ICBMs. But he puts it incorrectly *after* I had supposedly been given this assignment to draft the speech, something that never happened. As in the *New York Times* account, every one of the five passages from the speech that Beschloss quotes on the balance were by me, taken from my handwritten notes originally drafted for JFK and given to Stanley at my initiative.

I note this not from pride of authorship. As I've mentioned above, it makes me uncomfortable to realize that I've misinterpreted for more than half a century what I was really promoting in this instance. I've long thought, as I did at the time, that I was simply warning that we would act confidently with *conventional* force to assert our "rights and obligations" with respect to access to Berlin. We would not be deterred from that, I was saying, by the Soviet nuclear bluffs I was implicitly exposing. But they had never been threatening nuclear first use, over Berlin or anywhere else. *We* were. It didn't stand out in my mind that Khrushchev's bluffs had been precisely to counter our nuclear first-use threats, on which *we* were relying in the face of their real conventional superiority in Germany. I was participating in those nuclear threats without acknowledging it to myself.

All right, I'd joined the crowd. But in retrospect, it was much worse than that. From the perspective of one year later, my initiative and my provocative words were near disastrous. That wasn't clear right away— quite the contrary. The threats appeared at the time to have worked with spectacular speed. When I first learned soon after that Khrushchev's ultimatum on signing a peace treaty with East Germany, giving control of access to the East Germans, had been withdrawn during the Party Conference, I and some others in the Pentagon assumed that the Gilpatric speech had led to this decision. That was very gratifying to me to think. I felt for a long time afterward that I had contributed to ending the Berlin crisis in 1961.

I was disconcerted almost forty years later when an account written by my friend Seymour Hersh brought to my attention that "Khrushchev had publicly withdrawn his ultimatum that America negotiate a postwar peace treaty with Germany by the end of 1961" four days earlier than the Gilpatric speech, in his opening speech to the Party Congress. Thus, "the Gilpatric speech seemed to be Kennedy's response to the Soviet retreat."

Michael Beschloss had pointed out even earlier:

> By asking Gilpatric to make this speech [sic], Kennedy may have strengthened his own domestic political standing and reassured American allies, but he also provocatively undermined Khrushchev's position in the Kremlin and in the world.
>
> The Chairman's entire domestic and foreign strategy was based on creating the illusion of Soviet nuclear might. Now, as the world learned that the emperor had no clothes, Khrushchev must have imagined that the Third World and perhaps even Soviet allies, previously mesmerized by Soviet power, might begin turning away from Moscow. . . . Khrushchev had fashioned an illusion of Soviet strength most of all so that the United States would treat his country as an equal. Now Kennedy seemed to have deliberately chosen to humiliate him.

Khrushchev's first reaction was to go ahead with a thirty-megaton nuclear test explosion two days after the speech, soon followed by a fifty-eight-megaton explosion, the largest ever.

> The thirty-megaton blast and Malinovsky's tough language may have temporarily consoled the Party Congress delegates, but the

deeply serious problems created for Khrushchev by Gilpatric's speech remained. It pressured him to do something spectacular to change the world's perception of the nuclear balance between the Soviet Union and the United States.

Beschloss concludes:

> The speech violated the President's own rule against backing an enemy into a dangerous corner. Kennedy never gave sufficient thought to how Khrushchev might receive the speech.

Whether or not that was true for all the high officials who approved the address, I have to say that shoe fits me.

> Khrushchev almost certainly wondered why the President had decided to publicly humiliate him by rubbing his nose in the fact of Soviet inferiority, and amid a crucial Party Congress. Did the address foreshadow an American first strike against the Soviet Union?
>
> Khrushchev knew that his Kremlin and military critics would now demand that he relax his opposition to a huge Soviet military buildup. The forces set in motion by the Gilpatric speech and Kennedy's other efforts to demonstrate superiority compelled Khrushchev to look for a quick, cheap way to remake the nuclear balance of power. . . . As Khrushchev might have put it, by authorizing the Gilpatric speech, the President of the United States was playing with fire.

Within a few months Khrushchev had thought of a cheap, quick way to repay the humiliation and restore the balance. That wasn't the only or even the main aim or the triggering cause of his deployment of nuclear weapons to Cuba in 1962 (see page 202).

Nevertheless, in October 1961 I had done my part in greasing the skids toward the Cuban missile crisis.

* * *

When I visited Adam Yarmolinsky in his office next to McNamara's in early June 1962—after spending the first half of the year writing my Ph.D. thesis at RAND—he mentioned that he had been assigned to draft a commencement speech for McNamara to deliver in July at the University of Michigan, in Ann Arbor, his alma mater. McNamara had decided for this occasion that he wanted to give an unclassified version of a speech he had presented at the NATO conference in Athens on May 5. That had been drafted, Adam told me, by Bill Kaufmann.

Adam had rewritten Bill's speech considerably. He handed me his draft and asked me to read it for comments. I asked for and got the source document as well, the Athens speech, which was classified Cosmic Top Secret (NATO's Top Secret). McNamara had laid out, for the first time for the ears of our NATO allies, the "no cities," counterforce, coercive strategy first promoted at RAND and by Kaufmann himself, underlying my draft guidance that McNamara adopted the year before. The United States had concluded, he said, that in a nuclear war stemming from a major attack on the alliance, "our principal military objectives should be the destruction of the enemy's military forces"—not its civilian population—while retaining reserve forces capable of threatening its urban-industrial targets. This would give the Soviets "very strong incentives . . . to adopt similar strategies" to avoid urban targets of the alliance, providing the best hope of preserving the fabric of societies in the course of the war.

When I compared Yarmolinsky's draft for Ann Arbor with the Athens speech, I had a number of negative reactions. The least of these was that I thought the logic of the approach was spelled out more clearly in Kaufmann's original speech than in the new version. Adam's draft not only left out, necessarily, the classified figures for NATO and Soviet military forces and capabilities but, in an effort to reach a lay audience, it seemed to me to blur the rationale for the new approach, which was, after all, a striking departure from U.S. strategic planning heretofore.

Second, I questioned the diplomacy of the speech in alliance terms. That applied to the Athens version as well. Kaufmann, with little guidance given to him initially for a classified speech to NATO on the new strategy, had chosen to present it implicitly as an attack on the French independent nuclear force, which Charles de Gaulle was in the process of constructing. The speech emphasized the importance of centralized control to a strategy aimed at avoiding destruction of civilians in urban areas on both sides, leaving them unhit in initial attacks but threatened by U.S. forces held in reserve. Without naming the French force explicitly— which de Gaulle had no intention of coordinating with U.S. forces and which was known to be aimed *solely* at a few Soviet cities, principally

Moscow—Kaufmann drew attention to the contradiction that such a force posed for the very possibility of the U.S. strategy, which purported to have the best (or only) chance of "preserving the fabric" of Allied societies in nuclear war. For an uncoordinated French attack to destroy Moscow and some other cities at the outset of the war would mean "the destruction of our hostages—the Soviet cities," assuring catastrophic Soviet attacks in kind on cities of the alliance.

Kaufmann had added to this point a characterization of the projected Allied forces that seemed almost meant to offend the French, if not the British as well: "In short, then, limited nuclear capabilities, operating independently, are dangerous, expensive, prone to obsolescence, and lacking in credibility as a deterrent."

I didn't see the point of gratuitously insulting the two allies even in a classified speech among their colleagues, let alone in a public address. But both the critique of the role of the independent forces and the aggressive language persisted in Yarmolinsky's version.

When I questioned this, Adam told me that this followed McNamara's explicit guidance for his draft for Ann Arbor. McNamara had liked both Kaufmann's general frame and his specific language. He had delighted in sticking it to the French in Athens, and though he knew the French were unhappy about this, he wanted to do it again at Ann Arbor. (I never learned his motives for this. Like Kaufmann, he must have felt angry at de Gaulle.)

I felt strongly that this subject was totally unsuitable for public discussion. Even our Allied military commanders had never heard in any detail whatsoever how the United States actually proposed to fight a nuclear war. After all, General Curtis LeMay had spent more than a decade keeping all such matters as secret as he could even from the Joint Chiefs of Staff, as well as from all civilian officials.

I told Adam that I expected the American public, hearing of this for literally the first time, would be appalled.

My reaction may need a little explaining. Yes, I had been proud of the effort I had made the previous year in helping shape this very strategy that was being expounded. (Earlier this same week I had reviewed for Gilpatric the new JSCP-63—submitted for his approval for the first time by the JCS—and found that it had incorporated, in language at least, virtually all the changes I had proposed, over his signature, in 1961.) But that had been because I was rejecting and replacing an Eisenhower-era plan that seemed to me to be unequivocally much *worse*.

Moreover, in the spring of 1961 I had been working on guidance for what the JSCP explicitly said was for use in the event of a Soviet non-nuclear assault in Europe. I assumed, however, that it was actually for use as a retaliatory, second-strike plan, since I still believed that the Soviets had either a predominant strategic missile force or a parity in second-strike capability, either of which practically ruled out U.S. escalation to a first strike, regardless of our alliance commitment. So, for a desperate situation, "my" plan was, in my own understanding, the least awful way to respond to a Soviet surprise attack.

In this context, its prospects didn't have to look good, or even "tolerable," and they certainly didn't to me; they looked very probably catastrophic. To be acceptable for operational planning, as I was proposing, they had only to look less terrible than any available alternatives, including the previously existing plan. The strategy seemed to offer the *possibility* of avoiding catastrophes that would be even worse and more certain.

This was not a reassuring message to present to the public. Understandably, no attempt had ever been made to present it to them officially. But in 1962, it was going to have an even worse ring to it. In the context of a classified NATO audience at Athens, and in the light of the great imbalance of forces we had learned about in September 1961, McNamara was now describing this planning as a U.S. first-strike strategy, in fulfillment of our long-term commitment to NATO in response to a Soviet attack on Western Europe.

A high-level NATO audience was used to hearing—you might say they demanded—reiterations of our intent to attack the Soviet Union in that case (though they'd never heard in such detail just how we planned to do it). But it had never been forced on the attention of the American public that a large Soviet *non-nuclear* attack on *Europe*—not on the continental United States—would almost automatically trigger a full-scale U.S. nuclear attack on the Soviet Union, with the certainty of Soviet retaliation on the United States to the full limits of its capability.

Moreover, the U.S. public had never been given any real hint as to how limited that Soviet capability was in 1961–62, with respect to the U.S. homeland. Although the Kennedy administration had acknowledged in late 1961 that "there was no missile gap," and the Gilpatric speech (with my input) had even implied that we were significantly superior to the Soviets in strategic nuclear power, the public had never been told either officially or unofficially just how small the Soviet ICBM force was in those years. In fact, the real terms of that disparity have never entered public consciousness to this day. A scholar as authoritative as Richard Rhodes was still writing in 1995 that the Soviets had over forty ICBMs in 1961, ten times more than they actually had.

In Athens, McNamara had the intent of reassuring our military allies, on a highly classified basis, that we had a way of responding to a Soviet invasion of their countries that gave us enough assurance of surviving the war that we would indeed be willing, as we always said, to carry out our commitment of a nuclear first strike in that case. And moreover, the alliance should rely on the United States' way of doing this, rather than encouraging the growth of independent (French) forces that would only screw up the strategy and make it infeasible by hitting Soviet cities and central command and control at the outset.

However unlikely to work the plan probably seemed to our allies, McNamara's assured tone in describing it—and the fact that the United States was investing billions to implement it—may also have convinced some of them that McNamara actually believed in it and would carry it out in the event. Or at least, that would be the Soviet impression, and that might well scare the Soviets enough to keep them from encroaching on Western Europe. (McNamara and Kaufmann, I thought, were surely mistaken if they thought its logic was so compelling as to dissuade the French from pursuing their *force de frappe*, which it certainly didn't do.)

But these potential benefits, however speculative, didn't offer themselves at all to unveiling this strategy to the American public, especially in a first-strike context. The language of the Athens speech and Yarmolinsky's draft version seemed strongly to suggest that the American government put confidence in the results of a coercive strategy in a nuclear war—avoiding Soviet cities while threatening them with reserve forces as we attacked Soviet military forces. Any such confidence was bound to look bizarre, absurd.

I learned later that Bill Kaufmann had had exactly the same reactions as I did to the idea of presenting the substance of his classified Athens speech to the American public and the world in a public address. Yarmolinsky had asked him to do the job of declassifying his speech for this event, and he refused. He didn't believe that should be done, for all the reasons I felt. So Yarmolinsky did the job on his own.

After reading Yarmolinsky's draft, I handed it back to him and told him as firmly as I could that I thought this speech must not be given. McNamara would have to find another subject for his commencement address. As I was saying this in Adam's office, he got a call on the direct line from the secretary of defense. He said, "Yes, Bob. Well, I have Dan Ellsberg standing here with me just now, and he's read my draft and doesn't like it. He feels strongly that it shouldn't be given."

I could hear McNamara's voice on the other end but couldn't make out what he saying. I was feeling, I remember, a small glow that Adam would mention my name to McNamara, as an authority, without having to remind him who I was. (I'd been out of Washington for six months, and I'd met McNamara directly only once, half a year before that.) Adam said, "OK, Bob," and hung up. He said, "Bob says you should write it the way you think it should be."

Rats. That was not a job I wanted, especially after I'd spent one all-nighter commenting on the JSCP. But there was no question of turning it down. This was the first time I'd ever gotten a request directly from McNamara. The problem was that I didn't think *anything like* this speech should be given to the public, and Adam had already made clear to me that McNamara wanted something along the lines of the Athens speech, and that he specifically wanted parts including the crack at the French that I was particularly doubtful about.

Adam found me a desk in his suite of offices and I got to work. As I again compared Kaufmann's speech with Adam's much-revised draft, it again seemed to me that Bill's version was better worded and its logic followed more clearly. I made another copy of each and started out replacing some of Adam's paragraphs with Bill's. These were the days long before personal computers, or even Selectric typewriters with automatic erasure and correction. Secretaries made corrections on good copies by using white-out fluid and typing over it. I took a scissors and cut out the parts of Bill's draft that seemed well said and taped them where I wanted into Adam's version, cutting that apart for insertions. I rearranged Adam's sections and I wrote out sentences and paragraphs of transitions or exposition where I thought it was now needed.

What I thought I was doing was a kind of mock-up that I thought presented the argument that McNamara wanted better than Adam had done. If McNamara bought it, we then had a month before the speech was due to be presented. There would be time to do a really decent job— if I couldn't persuade them after all that this was a bad idea altogether.

I had told Yarmolinsky (not in detail) the nature of my reservations to publicizing the Athens speech. But McNamara hadn't heard them, and that's not what he had asked me for. I didn't think I had time both to write those out for him and to draft from scratch an entirely different speech that I thought would be more suitable. So I made the choice—in retrospect, a bad one—of simply editing Adam's draft, partly with the aid of Bill's original.

In the end, what I had was a speech that I thought read better than Adam's but was in fact closer to Bill's original Athens speech than Adam's had been. It didn't at all cure my most fundamental objections to the tone and substance. (Maybe my lack of sleep was taking its toll on my critical sense.) I had taken out parts of the original that I thought were, as I would have put it later, too Strangelovian. Not nearly enough, it turned out.

Still, I did cut out McNamara's presentation of the results of studies of a hypothetical nuclear war in 1966, four years away, in which he contrasted two possible courses of events. Where both sides confined their attacks to military targets, the United States might suffer 25 million deaths, the Soviets the same, and Europe somewhat fewer. But if both sides attacked urban-industrial targets as well, the United States might incur 75 million deaths, the Soviets at least 100 million, and Europe 115 million. He said, "While both sets of figures make grim reading, the first set is preferable to the second."

His argument that the U.S. strategy, under centralized (U.S.) control, had the best, or only, chance of attaining the first set of outcomes rather than the second set in a future nuclear war was what underlay his prior assertion that "in our best judgment, destroying enemy forces while preserving our own societies is . . . a not wholly unattainable objective."

This last phrase, along with two sets of figures he presented, would not seem to be greatly overselling the prospects of preserving societies by this new strategy (even though it really was essentially mistaken, as we'll see). In fact, reading these estimates (since declassified) fifty-five years later, it is hard to imagine how this presentation could have been in any way reassuring to an audience of hardened military professionals in Athens. It was clearly not suitable for the graduating class at the University of Michigan to hear, or for any other audience that had not become inured to RAND or JCS classified studies. I also omitted his too-revealing reference to Soviet cities that had not yet been hit as "hostages."

In the morning, I handed the cut-and-paste version with my interpolations to one of the office secretaries, who were all capable of retyping drafts at lightning speed. I gave the typed version to Adam, who said, "This is good," and sent it to McNamara. A little later that morning—I hadn't yet gone back to my hotel to sleep—Adam told me, "McNamara says it's fine. He's going to go with it."

I said with real concern, "Wait a minute! That's just a rough overnight draft! We've got four weeks before it's given, plenty of time to improve it."

Adam said, "No, he's done with it. He's satisfied. He doesn't change his mind about these things. That's the way it's going to go." I was unhappy but shrugged it off. I went back to my hotel to go to sleep.

In July, it was a disaster. The French, of course, were furious that McNamara's contemptuous dismissal of their force was aired publicly. The editorial and American public's response: about as bad as I'd foreseen. Khrushchev's reaction I learned only half a century later, from Aleksandr Fursenko and Timothy Naftali's *Khrushchev's Cold War*. Khrushchev had decided in May to secretly send missiles to Cuba, in part in reaction to [my] Gilpatric speech. According to Fursenko and Naftali, Soviet intelligence had apparently missed the Athens speech (surprisingly, as we generally thought that NATO was penetrated enough by the Soviets that a speech to the NATO Council was a secret channel to Moscow). But when Khrushchev read about the Ann Arbor speech,

> what McNamara said irritated the Soviet leader because the secretary of defense explained that in the future NATO should consider targeting Soviet military installations instead of cities. The U.S. government was making this argument because it wanted to discourage the French, the British, and the West Germans from building their own nuclear forces, which were inefficient and hard to control and bred Soviet concerns. Only the U.S. force was technologically sophisticated enough to hit the Soviet missile silos. But what Khrushchev heard was that McNamara was somehow trying to make nuclear war seem less bloody and therefore more acceptable. Minutes after outlining a new Berlin offensive, Khrushchev railed against McNamara at the July 1 [Presidium] meeting: "Not targeting cities—how aggressive! What is their aim?" he asked. Answering his own question, as he often liked to do, Khrushchev replied, "To get the population used to the idea that nuclear war will take place."

Ten days later, Khrushchev attacked the Ann Arbor speech publicly as seeking "to legalize nuclear warfare and thereby the death of millions and millions of people." He also said it was deceptive to the American people because bases in the United States were in or near large cities. "It will be *first of all* the civilian population that will fall victim to the weapons of mass annihilation."

Khrushchev was right. To underscore that point, just three months later when SAC planes were put on high alert in an ensuing crisis (see next chapter), many of these nuclear-loaded planes were deployed to civilian airports near major cities, making these cities high-priority targets; the same happened again in October–November 1969 under President Nixon. Meanwhile, of course, the French *force de frappe* did go ahead, with Moscow as its principal and immediate target, negating any possibility of a no-cities, controlled, "coercive" central war strategy. (In reality, the same remained true of SAC operational planning as well: see below).

Nevertheless, Khrushchev was bound to hear the McNamara Ann Arbor speech, like the Gilpatric speech before it, as a first-strike threat to him (the flip side of the first-strike *assurance* McNamara had been giving, in secret, to the NATO allies in Athens). The new speech, which I'd helped craft, must have confirmed him in his clever, reckless response to the one I'd contributed to earlier. By the time of the Ann Arbor speech in July, the Soviet medium-range ballistic missiles that were meant, among other aims, to counter American assertions of strategic superiority and warnings of possible U.S. first use or first strike over Berlin were already on their way to the Caribbean.

CHAPTER 12

My Cuban Missile Crisis

On Monday, October 22, 1962, along with most people in America, I watched President Kennedy on television announcing that the Soviets were installing "offensive" ballistic missiles in Cuba, preparing a capability to attack the United States. He said we would blockade Cuba—he called it a "quarantine"—starting Wednesday morning. Any launch of a single missile from Cuba "against any nation in the Western Hemisphere" would lead to "a full retaliatory response upon the Soviet Union."

That last bit sounded wild. "Full response?" That meant the SIOP—the plan for general nuclear war. I was caught by that, having written the guidance for that plan eighteen months earlier. Use it essentially as a first strike against the Soviet Union in the event someone—Cubans?—launched one missile against anyone? I wondered if the speechwriter had any idea what he was saying.

I went to the phone—I was at home in Malibu, California—and called Harry Rowen in the Pentagon. I asked him, "Could you use some help there?"

He said, "Why don't you come on over here—tomorrow." I made a reservation for early the next morning and packed a bag.

When I got to his office late Tuesday afternoon, Harry read me into the picture quickly. The group of principals called the ExComm, for "Executive Committee of the National Security Council," had been meeting with the president, and sometimes without him, several times a day for the past week, deciding what to do. Three or four working groups of staffers were supporting them. One, centered in the Pentagon, was coordinating plans for an air attack and invasion, probably a week away as I arrived.

Harry said to me, "Write a memo on what thirty-eight missiles could do to our strike-back ability." He gave me a map with the ranges of the medium-range ballistic missiles (MRBM) and intermediate-range ballistic missiles (IRBM), shown as circles on it. Both Washington and Omaha were within reach of the MRBMs, some of which were already operational. My first thought was that that meant the command posts in the Washington area and at Offutt Air Force Base in Omaha, SAC headquarters, could be hit with very short warning time: minutes— essentially no warning. That was really the most significant effect. It meant the Soviets could be confident of decapitation. But I knew what most didn't, even in the Pentagon: that wouldn't spare them from a full, quick retaliation from our massive surviving forces, thanks to delegation.

This ability to conduct a land-based no-warning attack on our command centers was not an insignificant effect. But it was nothing new; they could have accomplished this with cruise missiles from submarines. Therefore, we had never counted on protecting Washington or Offutt anyway. That was why the Pentagon had designed a system of alternate command posts, including at sea and airborne as well as underground, and why Eisenhower and Kennedy had delegated authority.

As for the threat to SAC's second-strike ability, Harry told me that bombers had already widely dispersed, including to more than thirty civilian airfields. (So much for the plans announced at Ann Arbor four months earlier of giving the Soviets maximum incentive to forgo targeting our cities.)

Thirty-eight missiles meant a big expansion, relatively, of their small strategic force. In Russia, they were starting to deploy their new silo-based ICBMs, the SS-7. Perhaps sixty sites were under construction, but only about ten, Harry told me, were operational.

Along with the four SS-6s at Plesetsk, for what they were worth, that meant that the Soviet first-strike missile force was at least doubling or expanding far more than that overnight. Yet it still didn't mean that they would escape total devastation if they struck first. A single surviving SAC base would assure that, and well more than one would survive. Aside from our theater forces, they would also be hit by Polaris missiles and carrier forces at sea, and surviving Atlas and Titan missiles. Fifty to a hundred missiles didn't give them a disarming first-strike force.

Nor did the vulnerable IRBMs (which were not delivered, because of the blockade) on unhardened fixed sites do much for their ability to strike second. The mobile MRBMs, if we really couldn't find all of them, would do more for their retaliatory capability. Of course, if the Soviets were allowed to base missiles on Cuba, they could quickly deploy a larger number of these from their current arsenal. A hundred or so IRBMs would make a big difference to their first-strike capability. Or so we calculated then, in days when it was assumed by our military that either side could "accept" tens of millions of deaths, though not hundreds of millions.

We have an unusual record of the Cuban missile crisis as a result of tapes Kennedy made of meetings of the ExComm. I wasn't surprised to read, years later when the tapes were transcribed, that McNamara had said at the second ExComm meeting one week earlier much the same as I had: that these missiles didn't affect our security decisively, or even significantly. "I'll be quite frank," he told the president. "I don't think there *is* a military problem . . . This is a domestic political problem."

The JCS didn't agree; they were itching to attack Cuba. But McNamara's point, and mine, was that the missiles in Cuba didn't affect us much more (despite the short warning time, which the JCS made much of) than did forty more ICBMs in the Soviet Union, which we were expecting in the next few months anyway. A year earlier, CINCSAC had been claiming that the Soviets already had a thousand ICBMs aimed at us. Forty, fifty, a hundred were not in that class of threat.

Walt Rostow at the State Department asked me to join a working group looking at "long-range plans": two weeks from now and more. (That designation "long range" for a two-week time span sounds like a joke, but that perspective is what defined this as a "crisis.") Harry also included me in his short-term invasion planning group. As far as I know, I was the only person to be in two of these groups (and the only outside consultant in any of them). Harry's boss, Paul Nitze, was in charge of another group planning our response if the Soviets blockaded Berlin if and when we attacked Cuba.

I was staying at the Dupont Plaza Hotel, where RAND people always stayed in those days. But we were working almost around the clock. Wednesday and Thursday nights I caught some sleep on a leather sofa in Nitze's office.

In Rostow's working group on Thursday morning, more than a dozen people were sitting around a long table at the State Department, reading the daily reports from the CIA on progress of the construction of the missiles and air defenses in Cuba; reports from the Pentagon on events on the blockade line; requests for information from the ExComm; and cables from embassies around the world on reactions to the crisis.

I found myself reading two cables that were almost identical, word for word, to the two simulated cables in the Berlin game I had participated in a year earlier. As in that game, students were now protesting our actions at the Free University in Berlin, and in the second report, large crowds were rioting around the American embassy in Delhi. As Walt Rostow was passing behind my chair, I turned to him and handed him the cables. He read them quickly. I said, "This shows how realistic the Berlin game was." He handed them back and said, "Or how unrealistic this is." One of his better lines.

We rarely saw, in the working groups, any cabinet-level members of the ExComm, who were meeting almost continuously at the White House or State Department. Once, on Saturday morning, Secretary of the Treasury C. Douglas Dillon dropped into the Rostow group during a break in the ExComm meetings. He didn't know me, but at one point, looking in my direction, he asked, "What is it we're offering? We've got to have something to offer him to get out."

I burst out, "We're offering not to hit his goddamn missiles!" He looked at me incredulously, snorted, and turned away.

It was wildly impudent of me—though no rank was being observed in the working groups, or, as it turned out, in the ExComm—and provocative, not really my style. I'm not proud of that memory. What's worse, I have to say that it did really reflect my expectations about how the crisis would come out, or ought to.

I was thinking all week—from Wednesday on, when the Soviets didn't choose to challenge the blockade—that Khrushchev *had* to back down without any real concession on our part. He was looking down the barrel of U.S. invasion forces that were fully primed to go on the following Monday or Tuesday, if not earlier. We had him outgunned at every level in the Caribbean: in the air, at sea, on the ground, in conventional weapons. And none of us, that I knew of, imagined that to redress that conventional imbalance, Khrushchev would allow any combat use of the nuclear missiles he was deploying.

That conventional superiority was reversed in Europe, in Berlin or Turkey, or in NATO as a whole. But our strategic nuclear superiority was so enormous that I couldn't believe he would really challenge it there either. I suspected that Dillon hadn't really absorbed, if he knew it at all, how much of a mirage the notion of Soviet superiority that we had all feared in the fifties had turned out to be.

It was precisely to repair that extreme strategic nuclear imbalance, I presumed, that Khrushchev had undertaken what seemed to be this desperate measure. But he had overreached. It might indeed have been a preparation to bargain over Berlin on more equal terms, or even to make new threats, and that was worth batting back, though I wouldn't have thought it was essential to do so. Even if we had accepted it, it wouldn't have changed significantly the risks for him of confronting us over Berlin.

That was pretty much what Nitze thought, and Harry; and so did the JCS. The difference was that the JCS *wanted* to attack Cuba, and I didn't, nor did I think that was needed to get the missiles out. I didn't even think it was essential to remove them, but I could understand the president's determination to get them out of there, even at some risk, which I (foolishly) thought was quite small.

The deployment obviously did confront Kennedy with a domestic political problem, after he had publicly rejected Republican claims that missiles would be coming and then that they actually arrived, following which he had given explicit notice to the Soviets that "gravest issues" would arise if they contradicted their assurances to him.[†] If he failed to act on his warning, the Republicans would charge, with good reason, that he had been both foolish and weak.

At that time, I hadn't yet come to recognize just how decisive domestic politics were in the calculations of presidents as they addressed foreign policy. But the external politics of this situation seemed enough to explain what Kennedy was doing so far in this crisis.

If he had backed down from his own warnings in the face of this provocative (though legal) Soviet move, I shared the view that our allies in Europe would have been impressed by both Khrushchev's boldness and Kennedy's timidity. They would fear that Khrushchev was not likely in the future to believe Kennedy's warnings or threats and that he was not wrong about this. Our allies would be less willing to commit themselves to threats—with respect to Berlin—that Kennedy was likely to back down from and that Khrushchev was not.

So though the blockade was an act of war, illegal in peacetime (Kennedy had chosen the word "quarantine" precisely not to admit an analogy to the Soviets' blockade of Berlin in 1948, which we had always described as illegal), I could agree that it was important for Kennedy to

show boldness not only for domestic reasons but for real alliance considerations as well. I took the defense of Berlin seriously. I wasn't in favor of
invading Cuba or attacking the missiles, nor did I think it would come
to that. But even if we did either, I didn't believe that Khrushchev could
afford to expand the conflict.

That Thursday afternoon, Rostow took me with him from the State
Department back to the Pentagon, where he was to meet with a CIA
specialist on Cuba. He was interested in expanding the blockade to cover
oil and other petroleum products. How long would Cuban supplies of oil
last, he wanted to know, before their economy ground to a halt? Six weeks,
he was told.

He was excited by that: more, it seemed to me, than was justified. He
said it would mean a "ticking clock" for Cuba. Back at Rostow's long-
range (two weeks) working group, I wrote a critical memo to him. An
alarm, I said, that rang after six weeks didn't seem to be related to the
timescale we were facing. All the missiles were expected to be operational within days, and the other working group I was on, Rowen's in
ISA, contemplated an invasion by the following Tuesday.*

Moreover, I said in the memo to Rostow, what we had heard of the
ExComm meetings that morning, which had led to a message to Khrushchev from JFK, indicated that while we were demanding that work on
the missiles be stopped and the missiles subsequently removed, no deadline was being set. We needed, I argued, to put a time limit on the process
explicitly if we wanted the Soviets to move out: something a lot shorter
than six weeks, more like days.

---

*Something I learned later from Carl Kaysen was that Rostow, in wartime, had a recur-
rent focus on stopping the flow of oil to an adversary. In World War II he had been one
of a number of economists in London headquarters (Kaysen was another) recommending targets for our strategic bombing with the objective of wrecking German war
production. Rostow had felt ever since then that "the great missed opportunity of the
war" had been a failure to concentrate bombing on German oil refining and storage.

Four years after the Cuban Missile Crisis, during Vietnam, Rostow pressed successfully in 1966—a year into the Rolling Thunder bombing campaign against North
Vietnam, which had failed to show much effect on the battlefield—for a major attack on
oil targets near Hanoi. He predicted it would be decisive in ending the North Vietnamese effort. It wasn't. The attacks had little effect at all; the North Vietnamese had
dispersed their supplies by that time. What I heard from Rostow in 1962 was part of his
career obsession with cutting off what General Jack D. Ripper of *Dr. Strangelove* would
have described as an enemy's vital fluids.

The transcripts later showed that John McCone, the director of the CIA and a Republican hawk on the ExComm, was making the same recommendation the next morning, and Bobby Kennedy actually delivered a forty-eight-hour ultimatum to the Soviet ambassador Anatoly Dobrynin the following night. I myself (unlike McCone) didn't want an ultimatum to be carried out, and I didn't expect it to be challenged.

But I have to admit that I don't recall spending any time thinking about what to do if it were challenged. At thirty-one, I was overconfident that a leader who was outgunned would back down under threat. And that seemed to be confirmed by Khrushchev, three days on. I wasn't the only one who drew wrong conclusions, as we'll see, about his reasons for doing that. (A number of my elders, Rostow and several on the ExComm—McNamara, Bundy, Johnson, and Taylor, among others—applied that mistaken lesson three years later to Ho Chi Minh.)

Friday evening I read a long six-part telegram from Khrushchev that showed a sober appreciation of the unacceptability of nuclear war between our two countries and that seemed to offer that he would remove the missiles from Cuba on the basis of nothing more than a no-invasion pledge by Kennedy. That was more or less what I had expected. That night I went back to the hotel to sleep for the first time in three days. Like most others, I thought the crisis was about to end. I saw no problem for Kennedy to accept this proposal.

As far as I knew, for us to pledge not to invade Cuba was no concession by the United States at all, since we had, I presumed, no intention of invading Cuba except for the presence of the missiles. It was, I supposed, a meaningless, face-saving "demand" that Khrushchev was including to cover the fact that he was retreating without having won anything at all by his adventure.

But the next morning, what seemed to be a totally contradictory message arrived, in the clear, demanding the withdrawal of our IRBMs (or, officially, NATO's IRBMs) in Turkey as well as the no-invasion pledge.

Still, I saw this as just a desperate last-minute attempt at haggling by Khrushchev. The very personal message of the day before seemed to me to show Khrushchev's realistic understanding of the intolerable position he was in. I saw no need to make that alliance-busting trade of missiles. Nor did almost any member of the ExComm. The word filtered down to us—confirmed by the transcripts of the discussion years later—that almost every member had strongly urged the president against it. And no indication came to us at the Pentagon that that proposal was delaying our preparations for a U.S. attack two days away. On the contrary.

From the beginning President Kennedy had felt sure that if he had to attack the missiles in Cuba, the Soviets would almost certainly retaliate by attacking our missiles in Turkey. (General LeMay had disagreed. This was the only occasion I can think of when I agreed with LeMay.) With the target date for an attack approaching on Saturday, October 27, Harry Rowen was asked by Secretary McNamara to lay out for the ExComm alternative options for a U.S. response to a Soviet non-nuclear attack on the U.S. missiles assigned to NATO in Turkey.

Harry called me in to work on this with him, and the two of us sat at opposite sides of his desk, each writing on yellow pads as fast as we could. The first option we presented was "No further U.S. response"—in effect, calling it "even," missiles destroyed in Turkey for missiles destroyed in Cuba, seeking to end hostilities there. We took some pride, I recall, in beginning with that, since we felt that few advisors in that era would have had the nerve even to include that as a policy option. Dean Acheson, for one, did not.[†]

Along with the next one, to hit the single plane or missile site from which the Soviet attack had been launched, we thought these two options (the first being unlikely to be adopted) were actually best, the only two unlikely to spur further escalations. But we weren't asked for recommendations, only for a range of alternatives.

The rest, all likely to be preferred by the JCS to these, followed fairly obviously. In ascending order: Retaliate against one Soviet IRBM site, or more than one. Or (especially if the Soviets had also attacked some of our bomber bases in Turkey) against several Soviet air bases in the region. If U.S. aircraft were used for any of these, rather than ballistic or cruise missiles, the JCS would demand attacks as well on the surface-to-air missiles and air defenses in the area.

If there was a Soviet response—or, as the JCS undoubtedly would have recommended, even without it—the United States could attack all the bases, missile sites, and defenses in the region. Or even—Generals Power and LeMay could be counted on to recommend this—full-scale attack on the Soviet Union.

That was, after all, what Eisenhower's plan for general war—SIOP-62, operational until recently—called for in these circumstances: conflict between armed forces of the Soviet Union and the United States. To be sure, the Kennedy guidance (which I'd drafted) changed that. Yet it was pretty much what NATO policy documents had always prescribed: an attack on one, Turkey, was an attack on all, to be responded to as if it were an attack on the United States directly.

And NATO planners and heads of state still rejected any notion of waging a war in Europe that treated the superpower homelands as sanctuaries; they still regarded deterrence as resting on an almost-immediate launching of a full U.S. attack on the Soviet Union in response to any Soviet attack on an ally. (Only days earlier, after all, President Kennedy had promised "full retaliation against the Soviet Union" as the response to a *single* IRBM fired from Cuba against the United States.)

On the other hand, NATO planning and policy-making had never contemplated circumstances exactly like the premise of our draft options: armed hostilities initiated by the United States against Soviet forces inside the territory of a Soviet ally. Some restraint in responding to a limited Soviet retaliation to that might seem in order. But not to SAC, or the USAF, or the JCS.

LeMay, in fact, would be sure to point out that if there were ever to be an occasion to disarm the Soviet Union—before it finally built up its missile forces to the scale SAC had been predicting for years—the Cuban missile crisis in 1962 was that time, perhaps the last. A Soviet attack on a NATO ally—no matter what the provocation, or the views of our European allies—would be an irresistible occasion for it, in the eyes of SAC and LeMay, and perhaps all the Joint Chiefs.

I believed it very unlikely that the Soviets would risk hitting our missiles in Turkey even if we attacked theirs in Cuba. We couldn't understand why Kennedy thought otherwise. Why did he seem sure that the Soviets would respond to an attack on their missiles in Cuba by armed moves against Turkey or Berlin? We wondered if—after his campaigning in 1960 against a supposed "missile gap"—Kennedy had never really absorbed what the strategic balance actually was, or its implications.

As I saw it, and I presumed he did also, Khrushchev was just as outgunned in strategic nuclear forces as he was, obviously, in conventional terms in the Caribbean. That meant to me that he *had* to back down. The long private telegram from him to Kennedy that I'd read the night before told me that he understood that. What some others in the ExComm (it came out later) had read as panicky on his part (Dean Acheson described it in print as "almost maudlin"), I saw as sober and realistic. Khrushchev had his feet on the ground, and he knew when a gamble had failed.

Ever since Wednesday morning, October 24—when, contrary to his threats on Tuesday, Khrushchev chose not to challenge the blockade line—I hadn't believed it would be necessary to carry out an air strike to get rid of the Soviet missiles in Cuba. Neither did Harry. I still didn't as we worked together on Saturday to take account of the repercussions of that possibility.

Nor did I believe it was necessary even to consider journalist Walter Lippmann's suggestion Thursday morning of trading away our missiles in Turkey, an option which I (like the majority of the ExComm, it turned out) strongly opposed for reasons of NATO solidarity.

That remained my view despite the Saturday-morning message from Khrushchev that seemed to take up Lippmann's proposal. Nitze relayed to us the sense from the ExComm that it represented a last-ditch bargaining move dictated by hard-liners in the Kremlin, presumably in opposition to his own inclination the night before to concede. Khrushchev could probably overrule that, if he remained in control. And Kennedy apparently was banking on that, having decided calmly to ignore that tough demand for a trade in favor of accepting the Friday night message, with no mention of our missiles in Turkey, as the ruling proposal.

All this was thrown in question by the gradual confirmation during the afternoon that a SAC U-2 over Cuba, which had been out of communication since the morning, had, in fact, been shot down by a Soviet-manned SAM. And, on the U.S. side, by President Kennedy's decision not to respond: contrary to his assurances to the JCS that any shoot-down of a reconnaissance plane would lead to immediate U.S. attacks on the attacking air defense sites and possibly more. That presidential reticence—or, as some military we were working with saw it, dismaying weakness—was explained as a desire not to derail Soviet acceptance of his latest proposal (which was sent before the attack on the U-2 had been confirmed).

But while the ExComm awaited a Kremlin response, and working groups kept working on plans for air attacks and an invasion now scheduled for two days away, a more ominous signal came down to the ISA offices. Harry was given a new task, which he passed on to me. This one came straight from McNamara.

I was to draft cables to our ambassador in Turkey, Raymond Hare, and to our ambassador to NATO, Thomas K. Finletter, conveying a presidential decision to remove the U.S. IRBMs from Turkey and "replace" them with Polaris submarines assigned to NATO in the eastern Mediterranean. As I understood the purpose of these drafts, this was to alert the ambassadors to the possibility, or likelihood, that a presidential decision to this effect would presently be forthcoming.

The brief instructions Harry passed on were that the Turks should be told that this would protect them from being targeted by the Soviets, if the crisis escalated, and that the Polaris submarines were a better deterrent to an attack on Turkey or NATO than the IRBMs, which were vulnerable, veritable lightning rods.

I was appalled. I had been given a file of previous cable exchanges with our Turkey and NATO ambassadors, on the subject of a possible missile trade—missiles being removed from both Turkey and Cuba— and I was entirely convinced by the ambassadors' judgments that this would have a devastating effect on our relations with the Turks and with other NATO governments in general.

The Turks, Hare had said in more than one cable, were proud of the possession of the IRBMs, and rather than being fearful of their targetability, they were particularly proud that these missiles put them on the "very front line" of the NATO military posture. "These are now Turkish missiles," Hare said. Indeed, "ownership" of the missiles (though not of the warheads, which the United States supposedly controlled) had been formally transferred to the Turks, which made the United States' unilateral reclaiming of them of questionable legality. The Turks had no desire or intention of giving them up—least of all under Soviet threat.

Moreover, if the United States were seen as disarming NATO of "its" weapons in the face of Soviet threats, it would appear to all of NATO that the United States was sacrificing the "defense" of Europe—its deterrent posture—in the interests of U.S. security. It would be understood as the precursor to a trade-off of the NATO missiles for the removal of the Soviet missiles on Cuba that threatened the continental United States, even though the White House and McNamara proposed to give no hint of this possibility at this time. This "precaution" they were taking—to keep the missiles from being attacked (and secretly, to keep them from being fired by the Turks)—was itself more than a hint of that.

This would be taken by Charles de Gaulle, and others, as confirming what he had been saying for some time: that the United States could not be trusted to put European interests with respect to security above its perception of its own security. Leadership of the alliance—which had always amounted to U.S. hegemony—might be lost to de Gaulle or a combination of France and Germany; the alliance itself might begin to dissolve. And Khrushchev could take advantage of this demoralization to press hard on Berlin.

All this made sense to me. (Although I didn't know it at the time, these same arguments had been pressed on Kennedy that very morning by McGeorge Bundy and others, persuading him to give up—at least for that moment—his inclination to accept Khrushchev's proposal Saturday morning of a public trade.) Nevertheless, I tried to craft language that would meet McNamara's directive to make the best case possible for the move, pretending that it was in the interest of the Turks themselves, not just of the United States—this in the face of Hare's reports that any such action would destroy their trust in the United States and the alliance.

I was usually pretty fast at drafting language—that was a major part of my job as a consultant from RAND in D.C.—but I found this agonizingly slow going. I typed lines and paragraphs, tore the paper out and threw it away, tried again. I simply didn't believe what I was writing, and I hated doing it. It was a bureaucrat's job, elaborating positions that had been dictated from above, even when you strongly disagreed with them personally. But I was a RAND consultant, not an official, not an employee.

I thought of saying I simply couldn't (wouldn't) do it, leaving the building if necessary—going back to California—but I put that out of my mind. It would have seriously embarrassed Harry Rowen with Nitze and McNamara. It was Harry who had brought me there and vouched for me. I tried to do it for him, not for them.

But I wasn't getting anywhere.

In real anguish, I was thinking of Kennedy and McNamara, *"They're blowing it."* The president was going to take away the Turkish missiles. He was going to make the deal that Khrushchev demanded that morning. He was going to snatch defeat—the breakup of the NATO alliance, yielding on Berlin as well as Cuba—from the jaws of victory. I felt sure that Khrushchev was on the verge of giving way. Kennedy was backing off, disastrously, *when he didn't have to.*

At one point, Nitze came by the desk where I was writing and asked, "How's it going?"

Uncharacteristically, I answered that query candidly: "Not so well. Slowly." I remember feeling very tired as well as frustrated. My mind was turning slowly. Everybody was getting tired. I said to him: "I can't stand writing logic that *Turks* can pick apart." I'm not proud of this now, but I said "Turks" with full chauvinistic overtones, and I wasn't kidding.

He said, "Well, keep at it," and walked off.

I kept at it. Half an hour later, Harry came by and put me out of my misery. He said McNamara had drafted the cables himself. It was embarrassing. Nitze must have told him he didn't have it yet. But I was relieved. Harry said to go home, and I went back to the hotel.

I've never forgotten my thoughts as I looked at my face in the mirror above the bathroom sink in my hotel room, clutching the sink in my hands. It was half dark, lit only from the bedroom behind me. I was feeling a kind of horror. I felt I had just been part of something shameful, a transaction that shamed my country. These words were almost aloud in my head as I looked at the mirror: "I'm never coming back here. I'm never going to be in this position again. I had to do this, try to do this, for Harry—he was under orders, it was his job—but I'm not working for Harry anymore. I'm done. I'm not coming back to this town."

I took off my clothes and fell into bed. The next morning, Sunday, I got up late. I had breakfast at the hotel and wandered into the ISA offices in the Pentagon about ten o'clock.

Everyone was celebrating, looking bemused. There'd been an announcement on the radio from Moscow an hour earlier that Khrushchev was in the process of removing the missiles from Cuba. He'd accepted Kennedy's proposal of the afternoon before. No mention was made of missiles in Turkey.

It was pretty much what I'd expected, before last night. I was glad to hear it, but I wasn't so surprised as the others, and I didn't feel any great jubilation. I felt relief, like everyone, but for a different reason: that McNamara's draft cables hadn't been acted on. I checked to see if they'd gone out. They hadn't—saving the day, as I saw it.

The NATO ministers were meeting at that moment, and the initial reports were that they were all joyously congratulating the United States for standing firm and triumphing. The Turks were especially happy.

CHAPTER 13

Cuba

The Real Story

Khrushchev had backed off; he had not only accepted the blockade but also removed his missiles, under threat of attack and without any compensating concession by JFK (except what I and most Americans assumed to be a meaningless promise not to invade Cuba). Harry Rowen had shared my confidence that the chance of *nuclear* war erupting from this confrontation was extremely low. I presumed President Kennedy and his lieutenants on the ExComm shared that confidence as well. Indeed, my notes reveal that sometime during that second week of the crisis, Harry had remarked to me, "I think the Executive Committee puts the chance of nuclear war very low, though they still may *overesti-* mate it by ten times. They may put it at one in a hundred." He himself, he told me, would have said the odds were "one in a thousand."

But the day after the crisis ended, on Monday, October 29, he informed me that his boss, Paul Nitze, had just told him that *he* had put the chance of some form of nuclear war, if we had struck the missiles in Cuba, as "fairly high." And his estimate of the risk, Nitze thought, was the *lowest* in the ExComm. Everyone else, he believed, put it higher.

Harry had asked him what odds he would have given. Nitze's answer: "One in ten."

I remember vividly my reaction that Monday to this news from Harry. It came in two parts.

First, puzzlement: Why would they put the risk that high? Nitze, of all people, was familiar with the new intelligence estimates. Could it be that he and the others, like the public at large, had not really absorbed the implications of the new intelligence, or didn't fully believe it?

But then came a second reaction, slightly delayed: *"One in ten?! Nuclear war . . . And we were doing what we were doing?!"*

What we had been doing, on recommendations of the ExComm, included the following:

- the blockade itself, at the risk of armed conflict with Soviet warships;
- forcing Soviet submarines to surface;
- high-level and low-level reconnaissance flights over Cuba;
- a large-scale airborne alert with significant risk of accidents involving nuclear weapons;
- continuing reconnaissance, even after several planes were fired on and one shot down on Saturday; and
- full preparations (if they were wholly a bluff, they fooled us) for invasion and airstrike.

With the exception of the dangerous airborne alert, every one of those actions was illegal under international law, a violation of the U.N. Charter (unless as an act of war sanctioned by the U.N. Security Council). More significantly, every one of them threatened at least conventional armed conflict with the Soviet Union. I myself had accepted the general wisdom that the stakes in this confrontation, in global political terms, were quite high: enough to justify certain risks. I was prepared to support non-nuclear threats, willing even to take some risks of conventional war. I was, in short, a Cold Warrior working for the U.S. Defense Department. My emotions Saturday night on the thought of an unnecessary missile trade made that as clear as could be, not least to myself.

But to be willing to take an estimated *10 percent* chance of nuclear war?! . . . In order to avoid a public trade of the Turkish missiles?

Who were these people I was working for? Were they all insane?

Later, Robert McNamara would reveal something of his state of mind on October 27, "the Saturday before the Sunday in which Khrushchev announced withdrawal of the missiles . . . and a U-2 was shot down . . . I remember leaving the White House at the end of that Saturday. It was a beautiful fall day. And thinking that might well be the last sunset I saw. You couldn't tell what was going to follow."

Could *I* have been that far off in my own belief that nuclear war was extremely unlikely? Could they have been right?

The answer to both is yes—though for different reasons than most of them supposed. The fact is that on Saturday, October 27, 1962, a chain of events was in motion that might have come close to ending civilization. How close? A handbreadth.

That is *despite* the fact, as I have come to believe, that both leaders, Khrushchev and Kennedy, were *determined to avoid armed conflict*— that both, in fact, were prepared to settle on the other's terms, if necessary, rather than go to war. And yet they each hoped, by threatening war, to achieve a better bargain. For the sake of a better deal they both were willing to postpone by hours or days the settlement that each was willing to make. And meanwhile, during those hours, their subordinates (unaware that they were supporting a pure bluff in a game of bargaining) were taking military actions that could unleash an unstoppable train of events, ultimately pulling the trigger on a Doomsday Machine.

*   *   *

A note: For more than half a century I have done my best to learn about this crisis and to learn from it. The scholarship of many others has been crucial to my current understanding of it, along with the opening of files both in America and Russia, both mostly decades after the events and continuing up to this moment. That will be evident from my endnotes to this chapter (and see my endnotes on Cuba in the introduction). But I have read all these contributions from the perspective of my classified nine-month study of nuclear crises, mainly this one, triggered precisely by my own participation in it and the challenge to understand how its dangers could have been (as I steadily discovered) so much greater than I believed at the time.

I intend to place on my website ellsberg.net/Doomsday/cubanmis silecrisis as many of my own files on the crisis as possible. I could, but probably won't at this point, write a book as long as this one solely on what I think I've learned from my study of the Cuban missile crisis, and what the evidence is for my conclusions so far. But I'm not going to present much of that evidence or reasoning here, or argue for it. What follows are my own inferences—many of them, I warn, unfamiliar and probably controversial even to scholars. And for the purpose of this book I'm going to focus mainly on what bears on the real risk of nuclear war.

For that reason I'll skip over not only the first nine days of the official crisis but its real origins: about which my understanding—not only in 1962 but in 1964 and for a decade or two after that—was flawed or mistaken in almost every important respect. In particular, that relates to Khrushchev's incentives to initiate his secret deployments to Cuba. Reducing the strategic imbalance (exposed by the Gilpatric speech and otherwise) was not the only or even main or triggering cause of his secret policy, as I and virtually all scholars and journalists had supposed for more than one decade and in important respects several decades.

It was not until 1975–76, with the report of the [Senator] Church Committee on covert operations including the massive 1962 Mongoose project against Cuba, and then a dozen years after that with investigative scholarship on U.S. contingency plans and exercise rehearsals for invading Cuba in 1962 by the historian James Hershberg, that I learned the basis in reality of Khrushchev's claims (especially in his 1970 memoir) that he had been anguished, with good reason, at the thought that he was about to "lose Cuba" to renewed U.S. aggression.[†] That realistic obsession was a major part of the answer—not once reflected in the Kennedy tapes of the meetings of the ExComm (many of whose members were not cleared either for Mongoose or the early October contingency plans for invasion)—of the question JFK disingenuously raised to his supposedly advisory group, "Why has Khrushchev done this?" For my own reflections on this and other matters relating to the early aspects of the crisis (which in reality began well before, almost a year before, October 16, 1962) see my website, ellsberg.net/Doomsday/cubanmissilecrisis.

*   *   *

By Thursday, October 25, the day after the blockade was instituted, Khrushchev decided that his effort had failed and that he would have to remove the missiles from Cuba. Despite his threats of defying "piracy," he didn't want to challenge the blockade, fearing that Kennedy's willingness to risk armed conflict with the Soviet Union on the high seas increased the credibility that the United States would attack the missiles if he didn't remove them. That, subsequently, would call for a response from the Soviets extending far beyond the Caribbean, raising even more risk of all-out war. Khrushchev had not entered into this project with a desire to encounter such risks.

His hope as of Thursday morning in Moscow was to withdraw with as little loss of face as possible, preferably with something to show for the effort—at the very least a non-invasion pledge, but probably a public trade for the Turkish missiles, or perhaps even more. Perhaps the IRBMs in Italy and Britain or all U.S. forces in Turkey, perhaps even concessions on Berlin. In the meantime he continued to press his forces in Cuba to continue the installation of the missiles on a crash basis. Presumably, his aim was to improve the terms of an eventual bargain, by increasing the stakes of any U.S. attack on the missiles, thereby increasing Kennedy's motivation to strike a deal.

The danger of this strategy lay in increasing U.S. military pressure to attack the missiles before they all became operational. And since that would likely be followed by invasion, Khrushchev might end up triggering the very event the missiles and other equipment had been intended to forestall. On the other hand, the stronger his hand, the more likely that Kennedy might seek a diplomatic solution. And there were "private" indications from the Kennedys that he was leaning in that direction.

The morning after the president's speech on October 22, Robert Kennedy had sent word by two separate channels to Georgi Bolshakov, a Soviet intelligence agent operating under journalistic cover, that his brother was open to removing the NATO missiles from Turkey in exchange for the removal of the missiles in Cuba. It is not clear when, if ever, this message reached Khrushchev. But, as the Soviet ambassador Anatoly Dobrynin would reveal in 1990, RFK delivered the same message to him in a private meeting on Thursday night. (That very morning Walter Lippmann had published a syndicated column suggesting such a trade. Although for a quarter century Lippmann was depicted as an interfering meddler, the Soviets had every reason to believe he had been writing with Kennedy's authorization—as was likely the case.)

On this basis, Khrushchev dictated a message to Kennedy, in the presence of the Presidium and with its suggestions, proposing that the crisis be resolved by a non-invasion pledge from the United States and the removal of "the weapons you call offensive" from both Cuba and Turkey. But this message was not sent Friday. Before it was sent, alarming indications came from a variety of sources, and in particular from Castro, that an invasion was imminent, possibly within the next twenty-four hours or the following day. In face of that, Khrushchev dictated—again in the presence of the Presidium—a longer message indicating that a pledge of non-invasion would be enough. There was no mention of

Turkey. After delays for coding, transmission, and decoding, that message arrived in sections at the White House and Pentagon Friday evening, though it had been sent that morning.

It was read happily by the Kennedys and much of the ExComm, who went to bed that night with relief. (Less so by the Joint Chiefs, who were eager to invade; a non-invasion pledge was anathema to them in any case, worst of all as a resolution of this crisis, which I suspect they regarded as the best justification for an invasion that would ever come along.) But by Saturday morning in Moscow, Khrushchev had come to doubt the imme-diate imminence of the invasion and decided to try for a better deal. Thus, with the agreement of the Presidium, he updated the earlier-composed message proposing a trade with the Turkish missiles and sent that.

The arrival of this second message caused confusion and consterna-tion among the ExComm Saturday morning. Had Khrushchev possibly been sidelined by a more hard-line faction? After much debate, it was decided that Kennedy should ignore this second letter and simply respond to the earlier message, agreeing to settle the crisis on the basis of a pledge not to invade Cuba. No one now had much hope that this would be sufficient to get the missiles out—not the Joint Chiefs, not McNamara, and not Kennedy. He now thought it unlikely that they would accept his latest offer, even though it purported to accept one that Khrushchev appeared to have proposed the night before.

When confirmation arrived on Saturday afternoon that an American U-2 had been shot down over Cuba that morning by a Soviet surface-to-air missile (SAM), the ExComm assumed this was a deliberate escalation by Khrushchev, a further signal that the Soviet position was hardening and that they were more willing to take risks and less prone to accept terms that had seemed possible even the night before.

And yet early Sunday morning, October 28, 1962, Moscow radio began broadcasting Khrushchev's full acceptance of Kennedy's proposal—withdrawal of the missiles in exchange for a non-invasion pledge. This unexpectedly rapid resolution, on these terms, came as an intoxicating surprise. The initial inferences drawn were that Khrushchev had simply given up on achieving his more favorable terms; Khrushchev's "loss of nerve," as Dean Acheson put it later. It appeared a victory for Kennedy's firmness throughout that week, evidenced not only in his public and private statements but also in the blockade and the urgent preparations for invasion. The lesson drawn was "Take a firm stand, prepare to back it up, and the Soviets will back down."

A different light was shed on this seven years later when Robert Kennedy's posthumous memoir of the crisis, *Thirteen Days*, revealed that on Saturday night he had met with Ambassador Dobrynin and conveyed what amounted to an ultimatum: the missiles must begin to be removed within forty-eight hours or the United States would remove them by force. This was accompanied by what amounted to a private deal: if the missiles were removed from Cuba, the missiles in Turkey would also be withdrawn in four or five months, though only if the Soviets did not reveal this explicit but secret understanding.

For military commanders who had regarded the failure of the crisis to lead to invasion as an intense disappointment, this last revelation was one more proof of Kennedy's weakness and "appeasement." Others found that the real lesson, after all, was the effectiveness of negotiation and compromise. A number of former members of the ExComm, in a joint column published in *Time* in 1982, maintained that it was the secret concession to Khrushchev that had led to a swift resolution of the crisis. Since then, it has been widely assumed that this secret offer was critical to ending the confrontation.

But that is almost surely untrue. The secrecy of the deal—RFK even rejected a proposal by Dobrynin the next day that the oral understanding be confirmed in writing—meant that it offered Khrushchev virtually nothing to soften the humiliation of his retreat. He couldn't even take credit for this deal to his own Presidium, let alone, say, to the Chinese—who mocked him for his craven surrender. It has since turned out that Khrushchev had announced his decision to concede to the Presidium before he received by phone, later in the same meeting, a report of RFK's threats and offer. In any case, I believe that this promise—even though it was meticulously carried out by the Americans—would have had no effect at all on Khrushchev's decision.

And yet the ultimatum by RFK wouldn't entirely explain Khrushchev's abrupt concession any more than the hollow offer of a secret deal. That ultimatum had allowed at least another day, perhaps two, for more bargaining. Even twenty-four hours—the time "requested" by RFK for a decision, though the hard deadline was forty-eight—allowed time for Khrushchev to stand on or reiterate his own latest demand for a public trade. Why hadn't he taken that time to renew his proposal, or at least ask for direct response to it?

Even in Moscow, some were struck by the special haste that Sunday. Fyodor Burlatsky, Khrushchev's speechwriter, later recalled for me some details of that day. "They were very, very nervous at this time," Burlatsky told me, speaking of the drafters of the October 28 message, with whom he had been in close touch. "This letter was not drafted in the Kremlin, nor in the Politburo. It was drafted at Khrushchev's dacha, by a very small group. As soon as it was done, they ran it to the radio station. That is to say, they sent it by car, very fast; as a matter of fact, the car ran into some trouble on the way, an obstruction, which delayed it. When it arrived, the manager of the station himself ran down the steps, snatched the message from the hands of the man in the car, and ran up the steps to broadcast it immediately." Burlatsky didn't know, he said, why they seemed in such a hurry.

In fact, there were good reasons for a sense of urgency in Moscow. One of these I learned from Robert F. Kennedy in 1964, in the course of a highly classified interagency study I was conducting of communication between governments in nuclear crises. He told me, in more detail than was made public in his memoir, that at the direction of his brother, on the evening of Saturday, October 27, 1962, he began a secret discussion at the Justice Department with Dobrynin by impressing on him the serious implications of the attacks that day on American reconnaissance aircraft.

"I said, 'You have drawn first blood, and that's a very serious matter,'" he told me he had said to Dobrynin. "I said the president had decided against advice—strongly from the military, but not only the military— not to respond militarily to that attack, but he [Dobrynin] should know that if another plane was shot at, we would shoot back. . . . I said we would be continuing to fly reconnaissance missions over Cuba—we had to. The shooting had to stop. If one more plane was shot at, we wouldn't just attack the site that had fired at it; we would take out all the SAMs and antiaircraft and probably all the missiles. And that would almost surely be followed by an invasion."

I asked Kennedy, "Did you name a deadline?"

He said, "Yes. Forty-eight hours."

I wanted to be sure I understood. "So he was giving them forty-eight hours—"

He cut in right away, correcting me. He said, "Unless they shot a plane sooner, in which case we would go right away."

"So there were *two* separate threats, or warnings," I said. "They had just two days to start removing the missiles or we would remove them. That's if no more planes were shot at, or shot down. But if we lost another plane, the attack would start immediately, right after that."

He said, "That's right."

The shooting down of the U-2 plane over Cuba on Saturday morning had certainly represented an ominous escalation of the crisis. (As it turned out, it was the first and only deliberate, acknowledged killing of an American soldier by Soviet troops in the entire Cold War.) But aside from the U-2, we were also flying low-level reconnaissance planes, criss-crossing the island every two hours, producing sonic booms and causing general panic. Cuban antiaircraft guns couldn't reach a U-2 at seventy thousand feet, but they could hit these low-level reconnaissance planes. Nevertheless, on Khrushchev's urging, the Cubans had refrained from firing before Saturday morning.

On Saturday this changed for Castro. Convinced that the recon flights were preparing for an imminent invasion, Castro rejected Khrushchev's cautions and ordered his antiaircraft to fire, damaging one low-flying plane. Given the assumption among the ExComm that Castro was a puppet under the iron control of Khrushchev, it didn't occur to anyone that the Cubans could take such action without Soviet authorization. Yet they had. At the same time, a Soviet-manned SAM had fired on the U-2, shooting it down. As transcripts of the White House meeting on October 27 make clear, no participant questioned that both firings represented a deliberate escalation, a change of orders by Khrushchev himself.

In reality, according to Burlatsky, "Khrushchev had given very strong, very precise orders that Soviet officers should make no provocation, initiate no attack in Cuba." In particular, the firing of the SAM that destroyed Major Anderson's U-2, he said emphatically, "was done absolutely without the direction of Khrushchev and the Soviet high command. In fact, it was against their orders, and Khrushchev was very apprehensive about the American reaction." All this has been confirmed by revelations, decades after the crisis, by other participants and Soviet files.

With no American advisor having guessed this possibility, RFK's mission Saturday evening was in part to induce Khrushchev to recognize the dangers of his supposed decision to escalate and to refrain from further attacks on reconnaissance planes, starting with the low-level flights scheduled for the next day.

This warning was no bluff. The October 27 transcript reveals that it conveyed accurately to the Soviets the consensus of the White House discussions that afternoon. (The Joint Chiefs were already furious that Kennedy had decided not to retaliate immediately for the attacks on our aircraft.) When he returned to the White House that night, RFK wrote:

"The President was not optimistic, nor was I. He ordered twenty-four troop-carrier squadrons of the Air Force Reserve to active duty. They would be necessary for an invasion. He had not abandoned hope, but what hope there was now rested with Khrushchev's revising his course within the next few hours. It was hope, not an expectation. The expectation was a military confrontation by Tuesday and possibly [Sunday] . . ."

But the warning almost surely had more impact than intended, for a reason the president and his advisors did not know and could not even imagine. Very simply, the deterrent warning was directed to the wrong party. Even if he could expect to control future SAM firings (which was in question at this point), Khrushchev knew he had no influence at all over the Cuban antiaircraft artillerymen who threatened low-flying flights. They had begun firing on Saturday morning on the direct orders of Fidel Castro, who was determined to defend the sovereignty of Cuban airspace, regardless of Soviet desires to avoid provoking American retaliation.

As Castro put it to Tad Szulc in 1984: "It was we who gave the order to fire against the low-level flights. . . . We had simply presented our viewpoint to [the Soviets], our opposition to low-level flights, and we ordered our batteries to fire on them." The Cuban gunners had never fired at live targets before; they were getting closer during the day on Saturday. Castro later said he was sure they would have destroyed at least one plane by Sunday.

As for the downing of the U-2, it wasn't immediately clear to Khrushchev how this had happened. All he knew was that it had not been done by his authority and was against his desire; he thought mistakenly it had come about under the influence of Castro, whom he berated the next day. In fact, the order came from the local SAM commander, a general. Though he was under orders not to fire without authorization from General Isa Pliyev, the commander in chief of Soviet forces in Cuba, he had been carried away by the action of the Cuban antiaircraft batteries wildly firing, for the first time, at low-level reconnaissance planes. Suspecting that an invasion was under way and unable to reach Pliyev, he had acted on his own authority and gave the order to fire.

As Khrushchev's son Sergei later told me, this was a turning point for his father. He knew things were getting out of his control; he could not control Castro, and now he had to wonder whether Soviet-manned SAMs were under his control. Even before he heard Dobrynin's account of his meeting with Robert Kennedy—which could only confirm his fears, and the urgency of acting on them—Khrushchev could only conclude that he might well lose both his missiles and SAMs, with heavy Soviet casualties and the likelihood of further escalation, soon after low-flying U.S. reconnaissance planes entered Cuban airspace on Sunday, perhaps at first light, less than twelve hours away in the Caribbean. If there was any way to avert this, it could only be to announce his acceptance of Kennedy's Saturday-night proposal and to start dismantling missiles before another shoot-down and the subsequent reprisal occurred.

That much I had come to know in my classified study in 1964. It seemed enough to explain why Khrushchev had folded his hand before the twenty-four or forty-eight-hour deadline Kennedy had sent his brother to deliver. *But there was even more that Khrushchev knew and Kennedy didn't*—secrets that Khrushchev had chosen not to reveal at the time and that remained unknown to any Americans (including me) for twenty-five years or more. First, that the number of Soviet troops in Cuba was not seven thousand, as we had at first supposed, or seventeen thousand, as the CIA estimated at the end of the crisis, but forty-two thousand. And second, that along with SAMs and ballistic missiles, they had been secretly equipped with over a hundred tactical nuclear weapons, warheads included.

So far as we knew, Khrushchev had *never* sent tactical (or until now, strategic) weapons with nuclear warheads outside the Soviet Union.[†] Yet not only had he done this, but also the Presidium had agreed to *delegate authority to local commanders to use them against an invasion fleet,* without direct orders from Moscow.

That delegation—by Soviets supposedly obsessed with centralized political control of the military—was virtually unimaginable to American intelligence analysts and officials. Yet it had been agreed to, throughout the period of deployment prior to Kennedy's speech on October 22, by the entire Presidium. This was reportedly on the theory that since these limited-range tactical weapons could not reach Florida or threaten other parts of the United States, their use by local Soviet commanders against an invasion force could be trusted not to escalate to all-out war—as fatheaded a belief by the Presidium as the earlier assurance by General Sergey Biryuzov to Khrushchev that IRBMs would look to overhead reconnaissance like palm trees. Although this prior authorization had been withdrawn following Kennedy's speech on October 22, it was understood by

Soviet commanders that in the heat of combat and with communications from Moscow interrupted, the new orders *not* to fire without explicit direction from Moscow were uncertain to be obeyed. (That would correspond to what actually happened with the SAM Saturday morning.)

When Robert McNamara learned about this in 1992, thirty years later, he noted: "We don't need to speculate what would have happened. It would have been an *absolute disaster* for the world . . . No one should believe that a U.S. force could have been attacked by tactical nuclear warheads without responding with nuclear warheads. And where would it have ended? In utter disaster."

Khrushchev knew the weapons were there, and he had no reason to believe that JFK knew that. Those weapons had not been intended as a deterrent but rather to defend against an invading fleet. (In fact, our reconnaissance had spotted only one weapon—during or after the crisis—which it regarded as "dual-capable," probably without a nuclear warhead.) Nevertheless, Khrushchev knew that by dawn's light on Sunday, low-flying reconnaissance planes would resume their flights over Cuba; that Castro could not be restrained from taking what he regarded as defensive measures; and that when one of those planes was shot down, it would trigger a U.S. attack on the SAMs, the missiles, and more than likely an invasion force that would have no idea what was in store for it. The invasion would almost surely trigger a two-sided nuclear exchange that would with near certainty expand to massive U.S. nuclear attacks on the Soviet Union.

Khrushchev's order to dismantle the missiles arrived in Cuba thirty-six hours ahead of RFK's ultimatum deadline. The dismantling began at five A.M. The race to the radio station for the public broadcast announcement, bypassing slower diplomatic channels, came a few hours later.

Khrushchev, as he expected, paid a heavy political price for withdrawing abruptly from what he had discovered to be Cuban roulette; yet surely he was wise to do so, without awaiting one more day's spin of the chamber. Explaining his decision suddenly to remove his forces from dangers to which he should never have exposed them, Khrushchev said later about that Saturday night, "A smell of scorching hung in the air."

The fact is, JFK and his brother never lived to know what Khrushchev had done about the Cuban defiance, or the insubordination of a SAM commander, or the tactical nuclear weapons on the island. But more was happening that neither leader knew that Saturday afternoon, while they were both still postponing agreement, haggling for better terms.

The same day that a Soviet SAM downed an American U-2, a Soviet submarine in the Caribbean, armed with a nuclear torpedo, believed it was being attacked by American destroyers.

It was 4:59 in the afternoon of October 27 that sonar operators on the American destroyer USS *Beale* detected the submerged Soviet submarine B-59 and began to bombard it with "practice" depth charges. A carrier, five destroyers, and several antisubmarine helicopters had their quarry cornered in a narrow sector of the Caribbean and were signaling, as they supposed, for it to come up and identify itself, a token of vulnerability and surrender. Otherwise they could wait it out until it had to come up amid them, running low on oxygen and electricity, to recharge its batteries.

The crews in the ships on the surface were exulting in their first live antisubmarine practice against a Soviet target. No one among the ships on the surface, nor any member of the ExComm that had directed this harassment, was aware or even suspected that the Foxtrot-class diesel submarine they were baiting was armed—for the first time in the operation of such vessels—with a nuclear-tipped torpedo, whose ten-to-fifteen-kiloton (Hiroshima yield) warhead was capable of destroying several or all of those ships in one blast. And the commander and crew in that submarine were coming to believe they were under attack.

The blockade had begun three days earlier with the utmost concern on President Kennedy's part about just such an encounter. The ten A.M. ExComm meeting on Wednesday, October 24, produced what Robert Kennedy later described as the most intense moment of the crisis, precisely on the issue of signaling procedures with respect to Soviet submarines.

At that same moment, as the quarantine became effective, the Strategic Air Command moved its alert level from Defense Condition (DEFCON) 3 to DEFCON 2—the level just below readiness for an imminent general nuclear war—for the first and only time in the Cold War. SAC Commander in Chief General Thomas Power had, on his own initiative, sent out the Execute orders for this change in the clear—uncoded—to intimidate the Soviets. Nearly 1,500 strategic bombers with nuclear weapons aboard were on alert around the world. And for the first time, one-eighth of SAC was on continuous rotating airborne alert, one nuclear-armed bomber taking off as another finished a tour and landed.

McNamara told the meeting that two ships, both possibly carrying offensive weapons, were approaching the quarantine line and that there were submarines close to each of them. The plan was for a destroyer to intercept one of the subs. McNamara and General Taylor explained that a brand-new signaling arrangement had been sent to the Soviets the night before. By dropping "practice depth charges"—in effect, hand grenades—which could supposedly even hit the submarine without causing it damage, we would signal to the submarine that it should surface. They presumed, they said, that the Soviets had received the message and passed it on, but they couldn't be sure. (In fact, the four submarines' captains in the Caribbean all denied in later interviews that they had received any such message.)

In his handwritten notes of that morning, Robert Kennedy said:

> These few minutes were the time of greatest worry by the President. His hand went up to his face & covered his mouth and he closed his fist. His eyes were tense, almost gray, and we just stared at each other across the table.

In later accounts, he quoted the president:

> "Isn't there some way we can avoid having our first exchange with a Russian submarine—almost anything but that?"
>
> "No, there's much too much danger to our ships. There is no alternative," said McNamara.

As Robert Kennedy observed:

> We had come to the time of final decision . . . I felt we were on the edge of a precipice with no way off. . . . One thousand miles away in the vast expanse of the Atlantic Ocean, the final decisions were going to be made in the next few minutes. President Kennedy had initiated the course of events, but he no longer had control over them.

Just then, John McCone, Director of Central Intelligence, broke in with confirmation that six Soviet ships approaching the quarantine line had stopped dead in the water or had reversed course. Robert Kennedy continues in his account: "The meeting droned on. But everyone looked like a different person. For a moment the world had stood still, and now it was going around again."

But unknown to Robert Kennedy in his lifetime or to any of the others on the ExComm for decades, the moment of truth had only been postponed.

There had been no interceptions or even signaling to submarines on Wednesday, the 24th. The president gave orders to lay off that day, lest we attack a vessel that had actually been ordered to return by Khrushchev. But the Navy energetically continued to track Soviet submarines in the area in succeeding days, with the intention, as McNamara had explained to the president, of harassing them to the point of their leaving the vicinity.

In the course of the next week, Navy destroyers, carriers, and helicopters had located precisely, at various times, three of the four Foxtrot submarines that had been dispatched to the Caribbean. *None* of them responded to the mock depth charge "signals" to surface and identify themselves. None of them, it turned out, interpreted the explosions as signals at all, not having received any information to this effect from Moscow, with which they were only intermittently in touch. Nor did they experience them as harmless.

All three, in fact, believed themselves at certain points to be under attack. On two of these submarines, the commanding officer ordered the "special weapon," the torpedo with a Hiroshima-size nuclear explosive power, to be readied for a retaliatory response. (Because the crew had not been told what they were carrying, it was referred to only as the "special weapon.") The second of these incidents actually occurred on October 30—two days after the world had concluded that the crisis was over. American surveillance and efforts to force Soviet submarines to surface continued until the quarantine was ended on November 20, but the submarines, still trying to evade detection, had not received messages as to whether war had begun or not.

Submarine B-130, under Captain Nicolai Shumkov—the same sub whose temporary detection six days earlier had brought President Kennedy's hand to his mouth—submerged suddenly on October 30 on being spotted by a destroyer, but could do so only slowly because two of its diesel engines had failed. The destroyer passed overhead, the sonar dome on its prow missing the conning tower on the sub's deck by only a few meters. Shumkov wondered whether the destroyer was trying to ram it, possibly to present it afterward as an accident. Unless, perhaps, they were already at war.

According to Shumkov, one of the depth charges landed a direct hit on the hull, and its explosion damaged the depth steering wheel. At the same time, he received a report from a compartment of the submarine, reporting that they experienced a leak (which was later repaired). As Shumkov said in a later interview: "When they blew up those grenades, I thought they were bombing us."

In the account by Peter Huchthausen, Shumkov ordered the flooding of four torpedo tubes, preparatory to firing, including the tube for the special weapon. He quickly got a call from the special weapon security officer in the forward torpedo tube, who warned him, "Sir, we can't arm that torpedo without specific instructions from the Special Weapons Directorate of the Main Navy Staff."

> Shumkov cut him off: "Why the hell don't you dial the headquarters on your little telephone and ask them? Or doesn't it work a hundred meters below the sea?" He ordered the young officer, "Look, just do as you're told, and I'll handle the permission." As the conversation ended, Shumkov pulled his Exec Frolov by the arm out of earshot from the others and whispered, "I have no intention of arming or shooting that weapon. We'd go up with it if we did. That conversation was for *his* ears," and he nodded over at the *zampolit* [the Communist Party political officer], who was looking at the depth gauge. "Regardless of what happens I know he'll report what I was or wasn't prepared to do."
>
> Frolov stared at the captain for a moment, then slowly nodded in full understanding. The skipper was covering his ass by appearing ready to fire the special torpedo, but in fact he had no intention of firing anything. The *zampolit* would report it all, if they survived.

What seems significant about this story is that it implies Shumkov believed it would look better for him—in the political officer's report to his superiors—if he had appeared ready to use the special weapon against his pursuers, despite the absence of any authorization from Moscow.

Such a judgment would have been sound, considering the reception the four captains got when they returned to port, which was even colder than they expected, three of them having been discovered by American antisubmarine forces and having chosen eventually to surface under the guns of those forces rather than to suffocate or go down (or to use their weapons, starting with the special one). The day after they returned to port, they were debriefed at a commission that was "aimed exclusively at uncovering violations of orders, documents, or instructions by the commander or by the personnel." The commanders were especially criticized for "violating the conditions of secrecy by surfacing." Or as some other superiors at the commission told them, rather than surface, *they should have violated their written orders under the circumstances.* Despite the lack of authorization from Moscow, they should have used their weapons, *starting with the "special weapon."*

It was not until forty years later that American scholars and former officials first heard of this latter choice as even a possibility. It was to them an unimagined response to the conditions that McNamara's directive and the Navy's practices had been imposing on Soviet submarines, which were, unknown to U.S. intelligence and decision makers, armed with nuclear warheads.

Conditions on the submarines, meanwhile, were hardly conducive to sound judgment. These were Foxtrot-type subs, which were meant for the Northern Circle. They had never been in warm water before, and their ventilators had broken down. It was 140 degrees Fahrenheit in the main compartments. The coolest part of the sub was 113 degrees, next to the torpedoes, and the crew would take turns going there for a few minutes to recover. Carbon dioxide was building up, because they hadn't been able to go up and snorkel and get more oxygen and some cool air. Crew members were dropping.

At the Havana conference on the fortieth anniversary of the crisis in 2002—before an audience that included Robert McNamara, McGeorge Bundy, and naval officers from the Soviet Alfa group of hunter-killer submarines—Vadim Orlov, chief of the special signals intelligence detachment on the B-59, described conditions underwater that Saturday afternoon from the point of view of men in a barrel, or rabbits in a cage.

For some time we were able to avoid them quite successfully. However, the Americans were not dilettantes either. . . . [Starting at 4:59 P.M. on Saturday, October 27] they surrounded us and started to tighten the circle, practicing attacks and dropping depth charges. They exploded right next to the hull. It felt like you were sitting in a metal barrel, which somebody is constantly blasting with a sledgehammer. . . .

The temperature in the compartments was 45-50 C, up to 60C [113–122 degrees Fahrenheit, up to 140] in the engine compartment. The level of CO_2 in the air reached a critical mark, practically deadly for people. One of the duty officers fainted and fell down. Then another one followed, then the third one. . . . They were falling like dominoes. But we were still holding on, trying to escape. We were suffering like this for about four hours. The Americans hit us with something stronger than the grenades [depth charges]—apparently with a practical depth bomb. We thought—that's it—the end.

After this attack, the totally exhausted Savitsky, who, in addition to everything, was not able to establish connection with the General Staff, became furious. He summoned the officer who was assigned to the nuclear torpedo and ordered him to assemble it to battle readiness. "Maybe the war has already started up there, while we are doing somersaults here"—screamed emotional Valentin Grigorievich, trying to justify his order. "We're going to blast them now! We will die, but we will sink them all—we will not disgrace our Navy!"

Orlov's account continues:

But we did not fire the nuclear torpedo—Savitsky was able to rein in his wrath. After consulting with Second Captain Vasili Alexandrovich Arkhipov and his deputy political officer Ivan Semenovich Maslennikov, he made the decision to come to the surface.

But there was more to that story. At least two officers were required to agree on the firing of the special weapon: the captain and the political officer, in this case Maslennikov. According to Orlov, Maslennikov agreed with Savitsky's order to fire. On another sub that would have been sufficient. These two each had half of a key that was required to fire the special weapon. (The special weapons officer next to the torpedo also had a key.)

But on this submarine, a third concurrence was required, because the chief of staff of the brigade, Vasili Arkhipov, was traveling with them. In terms of command on the vessel, Arkhipov—who was of the same rank as Savitsky—was second to the commander, Savitsky. Nevertheless, for this decision, because of his role in the brigade, Arkhipov's agreement was also required. And he withheld it. He did so on the grounds—which Savitsky and Maslennikov understood as well as he, but which they chose to ignore under the circumstances—that Moscow had not authorized it.

Had Arkhipov been stationed on one of the other submarines (for example, B-4, which was never located by the Americans), there is every reason to believe that the carrier USS *Randolph* and several, perhaps all, of its accompanying destroyers would, within minutes of the agreement by Savitsky and Maslennikov, have been destroyed by a nuclear explosion. Or if not destroyed, then drenched in a lethal bath of radioactive water that would incapacitate crew members almost immediately and kill them soon after.

The source of this explosion would have been mysterious to other commanders in the Navy and officials on the ExComm, since no submarines known to be in the region were believed to carry nuclear warheads. The clear implication on the cause of the nuclear destruction of this antisubmarine hunter-killer group would have been a medium-range missile from Cuba whose launch had not been detected. That is the event that President Kennedy had announced on October 22 would lead to a full-scale nuclear attack on the Soviet Union.

Savitsky and Arkhipov are now both dead and cannot testify further; but Arkhipov's widow, Olga Arkhipova, says he told her they came close to firing the nuclear torpedo. Had that happened, we would probably not be reading this. The fear of Robert McNamara on October 27, 1962, that he might not see another sunset would have been realized. Olga Arkhipova in 2012 was justly proud that her husband, Vasili Alexandrovich, had, since the Havana conference ten years earlier, become known as "The Man Who Saved the World."

But there was even more going on that Saturday.

During the morning, while McNamara was in the tank with the Joint Chiefs, word came through that an American SAC U-2 under General

Power had wandered into Soviet airspace. The story was that it was a weather plane that went off course. Most of us—and I suspect the president—assumed that Power was playing a game, and that he, like his boss LeMay, wanted to go to war.

When he received this news (according to a 1975 oral history interview with Air Force General David Burchinal), McNamara rushed out of the Pentagon meeting "yelling hysterically 'this means war with the Soviet Union.'" In the height of the crisis, the Russians might have assumed this was a reconnaissance plane preparing for an all-out attack. In a message to Kennedy on October 28 agreeing to dismantle his missile sites on Cuba, Khrushchev expressed concern that the American intruder could have "easily" been mistaken "for a nuclear bomber, which might push us to a fateful step."

The U-2's pilot had been confused by the northern lights over the pole and gone in the wrong direction. By the time he realized his mistake, he was over the Chukot Peninsula in the Soviet Union. Running out of fuel, the pilot turned around and proceeded to glide for miles, unaware that MiGs were coming after him, attempting to intercept him and shoot him down. Meanwhile, Alaskan Air Command scrambled F-102A fighters to protect the U-2. These fighters, designed to confront not MiGs but Russian bombers coming over the pole, were armed only with nuclear air-to-air missiles. Fortunately they did not encounter the MiGs, and the U-2 coasted safely home.

Roger Hilsman, chief of the Bureau of Intelligence and Research at the State Department, happened to be in the White House when word of this incident arrived. In a panic, he rushed in to tell the president there was a U-2 over Russia being pursued by MiGs. Kennedy, very cool, responded from his rocking chair (as Hilsman reported) with an old Navy joke: "There's always some son-of-a-bitch who didn't get the word."

If, on Saturday, Khrushchev had reason to believe he was losing control over his own forces in Cuba, he had similar grounds to doubt his counterpart's control over events. In their meeting that night, Robert Kennedy told Dobrynin, among other things, "[Those favoring diplomacy are] losing momentum. . . . It's going to be hard to stop this process. The generals are itching for a fight. They want to go." The message that Khrushchev took from Dobrynin's account was that if this crisis continued to escalate, Kennedy might well face a coup.

*   *   *

Yes, the world of humans came very close to ending in October 1962. Closer than anyone in high office in the United States imagined at the time, or for some forty years afterward. Certainly far closer than I could have conceived. This was not because the two opposing leaders were rash or reckless or insensitive to the potential dangers. Both, in fact, were cautious to a degree that neither could know, more cautious than the world or most of their associates could realize. Furthermore, they both shared an extreme abhorrence for the idea of nuclear war, which they recognized as potentially the end of civilization and even of humanity.

On that terrible Saturday night, October 27, when the fate of the world hung in the balance, Robert Kennedy described his brother's thoughts that evening in the Oval Office:

> The thought that disturbed him most, and that made the prospect of war much more fearful than it would otherwise have been, was the specter of the death of the children of this country and all the world—the young people who had no role, who had no say, who knew nothing even of the confrontation, but whose lives would be snuffed out like everyone else's. They would never have a chance to make a decision, to vote in an election, to run for office, to lead a revolution, to determine their own destinies.

Khrushchev saw the stakes in identical terms. In his personal letter to the president on October 26, he wrote:

> Mr. President, we and you ought not now to pull on the ends of the rope in which you have tied the knot of war, because the more the two of us pull, the tighter that knot will be tied. And a moment may come when that knot will be tied so tight that even he who tied it will not have the strength to untie it, and then it will be necessary to cut that knot, and what that would mean is not for me to explain to you, because you yourself understand perfectly of what terrible forces our countries dispose.
>
> Consequently, if there is no intention to tighten that knot and thereby to doom the world to the catastrophe of thermonuclear war, then let us not only relax the forces pulling on the ends of the rope, let us take measures to untie that knot. We are ready for this.

Neither saw the stakes in Cuba as high enough to justify even a moderately low risk of nuclear war, and both were determined to find a peaceful resolution of the crisis. In fact, as I said earlier, I believe that each leader was—contrary to his public declarations, and in Kennedy's case, secretly from almost all his advisors—*determined*, to the extent that he had control over events, *not* to go to war, not to permit armed conflict to arise between American and Soviet forces under any circumstances. I believe that each of them, from an early stage in the public confrontation (and earlier, for Kennedy), was determined to end the crisis *on the other's terms, if necessary*, rather than let events escalate to actual combat. And yet the world came close to nuclear war.

Each was directing his military to carry on provocative activities—on the Soviet side, making the missiles operational on a crash basis in Cuba and sending submarine patrols in the Caribbean; on the American side, pursuing all preparations for an invasion of Cuba and pressing aggressive low-level aerial reconnaissance over Cuba while harassing Soviet submarines. Each of them was prolonging the crisis day by day while they haggled over the resolution of the conflict, each hoping to achieve better terms than he was prepared, at bottom, to accept. If Khrushchev had not, surprisingly, initiated an abrupt, humiliating withdrawal of his missiles Sunday morning—without even waiting for an official American response to his proposal of Saturday morning, which Kennedy had argued to his advisors was "very reasonable"—there was every likelihood of the fuse to all-out war being lit by that afternoon.

How close did that come? As close as the unpredictable decision of one man to overrule two others on a Soviet submarine, or the inaccuracy of Cuban antiaircraft gunners (improving every hour) on their first day of firing at live targets. Far greater than one in a hundred, greater that day than Nitze's one in ten. And that was for reasons which I didn't know, and no other Americans knew, for thirty and in some cases forty years. The world has yet to absorb the lessons of this history—the story of how the existence of humanity was placed in great, unjustifiable danger by men who had no intention of doing that, men who recoiled from ending human history, or from taking what they saw as a high or even significant risk of doing so.

A primary lesson I draw from this episode is that the existential danger to humanity of nuclear weapons does not rest solely or even mainly on the possibility of *further* proliferation of such weapons to "rogue" or "unstable" nations, who would handle and threaten them *less* "responsibly" than the permanent members of the Security Council, nor does it rest merely on the vagaries of the smaller and more recent nuclear weapons states of Israel, India, Pakistan, and North Korea (though these do enhance the dangers).

What a true history of the Cuban missile crisis reveals is that the existence of masses of nuclear weapons in the hands of leaders of the superpowers, the United States and Russia—even when those leaders are about as responsible, humane, and cautious as any we have seen—posed then, and still do, intolerable dangers to the survival of civilization.

Just such leaders in both countries—each presiding over nuclear forces much smaller then than at present, despite the reductions of the last two decades—came horrifyingly close to possibly launching those forces, something that neither remotely contemplated at the start of the crisis. For several crucial days, I believe, Kennedy and Khrushchev were each privately prepared *to back down*, "but not yet," as they sparred with forces armed with thermonuclear weapons. If their bargaining had gone on one more day, then nearly all then-living humans might have died from it, and few if any now alive would ever have existed. Yet—have we had a president since World War II who would have acted in those circumstances *more* responsibly, more prudently? Do we have such a president now? Does Russia?

Let me give one last quote from the one who finally did back down, just in time, with the advantage of knowing what the other did not. Khrushchev told Norman Cousins, a few months after the crisis, his reaction at the time:

> When I asked the military advisors if they could assure me that holding fast would not result in the death of five hundred million human beings, they looked at me as though I was out of my mind, or what was worse, a traitor. The biggest tragedy, as they saw it, was not that our country might be devastated and everything lost, but that the Chinese or the Albanians might accuse us of appeasement or weakness.
>
> So I said to myself, "To hell with these maniacs. If I can get the United States to assure me that it will not attempt to overthrow the Cuban government, I will remove the missiles." That is what happened, and now I am reviled by the Chinese and the Albanians. . . .

They say I was afraid to stand up to a paper tiger. It is all such nonsense. What good would it have done me in the last hour of my life to know that though our great nation and the United States were in complete ruins, the national honor of the Soviet Union was intact?

That last line, indeed the whole quote, deserves to be studied by all those whose fingers hover over the trigger to a Doomsday Machine.

PART II

THE ROAD TO DOOMSDAY

CHAPTER 14

Bombing Cities

Where did the road to doomsday begin?

The fission-bomb mechanism that made it possible was first envisioned by theoretical physicists. It was then tested in the desert at Alamogordo, New Mexico. Its potential was finally revealed to the world in Hiroshima and Nagasaki. But before that, when and how did it become possible to imagine that setting fire to cities and burning civilians from the sky was not only an acceptable but also a necessary way to wage war? What change in consciousness transformed what had previously been regarded as an unspeakable war crime into the official policy of the world's leading democracies?

That change preceded the formal dawn of the nuclear era, but it relied on two crucial developments, which happened to converge in World War II: first, the belief by some militarists that airpower was the key to victory; and second, the increasing willingness by civilian leadership and air commanders to regard cities—which is to say, civilian populations—as legitimate military targets. Each of those developments has its own particular history.

The beginning of World War II in Europe provides an available benchmark as to what the conscience of humanity up to that time deemed natural and reasonable when it came to waging war. On September 1, 1939, the day Hitler invaded Poland—marking the official outbreak of

World War II—President Franklin D. Roosevelt addressed this appeal to all the belligerent states:

> The ruthless bombing from the air of civilians in unfortified centers of population during the course of the hostilities which have raged in various quarters of the earth during the past few years, which have resulted in the maiming and death of thousands of defenseless men, women and children, has sickened the hearts of civilized men and women and has profoundly shocked the conscience of humanity.
>
> If resort is had to this form of human barbarism during the period of the tragic conflagration with which the world is now confronted, hundreds of thousands of innocent human beings who have no responsibility for, and who are not even remotely participating in, the hostilities which have now broken out, will lose their lives.
>
> I am therefore directing this urgent appeal to every Government which may be engaged in hostilities publicly to affirm its determination that its armed forces shall in no event, and under no circumstances, undertake the bombardment from the air of civilian populations or of unfortified cities, upon the understanding that these same rules of warfare will be scrupulously observed by all of their opponents. I request an immediate reply.

The very next day, Britain (before it had formally declared war on Germany) gave that affirmation, declaring that the British and French would "conduct hostilities with a firm desire to spare the civilian population" and had already sent explicit instructions to the commanders of their armed forces prohibiting the bombardment "of any except strictly military objectives in the narrowest sense of the word."

This was shortly followed by a similar agreement from Germany. In fact, none of these governments, at least at the highest levels, had any plan or intention at this time to pursue the deliberate bombing of cities. That included the government of Adolf Hitler.

Roosevelt's message was not an appeal to a new standard of conduct in war. Quite the contrary, he was reaffirming the importance of what was regarded as an international norm, part of the common law of international relations, despite recent violations of it by fascist powers that had been widely and strongly condemned.

The British instructions, referenced in their reply to FDR, included the following three principles, "enunciated in Parliament by the Prime Minister in June 1938": (1) "It is against international law to bomb civilians as such and to make deliberate attacks on the civilian population"; (2) "Targets which are aimed at from the air must be legitimate military objectives and must be capable of identification"; and (3) "reasonable care must be taken in attacking those military objectives so that by carelessness a civilian population in the neighborhood is not bombed." Britain introduced these three principles in a League of Nations Assembly resolution, which was unanimously adopted on September 30, 1938.

Nevertheless, a significant minority of the air services of Britain (Bomber Command) and the U.S. Army Air Forces (USAAF) had for a generation been preparing and hoping for a much broader bombing strategy targeting industry and population, violating these international restrictions. They found FDR's multilateral agreement constraining and regrettable. But no one, neither the British nor Hitler, wanted to be seen *initiating* the process of city-bombing that FDR's appeal had denounced.

FDR's reference to the "ruthless bombing . . . during the past few years" pointed to the Japanese bombing of Chinese cities, beginning with an attack on Shanghai in 1937, and the bombing of Spanish cities, Barcelona, Granollers, and Guernica, by Italian and German fascist forces in 1937–38. Actually, five years earlier, in January 1932, Japanese carrier aircraft had bombed the Chinese section of the International Settlement in Shanghai, causing a thousand deaths in what Barbara Tuchman described as "the first terror bombing of a civilian population of an era that was to become familiar with it."

The bombing of the city center of Guernica by German Condor Legion aircraft on April 26, 1937 (the German role being clandestine and denied by the supposedly neutral Nazi government), became and has remained ever since iconic for civilian suffering from such attacks, especially after it inspired the Picasso painting. But nothing has ever expressed the general, gut-felt moral revulsion against city-bombing better than a virtually unknown article, from firsthand experience, by America's most famous writer at the time, Ernest Hemingway, in July 1938. It's still little known because he wrote it, by request, for the Soviet newspaper *Pravda*, which published it in Russian; his manuscript in English didn't surface for forty-four years. It conveys in words the same surreal images that Picasso had rendered on canvas the year before. His lead sentence:

"During the last fifteen months I saw murder done in Spain by the Fascist invaders. Murder is different from war." Hemingway was describing what he had seen of fascist bombing of workers' housing in Barcelona and shelling of civilian cinemagoers in Madrid.

> You see the murdered children with their twisted legs, their arms that bend in wrong directions, and their plaster powdered faces. You see the women, sometimes unmarked when they die from concussion, their faces grey, green matter running out of their mouths from bursted gall bladders. You see them some-times looking like bloodied bundles of rags. You see them sometimes blown capriciously into fragments as an insane butcher might sever a carcass. And you hate the Italian and German murderers who do this as you hate no other people.
>
> ... When they shell the cinema crowds, concentrating on the squares where the people will be coming out at six o'clock, it is murder.
>
> ... You see a shell hit a queue of women standing in line to buy soap. There are only four women killed but a part of one woman's torso is driven against a stone wall so that blood is driven into the stone with such force that sandblasting later fails to clean it. The other dead lie like scattered black bundles and the wounded are moaning or screaming.

Hemingway's moral and emotional reaction that what he was witnessing was criminal, murder, even in wartime, reflected the general values of that period that underlay the appeal by President Roosevelt a year later, and that were in fact proclaimed by the American and British governments (increasingly disingenuously) to their publics consistently throughout the war that followed.

In any case, the agreement of September 1939 did not hold. Hitler's bombing of London in 1940, the Blitz, was an obvious breach. But a full year after the Blitz, largely for operational reasons, the civilian and mili-tary leaders of Britain officially and deliberately, though secretly from their public, adopted and expanded the tactics of Hitler's attack on London as their primary basis for attacks in Germany from early 1942 on. In time, likewise for operational reasons (not because of a newly discov-ered effectiveness of these tactics nor because USAAF commanders had rejected their initial antipathy to such "terror" attacks, but because they found it difficult to do anything else in bad weather or at night), the United States also joined in. Particularly in Japan, from early 1945, the targeting of cities with the aim of causing maximum civilian casualties— what FDR had termed a "form of human barbarism"—became really the only form of attack waged by the bomber forces under General Curtis LeMay.

This policy was kept secret throughout the war from the citizens of Britain and the United States because the public posture of Churchill, Roosevelt, and then Truman was that they were observing, as well as could be done under the circumstances, the very old principles of the immunity of noncombatants, civilians, from deliberate attack. That was a lie.

Instead, midway in World War II, these two democratic liberal governments secretly adopted Hitler's tactics of terror bombing civilians and obliterated the distinction between combatants and noncombatants in their bombing operations. They were thereby rejecting the principles of "just war" doctrine, which they and their successors have continued to this day to publicly endorse. How this came to be, and why, is crucial to understanding nuclear war planning today.

*   *   *

The principles of "just war," codified by international jurists starting with Hugo Grotius in the seventeenth century, reflected a "civilizing" response to the more destructive religious wars of the past, particularly the Thirty Years' War in Germany. The restrictions on war—above all, against deliberate killing of noncombatants—were contrasted to the wars of the barbarians, Genghis Khan, Tamerlane, and others, who had regularly put cities to the sword, killing all males, killing or enslaving all women and children, sometimes even constructing pyramids of the skulls of their victims.

The seventeenth through the nineteenth centuries saw the adoption of notions first articulated by Augustine for the Catholic Church and later elaborated by Thomas Aquinas in the Middle Ages. The so-called just-war doctrine established conditions under which war could be legitimately undertaken (*jus ad bellum*). This called for a just cause, usually national defense or a declaration by competent authority. But there were also conditions regarding the just means of waging war (*jus in bello*)— in other words, restrictions on the kinds of violence that even a Christian monarch could order or a Christian soldier could obey. These

Catholic doctrines were taken up by most of the Reformation churches and later by secularized international law.

Even a legitimate authority acting in self-defense could not do simply anything in the way of violence to an enemy. Such forces were obliged to respect an absolute distinction between combatants and noncombatants, with noncombatants—essentially, civilians—to be absolutely immune from deliberate attack.

By and large, these principles continued to be observed up to the outset of World War II. In his 1939 appeal, Roosevelt was really doing nothing more than reminding the various belligerents of the clear-cut principles of civilized behavior in warfare at that time: norms of international law. Thus it was not surprising that the various belligerents, even Nazi Germany, would give formal acceptance to this appeal, though the Japanese in China and the Germans in Spain had already clearly violated its principles.

But long before World War II, something had been happening in the nature of warfare to erode elite commitment to those norms. A century after Grotius, the French Revolution led for the first time to conscription on a mass basis. Earlier wars since the Middle Ages—except religious wars which were particularly barbaric—had been fought by small numbers of mercenaries, often foreigners, working for a prince, a warlord of some sort, or a small state. The French Revolution introduced a spirit of patriotism, a feeling of widespread enthusiasm and support for a cause, which made it possible to mobilize a whole nation in a way that had not been possible in the previous several hundred years.

This coincided more or less with the dawn of industrialization, affording the possibility of arming these masses, transporting them, and supplying them with cannons, and later Gatling guns and machine guns. In particular, the use of railroads, for the first time in our Civil War, made possible an enormous increase in the range, extent, and destructiveness of war. These developments worked together to make the whole nation become a participant in a war between states.

All this helped plant the deadly seeds that later flowered in the doctrine of strategic bombing: the notion that nearly every citizen of the opponent's country was a legitimate target, since many of them could be said to be contributing in some way or another to military operations. That began most obviously with those in war industries, making munitions, but it also applied to those in basic industries that fed into the war machinery: steel, energy, coal and oil, transportation, and communications. This blurred the distinction between combatants and noncombatants, but the implications of this change were not immediately expressed.

One of the first applications of this changed perception was Sherman's march through Georgia, destroying harvests, stores, and infrastructure along the way. Sherman is often remembered for his statement "War is hell," and this was not just an observation. His theory of war was that it should be made as close to hell as possible for one's opponents so they would end it quicker. And the innovation that he introduced— which was observed from Europe as an act of barbarism and is so remembered in the South to this day—was to allow his troops to attack the city of Atlanta as a whole, destroying most of its stores and burning the city. He then moved from Atlanta to the sea, burning stores, fields, and logistic supplies as he went, partly to destroy the supplies of the armies opposing him, and partly—quite explicitly and openly—to punish and terrorize the population, to make them realize that they must pay a price for supporting this secession or in allowing their leadership to continue the war.

Despite this precursor to the era of total war—the large-scale military attack on the economy and social order of an opponent—this strategy was not really implemented in World War I, which by and large remained a traditional war of soldiers battling other soldiers. Most of the huge number of people who died directly from military operations in World War I were military. Between nine million and thirteen million soldiers died out of perhaps sixty-five million troops worldwide.

In the minds of a lot of soldiers and their generals, there was a potential in this experience for erosion of the moral significance of the distinction between combatants and noncombatants as a basis for restraint in warfare. Military men in World War I could see the deaths of soldiers on the fields of France and Belgium and elsewhere as very like massacres, even though these people were wearing uniforms.

On the first day of the Battle of the Somme, July 1, 1916, twenty thousand British soldiers died; another forty thousand were wounded or missing. Within a few months, there were over a million casualties on both sides in that campaign, which moved battle lines a few miles from time to time, one way or the other. The next year in the Passchendaele campaign, General Sir Douglas Haig sent men into fields in Flanders in an area where shelling had destroyed the dikes. The arrival of the rainy season turned the fields into bogs of mud several feet deep. Every shell hole became a pool of water; some craters were small lakes, deep enough to drown a man. It was a literally impassable barrier, bounded on both sides—a few hundred yards apart—by barbed-wire barricades covered by machine guns. And day after day, month after month, Haig, advised by a general staff that almost never visited conditions at the front from their headquarters in the rear, continued to send men through this mud into the wire and the machine guns, dying ten thousand at a time in a morning.

Airmen flew over that battlefield in various roles: reconnaissance, artillery spotting, sometimes dropping grenades. Almost inevitably, as they looked down at troops dying in the mud below them or huddled against artillery in fetid trench-lines that scarcely moved from one month to the next, the spectacle impelled them to think: there has to be a better way of fighting war than this.

For such airmen, and the designers and producers of large aircraft, the answer was plain: it was the airplane itself, planes of longer range and heavier bombload than were available before the Great War ended. Such aircraft would offer the possibility of moving over that barbed wire and even beyond the stalemated battle lines to attack the vulnerable civilian economy that supported the troops. This was the vision of so-called strategic bombing—overflying or bypassing battlefronts with long-range bombers to attack targets far in the rear of the engaged ground forces.

One of the earliest champions of this concept was an Italian general named Giulio Douhet, who was later briefly Mussolini's first commissioner for air and a long-term associate of a manufacturer of bombing aircraft, Giovanni Caproni. Douhet laid down a number of principles that were called, quite appropriately, "doctrine," since they came to be held among a body of military airmen with the tenacity and fervor of a religious faith. They were beliefs that were a requirement and badge of membership in what might well be described as a cult of airpower.

One of those principles was that the characteristics of the bomber gave an overwhelming advantage to the side that struck first in massive force. There were controversies as to what should be struck first, but Douhet's emphasis was on bombing cities for what he called the "morale effect"—paralyzing the other side's will, not simply its capability to carry on the war.

Douhet's recommendations clearly breached the principles of just-war doctrine embodied in international law—specifically, the unconditional proscription against any deliberate killing of noncombatants. Nevertheless, among airmen like Douhet in Italy, Lord Trenchard in Britain, and General Billy Mitchell, the chief of American air operations in France, the idea of the "strategic" use of airpower pointed to a better way of waging war.

In the Continental powers, whose armed forces were dominated by the army, this was not the answer to avoiding the battlefield deadlock that ground war seemed to have become. Nazi Germany in its blitzkrieg attack on France showed the effective use of tanks and close support aircraft together as combined arms of a ground commander. But the theory that offered itself to some airmen was that airpower, if properly used, might win the war *by itself*, or at least prove a decisive element.

What Douhet envisioned (with the encouragement of Caproni, who sought to sell large aircraft to all the parties, including the United States) was a bomber that could carry a significant bombload—a ton or more of explosives—deep into the enemy territory and drop it on their capital and other major cities. The main notion of Douhet and others was that with a relatively small number of bombs measured in hundreds to thousands of tons, you could cause such panic as to totally disorganize the enemy's centers, and cause enormous political pressure on the rulers to end a war. A somewhat larger tonnage, if necessary, would actually annihilate those cities.

The airmen who proposed such a strategy—regarded by nearly everyone else as unconscionable barbarism—had a compelling desire to have an independent air force, to get out from under the operational control of the army. Airmen felt infantry and artillery staffs didn't understand the potentiality of airpower. They didn't understand the machines, didn't have the vision to see what could be done with long-range heavy bombers. Furthermore, the kind of bombers that these men wanted to fly and thought would be effective were extremely expensive. This meant that only quite rich nations could afford such a bombing force, and even in those nations, it would be competing for resources against other military services, with their tanks, artillery, and battleships. So from early on, the airmen had an obsession that they must have a separate air force, which would have its own bureaucratic base to fight for its proper share of the budget.

Secondly, to justify a separate service, they wanted higher levels of command and budget authority to share their own belief in the decisive, war-winning potential of their strategic mission independent from the conduct of battlefield combat. This gave them a strong incentive to believe and fervently propagate as an article of faith a doctrine that had not ever been tested and which had little evidence to support it: the belief that enough planes capable of carrying a heavy load of bombs over a long distance could effectively and quickly win a war. Douhet's theories appealed to airmen in every country in the world, but in the end, only the political leadership in Britain and America endorsed the idea of building up a force for this purpose.

The word "strategic" as used here was introduced to refer to an independent role for the air force beyond what were described as battlefield targets. The latter role was called tactical bombing, and it was used in close association with the army. This new use of the word "strategic" is reflected in our reference to strategic nuclear weapons—for long-range delivery, generally heavier warheads—versus tactical or "battlefield" nuclear weapons of shorter range and relatively lower yields. Both usages come out of this airpower doctrine: the strategy of aiming at the economy or the civil society of the enemy.

This strategy was conceived as being effective militarily in two distinct ways. Very early on, both Douhet and Trenchard, the "father of the Royal Air Force," emphasized the idea of breaking civilian morale and will to support the war, though Trenchard also urged destroying the productive capability of the enemy. In the U.S. Air Force, before and during World War II, a different form of the doctrine took hold, which was that you would aim quite precisely at industrial targets that were civilian but which had a direct bearing on war-fighting capability—for example, aircraft factories.

The Americans believed that their Norden bombsight permitted them to bomb with extreme accuracy—what they called "pickle-barrel bombing," from the conceit that you could land a bomb in a pickle barrel. In fact, they would practice in their training to hit not just a particular industrial complex but a particular corner of a particular building. They believed they could land these bombs on the average with what we would now call a circular error probability (CEP)—a miss distance—of less than a hundred yards. That meant they expected that half the bombs aimed at a particular point would land within a hundred yards of that point, half outside that circle. That was actually fairly far away for the relatively low-yield bombs of those days, dropped from planes at lower altitudes. A five-hundred-pound bomb at a distance of a hundred yards would not necessarily do any damage to what you were aiming at. But a

CEP of a hundred yards meant that if enough bombs were dropped, a fair number of them would get closer than that.

They also drew on another premise of Douhet's doctrine, which was that there was really no defense against bombers sent in sufficient numbers. As the British prime minister Stanley Baldwin said in 1932, "The bomber will always get through." The Americans thought that the precision of the Norden bombsight would permit them to bomb from extremely high altitudes, above the effective levels of enemy defenses. In any case, they believed, only a small number of bombers had to get through to have a decisive effect on industry or civilian morale.

Of course civilians would be killed, even if they weren't the designated targets. Some bombs would miss the targeted factories. And civilians who worked in those factories would die (though in industrial war, airpower advocates would deny them noncombatant status). But any attack aimed directly at civilian targets, whether to impede the economy or for the sake of undermining morale, would blatantly violate earlier principles of warfare.

However, the moral justification of any of this was clear in the minds of these strategists: Better to kill a few civilians and get the war over with quickly than to observe scrupulously and meticulously a distinction between civilians and military and thereby doom both countries to a repetition of World War I. In other words, it was their ethical conviction that this was the most humane, indeed the only moral way to carry on a modern war. Fewer people would be killed overall, on both sides, from this approach.

This justification was based on the assumption that the bombing would be effective quickly with relatively small numbers of bombs. And that belief depended on several other beliefs that British and American planners held:

- that British and American bombers could sustain the loss rates from defenses flying in daylight;
- that they could bomb accurately enough in daytime to destroy enemy bases and factories;
- that they could find towns and industrial targets accurately at night, if necessary, and still destroy factories;
- that, for the Americans, those B-17s flying in mass formations above antiaircraft fire had enough armament (they were called "Flying Fortresses") to ward off enemy fighters and keep losses

low in daytime, without needing long-range interceptors to defend them;

- that, while dodging defenses in poor weather over the European continent, American bombardiers could achieve the pickle-barrel accuracy they demonstrated in straight runs over the Arizona desert without cloud cover;
- that with attainable accuracy, American bombers could destroy critical bottlenecks and vulnerabilities in German industrial networks that would cripple war production;
- that through the use of high explosives and incendiaries, British bombers flying at night could "de-house" a huge fraction of the German population, destroying German will to fight; and
- that the morale of the German population (and later, the Japanese) was far more fragile under bombing than that of the Chinese, Spanish, or British had proved to be.

Each of these assumptions, every one of them—all articles of faith among strategic-bombing enthusiasts—was decisively disproven by experience in the first years of World War II. But the bombing continued, and greatly increased.

* * *

For the first couple of years of the war (the Americans didn't come into the European theater until 1943), the British were bombing as the major part of their war effort. In fact, after their troops were forced off the continent at Dunkirk in 1940, it was the only offensive effort they could take. And making that effort, effective or not, was prompted by strong political motivations. They had to counter the general conviction in the world that Hitler was bound to win the war, especially after his early successes in Russia in 1941. In 1940–41 it was particularly important to the British to show their potential American allies that they were fully in the fight, that they were an ally worth supporting; likewise, after mid-1941, to show the Soviets that the British were taking and inflicting losses in fighting Germans, even if not comparable to those on the eastern front. Bomber Command offered itself as the only force that could deliver either message. After the United States was attacked at the end of 1941, it was still important to show that aid to Britain was as important to America as its own competing rearmament.

Lord Trenchard, who had managed to achieve independent status for the British air service in World War I (not achieved by USAAF until it became USAF in 1947), agreed with Douhet that strategic bombing should aim not only at enemy productive installations but at the morale of the civilian population. (The word he used for morale, incidentally, was "moral effect," as in, "the moral effect is to physical effect as twenty to one." This makes a peculiar impression on an American reader, since the "moral" objective it refers to involves the deliberate killing of civilians.) So the agreement that Britain made on September 2, 1939, the day after Roosevelt's appeal, that they would not bomb civilian populations, was potentially quite a restriction on what Bomber Command was really preparing itself to do in terms of producing heavy bombers, such as the four-engine Lancaster that came into operation in early 1942.

Hitler had not bought into this doctrine of strategic bombing, nor had he ever prepared for it. Indeed, he had *no* four-engine bombers: the heavy bombers of the type that Britain and America had been designing since the 1930s. In Germany, France, Russia, and Italy, the predominant army officers and the political leadership looked at these doctrines and said, "Nonsense, civilians won't collapse that easily. It's too expensive; you won't get much effect. The way to use airplanes is in close support of troops and tanks."

From the point of view of the British and American air forces, this thinking was simply service bias, hidebound and anachronistic. But in retrospect it was right. In terms of cost and effectiveness, the air force tenets were simply wrong. In any case, only Britain and America had really prepared themselves in the way of designing heavy bombers for long-range heavy bombardment. And this was not a response to Hitler's aggressions; it started well before Hitler came to power.

Hitler, for his part, really didn't want to invite reciprocal attacks early on in the war, if ever. Nevertheless, in the first month of the war, his planes—short-range and medium-range bombers—attacked the heart of Warsaw, which his troops had surrounded. It was technically true that the legal prohibition over the last two hundred years of deliberately harming civilians had a practical exception, which was that cities under siege that did not surrender—cities that defended themselves—could be bombarded by artillery as an example to others and to make them surrender. Hitler apparently conceived of this air attack as part of a siege operation, though this time carried on from the air rather than by artillery. Thus, the Nazis defended it, perhaps sincerely, as not being in contradiction to their assurance to FDR at the start of the month. Nevertheless, for intimidating political effect to show his ruthlessness, the Germans publicized films of dive-bomber attacks on the center of Warsaw and on fleeing refugees on roads. (Hitler—or rather the German people—later paid heavily for this propaganda success.)

However, Hitler did not want to start "strategic" bombardment of cities outside the battle area. He understood the British were preparing for it. He understood that his cities were vulnerable, and he didn't want German civilian morale and support to be tested by that kind of bombardment. The next year he actually signed an order in the battle for France—and later, prior to the Blitz, in the preparations for attacking Britain—that no attacks on cities should be made unless with his express permission.

Indeed for the first eight months of the war, both sides felt it was worthwhile to avoid starting a process of reprisals on cities. Even after the attack on Warsaw, and throughout the spring of 1940, the British high command was not ready to "take the gloves off." That was the phrase the British used for the decision allowing Bomber Command to use its bombers the way Trenchard wanted—and the way his friend Winston Churchill (his superior as secretary of state for air and war in 1919, when Trenchard had been chief of the air staff) wanted.

Hitler had regarded his attack on Warsaw as a demonstration of the fate of "defended" cities. Likewise, when the Germans bombed the center of Rotterdam on May 14, 1940, that city was under siege. Holland was still refusing to surrender, though negotiations were under way. The German ground commander, General Rudolf Schmidt, called for a bombing strike. But while the bombers were on their way, Schmidt tried to call them off because the garrison, he had learned, was on the verge of surrender. It was too late. Half the bombers did not get the message. Though Schmidt put up red flares as a warning that they should go back, the pilots didn't understand and they destroyed the city center of Rotterdam. This occasioned a rare apology by the German military to the Dutch people.

The initial word from the Dutch press was that thirty thousand people had died. In fact, it was just under a thousand. Nevertheless, the larger figure created an enormous sensation and Britain announced that they would not be bound by the promise that they had made to FDR, nor by the policy they had followed up to that point. The *day after* the bombing of Rotterdam, May 15, the British cabinet sent bombers into Germany for the first time against strategic targets in densely populated areas. The gloves were off.

* * *

I had long been following the phenomenon of strategic bombing, first horrified by the Nazi bombing of London, then following up when I had access to classified studies at the Air Force–sponsored RAND Corporation. One of the best accounts on the movement toward strategic bombing, which had a great influence on me when I read it at RAND, is *The Road to Total War: Escalation in World War II*, by Fred Sallagar; the unclassified RAND Report R-465-PR is dated 1969, but I first read it as an internal document about ten years before that.

I had a number of talks about it with Fritz Sallagar, as we knew him. He was looking for lessons from World War II that might suggest how nuclear escalation could develop and proceed in a conventional war that turned nuclear. He was particularly concerned with the possibility of keeping such a war limited and under control. One of his themes was how often escalation developed in terms of misunderstandings, misinterpretations, and failures of command and control—as with the bombing of Rotterdam just described. That had served as the trigger and justification for Winston Churchill—who had come into office only four days earlier—to unleash the RAF for bombing civilian areas in Germany, something he had long believed in doing. As he said to the minister of aircraft production on July 8, 1940: "There is one thing that will bring [Hitler] back and bring him down, and that is an absolutely devastating, *exterminating attack* by very heavy bombers from this country upon the Nazi homeland. We must be able to overwhelm them by this means."

Nevertheless, it was crucial in the minds of the British public and many officials that this new British policy was introduced in the context of reciprocity. Said Churchill, "This is the way to pay them back; it's legitimate for us to do so, and in fact it's virtually obligatory for us to do so. If he's starting this form of warfare, it's necessary for us to do the same."

On the day the German attack on France and the Low Countries commenced, planes bombed the German university town of Freiburg. The Nazis denounced this as a violation of the Allies' assurance they would not initiate bombing of undefended cities. The bombing was, in fact, a mistake by *German* Luftwaffe planes, which, after a navigational error, thought they had bombed a target in France. (It took forty years for the German commander in charge to acknowledge this mistake and false report in 1980.)

The propensity for such costly errors was further demonstrated on the night of August 24, 1940, when German bombers drifted off course during a planned attack on oil refineries on the Thames and ended up bombing houses in London. Hitler, at this point still trying to avoid reprisal, had in fact issued the strictest orders that no bombs should fall on London, while reserving that as a possibility for later on. Nevertheless, this initial attack prompted the first British attacks on Berlin the next day, August 25, and then the day after that, followed by six attacks within the next ten days.

After the fifth of those, Hitler was saying, "We will pay back a hundredfold if you continue this. If you do not stop this bombing, we will hit London." Churchill kept up the attacks, and two weeks after that first attack, on September 7, the Blitz commenced—the first deliberate attacks on London. This was presented by Hitler as his response to British attacks on Berlin. The British attacks, in turn, were presented as a response to what was believed to be a deliberate German attack on London.

In the beginning of the British strategic bombing, there was some debate between factions that believed in targeting civilian morale and a more dominant part of the Air Staff and even the Bomber Command that still adhered to what we could call the American doctrine. The latter was associated with General Billy Mitchell, who pushed the idea that industries were the things to hit, not people per se. The trouble was that as early as 1940, the British had discovered conclusively that Douhet's notion that you could afford to ignore defenses, that the bomber would always get through, was wrong. They were losing so many planes to daylight raids that they had to switch to night bombing.

The Germans initially had little capability for night interceptors; their fighters didn't have the proper radar. As a result, British planes were fairly safe at night. The trouble was that in moving to night bombing, they rather quickly discovered not only that they could not identify or hit a factory at night, but also that they had great difficulty finding a small- or medium-size town. British nighttime navigation capability, even when there was a bright moon, proved to be much less reliable than they had imagined.

Although these navigational methods would improve over time, there was an additional problem. Even if they found the right town, hitting something specific within that town, either finding it or managing to drop their bombs on it while taking evasive action in the face of antiaircraft flak, was impossible. Later photoreconnaissance showed that no more than one-third of their planes' bombs were getting within five miles of their targets.

Freeman Dyson was a physicist and later a nuclear bomb designer who in World War II was a young mathematician doing operations research on the British bombing campaign. He described one of the early results of a photoreconnaissance mission, which showed photographs of where the bomb damage actually was in relation to the target. The briefers had made a three-mile circle on the map around the targeted factory, in preparation for showing the results to higher command. He recalls somebody saying, "You know, there aren't too many bombs within that circle; maybe you'd better use a five-mile circle."

With high explosives, a 500- or 750-pound bomb, exploding even a hundred yards away, had essentially no effect on the target. So if they were hitting a mile or five miles away, people at the target wouldn't even be aware that they were under attack. Analyses of the results were based on the bombing crews' reports that they had annihilated this or that factory, or had just destroyed a particular wing of the factory. It wasn't until separate missions were sent with Spitfires for photoreconnaissance—well into the war—when analysis revealed that they weren't hitting *anything* they were aiming at, unless by accident.

In the summer of 1941, with the United States not yet in the war but the Russians now under Nazi attack, the British really wanted very much to keep bombing Germany. In recognition of the impossibility of destroying individual factories at night, they moved to a different kind of target. Instead of worrying about whether they should hit oil refineries or ball bearings factories, the RAF shifted their focus to transportation targets.

These targets had always been conceived as important from the earliest thinking about strategic bombing. But the reason they became primary targets at this particular time was that railheads, marshaling yards, and junction points for trains were in the middle of cities. If you took those as a target, you would not necessarily hit them but you would certainly hit something; the bombs would not land in a field, as most did when they were aimed at factories on the edges of town. And there would be what they called a "bonus": people would get killed—civilians, yes, but still enemies. Perhaps war workers, at least some of them.

Among the decision makers and planners, some believed such enemy people should be the true targets anyway, but in 1941 that was still a minority attitude within the RAF.

Sallagar presents an account in the air offensive history of the British based on official documents:

> If there was to be any strategic bombing at all, civilians would be killed—hospitals, churches and cultural monuments would be hit. The Air Staff, as represented by its Vice-Chief, Sir Richard Peirse, believed that what was inevitable was also desirable, but only insofar as it remained a byproduct of the primary intention to hit a military target in the sense of a power station, a marshaling yard or an oil plant.

In short, it was all right or even good to kill civilians, but only if you didn't "intend" to hit those people—you were aiming and intending only to hit the power plant. Meanwhile,

> Bomber Command, as represented by its Commander-in-Chief, Sir Charles Portal, already believed by September 1940 that this byproduct—human beings—should become the main or end product. He believed this had already been justified by previous German actions [the Blitz] and would be further justified as a strategy in the outcome.

(Curiously, this belief was not tempered by the actual failure of the London Blitz to achieve any of its objectives with respect to British morale or production.)

Sallagar cites a new British directive in late 1941 identifying objectives in large towns, with the primary aim of causing heavy material destruction. It instructed Bomber Command "to employ a high proportion of incendiaries and to focus their attacks to a large extent on the fires with a view to preventing the firefighting services from dealing with them, thereby giving the fires every opportunity to spread." Sallagar comments, "If the Air Staff was still reluctant to come out openly in favor of attacking civilians, at least it was willing to adopt the German tactics that had proved so successful in killing civilians in British cities."

At the same time, Joseph Goebbels, the Nazi propaganda minister, was publicizing in enormous detail the horrific effect of what the Germans called terror raids. It was easy to discount his claims as enemy propaganda. But unimpeachable accounts were also coming from bishops in occupied territories or Germany itself that many civilians were dying under the bombs and incendiaries. On the basis of such accounts, which were in fact quite accurate, the American Jesuit John Ford and the British pacifist Vera Brittain strongly condemned what was happening. But their interpretation and critique of Allied bombing policies was not believed or accepted by most Americans or English citizens because it was invariably strongly denied by British and American authorities.

To the end of the war, when questions about this policy were raised in Parliament and Congress, both the American and the British authorities on every occasion responded with some version of this formula: "Yes, some innocent people are being killed in warfare. That is the nature of war. It has always happened. Indeed, although it is unhappy and deplorable that these people are being killed, the fact is that the Germans did start this type of operation. They are fighting an aggressive war. They started it and they are getting back what they have given to us."

Of course, the civilians who were being killed were not precisely the ones who "gave it to us." The fact that members of the German public were not exactly in democratic control of their country's policy was glossed over. But they were seen as having been supportive of Hitler's policy when he was winning, and that was largely true. So they deserved this regrettable but inevitable punishment. But "we are doing our very best, in view of our own basic values, *to minimize civilian casualties*, while we are hitting war factories, oil reserves, port facilities as accurately as we possibly can in the face of antiaircraft fire."

This was false. Nevertheless, through 1941 many people at the top in the U.K. were still fooling themselves as to what they were actually doing and why they were doing it. But there came a time when they stopped deceiving themselves, though they continued to lie to the public for the rest of the war. The era of modern warfare in an important sense—the essential precursor, I believe, to the era of nuclear danger we still inhabit—began on February 14, 1942.

It was not that city-bombing began on that date, as we saw in Shanghai, Guernica, and elsewhere. But deliberate bombing of urban populations as the *principal* way of fighting a war by a major industrial power can be said to have started on February 14, 1942, with a specific British directive I first encountered in Sallagar's manuscript, which I read in my office at RAND in 1959.

The document was an Air Staff directive later confirmed by the Joint Chiefs of Staff and the civilian Defense Committee:

> TO THE BOMBER COMMAND:
> The primary object of your operations should now be focused on the morale of the enemy's civil population, and in particular of the industrial workers. With this aim in view, a list of selected area targets ... is attached.

The primary targets listed were four important cities in the Ruhr-Rhineland area. It was the start of the practice of naming cities as targets: not factories, not specific blocks, but cities. Of course in those days high explosives couldn't destroy a whole city. It took hundreds of planes on many return missions to do that. Nuclear weapons made it possible to destroy whole cities with a single plane, and when nuclear weapons plans began to be written after the war, they designated *only* entire cities as targets. But that practice really started with this directive, and its handwritten addendum by the chief of the Air Staff, who "wanted no misunderstanding on whether the air offensive was to be directed against cities or against specific objectives." He penciled an explanatory note for the guidance of the new chief of Bomber Command, General Arthur Harris, who was to take command the following week:

> Ref. the new bombing directive. I suppose it is clear that the aiming points are to be the built-up areas, not, for instance, the dockyards or aircraft factories. ... This must be made clear if it is not already understood.

Sallagar notes that "there was little danger that Air Marshal Harris would misread the intent of the directive, for it accorded with his own preference." Bomber Harris, as he came to be known, had believed for years—in particular, since he studied with admiration the German attack on Coventry—that the notion of destroying a specific industry was not only infeasible but also would not have the desired effect. He believed that his bombers could only hit large areas, that this had a bigger effect on productivity than destroying individual factories, and this was the correct way to fight the war—to destroy as large a part of as many German cities as possible.

> [The air-war historians] Webster and Franklin refer to February 14, 1942 when this directive was issued as "a pregnant date in air history." It was indeed, for it ushered in an onslaught on Germany that made the Luftwaffe attacks on London seem puny by comparison.

For every ton of bombs dropped on England in the nine months of the Blitz, England and the United States, mainly England, eventually dropped a hundred tons of bombs on German cities. More than half a million Germans—civilians—were killed.

> For the first time, a bombing directive had singled out the parts of cities where civilians were housed most densely as the primary objective of individual attacks and of the overall campaign. Except for inescapable diversions [such as supporting the Normandy invasion,] it was to remain the primary objective for Bomber Command for the remaining years of the war.

The largest part of the tonnage dropped by the British through the rest of the war was directed at the centers and most built-up parts of cities—not at factories or military installations, which tended to be on the outskirts—although high officials continued, falsely, to deny this to Parliament and the public every year of the war.

When it came to killing civilians, practice preceded intention; but a change in intention did make quite a difference. It was possible to kill more people from the air than the Germans had succeeded in doing in the London Blitz or the British had attempted to do by the end of 1941. The February 14, 1942 decision was the British authorization and directive to do just that.

CHAPTER 15

Burning Cities

Early on in the course of trying to attack cities at night, the RAF discovered that high explosives did not get the desired effects, even when they were targeting housing. To begin, they chose the built-up portions of *workers'* housing on the grounds that these houses were closer together so the fire would spread faster that way and the bonus damage would be greatest—a bomb missing one house would hit another. It wouldn't fall in the yards that separated houses in middle-class or upper-class suburbs.

They began to discover that fire, not high explosives, was a better way to destroy a city. In fact, delayed-action high-explosive bombs came to serve the purpose of discouraging firefighters from going after the incendiary bombs when they first hit the ground. By this time, the RAF was using magnesium-thermite bombs that couldn't be put out with water. They had to be smothered with sand. Water would just intensify the flames or cause them to explode. But they could be extinguished if firefighters responded quickly with sand.

In 1943 the RAF successfully tested a theory that had been conceived some time before: that the best way to destroy large parts of cities was to harness the forces of nature by appropriately designed technology and tactics. Specifically, it was hoped that a "firestorm" could be created, a kind of fire that would change the local winds—in effect, altering the area's weather. If enough planes were sent in en masse to do patterned area bombing with incendiaries, a lot of little fires would start simultaneously throughout a large area. This would be helped by first dropping high-explosive bombs, which would break up the structures and make for better kindling, and also block fire trucks from the streets. The fire departments would be unable to deal with the many small fires, which would spread and join together until they became a mass fire. A large part of the city would burn uncontrollably.

As this happened, super-heated air would rise rapidly in a strong updraft, thus creating a low-pressure area, sucking in winds from the surrounding area. In effect, the fire would create its own draft, changing wind patterns. And the new oxygen coming in would feed this fire like bellows on a hearth, turning the entire city into a furnace. That was the theory. After many attempts, success finally came in Hamburg on the night of July 27, 1943, in Operation Gomorrah. It was proven that with this effect, temperatures could rise up to 1500 degrees Fahrenheit. Everyone died in the area within the circle of fire, fed by winds coming from all directions, at up to 150 miles per hour.

Those in shelters died from asphyxiation, if not from heat. The calcium carbonate in cement decomposes and the silicate sand in concrete can melt at this temperature, causing buildings to collapse. Asphalt melted and firefighters were trapped; their equipment bogged down on the street, preventing them from moving. People fleeing the flames were stuck in the asphalt and became flaming torches. The radiant heat itself without the visible flame was so intense that it crossed fire-breaks and streets and spread the fire within this zone of death. About forty-four thousand civilians died in Hamburg.

A German doctor who examined shelters after the attack reported:

> Bodies were frequently found lying in a thick, greasy black mass, which was without a doubt melted fat tissue. . . . All were shrunken so that clothes appeared to be too large. These bodies were *Bombenbrandschrumpfleichen* ("incendiary-bomb-shrunken bodies"). . . . Many basements contained only bits of ashes and in these cases the number of casualties could only be estimated.

Just how deliberate these tactics were has been laid out by Freeman Dyson:

> I arrived at the headquarters of the Royal Air Force bomber command just in time for the big raids against Hamburg. On

the night of July 24 [1943] we killed forty thousand people and lost only twelve bombers, by far the best we had ever done. For the first time in history we created a fire storm, which killed people even inside shelters. The casualties were about ten times as numerous as in a normal attack of the same size without a fire storm.

Nobody understands to this day why or how fire storms begin. In every big raid we tried to raise a fire storm, but we succeeded only twice, once in Hamburg and once two years later in Dresden. Probably the thing happens only when the bombing releases a preexisting instability in the local meteorology.

Elsewhere he says:

The Dresden fire storm was the worst, but from our point of view it was only a fluke. We attacked Berlin sixteen times with the kind of force that attacked Dresden once. We were trying every time to raise a fire storm. There was nothing special about Dresden except that for once everything worked as we intended. It was like a hole-in-one in a game of golf. Unfortunately Dresden had little military significance and anyway the slaughter came too late to have any serious effect on the war.

The RAF attacked Dresden with magnesium bombs the night of Ash Wednesday, February 13, 1945. U.S. bombers attacked with explosives and incendiaries in daylight the next morning, Valentine's Day, and the day after, but used blind bombing through smoke and thick clouds.

Kurt Vonnegut's *Slaughterhouse-Five* is a surrealistic account of the Dresden attack, which he experienced as a prisoner of war in a slaughterhouse where the prisoners were kept at night. He came up in the morning to empty out shelters filled with dead people shrunk to the size of large gingerbread cookies—*Bombenbrandschrumpfleichen*—their bodies dehydrated from the heat of the firestorm, which again reached 1500 degrees Fahrenheit.

Dresden, the seventh-largest city in Germany, had not previously been hit. It was a historic university town, and at that particular time it was filled with refugees who were fleeing the Russian armies coming into Germany. As a result, an unknown number of people were in

Dresden, filling its public buildings and houses. It's still not known accurately how many were killed in the raid. For a long time estimates ran as high as one hundred thousand or even half a million people. When I visited a diorama of the fire in Dresden in 2016, I was told that researchers now believed the early estimate by the police was correct, about 25,000. For propaganda, Goebbels had added a zero to that estimate, and the world's shock was considerably affected by the estimate of 250,000. Actually, the body count was higher in a number of other German cities, starting with 40,000 to 50,000 in the firestorm in Hamburg.

The much greater controversy that arose around the Dresden attack at the time (which has persisted) was partly due to the inflated impression of an unprecedented massacre, partly to the feeling that the war in Europe was now nearly over and this attack was unnecessary, but particularly to an Associated Press report on February 18, 1945, that paraphrased an RAF briefing officer to the effect that "Allied Air Chiefs" had made "the long-awaited decision to adopt deliberate terror bombing of German population centers as a ruthless expedient to hasten Hitler's doom."

The phrase "terror bombing" in a supposedly official release (the briefing officer had not actually used those words, though confirming that "morale"—the official euphemism—had been among the targets) struck terror in the British and American high commands, especially their public affairs officers. They had carefully avoided use of that term to their home audiences, since it was the description long used by Nazi propaganda (in this case, apt) and by the few religious and parliamentary critics of "area bombing." They denied any such intention as terrorizing, or that there had been any change in their tactics or targeting. (This latter denial of any change, of course, was accurate. On February 3, 1945, General Spaatz, Commander of U.S. Air Forces in Europe, had sent 900 bombers on a blind radar-guided attack on Berlin, estimating that 25,000 civilians had died, though they failed to generate a firestorm.)

On February 21, the day before Operation Clarion sent thousands of U.S. planes along with the RAF to bomb and strafe targets of opportunity across Germany, Austria, and Italy, including small cities like Heidelberg, Gottingen, and Baden-Baden, Spaatz told his generals: "Special care should be taken against giving any impression that this operation is aimed, repeat aimed, at civilian populations or intended to terrorize them." The next day, Secretary of War Stimson told reporters,

"Our policy never has been to inflict terror bombing on civilian populations."

The uproar provoked Prime Minister Churchill—who had endorsed the idea of "exterminating" attacks five years earlier and had backed Bomber Command tactics consistently ever since—to write a secret memorandum to his military staff on March 28, 1945, breaking ranks with Bomber Harris:

> It seems to me that the moment has come when the question of bombing of German cities *simply for the sake of increasing the terror*, though under other pretexts, should be reviewed. . . . The destruction of Dresden remains a serious query against the conduct of Allied bombing. . . . I feel the need for more precise concentration upon military objectives, such as oil and communications behind the immediate battle zone, rather than on *mere acts of terror and wanton destruction*, however impressive.

Neither the Air Staff nor Harris took this defection by Churchill lying down. The next day, March 29, Harris responded to the Air Ministry:

> I . . . assume that the view under consideration is something like this: no doubt in the past we were justified in attacking German cities. But to do so was always repugnant and now that the Germans are beaten anyway we can properly abstain from proceeding with these attacks. This is a doctrine to which I could never subscribe. Attacks on cities like any other act of war are intolerable unless they are strategically justified. But they are strategically justified in so far as they tend to shorten the war and preserve the lives of Allied soldiers. To my mind we have absolutely no right to give them up unless it is certain that they will not have this effect. I do not personally regard *the whole of the remaining cities of Germany* as worth *the bones of one British Grenadier.*

In face of such views and pressure from his chiefs of staff, Churchill *withdrew* his internal memo to the Air Staff and replaced it four days later with one reworded to omit any talk of "terror" or "wanton destruction."

* * *

At the Casablanca Conference in 1943, attended by FDR and Winston Churchill, it had been agreed that the British would pursue night bombing while the Americans would focus on daylight precision bombing in a joint coordinated operation. Churchill tried hard at Casablanca to get the Americans to participate in the RAF night-bombing "area" attacks, but the Joint Chiefs of Staff refused. At the time, many American air officers regarded what their allies the British were doing as mass murder.

Moreover, they continued to believe that with their Norden bomb-sight, their high-flying bombers were capable in daylight of doing what the British had tried and failed to do early in the war: hit and cripple specific, key German industrial targets. The British were skeptical of this, and after a long while, when the Americans eventually did their own photoreconnaissance, they discovered that the British had been right. The super-secret Norden bombsight (whose development had cost half as much as the Manhattan Project) required visual sighting of the target, impossible through clouds. In actual combat conditions, dodging flak and fighters, and with frequent cloud cover—none of which they had encountered in their bombing practice in Arizona—American bombar-diers weren't hitting what they were aiming at in their high-altitude "precision" bombing. Their actual bomb patterns on the ground and their effect on the civilian population of cities weren't all that different from the British area bombing.

Furthermore, the attempt to conduct raids in daylight, deep into Germany without a fighter plane escort, was causing enormous losses in the air. At Schweinfurt and Regensburg on August 17, 1943, 60 American bombers were lost out of 346 and more than 60 others so badly damaged they never flew again. They were losing unsustainable numbers of planes. A second raid to the ball-bearing works at Schweinfurt in October lost another 60 planes, 22 percent of the mission, after which such raids were suspended for four months.

So the American air force resorted to night bombing too. And in due course they discovered what the British had already learned three or four years earlier: they couldn't hit anything at night except large areas. By the spring of 1945, the American air force had not completely turned to area bombing, as the RAF had since 1942. But there was more and more "blind bombing" through clouds in bad weather, which scarcely pretended to be targeted on specific factories or even narrow sectors of cities.

The technique of using American or British ingenuity to annihilate urban populations by fire had emerged from turning some specialized peacetime knowledge on its head. Fire insurance executives, who were experts in averting the spread of fires (to keep rates down), proved inventive in advising how to reverse that process. American economists like Walt Rostow and Carl Kaysen (later senior colleagues of mine in the government) came to London air headquarters as experts in how an economy worked, how it hung together and what its nodes of interdependence or bottlenecks were, and thus how it could be dismantled by bombing. This gradually merged with the unacknowledged quest of Bomber Command: how to destroy a society. Operations analysts turned to questions of what the mix should be of explosives and different sorts of incendiaries for the most efficient, cost-effective ways to burn German workers and their families alive.

City burning, in other words, was becoming something of a science. The M-50 thermite incendiary used in Europe had excessive penetration. In Japan, it would often pass entirely through a structure and ignite in the earth beneath it. The most effective weapon for Japan was the M-69, a small incendiary bomb, many of which were dropped in a single casing. The casing was designed to release thirty-eight incendiary bombs made to fall in a random pattern. Delayed-action high-explosive bombs would also be included, exploding minutes to hours after landing, to deter and obstruct firefighters. People became conditioned to stay away from these little thermite or napalm bombs when they first landed and could still be smothered fairly easily with sand.

*　*　*

Enter Curtis E. LeMay into history. About the same time that Dresden was being hit by the Americans and British, Air Force Chief of Staff Hap Arnold and Vice Chief Lauris Norstad were reconsidering the bombing strategy in Japan. They suspected firebombing, as in Dresden, was the way to go, and they believed that LeMay was their man.

This was not a new idea in the USAAF for Japan. Just the opposite. The effects of the Great Kanto earthquake and resulting fires in Tokyo and Yokohama in 1923 had attracted the attention of American airpower theorists as to what bombing could do in Japan. Just a year later, in 1924, having examined these effects, General Billy Mitchell reported that an American aerial offensive would be "decisive" because Japan's cities were "congested" and built from "paper and wood or other inflammable structures." In the 1930s, Mitchell said that "these towns . . . form the greatest aerial targets the world has ever seen. . . . Incendiary projectiles would burn the cities to the ground in short order."

Studies at the Tactical Air Warfare School in the thirties of possible air campaigns against Japan were different from prospective strategies of "precision bombing" in Europe. Japan was not then an enemy nation. But those studies were reflected when, on November 15, 1941—three weeks before Pearl Harbor—General George Marshall held an "off the record" briefing for seven senior journalists in Washington, including Robert Sherrod and Ernest K. Lindley. Their record of the briefing paraphrased Marshall as promising that if war with the Japanese did come, "we'll fight mercilessly. Flying Fortresses [B-17s] will be dispatched immediately to set the paper cities of Japan on fire. There won't be any hesitation about bombing civilians—it will be all-out."

Historian John Dower recounts, "On November 19th, four days later, Marshall instructed his staff, again in graphic language, to investigate plans for 'general incendiary attacks to burn up the wood and paper structures of the densely populated Japanese cities.'"

Despite this long-term vision of producing the man-made equivalent of the 1923 earthquake and firestorm in Japan, by the time the XXI Bomber Command—based on the Marianas in October 1944—was at last in range of the paper-and-wood housing in Japan, it still pursued "precision attacks" against Japanese industrial targets, particularly the aircraft industry. Its commander, Brigadier General Haywood S. Hansell, was a major architect of the Air Force doctrine of daytime high-altitude precision bombing. Hansell opposed firebombing as morally repugnant and militarily unnecessary. But his replacement on the Air Staff in Washington, Major General Norstad, came to prefer massive destruction of Japanese cities by firebombing to precision bombing. On January 6, 1945, Norstad visited Hansell's headquarters in Guam and abruptly relieved him of command, replacing him with LeMay.

General LeMay was a very brave man physically. He was an outstanding commander who enforced strict discipline and earned great loyalty. Among other things, he initiated tactics of forcing the people flying under his European command to fly in tight formation with no evasive action in the face of flak. Anyone who dropped out and returned to base would be court-martialed. He himself would fly the lead plane (as he did in the costly Regensburg raid, when he lost 24 B-17s out of 146). Everybody following was to drop their bombs in a pattern when he dropped his. The idea was to fly straight through the flak without any evasive action and thereby do the job, destroy the target, without having to return and run the risks again. He became known, he said, as "Iron Pants" (elsewhere, "Iron Ass") for his own willingness and ability to fly a straight course through heavy antiaircraft fire. Fewer repeat missions did become necessary, overall losses went down, and "no evasive action" became the rule in the whole Eighth Air Force.

Soon after taking over XXI Bomber Command, LeMay discovered for himself, as his bosses had suspected earlier, that Hansell's precision bombing of steelworks and bridges with B-29s, which LeMay continued for some weeks, was not working. He initiated trial runs with incendiaries, which his superiors had been calling for, and got impressive fires started. Without being directly ordered to do so, he decided to go all out to burn Tokyo.

As he prepared for a fire raid over Tokyo scheduled for the night of March 9–10, 1945, he wanted very much to fly the lead plane, but reluctantly he had to send his subordinate General Thomas Power in his place. LeMay couldn't subject himself to possible capture because he knew, almost alone in his theater, of an upcoming operation with the military code name Firecracker—the dropping of atomic bombs, whatever they were. (In early July, four cities were taken off the list of cities scheduled for bombing, so as to provide undamaged targets that would allow a full demonstration of the lethality of the atom bombs.)

His memoir, *Mission with LeMay*, was written with the novelist MacKinlay Kantor, apparently on the basis of endless tapes. The book runs to six hundred pages, all in the first person in LeMay's voice in the form of a stream of consciousness. Nothing better illustrates how far we had come by 1945 from FDR's denunciation of city-bombing as cruel, inhumane, barbaric, and savage, just six years earlier.

LeMay speaks at some length on the tactical considerations that went into what made his reputation for "courage"—the most daring gamble by an American air commander during the war. He had concluded that the Japanese did not have as much antiaircraft capability at low altitude as the Germans had, so that by going in low, he could achieve a number of benefits and perhaps not lose a lot of planes. If he were wrong—if they turned out to have antiaircraft capabilities that had not yet been spotted—he was afraid he could lose a lot of planes and it would go down in history as LeMay's great blunder.

The instructions he briefed to the crews just before the raid were unique in the history of bombing up until that time. The enormous B-29s were designed to fly at very high altitude, very fast, and in a tight bomber stream to deal with fighters with their coordinated guns. The tactics he prescribed that night were ones the crews had never heard of before. They were not to convoy. They were not to go up to high altitude. They were not to circle around, using up fuel, until others got in place for an enormous stream that was to go high over the city. Instead they would crisscross the city from their bases by the most direct route. Therefore they would save a great weight of fuel, which would go into extra bombload.

Most dramatically, they were to strip the planes of guns and ammunition, thus saving another ton and a half of weight for bombs. By these tactics, he counted on increasing the bombload of his 334 planes by over 50 percent. They could each go in with six to eight tons of bombs, mostly incendiaries.

LeMay determined that he wouldn't inform General Arnold of his plans—thus protecting his superior from blame if the mission were unsuccessful. The development of the B-29s was Hap Arnold's pet project; he considered them the key to the future of the Air Force. But their development and production had cost more than the Manhattan Project, and they'd had technical problems that had kept them out of the war in Europe. Partly due to the weather over Japan—almost constant overcast, and a jet stream at high altitude of two hundred miles an hour that made accurate bombing impossible coming or going—they hadn't shown much for their money.

LeMay's superiors in Washington desired above all to prove that the 29s could do a big job and keep strategic bombing in the war in the Pacific, which would make the case for getting an independent air force and keeping strategic bombing after the war. What LeMay was sparing his bosses from knowing was not the deliberate firebombing of civilians; he knew that was what they wanted, really what they had sent him there for. What he chose to conceal from them until the last moment was the radical tactics he was going to employ, potentially dangerous to costly aircraft and crews though possibly essential to the "results" they wanted. He planned to take personal responsibility for the tactics and their possible failure.

In the Kantor-transcribed staccato flow of words (ellipses below as well as italics are from the original text), LeMay reflects:

. . . Plenty of strategic targets right in the primary area I'm considering. All the people living around that Hattori factory where they make shell fuses. That's the way they disperse their industry: little kids helping out, working all day, little bits of kids. I wonder if they still wear kimonos, like the girls used to do in Columbus in those Epworth League entertainments, when they pretended to be Geisha girls, with knitting needles and their grandmother's old combs stuck in their hair.

. . . Ninety percent of the structures made of wood. By golly, I believe Intelligence reports said ninety-*five*! And what do they call that other kind of cardboard stuff they use? *Shoji.* That's it.

. . . Each type of weapon has some good points as well as some bad points; but if I now had my choice, and had available an overwhelming quantity of any type of fire bomb which could be employed, I wouldn't stick to one particular type. No. Of course magnesium makes the hottest fire, and it'll get things going where probably the napalm might not. But the napalm will splatter farther, cover a great area. We've got to mix it up. We're not only to run against inflammable wooden structures. We're going to run against masonry too. That's where the magnesium comes in handy.

. . . No matter how you slice it, you're going to kill an awful lot of civilians. Thousands and thousands. But if you don't destroy the Japanese industry, we're going to have to invade Japan. And how many Americans will be killed in an invasion of Japan? Five hundred thousand seems to be the lowest estimate. Some say a million.

. . . We're at war with Japan. We were attacked by Japan. Do you want to kill Japanese, or would you rather have Americans killed?

. . . Crank her up. Let's go.

LeMay's recollections in 1965 that civilian casualties were a regrettable, unavoidable side effect of attacks intended to destroy "home factories" were as disingenuous as the RAF euphemisms about housing and industry being the objective when German cities were blanketed with incendiaries. (Moreover, in reality, the home-factory system had been abandoned by the Japanese in late 1944.) Many years later, Roger Fisher, a long-term Harvard law professor—who had been a close friend and consultant to my boss John T. McNaughton when I was working on Vietnam in the Pentagon—mentioned to me that he had been General LeMay's "weather officer" in Guam at the time of the Tokyo raid. That got my attention, and I asked him what he remembered of that night. He told me, "I briefed that day, as usual, on the weather to be expected over the target, and he asked me a question I'd never heard before. He asked, 'How strong are the winds going to be at ground level?' I started to tell him we could predict the winds at high altitudes, with reconnaissance flights, and even at intermediate altitudes if we dropped balloons, but we had no way of knowing what the ground winds would be. But he broke in and asked me, 'How strong does the wind have to be so that people can't get away from the flames? Will the wind be strong enough for that?'"

"What did you tell him?"

"I didn't know what to say. I stammered something about how I didn't know the answer to that, and I left and went to my quarters. I didn't go near him again that night. I had my deputy deal with him. It was the first time it had entered my head that the purpose of our operation was to kill as many people as possible."

LeMay's instructions were very frightening to the bomber pilots when they heard them at the briefing. Incredible. Going in at low altitude, almost naked of guns; they had never heard anything like this. He hated to send them in by themselves, he said, without him in the lead. But they went.

Again, LeMay from *Mission with LeMay*:

> [Up]drafts from the Tokyo fires bounced our airplanes into the sky like ping-pong balls. A B-29 coming in after the flames were really on the tear would get caught in one of those searing updrafts. The bombers were staggered all the way from five to nine thousand feet, to begin with. But when the fires sent them soaring, they got knocked up to twelve and fifteen thousand feet.
>
> According to the Tokyo fire chief the situation was out of control within thirty minutes. It was like an explosive forest fire in dry pine woods. The racing flames quickly engulfed ninety-five fire engines and killed a hundred and twenty-five firemen.

The airmen found the glow of the flames lighting the sky. The clouds, they said, looked like cotton wool dipped in blood from a hundred and fifty miles away. It was a false dawn over Japan.

The Tokyo fire was not, by definition, a classic firestorm (though it's usually described as such), drawing winds into a defined area from all directions. There was a ground wind blowing. If Fisher had been able to predict it, LeMay would have found the answer to his question very reassuring. The effects of the wind went far beyond his requirement. The Japanese called it a red wind, *akakaze*, whose speed got to be quite high, twenty-eight miles an hour. This meant that the blaze moved ahead of the wind and developed a kind of mass fire—akin to a firestorm— known as a sweep conflagration, a tidal wave of flame which planners had hoped to get before, but the wind conditions had to be exactly right. And on this night they were.

This moving wall of flame rose hundreds of feet in the air. It projected radiant heat, invisible infrared rays, ahead of it that would knock people down and burn them before the flames even reached them. It had all the effects of the firestorms in Hamburg and Dresden, but winds acting as a bellows produced temperatures even more intense than in those conflagrations, eighteen hundred degrees Fahrenheit. People fleeing suffocation in the shelters took to the streets to escape and became blazing torches unable to move in the melting asphalt. Tokyo, like Venice, was covered with canals, to which mothers raced with their children to get away from the heat. The smaller canals began to boil, and families boiled to death by the thousands.

Between eighty thousand and a hundred and twenty thousand people were killed that night. Many of the crews of the bombers had to put on their oxygen masks, at five thousand feet, a mile above the flames, to keep from vomiting from the sweet, sickening smell of burning flesh.

LeMay continues:

> Contrary to supposition and cartoons and editorials of our enemies, I do not beam and gloat where human casualties are concerned.
>
> I'll just quote AAFWW II [Army Air Force World War II] volume V, page 627, and let it go at that. "The physical destruction and loss of life at Tokyo exceeded that at Rome . . . or that of any of the great conflagrations of the western world— London, 1666 . . . Moscow, 1812 . . . Chicago, 1872 . . . San Francisco, 1906 . . . Only Japan itself, with earthquake and fire of 1923 at Tokyo and Yokohama, had suffered so terrible a disaster.

No other air attack of the war, either in Japan or Europe, was so destructive of life and property."

The italics are my own. [LeMay's.]

General Arnold wired me, "Congratulations. This mission shows your crews have got the guts for anything." It was a nice telegram but I couldn't sit around preening myself on that. I wanted to get going, just as fast as was humanly possible.

It would be possible, LeMay thought, "to knock out all of Japan's major industrial cities during the next ten nights." And he set out to burn the next most populous seventeen cities in succession. After that, the next fifty.

*   *   *

The new campaign was not a secret from the American public. *Time*, in its issue dated March 19, 1945 (released March 12, two days after the Tokyo firebombing), had an accurate account of the tactics, the incendiary bombloads, and the operation's intent. The lead, under the heading "Firebirds' Flight":

A dream came true last week for U.S. Army aviators: they got their chance to loose avalanches of fire bombs on Tokyo and Nagoya, and they proved that, properly kindled, Japanese cities will burn like autumn leaves.

Giving LeMay's estimate that fifteen square miles of the city had been totally destroyed, *Time* noted:

Never before had there been an incendiary attack of comparable scale. The Luftwaffe's "great fire raid" on the City of London (Dec. 29, 1940), made with a maximum of 200 tons of incendiaries, burned not more than one square mile. Major General Curtis E. LeMay's Marianas firebirds were in another league.

No estimates of Japanese casualties appeared in this story, but not because of American sensitivities to the deaths of their enemy. Another story in the same issue, describing the success of American troops in the Pacific digging Japanese troops out of their holes and bunkers with napalm and flame-throwers, was titled "Rodent Exterminators."

After further raids on Tokyo in May, the *New York Times* was reporting casualty estimates for Tokyo civilians that were actually exaggerated. Under a three-line headline claiming TOKYO ERASED, SAYS LEMAY was this headline on an independent article:

> *51 Square Miles Burned Out*
> *In Six B-29 Attacks on Tokyo*
> *LeMay Backs Figures With Photos of Havoc*
> *—1,000,000 Japanese Are Believed*
> *to Have Perished in Fires*

John W. Dower notes that in the accompanying article,

> only in the eleventh paragraph, on an inside page, did it get to the astonishing estimate of fatalities—and suggest that the subhead may in fact have been restrained. "It is possible," the *Times* reported, "that 1,000,000, or maybe even twice that number of the Emperor's subjects, perished." The remainder of the article focused on the dates of the six raids and number of B-29s lost.
>
> The fatality estimate for Tokyo was exaggerated by a factor of ten or twenty, but more suggestive in retrospect is how casually such a staggering number of projected Japanese civilian deaths could be reported, and tucked away, by this date. It did not even qualify as the lead story.

When Truman later mentioned that neither the prospect nor the actual use of the atom bomb ever gave him a moment's hesitation or a night's troubled sleep, that seemed odd to many Americans, including myself when I first read it. After all, he might have said that it was a difficult, in fact anguishing, moral problem, a grave decision, but that there was just no way around it. How could it not be a moral challenge?

But Truman sometimes went on to mention something that was scarcely clear to many Americans then, and still is not: that we had long been killing more people than that in the course of our non-nuclear firebombing attacks. And that was true—not only for Truman but also for FDR before him. For five solid months before August 1945, the U.S. Army Air Force had been deliberately killing as many Japanese civilians as it could.

The atomic bomb simply did it more efficiently, one bomb doing what it took three hundred bombers to do in March. But we had three hundred bombers, and more, and they had been doing the same job, night after night, city after city, some sixty-seven of them before Hiroshima. The United States Strategic Bombing Survey reported, shortly after the war, "It is probable that more persons were killed in one six-hour period . . . than in any other recorded attack of any kind."

Contrary to Stimson's highly influential but totally misleading account in *Harper's* in February 1947, "The Decision to Use the Atom Bomb"— written for Stimson by McGeorge Bundy while he was in the Society of Fellows, and a successful propaganda counter to the impact of John Hersey's *New Yorker* report "Hiroshima" in August 1946—there was no moral agonizing *at all* among Truman's civilian or military advisors about the prospect of using the atom bomb on a city.[†] That moral threshold had been crossed long before. There was, in reality, *no debate or even discussion whatever in official circles* as to *whether* the bomb would or should be used, if it were ready in time before the war ended for other reasons.

One such foreseeable reason for Japanese surrender *before* the bomb was dropped would be the announcement at Potsdam in July of the scheduled Soviet entry into the war against Japan on August 8. The Soviets wished but were not permitted to sign the Potsdam Declaration, which would have announced the end of their neutrality with Japan (and unavailability of the Soviets as a mediator with the United States, which—we knew from intercepted communications—the Japanese were counting on to get better surrender terms). Another possible ending might come—as recommended by the Combined Chiefs of Staff and by virtually *all* civilian advisors except Byrnes—from informing the Japanese (before the Soviets entered the war in August) that they would be permitted to keep the imperial institution and Hirohito as emperor, as the United States intended. Neither of these possibilities, both well known by high-level insiders, was mentioned in the Stimson article.

Seventy years of public controversy about "the decision to drop the bomb" have been almost entirely misdirected. It has proceeded on the false supposition that there was or had to be any such decision. There was *no new* decision to be made in the spring of 1945 about burning a city's worth of humans.

The atom bomb did not start a new era of targeting or strategy or war making in the world. Annihilation of an urban civilian population by fire had already become the American way of war from the air, as it had been the British way since late 1940.

Thus, there is an ironic undertone to the judgment on the atomic bombings by Admiral William D. Leahy, chief of staff to Presidents Franklin Roosevelt and Harry Truman, in his postwar memoir:

> It is my opinion that the use of this barbarous weapon at Hiroshima and Nagasaki was of no material assistance in our war against Japan. The Japanese were already defeated and ready to surrender because of the effective sea blockade and the successful bombing with conventional weapons.
>
> The lethal possibilities of atomic warfare in the future are frightening. My own feeling was that in being the first to use it, we had adopted an ethical standard common to the barbarians of the Dark Ages. I was not taught to make war in that fashion, and wars cannot be won by destroying women and children.

There is no record of Admiral Leahy—or anyone else in the U.S. government—having expressed such an opinion to his immediate boss FDR in the last month of the president's life, nor to his next boss, Harry Truman, about the prior four months of destroying women and children in Japan. Those direct attacks on Japanese civilians had begun under Roosevelt, Stimson, and Leahy when, as their subordinate General LeMay put it, "we scorched and boiled and baked to death more people in Tokyo on that night of March 9–10 than went up in vapor at Hiroshima and Nagasaki combined."

LeMay himself was convinced that fire bombing had brought the Japanese to the point of surrender and that the atom bomb was in no way necessary. That last opinion was not at all confined to Air Force commanders, though Navy commanders, with reason, put more emphasis on the effects of the submarine blockade. The judgment that the bomb had not been necessary to victory—without invasion—was later expressed by Generals Eisenhower, MacArthur, and Arnold, as well as Admirals Leahy, King, Nimitz, and Halsey. (Eisenhower and Halsey also shared Leahy's view that its use was morally reprehensible.) In other words, *seven of the eight officers of five-star rank* in the U.S. Armed Forces in 1945 believed the bomb was not necessary to avert invasion (that is, all but General Marshall, chief of staff of the Army, who alone still believed in July that invasion might have been necessary). Likewise, the U.S. Strategic Bombing Survey for the Pacific War concluded in July 1946 (in a report primarily drafted by Paul Nitze):

> Based on a detailed investigation of all the facts and supported by the testimony of the surviving Japanese leaders involved, it is the Survey's opinion that certainly prior to 31 December 1945 and in all probability prior to 1 November 1945, Japan would have surrendered even if the atomic bombs had not been dropped, even if Russia had not entered the war, and even if no invasion had been planned or contemplated.

Whether that was true or not, the U.S. Army Air Force came out of the war convinced it had won the war in the Pacific by burning masses of civilians to death. Certainly that was the conclusion of Curtis LeMay. In contrast, his civilian superiors, Truman and Stimson, denied to the end of their lives that the commanders and forces under their authority had ever violated the code of *jus in bello* by deliberately targeting noncombatants. In LeMay's eyes, that was something of a semantic question. In a lengthy interview with historian Michael Sherry, he said, "There are no innocent civilians. It is their government and you are fighting a people, you are not trying to fight an armed force anymore. So it doesn't bother me so much to be killing the innocent bystanders."

In the early sixties, my RAND colleague and friend Sam Cohen told me he had once been in a meeting at Air Force Systems Command when its commander, General Bernie Schriever (who pressed the development of our ICBM) asked LeMay, "What is your requirement for a large warhead?" That is, what's the largest yield you need, what would be "large enough"? LeMay answered, "One bomb, for Russia."

In the ensuing discussion, Sam told me he had argued for the development of smaller bombs, more usable in limited wars like Korea, that would cause fewer unintended victims. He was a physicist and bomb designer who liked to be known as the "father of the neutron bomb." LeMay, who had a friendly, fatherly feeling toward Cohen, drew him into an adjoining empty room, just the two of them, put his arm around his shoulders and told him, "Sam, war is killing people. When you kill enough of them, the other guy quits."

Whether or not they consciously shared it, General LeMay's viewpoint was well known to the presidents—Truman, Eisenhower, Kennedy, and Johnson—who placed him and kept him in charge of nuclear war plans and implementing forces that embodied that perspective for fifteen years, as commander of the Strategic Air Command and later chief of staff of the U.S. Air Force.

CHAPTER 16

Killing a Nation

In August 1945 the atom bomb was simply fitted into a long, secret pattern of war making by the massacre of civilians. The atomic attacks *seemed* to vindicate that pattern by the sudden ending of the war against Japan that followed almost immediately and which, so far as the public and troops knew (in ignorance of our secret intercepts of Japanese communications), had no other way of being achieved. The military service that delivered the bomb had no trouble, after all, winning its independence from the other services soon after the war, and no great resistance to accepting its own subsequent domination by the Strategic Air Command, built up and commanded in turn by Generals Curtis LeMay and Thomas Power, an organization which was committed to the tactics of extermination perfected in the last six months of World War II.

But against what adversary was it now directed? As World War II came to an end, only one country was left with the population, armed forces, and industrial and scientific strength to challenge the United States militarily: the Soviet Union—despite having suffered virtually unprecedented wartime destruction and casualties. Moreover, it was ruled by a dictator as ruthless as Hitler and by a single party more cohesive and competent than the Nazi Party; it already occupied half of Europe and had the military strength to take over the other half. Increasingly, and with various underlying motives, some high-level members of the Truman administration came to adopt and promote a fear that the Soviet Union intended to do just that.

This was not a new perspective to General Leslie Groves, who was in charge of all aspects of the atomic Manhattan Project. As early as 1944, the Polish physicist Joseph Rotblat, having dinner with Groves at Los Alamos, had been shocked to hear the fervently anti-Communist general say to him that, in his eyes, the project had always been aimed at confronting the Soviets. The Army Air Corps had a similar view. Looking for a target system that would justify a large postwar force of strategic bombers and thus an independent Air Force, it turned its eyes to the Soviet Union.

On August 30, 1945, just two weeks after Japan surrendered, Major General Lauris Norstad, assistant chief of Air Staff for plans, sent General Groves a document identifying for possible future atomic attack fifteen "key Soviet cities," headed by Moscow, and twenty-five "leading Soviet cities," including Leningrad, and specifying the number of atomic bombs needed to destroy each. Moscow and Leningrad would require six apiece.

But the United States didn't have six atomic bombs in 1945. At the end of the year it had two. By June 30, 1946 (the end of the fiscal year), nine bombs were in the stockpile. The first official war plan against the Soviet Union, in November 1947, called for hitting twenty-four Soviet cities with thirty-four bombs. But there were only thirteen bombs in the U.S. arsenal at that time, perhaps only seven complete weapons. The war planners didn't know that. It was a super secret. President Harry Truman himself wasn't formally briefed on the number until April 3, 1947, when he was shocked to find out it was so small.

Two months earlier the Joint Chiefs of Staff had told the secretaries of war and Navy that the supply of atomic weapons was "inadequate" to meet U.S. security requirements. Until late 1948, all the weapons produced—all Nagasaki-type plutonium implosion bombs—were in many ways hand tooled, considered as "laboratory weapons." The JCS evaluation of the Bikini Atoll tests in the summer of 1946—which had used up two of the nine weapons available that year—"concluded that because of the scarcity of fissionable material, the bomb would have to be used as a 'strategic' weapon against urban industrial targets." But General LeMay, then in charge of Air Force research and development (in which capacity he supported the creation of Project RAND), summarized the report's main conclusions:

1. Atomic bombs in numbers conceded to be available in the foreseeable future can nullify any nation's military effort and demolish its social and economic structures.
2. In conjunction with other mass destruction weapons it is possible to depopulate vast areas of the earth's surface, leaving only vestigial remnants of man's material works.

In October 1947, a report on longer-run bomb requirements was sent to the Atomic Energy Commission (AEC), which was now in charge of all aspects of bomb production, from the Joint Chiefs by their de facto Chairman, Admiral William D. Leahy. Two years earlier as Truman's chief of staff, as Leahy recounted in a memoir, he had privately deplored dropping either the Nagasaki or the Hiroshima bombs on cities, believing that "in being the first to use it, we had adopted an ethical standard common to the barbarians of the Dark Ages. I was not taught to make wars in that fashion, and wars cannot be won by destroying women and children." Now he reported to the AEC that a "military requirement exists for approximately 400 atomic bombs of destructive power equivalent to the Nagasaki bomb" to be dropped on approximately one hundred urban targets. The target date for achieving that capability for "killing a nation"—a concept that arose in the Air Staff that prepared the recommendations—was January 1, 1953.

By mid-1948, Air Force plans were coming into line with the stockpile, though that was far below what the JCS regarded as adequate. The plan at that time was to hit twenty cities with fifty bombs. There were fifty bombs in the arsenal on June 30, 1948. Moscow would be hit with eight bombs, Leningrad with seven.

General LeMay became head of SAC in October 1948. He drew up its Emergency War Plan (EWP), which called for SAC to "increase its capability to such an extent that it would be possible to deliver the entire stockpile of atomic bombs, if made available, in a single massive attack." Primary objectives would be urban industrial concentrations and government control centers. Secondary objectives included petroleum production; two-thirds of that was within sixteen Soviet cities. The plan entailed strikes on seventy Soviet urban areas with 133 atomic bombs. Estimates said the plan might kill 2.7 million people in the seventy target cities, with four million additional casualties.

A year later, in October 1949, the target annex for the Emergency War Plan called for attacks with 220 bombs on 104 urban targets, plus a reattack reserve of 72 weapons. The 292 bombs required for this were available by June 30, 1950. The AEC, with three separate budget increases for bomb production by Truman after the Berlin blockade in 1948–49 and the first Soviet atomic test in August 1949, was now turning out Nagasaki-type bombs on a production line. The era of "nuclear scarcity," in Pentagon terms, was giving way to "nuclear plenty." The 400 bombs required for killing a nation were in the stockpile by January 1, 1951, two years ahead of schedule. But by this time, the targets requiring atomic attack, in the eyes of Air Force planners, had expanded manyfold.

For the first four years of the nuclear era, the JCS, the newly independent Air Force, and the newly formed Strategic Air Command had been making plans for attacking a nation that posed no military threat, conventional or atomic, to the homeland of the United States. These were *only* first-strike plans, in later terms, though not thought of as such at the time because there was no adversary that could strike second.

America had a monopoly of atomic weapons, which President Truman and General Groves (though not the nuclear scientists, if they had been asked) expected to last for a generation or more. He and Truman foolishly believed that by a highly secret program of purchase and diplomacy, they had succeeded in controlling all the known high-grade sources of uranium. (Groves had overlooked, he said later, high-grade supplies of ore in East Germany, occupied by the Soviets.) That program was, in their eyes, the critical "atomic secret." It was in that mistaken belief that Truman had sought and achieved the consent of the Senate to commit the United States, for the first time, to the defense of Western Europe by NATO.

Scientists had pressed for international control of uranium supplies, research, and all enrichment and possession of fissile material for energy, predicting in 1945 that otherwise the Soviets would have a bomb in about four years. Four years later, in September 1949, U.S. intelligence flights detected evidence that the Soviets had conducted a test of a Nagasaki-type plutonium implosion bomb. (It was, in fact, a replica of the Nagasaki bomb, based on blueprints supplied by Klaus Fuchs, a Soviet spy at Los Alamos.) Truman, Groves, Congress, the American public, and our NATO allies were shocked.

The JCS, however, didn't panic. They soon correctly estimated that it would be years before the Soviets had the means of delivery or sufficient weapons to threaten the United States itself. But in SAC planning, urban-industrial areas now ceded the very highest priority for an attack to a target system related to the future Soviet delivery of atomic weapons on the United States and its allies. That implied an almost unlimited multiplicity of urgent targets for an American atomic attack—above all, airfields, of which there were eleven hundred in the USSR, most in or near cities. By 1953, General LeMay had identified 409 airfields that could be used for a nuclear attack, along with nuclear production facilities of all kinds sprawled across the USSR.

In the fall of 1949, the production of fissile material was again accelerated, to provide warheads for an expanding set of targets and weapons of all kinds to deliver them. When Truman left office in early 1953, a thousand atomic weapons were in or scheduled shortly to be in the U.S. stockpile. At the end of his two terms, President Eisenhower bequeathed to the Kennedy administration eighteen thousand nuclear weapons.

While the target system remained essentially what it was in the early fifties, the eighteenfold increase in the *number* of nuclear weapons— many of them now shorter-range "tactical" weapons averaging the yield of the Nagasaki bomb—did not begin to measure the meaning to human survival of the change in the *nature* of the strategic weapons, more than ten thousand of them, carried by SAC and the Navy. The meaning of "nuclear" had changed, in a way largely hidden, deliberately, from the people of America and the world. The great majority of the weapons in the nuclear arsenal that President John F. Kennedy inherited in 1961 were not "atomic" weapons of the type used on Japan in 1945 and later tested at Bikini and Nevada, based on fission of isotopes of the heavy elements uranium or plutonium. Until the early fifties, those A-bombs had been the only kind of nuclear weapons in existence. But by 1961 virtually all SAC's weapons were "thermonuclear" weapons—hydrogen bombs, or H-bombs, based on the fusion of heavier isotopes of hydrogen— which were first tested in November 1952.

It was that change, I discovered in 1961, that explained what had been a striking puzzle to me earlier in the year. In the course of reviewing Top Secret documents associated with various JSCPs in the fifties, as background for drafting guidance for the JSCP under the Kennedy administration, I had seen successive estimates for Soviet casualties in general war that in the early years of the decade seemed surprisingly "low" for the nuclear era: a few million deaths, then ten million, then up to thirteen million or so by 1955. But from that year to the next, 1956, there was a sudden *tenfold* jump in the estimates—an order-of-magnitude increase, as RAND analysts would put it—to a hundred and fifty million Soviet dead. By 1961, as I had already learned, the JCS forecast was for more than two hundred million in the Soviet bloc alone. Why this increase? Why just then?

My shock at this, described in the prologue and chapter 9, was accompanied by questions in my mind: How and why had any planners or decision makers proposed this increase? Had someone concluded that "killing a nation" with four hundred atomic bombs that would kill tens of million Russians was *not* enough devastation for deterrence? Or perhaps that the fulfillment of our commitment to NATO to respond to or preempt a Soviet ground invasion absolutely required this much additional "collateral damage"? On what basis might they have reached either of those judgments?

The reason for the jump, from one year to the next, in the number of deaths we were preparing to inflict in a war against Russia—from numbers that were huge but still less than Soviet fatalities in World War II (though inflicted in days and months rather than years), to levels that were totally unparalleled in human history—turned out to be neither of the above explanations. It was much simpler.

There was no new judgment of the necessity for the dramatic change in the planned-for effects of our attack. The war planners were simply assuming, correctly, that SAC meant to replace their atomic weapons of the first decade of the nuclear era with the newly available H-bombs, thermonuclear warheads, against essentially the same ever-expanding target system. That entailed SAC's preparedness to kill ten times or more the number of people as before. Not tens but hundreds of millions of dead, perhaps a billion, largely from radioactive fallout from hydrogen bombs, of which hundreds in the SAC arsenal were a *thousand times* larger in yield than the atom bombs of World War II.

This change was introduced not because it was judged by anyone to be necessary, but because it was simply what the new, more efficient nuclear bombs—cheaper but vastly larger in yield than the old ones—could and would accomplish when launched against the same targets. (One contributing factor in this increase in casualties was the fact that nearly all the nuclear targeting in the late fifties and early sixties planned ground-burst explosions of thermonuclear weapons, deliberately creating greater radioactive fallout and "bonus" casualties in the Sino-Soviet bloc—though, regrettably, also among their neighbors, including our allies and neutrals.)

These estimates of U.S.-inflicted deaths were so secret and so closely held, even in SAC and the Pentagon, that very few Americans outside or *within* the government were aware of the drastic change in the meaning of "nuclear war" that had occurred in the late fifties or how it had come about. In the interests of allowing atmospheric tests of thermonuclear weapons to be carried on in the continental United States, despite their predictable effects on "downwinders" in Nevada and Utah, President Eisenhower had done his best to maintain that lack of awareness in the public about the changes in nuclear weapons and their effects. He told Gordon Dean, chairman of the AEC, to leave the terms "thermonuclear," "fusion," and "hydrogen" out of press releases and speeches and to "keep them confused about 'fission' and 'fusion.'" But as I discovered to my surprise in the spring of 1961, the JCS, the Joint Staff, and President Eisenhower himself were aware of the horrific potential consequences in Eurasia of their preparations.

Eisenhower had been "appalled" in late 1960 by the prospects of "overkill" (reported to him by his science advisor George Kistiakowsky) in SIOP-62—especially by its uneconomic redundancy of target coverage, but surely not only by that. He told his naval aide that the presentation "frighten[ed] the devil out of me." Nevertheless, he approved the plan and passed it on to Kennedy. When in July 1961 JFK was briefed on the projected results of a 1963 exchange, he commented in shock on leaving the briefing room, "And we call ourselves the human race!" But he made that comment to Secretary of State Dean Rusk, not to the JCS and certainly not to the public; and that all-out "option" remained in the plans throughout his brief time in office and throughout that of Lyndon Johnson.

President Nixon in 1969 was reportedly likewise "appalled" to learn in January 1969 in his first briefing on the SIOP that the only available options were for massive nuclear strikes involving thousands of weapons, some killing ninety million Russians in hours. His national security assistant Henry Kissinger said that such plans were not the basis for "politically plausible," sufficiently credible threats. Later in the spring he asked in a meeting, how can "one rationally . . . make a decision to kill eighty million people?" But his efforts in the next eight years to add less murderous options to the plans (like the efforts of Robert McNamara before him, with my help) came to little or nothing.

In 1973, midway in his abortive search for more limited and credible alternatives, Kissinger asserted in another meeting, "To have the only option that of killing eighty million people is the height of immorality." (It was not, in fact, the only option in the plan; all the others killed many more.) But his private judgments about morality remained entirely secret from the American public until declassified decades later. Presidents Ford, Carter, and Reagan all multiplied alternatives for "limited nuclear options" that would be less apocalyptic, but as General Lee Butler, the last commander of SAC, has revealed, the war planners in Omaha and the Pentagon never took any of these proposals seriously, either in their operational planning or in rehearsals for the war they expected and planned to be "all-out."

Of course, none of these officials, civilian or military, ever hoped or perhaps expected circumstances to arise that would compel them to carry out any of these plans. But they also knew the chances of that occurring were more than zero. It was always a possibility, a risk—hopefully a remote one.

At the same time, they did not see themselves as presiding over a Doomsday Machine that might kill nearly everyone.[†] Nevertheless, the risk the presidents and Joint Chiefs were consciously accepting, however small they saw the probability of carrying out the SIOP, involved the possible ending of organized society—the very existence of cities—in the northern hemisphere, along with the deaths of nearly all its human inhabitants.

As the British historian Edward P. Thompson summed it up somberly, this outcome would not (probably) mean the "extermination of all life." It would "mean only the extermination of our civilization. A balance sheet of the last two millennia would be drawn, in every field of endeavor and of culture, and a minus sign be placed before each total."

From 1961 on, I thought of that decision-making by responsible authorities in the United States and its NATO allies, as well as in the Soviet Union, in the same way that I thought of the Vietnam War eight years later: as something that needed to be resisted but that remained to be understood.[†] As I studied over subsequent decades the history of the nuclear era, I learned that the prospect of a threat to the existence of civilization and even our species—not only in the northern hemisphere—had been foreseen, in great secrecy, at the very onset of the Manhattan Project.

Specifically, the possibility of thermonuclear weapons, a thousand times more powerful than the fission weapons (and ultimately cheaper and more numerous), loomed in the minds of the Manhattan Project scientists from the beginning. It was seen eventually by some of them as a challenging and exciting prospect, both inevitable and desirable; by others, in anguish, as a danger they urgently desired (but failed) to prevent.

However, at the very same time—in fact, on the same afternoon in July 1942—that the top theoretical minds of the Manhattan Project were introduced to the prospect of H-bombs as a result of their efforts, they were exposed to the possibility of a much less likely but more imminent and almost unimaginably more serious threat to all life on the planet. Secretly, they accepted that risk.

This little-known story (in the next chapter) reveals something about actual decision-making under uncertainty at high levels, especially under cover of secrecy, that we humans are understandably resistant to recognizing in our leaders. It reveals the original readiness to gamble with nuclear disaster—a willingness to undertake small and sometimes not-so-small risks of ultimate catastrophe—that leading officials in nuclear superpowers have been exhibiting ever since. It is not good news.

CHAPTER 17

Risking Doomsday I
Atmospheric Ignition

As we have seen, the creation of a nuclear Doomsday Machine depended on a willingness to regard cities as legitimate targets for mass destruction; that was fully accepted by our ally, Britain, as early as 1942, and by our own leaders and air force by 1945. But the construction and maintenance of such a machine also drew on a willingness, at least on the part of certain human beings, to undertake vast, even incalculable risks that went far beyond the potential of "killing a nation." This propensity was demonstrated before the first atomic bomb was tested on living targets.

In the late winter of 1941, Enrico Fermi passed on to Edward Teller his thoughts about the possibility of a fusion bomb a thousand times more powerful than the fission bomb they were about to consider. To cause atoms of the lightest element, hydrogen, to fuse together, thereby releasing a vast amount of energy, would require extraordinarily intense heat. Within the heart of the sun, fusion of hydrogen was self-generated by the ongoing heat and pressure of the sun itself. On earth, if it were possible at all, the fusion of hydrogen would require a fantastic amount of heat and pressure to start the process. But an atom bomb—which depended for its energy on splitting, or fissioning, the atoms of the heavy element uranium—might do the job.

This discussion with Fermi lighted a fire in Teller's mind that never subsided. The pursuit of this obsession so consumed him during the Manhattan Project that he was shunted aside by Robert Oppenheimer to a subproject on "future superweapons" and didn't contribute much to the actual project of developing an atomic weapon before the end of the war.

It was on the second day of the first meeting of the proto–Manhattan Project, July 7, 1942, in a locked classroom at the University of California, Berkeley, with heavy wire screens on the windows to keep out intruders, that Teller covered a blackboard with his calculations on the process that might lead to the ignition of a thermonuclear fusion weapon.

First, he laid out the process understood in principle by all those in attendance, starting with the fission by a single neutron of one atom of U-235, which, in splitting, would emit two or more neutrons. That would in turn start a chain reaction of successive fissioning and emissions that would, in milliseconds, cause an explosion a thousand times more powerful than the blast of a ton of TNT. That was supposedly the end result their main project was aiming for.

But the point of Teller's presentation, triggered by his conversation with Fermi, was a calculation of the heat that would be built up in this process. It would be enough, he proposed to show, that the resistance to the fusion of two or more atoms of hydrogen would be overcome, leading to the emission of energy another thousand times greater (a million times that of TNT). His figures on the board did show that.

But to these assembled minds it also showed something else, something Teller himself quickly pointed to. The scientists looked at the blackboard scribblings with a wild surmise. Heat that intense, greater than that at the center of the sun, would not only fuse hydrogen atoms. It would break the Coulomb barrier between atoms of hydrogen in water and nitrogen in the air. It would ignite virtually instantaneously all the hydrogen in the oceans and set the air around the globe afire. The earth would blaze for less than a second in the heavens and then forever continue its rounds as a barren rock.

None of them, coming together in Berkeley, had doubted the theoretical feasibility of an atomic explosive. The problems, possibly insurmountable at least in time for practical use in World War II, were technical: for example, could the mass be held together long enough for the fission chain to generate a full explosion? Now it appeared that the practical challenge of making the bomb was not the only issue. Making it workable might not be such a good idea.

They began to go over the stages of Teller's calculations. Before long they discovered a mistake. He had omitted consideration of one part of the process that bore, critically, on the speed of cooling: the transmission of heat to the atmosphere. Still, these corrections did not eliminate the possibility that the feared reaction might still occur.

Among those present for this presentation was Hans Bethe, who was the greatest theoretical physicist among the group, and whose later Nobel Prize was precisely for his work on the thermonuclear reactions in the sun. His initial instinct was that this result was "impossible."

However, others didn't come out with that result. ("Certainty," Nuel Phar Davis wrote in his account of this episode, "is a state of mind based on not having to depend on someone else's calculations.") Fermi, in particular, the greatest experimental physicist present, did not agree with Bethe's assurance of impossibility. Eventually Oppenheimer concluded that Arthur H. Compton, in charge of the whole project, needed to be told of this danger at once. Meanwhile, everything had to be put on hold. But Compton was on vacation with his family at a lake in Michigan. Oppenheimer managed to reach him by phone and, in an anxious voice, told Compton that he must come to see him immediately. He couldn't tell him why. They agreed that Oppenheimer would take the next available train. (Scientists essential to the project were forbidden by government orders to travel by plane, for safety reasons.) What happened next was recounted by Compton in his memoir:

> I'll never forget that morning. I drove Oppenheimer from the railroad station down to the beach looking out over the peaceful lake. There I listened to his story. What his team had found was the possibility of nuclear fusion—the principle of the hydrogen bomb. This held what was at the time a tremendous unknown danger. Hydrogen nuclei, protons, are unstable, for they could combine into helium nuclei with a very high temperature. But might not the enormously high temperature of an atomic bomb be just what was needed to explode hydrogen? And if hydrogen, what about the hydrogen of sea water? Might the explosion of an atomic bomb set off an explosion of the ocean itself?
>
> Nor was this all. The nitrogen in the air is also unstable, though in less degree. Might it not be set off by an atomic explosion in the atmosphere?
>
> These questions could not be passed over lightly. Was there really *any chance* that an atomic bomb would trigger the explosion of the nitrogen in the atmosphere or of the hydrogen in the

ocean? This would be the ultimate catastrophe. *Better to accept the slavery of the Nazis* than to run *a chance* of drawing the final curtain on mankind!

Let's step back for a moment and consider that last proposition. It seems sensible enough, one might even say obvious. Yet in the countless books about the Nazis and World War II, I don't believe that there is a comparable statement to be found anywhere, in any official record, memoir, or scholarly history. Nor in a newspaper editorial or letter to the editor. Something worse than Nazi occupation?

Being enslaved by Nazis was actually not a near-term danger for Americans, but it *was* for their wartime allies, the British and Russians. In June 1942, just before the six-month battle of Stalingrad was to begin, a Nazi victory in Russia looked more than possible, on top of their success in occupying all of Europe. And at the time of Compton's judgment, the Nazis had begun the process of murdering two million Polish and six million Jewish civilians in their occupied lands, along with twenty-seven million Soviet soldiers and civilians. Could there really be something worse, something so bad that "a chance" of it was worse than accepting the slavery of the Nazis?

Well, yes. Compton's instant judgment was that what they might be bringing about—the possibility of ending life on earth—was such a prospect, one they should not risk at any cost.

Strikingly, Adolf Hitler's own reaction to this possibility was not different. Just weeks prior to this, in June 1942, his minister of armaments, Albert Speer, was confirming Hitler's view that there was "not very much profit" in pursuing an atom bomb project during the war, mainly because it would not be successful within Hitler's two-year deadline for victory, but also for another reason:

> Actually, Professor Heisenberg had not given any final answer to my question whether a successful nuclear fission could be kept under control with absolute certainty or might continue as a chain reaction. Hitler was plainly not delighted with the possibility that the earth under his rule be transformed into a glowing star.

Following this discussion, Speer reported, "on the suggestion of the nuclear physicists we scuttled the project to develop an atom bomb . . .

after I had again queried them about deadlines and been told that we could not count on anything for three or four years."

In ignorance of this German decision that month against a bomb project, and facing the possibility that earth might become forever a barren rock after a very brief glow, Compton and Oppenheimer "agreed there could be only one answer. Oppenheimer's team must go ahead with their calculations. Unless they came up with a firm and reliable conclusion that our atomic bombs *could not* explode the air or the sea, these bombs must *never* be made."

Facing, indeed, possibilities that no human being had ever confronted before, one would like to think that this was an inevitable judgment. It turns out, that was far from being so. In fact, Compton didn't entirely hold to it himself.

The Manhattan Project did continue, at full blast (so to speak), but *not* because further calculations and partial tests proved beyond doubt that there was no possibility of what became known as "atmospheric ignition." Some scientists may have come to trust Bethe's calculations, or really, his initial gut feeling, that this result was "impossible." But many others did not.

As months went by, with the work having resumed on a crash basis, no one, including Bethe, was able to convince most others that the ultimate catastrophe was "not possible": which Compton, in charge of the project, had laid down, seemingly reasonably, as the definite condition for pursuing the work. Very unlikely, yes. But not impossible.

Just how unlikely? Was the risk, in some sense, "negligible"? How low was it? And just how low would the risk *have* to be—of killing everybody, every living thing?—to be acceptable? In a later interview with the novelist Pearl S. Buck, Compton recounted the story above (in almost identical words) and then added, according to Buck, that while the work went on for the next three months,

> scientists discussed the dangers of fusion but without agreement. Again Compton took the lead in the final decision. If, after calculation, he said, it were proved that the chances were more than approximately three in a million that the earth would be vaporized by the atomic explosion, he would not proceed with the project. Calculation proved the figures slightly less—and the project continued.

Say what? How does one arrive at a precise upper limit of "three in a million"? What is it derived from, and what does it mean? In this case, it meant: "Small, very small. We don't know exactly." Most of the senior theorists did believe the chance was very small, but not zero. When Compton had been assured that the risk was not more than the "three in a million" chance (which he had more or less pulled out of the air as the upper limit to be accepted for continuing the work), he decided, contrary to his initial reaction, that although it was *not* "no chance," it was low enough to resume research. All the others went along with that. As Peter Goodchild puts it, "Once Bethe's calculations had relegated atmospheric ignition to a *remote possibility*—at least for the time being—the group returned to the issue at hand [designing a fission bomb]."

"For the time being"—meaning, awaiting further calculations, hopefully that would prove the possibility was zero (as Compton had initially demanded of Oppenheimer), prior to conducting an actual explosion. But calculations before the test never did demonstrate that.

Nearly every account to be found of the problem of atmospheric ignition describes it, incorrectly, as having been proven to be a strict non-problem—an impossibility—soon after it first arose in the initial discussion of the theoretical group, or at any rate well before a device was actually detonated.

I know this to be untrue because I heard that from the lips of the official historian of the Manhattan Project, David Hawkins, who had been hired to write an ongoing, highly classified account of the process from its earliest days. When I questioned him at the University of Colorado in 1982, he elucidated an often-quoted statement from his own eventually declassified 1945 history: "The impossibility of igniting the atmosphere was thus assumed by science and common sense." "Impossibility" in that passage, he explained to me, "didn't mean no possibility." It meant "for practical purposes" a "negligible" chance: "enough assurance to proceed with the work."

He told me that he had "done more interviews with the participants on this particular subject, both before and after the Trinity test, than on any other subject" in his research. What the problem did become, he said, was a nonsubject for further discussion by the project's leaders with the other researchers. "They had to keep batting it down. Younger researchers kept rediscovering the possibility, from start to finish of the project." When they brought it up privately to a senior theorist, with considerable anxiety, they would be told, "We've looked into that; it's been taken care of; don't worry about it."

Prior to the detonations at the Trinity site, Hiroshima, or Nagasaki, Hawkins told me firmly, they never confirmed by theoretical calculations that the chance of atmospheric ignition from any one of these was zero. Even if they had, the experimentalists among them would have recognized that the calculations could have been in error or could have failed to take something into account. That was very much in Enrico Fermi's mind, and even Edward Teller's, on the eve of the first test.

Most accounts of the Trinity test on the early morning of July 17, 1945, recount that Fermi offered to accept bets the night before as to whether atmospheric ignition would occur. He said, "I feel I am now in a position to make book [that is, to accept bets at fixed odds] on two contingencies: 1) that the explosion will burn New Mexico; 2) that it will ignite the whole world."

Too bad that the actual odds Fermi offered that night on these events are lost to history. Whether anyone placed money with Fermi and what odds he did offer seem never to have been reported. There are strong hints that his odds for total atmospheric ignition were much higher than three in a million. He would hardly have offered to "make book" on the basis of odds like that.

Accounts agree that when General Groves, the military officer in charge of the Manhattan Project, heard about this offer, he was angry; he feared it would upset the enlisted men. He had himself prepared a draft news release in case the explosion was larger than expected and destroyed Oppenheimer and the other observers. It mentioned simply an "accidental explosion." He was disconcerted that Fermi's reported bets would imply to some that he might need a different press bulletin: "We've lost New Mexico." (If Fermi had won the second bet, about the end of life on earth, no bulletin would be necessary.) But on second thought, Groves concluded that Fermi was joking.

As a consequence of his reaction, many accounts describe Fermi's offer as "a joke, intended to relieve the tension." It's unclear how anyone's tension could have been relieved by this particular jest. But as William Laurence of the *New York Times*, permitted to chronicle the whole process and the testing of the bomb, put it at the time and in a retrospective later, "many of the scientists did not believe he was joking." Indeed not: numerous accounts mention how anxious many of the participants were that night, especially the younger ones. That probably included those who had hit upon the possible phenomenon themselves and whose concerns had been met simply with formulaic assurances.

As Peter Goodchild recounts, Fermi's expression of uncertainty about the occurrence of atmospheric ignition had been neither a joke nor a last-minute tremor:

> In the final weeks leading up to the test Teller's group were drawn into the immediate preparations when the possibility of atmospheric ignition was revived by Enrico Fermi. His team went to work on the calculations, but, as with all such projects before the introduction of computers, these involved simplifying assumptions. Time after time they came up with negative results, but Fermi remained unhappy about their assumptions. He *also worried whether there were undiscovered phenomena that, under the novel conditions of extreme heat, might lead to unexpected disaster.*

As the test approached, Teller himself, Goodchild reports, "searched for and tested out hypotheses about such phenomena on anyone who would listen." He was still doing this with Oppenheimer's aide Robert Serber in the evening hours before the test. (Serber advised him to deal with the possibilities by bringing along a bottle of whiskey.)

In 1982, Thomas Powers reported an interview with Stan Ulam, who in 1951 was the progenitor of the H-bomb along with Teller, that finally gives a sense of the measure of Fermi's uncertainty that night. According to Ulam:

> Before the Trinity test, the physicist George Breit was given the job of estimating the chances that a nuclear bomb would ignite the earth's entire atmosphere. The chance of this was very small, but after all, said Ulam, "the stake is infinite. . . . Fermi did the same calculations too." He wanted to be sure. Theoretically, if the temperatures created by a nuclear explosion were high enough, the nitrogen in the atmosphere might spontaneously ignite. Fermi confirmed Breit's calculations: such temperatures don't exist in nature. On the long drive to Alamogordo for the Trinity test, Fermi joked about his conclusions. "It would be a miracle if the atmosphere were ignited," he said. "I reckon the chance of a miracle to be *about ten percent.*"

As Sam Allison, a physicist who had been assigned to "ride herd" on the final stages of the project, was counting down the last seconds over a loudspeaker, "Ten, nine, eight..." Davis reports that another young physicist had the responsibility of deciding whether to push a button that would abort the process. In those last seconds, he turned to Oppenheimer and said, "What if I just say this can't go on and stop it?"

Oppenheimer looked at him coldly and said, "Are you all right?" As Allison continued his countdown, "...five, four..." he was thinking partly, he told Davis, of "Fermi's qualms," which he shared. It had been his job, assigned by Oppenheimer, for the past six months to make sure that the project was moving ahead on schedule. But now, "for him it was no justification to say he had done what someone had told him to do; what right had he to participate in an experiment that might kill off the human race?" Seconds later, as the great light was followed by a blast wave that shook the bunkers and eventually subsided, Allison was musing, "Still alive.... No atmospheric ignition."

Others watching ten miles away from ground zero had the same feeling of relief, for the same reason, having spent seconds before that fearing the opposite. One of these was James Conant, the president of Harvard who had oversight over the Manhattan Project as chairman of the NDRC. As Allison's final countdown was echoing over a loudspeaker Conant whispered to Groves that he "never imagined seconds could last so long." In his words:

> Then came a burst of white light that seemed to fill the sky and seemed to last for seconds. I had expected a relatively quick and light flash. The enormity of the light quite stunned me. My instantaneous reaction was that something had gone wrong and that the thermal nuclear transformation of the atmosphere, once discussed as a possibility and jokingly referred to a few minutes earlier, had actually occurred.

His thought at that moment was, "The whole world has gone up in flames."*

---

*I was told by the daughter of a scientist who had experienced the test lying near James Conant that when the preternaturally intense white light first enveloped them, Conant's first thought, he said later, was, "Fermi was right." It was my hearing this comment at a

In short, the first Trinity test at Alamogordo constituted a conscious gamble by the senior scientists at Los Alamos and their immediate superiors: a gamble with the fate of every sentient being on the face of the planet and in the atmosphere and the depths of the oceans. It is noteworthy that it was the scientists alone who took on themselves the responsibility for this gamble. On the basis of any documentation that has survived or any recorded memories, there is no evidence that the possibility of atmospheric ignition was ever made known to the president or anyone else in Washington, D.C., outside the Manhattan Project, either in 1945 or in the three years since it had first been raised to Compton by Oppenheimer in July 1942.

If it had been made known to top civilian officials—as it *was* exposed to Hitler, that same month in 1942, by Speer—how would they have reacted? Would President Roosevelt have sided with Compton's first reaction: that "no chance" of this event was acceptable, no matter how small the probability? Or with his judgment shortly after that the risk was sufficiently small that continued development work was appropriate?

Probably the latter, since only the research was in question at that point, and for the next several years. After all, in June 1942, the scientists had every reason to fear that the Germans might develop the bomb before we did, and for the policy makers there was still a lively concern that Germany might win the war without a bomb. But none of that was still true in July 1945, when the effort had come to the point of actually detonating a test device without having put entirely to rest the possibility of atmospheric ignition.

Might President Truman or Secretary of War Henry Stimson—if they had been aware of the possible loss of all life on earth, forever!—have demanded odds better than three in a million, let alone Fermi's "ten percent"? As it was, in ignorance of any reason for anxiety as they awaited reports at the Potsdam Conference in Germany, hoping for news that would strengthen their hand in negotiations with the Soviets, they learned of its success without Sam Allison's sense of relief. And they were equally ignorant of some scientists' continued cause for apprehension about the longer-term effects of this result, and still more about the experiments on humans that lay just ahead in Japan.

---

reception at the University of Colorado Boulder in 1982 that first attracted my attention to this issue and led to my talk with David Hawkins a few days later.

Part of that concern—for some the smaller part—had to do with the people who would be killed by those further explosions. Allison had qualms about that prospect within minutes after the test, as soon as his fears of burning everyone on earth had dissipated. "Oh, Mr. Conant," he said, in anguish, "They're going to take this thing over and fry *hundreds* of Japanese." His estimate was low by three orders of magnitude, a thousand times.

At the May 31 meeting, Oppenheimer had estimated that the first bomb would kill about twenty thousand people. It immediately killed four times that many, but that was still fewer than the hundred thousand who had been burned alive in one night by the Tokyo firebombing. The readiness of the highest civilian and military officials to allow General Curtis LeMay to multiply that scale of civilian death several times over had been thoroughly tested in the months since. They had all passed that test. Likewise, by late July the scientists had demonstrated their own readiness to take a sufficiently small chance (for Fermi, not so small) of burning up all life on the planet.

According to Albert Speer, this would not have surprised Adolf Hitler. In June 1942, Hitler occasionally "joked that the scientists in their unworldly urge to bare all the secrets under heaven might some day set the globe on fire. But undoubtedly a good deal of time would pass before that came about, Hitler said; he would certainly not live to see it." Actually he died, by his own hand, only ten weeks before the Trinity experiment.

Those who undertook that gamble in July 1945 did not appear to fit the stereotype of the "mad scientist": though in the light of this long-unknown history, the notion is not so far removed from reality. But though they did expect to win that particular bet, with high probability, they were also aware—again more so, it seems, than their civilian superiors—that they were simultaneously engaged in a longer-term gamble imperiling the survival of humanity.

First, some of them (not all) were convinced that even a unilateral U.S. test, still more the unwarned use of the bomb on cities in wartime— in the absence of collaboration with the Soviets and of international controls—virtually assured a desperate postwar nuclear arms race with the Soviets. Second, nearly all understood that such a race would probably lead in a few years' time to the production of thermonuclear weapons on both sides. Bombs with a million times the explosive power of the largest blockbusters of World War II; thousands of them. These two developments together—the latter recognized in July 1942 at the same moment as the possibility of atmospheric ignition—foretold the distinct possibility of destroying the whole of human civilization. Total incineration of the world of cities of the last four thousand years. And with a probability of a lot more than three in a million.

Back in Washington, James Conant wrote up his notes on the Trinity test for his boss, Vannevar Bush. Conant concluded by suggesting that his first few seconds' sense that they had participated in the destruction of humanity might have been prescient. "My first impression remains the most vivid, a cosmic phenomenon like an eclipse. The whole sky suddenly full of white light like the end of the world. Perhaps my impression was only premature on a timescale of years!"

George Kistiakowsky's reaction to the flash was much the same as Conant's. He told the *New York Times* reporter who had witnessed the spectacle from ten miles farther away that it was "the nearest thing to Doomsday one could possibly imagine."

That was mistaken. More than three years earlier, Enrico Fermi had stirred Edward Teller to imagine—and for the next nine years, obsessively to pursue—an explosion a thousand times nearer to Doomsday than the one they witnessed at Alamogordo.*

---

*The yield of the first droppable H-bomb tested by the United States in 1954 was fifteen megatons. That is a million times more explosive power than the largest blockbusters in World War II. The largest warhead ever tested, fifty-eight megatons, was detonated by the Soviets in 1961. The yield was 250 percent greater than the largest yield that had been predicted for it, six megatons, resulting—along with an unexpected shift in wind—in heavy radioactive fallout contaminating inhabitants of the Marshall Islands and the crew of the distant Japanese fishing boat Lucky Dragon, one of whom died. The reason for the great underestimate of yield, with its serious human consequences, was precisely the kind of scientific error or unforeseen reactivity that Fermi had feared in connection with the possibility of atmospheric ignition from the Trinity test. Los Alamos bomb designers had neglected (or greatly underestimated) the contribution to the production of neutrons and to the yield from one of the isotopes included in the hydrogen fuel, lithium-7, which had been thought to be relatively inert but proved not to be under the unprecedented conditions of the dry-fuel thermonuclear detonation. (See Alex Wellerstein, "Castle Bravo Revisited," *Restricted Data*, June 21, 2013, and comments: blog .nuclearsecrecy.com/2013/06/21/castle-bravo-revisited/.)

CHAPTER 18

Risking Doomsday II
The Hell Bomb

In July 1942, on the way to the U.C. Berkeley conference that preceded the formal launch of the Manhattan Project, Edward Teller shared a train compartment with his close friend Hans Bethe. During the trip, he told Bethe that "the fission bomb was all well and good and, essentially, was now a sure thing. He said that what we really should think about was the possibility of igniting deuterium by a fission weapon—the hydrogen bomb." This was the idea that Teller would lay out on the blackboard in Berkeley's Le Conte Hall—simultaneously introducing the possibility of atmospheric ignition. The theorists present spent most of the remaining four weeks of the conference discussing the concept of Teller's "Super," some of them with a sense of foreboding.

Goodchild recounts:

> Hans Bethe recalled talking to his wife [also a physicist, though not cleared for this], who knew in broad terms what they were discussing, "and on a walk in the mountains in Yosemite National Park she asked me to consider carefully whether I really wanted to continue to work on this. Finally, I decided to do it." For Bethe, the Super was a terrible thing, but its development was inextricably linked to the German threat, and to the fission bomb. This was, after all, to be the indispensable trigger

for a thermonuclear reaction and, because of the Germans, they were committed to developing a fission weapon anyway. So for the time being, any moral dilemma associated with the Super itself could be held in abeyance.

But in June 1945, a month before the Trinity test in New Mexico, for some of the scientists who understood (unlike any of the decision makers in Washington) that what was about to be tested was a potential trigger to a hydrogen bomb—and trigger to a thermonuclear arms race with the Soviet Union—facing up to that moral dilemma could no longer be postponed. With most of those at Los Alamos preoccupied with the last-minute technical issues of producing and testing the fission bombs, some scientists in the Chicago lab of the Manhattan Project focused then, belatedly, on the long-run implications of nuclear weapons in a committee chaired by James Franck and strongly influenced by Leo Szilard.

They concluded, in a report that never reached the president, that using the bomb against Japan, especially without warning and without direct Soviet participation in the testing, would make international control of the weapon very unlikely. In turn, that would make inevitable a desperate arms competition, which would before long expose the United States to uncontrolled possession by adversaries of thermonuclear weapons. As a result, some of them said in a prescient pre-attack petition to President Truman, "the cities of the United States as well as the cities of other nations will be in continuous danger of sudden annihilation."

Szilard was the driving force behind this petition. Its many signers in the project tried to caution the president—on both moral grounds and considerations of the long-run survival of civilization—against beginning this process by using the bomb against Japan *even if its use might shorten the war and save the lives of American troops.*

But their petition was sent "through channels" and was deliberately held back by General Leslie Groves, director of the Manhattan Project. It never got to the president, or even to Secretary of War Henry Stimson, until after the bomb had been dropped. There is no record that the scientists' concerns about the *future* impact of nuclear attacks on Japan were *ever* made known to President Truman before or after his decisions. Still less were they made known to the American public.

At the end of the war the petitions and their reasoning were reclassi-fied secret to keep them from public knowledge, and their existence was unknown for more than a decade. Several project scientists later expressed regret that they had earlier deferred to the demands of the secrecy managers—for fear of losing their clearances and positions, and perhaps facing prosecution—and had collaborated in maintaining public ignorance on this most vital of issues.

One of them, Eugene Rabinowitch—a physicist who had been rappor-teur for the Franck Committee and who after the war founded and edited the *Bulletin of the Atomic Scientists* (with its Doomsday Clock)—had in fact, after the German surrender in May, actively considered breaking ranks and alerting the American public to the existence of the bomb, the plans for using it against Japan, and the scientists' views both of the moral issues and the long-term dangers of doing so.

Rabinowitch first reported this in a letter to the *New York Times* published on June 28, 1971. It was the day I submitted to arrest at the federal courthouse in Boston, so I didn't see it that day or for many years afterward. For thirteen days before it was published, my wife and I had been underground, eluding the FBI while distributing the Pentagon Papers to seventeen newspapers after injunctions had halted publication in the *New York Times* and the *Washington Post*.

The Rabinowitch letter began by saying it was "the revelation by the *Times* of the Pentagon history of U.S. intervention in Vietnam, despite its classification as 'secret'" that led him now to disclose the following for the first time:

> Before the atom bomb-drops on Hiroshima and Nagasaki, I had spent sleepless nights thinking that I should reveal to the Amer-ican people, perhaps through a reputable news organ, the fateful act—the first introduction of atomic weapons—which the U.S. Government planned to carry out without consultation with its people. Twenty-five years later, I feel I would have been right if I had done so.

Rereading this, still with some astonishment, I agree with him. He was right to consider it, and he would have been right if he had done it. He would have faced prosecution and prison (as I did, at the time his letter was published), but he would have been more than justified, as a citizen and as a human being, in informing the American public and burdening them with shared responsibility for the fateful decision (even though, as he said later, he had no expectation that they would have demanded a different decision).

In the fall of 1949 another moment of truth had arrived on the path to an H-bomb. Edward Teller, after seven years of intense effort, was still no further toward solving the problem of igniting thermonuclear fuel with an A-bomb. But immediately after the September announcement that the Soviet Union had tested a fission bomb, Teller enlisted some prominent former members of the Manhattan Project, still at or consulting for Los Alamos, to join him in promoting a crash program for an H-bomb, to regain "superiority" over the Soviets (having just lost our monopoly).

The General Advisory Committee (GAC) of the Atomic Energy Commission, chaired by Oppenheimer, was asked to consider this proposal in October 1949. Its members unanimously rejected a crash program in the strongest terms. All hoped "that by one means or another, the development of these weapons can be avoided. We are all reluctant to see the United States take the initiative in precipitating this development. We are all agreed that it would be wrong at the present moment to commit ourselves to an all-out effort toward its development." The reasons for rejecting a high-priority program of development included practical grounds of cost, feasibility, and alternative uses for scarce resources (including tritium, needed for smaller, tactical fission weapons). All agreed such a weapon was not needed for deterrence of a nuclear attack, whether the Soviets went ahead and developed it or not. "Reprisals by our large stock of atomic bombs would be comparably effective to the use of a super."

But they all went far beyond this to urge the United States to make a commitment virtually without precedent (still!) *not* to develop such a weapon. "The majority feel that this should be an unqualified commitment. Others [Enrico Fermi and I. I. Rabi] feel that it should be made conditional on the response of the Soviet government to a proposal to renounce such development."

In arguing for either form of a commitment, all the members present raised moral issues in language I've never seen in any other official classified document opposing an impending development. (Never, for example, in the seven thousand pages of the Pentagon Papers on the calamitous *U.S. Decision-Making in Vietnam, 1945–68*.) No other secret proposal before the U.S. government has ever, to my knowledge, been condemned by insiders in such terms, nor has one ever deserved it more.

The majority addendum was written by Conant and signed by Hartley Rowe, Cyril Smith, L. A. DuBridge, Oliver Buckley, and Oppenheimer. It said, in part:

> We base our recommendation on our belief that the extreme dangers to mankind inherent in the proposal wholly outweigh any military advantage that could come from this development. Let it be clearly realized that this is a super weapon; it is in a totally different category from an atomic bomb. The reason for developing such super bombs would be to have the capacity to devastate a vast area with a single bomb. Its use would involve a decision to slaughter a vast number of civilians. We are alarmed as to the possible global effects of the radioactivity generated by the explosion of a few super bombs of conceivable magnitude.

Fermi and Rabi, though recommending a conditional rather than unconditional commitment not to proceed, were if anything even more unreserved in their reasons for opposing initiating development of a Super altogether, not only a crash program.

> By its very nature it cannot be confined to a military objective but becomes a weapon which in practical effect is almost one of genocide. It is clear that the use of such a weapon cannot be justified on any ethical ground which gives a human being a certain individuality and dignity even if he happens to be a resident of an enemy country.
>
> The fact that no limits exist to the destructiveness of this weapon makes its very existence and the knowledge of its construction a danger to humanity as a whole. It is necessarily an evil thing considered in any light.
>
> For these reasons we believe it important for the President of the United States to tell the American public, and the world, we think it wrong on fundamental ethnical principles to initiate a program of development such a weapon.

Secretary of State Dean Acheson and AEC Commissioner Lewis Strauss did not agree, nor did the Democratic majority chairmen of the Senate Foreign Relations Committee and the Joint Congressional Atomic Energy Committee. On January 31, President Harry Truman announced publicly that he had directed the AEC "to continue with its work on all forms of atomic energy weapons, including the so-called hydrogen or super-bomb."

The GAC had also recommended "that enough be declassified about the super bomb so that a public statement of policy can be made at this time." But that recommendation went the way of a pledge not to initiate the development.

Oppenheimer and Conant, having been overruled on this vital issue, thought of resigning from the GAC, but Acheson—precisely because he didn't want the public to be aware of any opposition to the program or to inquire about the reasons for it, urged them not to. So they didn't. Nor did Fermi or Hans Bethe—who also strongly opposed the development prior to Truman's decision—cease to be active consultants on it. Nor did anyone else, to my knowledge, leave the program: with one exception I learned of many years later. Surprisingly enough, that was my father.

As I have previously related, my father had spent the war designing factories to build bombing planes and engines for them. When the war ended, he accepted an offer to oversee the buildup of the plutonium production facilities at Hanford, Washington. That project was being run first by DuPont, then by General Electric under contract with the Atomic Energy Commission. To take the job of chief structural engineer on the project, Dad moved from the engineering firm of Albert Kahn, where he had worked for years, to what became Giffels & Rossetti. As he later told me, that engineering firm had the largest volume of construction contracts in the world at that time, and his project was the world's largest. I grew up hearing these superlatives.

The Hanford project gave my father his first really good pay.

But while I was away as a sophomore at Harvard, Dad left his job with Giffels & Rossetti, for reasons I never learned at the time. He was out of work for almost a year. Then he went back as chief structural engineer for the whole firm. Almost thirty years later, when my father was eighty-nine, I happened to ask him why he had left Giffels & Rossetti. His answer startled me. He said, "Because they wanted me to help build the H-bomb."

This was a breathtaking statement for me to hear in 1978. That year I was in full-time active opposition to the deployment of the neutron bomb—a small H-bomb—that President Jimmy Carter was proposing to send to Europe. The N-bomb had a killing radius from its output of neutrons that was much wider than its radius of destruction by blast. Optimally, an airburst N-bomb would produce little fallout. Its neutrons would kill humans either outside or within buildings or tanks, while sparing structures, equipment, or vehicles. The Soviets mocked it as "a capitalist weapon" that destroyed people but not property. But they tested such a weapon too, as did other countries.

I had opposed developing or testing that concept for almost twenty years, since it was first described to me by my friend and colleague at RAND Sam Cohen, who liked to be known as the "father of the neutron bomb." He wanted me to evaluate the strategic implications of such a weapon, hoping I would support his campaign for deploying it. To his great disappointment, after studying his earnest descriptions of its properties, I told him I thought it would be too dangerous to develop or possess.

I feared that, as a low-yield, tactical battlefield weapon with limited and seemingly controllable lethal effects, it would be seen, delusionally, as usable in warfare, making U.S. first use in pursuit of "limited nuclear war" more likely. It would be the match that would set off an exchange of the much larger "dirty" weapons with widespread fallout, which made up the bulk of our own arsenal and were all that the Soviets then had.

In the year of this 1978 conversation with Dad, I was arrested four times in Colorado while blocking the railroad tracks at the Rocky Flats nuclear weapons production facility, which produced all the plutonium triggers for H-bombs and was going to produce the plutonium cores for neutron bombs. One of these arrests was on Nagasaki Day, August 9, 1978. The "triggers" produced at Rocky Flats were, in effect, the nuclear components of A-bombs, plutonium fission bombs of the type that had destroyed Nagasaki on that date in 1945.

Every one of our many thousands of H-bombs, the thermonuclear fusion bombs that arm our strategic forces, requires a Nagasaki-type A-bomb as its detonator. I doubt that one American in a hundred knows that simple fact, and thus has a clear understanding of the difference between A- and H-bombs, or of the reality of the thermonuclear arsenals of the last fifty years.

Our popular image of nuclear war—from the familiar pictures of the devastation of Nagasaki and Hiroshima—is grotesquely misleading. Those pictures show us only what happens to humans and buildings when they are hit by what is now just the detonating cap for a modern nuclear weapon.

The plutonium for these weapons came from Hanford and from the Savannah River Site in Georgia and was machined into weapons components at Rocky Flats in Colorado. The poet Allen Ginsberg and I, with many others, blockaded the entrances to the plant on August 9, to interfere with business as usual at the bomb factory on the anniversary of the day a plutonium bomb had killed fifty-eight thousand humans. (About one hundred thousand had died by the end of 1945.)

I had never heard before of any connection between my father and the H-bomb. He wasn't particularly wired in to my antinuclear work or to any of my activism since the Vietnam War had ended. I asked him what he meant by his comment about why he had left Giffels & Rossetti.

"They wanted me to be in charge of designing a big plant that would be producing material for an H-bomb." He said that DuPont, which had built the Hanford Site, was to have the contract from the Atomic Energy Commission. That would have been for the Savannah River Site. I asked him when this was.

"Late '49."

I told him, "You must have the date wrong. You couldn't have heard about the hydrogen bomb then—it's too early." I'd just been reading about the whole H-bomb controversy and the GAC report in Herb York's recent book *The Advisors* (New York, 1976). The GAC meeting on the issue of a crash program had been in October 1949. I said to Dad, "Truman didn't make the decision to go ahead till January 1950. Meanwhile the whole thing was super secret. You couldn't have heard about it in '49."

My father said, "Well, somebody had to design the plant if they were going to go ahead. I was the logical person. I was in charge of the structural engineering of the whole project at Hanford after the war. I had a Q clearance."

That was the first I'd ever heard that he'd had a Q clearance—an AEC clearance, higher than Top Secret, for nuclear weapons design and stockpile data. I'd had that clearance myself in the Pentagon—along with close to a dozen other special clearances above Top Secret—after I left the RAND Corporation for the Defense Department in 1964. It was news to me that my father had ever had any security clearance, but it made sense that he would have needed it for Hanford. I said, "So you're telling me that you would have been one of the only people in the country, outside Los Alamos and the GAC, who knew we were considering building the H-bomb in 1949?"

He said, "I suppose so. Anyway, I know it was late '49 because that's when I quit."

"Why did you quit?"

"I didn't want to make an H-bomb. Why, that thing was going to be a thousand times more powerful than the A-bomb!"

I thought, score one for his memory at eighty-nine. He remembered the proportion correctly. That was the same factor Oppenheimer and the others predicted in their report in 1949. They were right. The first explosion of a droppable H-bomb, almost five years later, had a thousand times the explosive power of the Hiroshima blast.

My father went on: "I hadn't wanted to work on the A-bomb either. But then Einstein seemed to think that we needed it, and it made sense to me that we had to have it against the Russians. So I took the job, but I never felt good about it.

"Then when they told me they were going to build a bomb a thousand times bigger, that was it for me. I went back to my office and I said to my deputy, '*These guys are crazy*. They have an A-bomb, now they want an H-bomb. They're going to go right through the alphabet till they have a Z-bomb.'"

I said, "Well, so far they've only gotten to N."

He said, "There was another thing about it that I couldn't stand. Building these things generated a lot of radioactive waste. I wasn't responsible for designing the containers for the waste, but I knew they were bound to leak eventually. That stuff was deadly forever. It was radioactive for twenty-four thousand years."

Again he had turned up a good figure. I said, "Your memory is working pretty well. It would be deadly a lot longer than that, but that's about the half-life of plutonium."

There were tears in his eyes. He said huskily, "I couldn't stand the thought that I was working on a project that was poisoning parts of my own country forever, that might make parts of it uninhabitable for thousands of years."

I thought over what he'd said; then I asked him if anyone else working with him had had misgivings. He didn't know. "Were you the only one who quit?" He said yes. He was leaving the best job he'd ever had, and he didn't have any other to turn to. He lived on savings for a while and did some consulting.

I thought about Oppenheimer and Conant, both of whom had recommended dropping the atomic bomb on Hiroshima but who—that same month Dad was resigning—along with Fermi and Rabi had expressed internally their opposition to the development of the "superbomb" in the most extreme terms possible. It was, they had said, potentially "a weapon of genocide" which carried "much further than the atomic bomb itself the policy of exterminating civilian populations . . . whose power of destruction is essentially unlimited . . . a threat to the future of the human race which is intolerable . . . a danger to humanity as a whole . . . necessarily an evil thing considered in any light." Not one of these men had risked their status in the nuclear establishment by sharing with the American public at the time their expert judgment that the president's course fatally endangered humanity. Nor had they refrained from supporting it, once Edward Teller and Stan Ulam had come up with a design that would work early in 1951.

I asked my father what had made him feel so strongly, to act in a way that nobody else had done. He said, "You did."

That didn't make any sense. I said, "What do you mean? We didn't discuss this at all. I didn't know anything about it."

Dad said, "It was earlier. I remember you came home with a book one day, and you were crying. It was about Hiroshima. You said, 'Dad, you've got to read this. It's the worst thing I've ever read.'"

I said that must have been John Hersey's book *Hiroshima,* in 1946. I didn't remember giving it to him.

"Yes. Well, I read it, and you were right. That's when I started to feel bad about working on an atomic bomb project. And then when they said they wanted me to work on a hydrogen bomb, it was too much for me. I thought it was time for me to get out."

I asked if he had told his bosses why he was quitting. He said he told some people, not others. The ones he told seemed to understand his feelings. In fact, in less than a year, the head of the firm called to say that they wanted him to come back as chief structural engineer for the whole firm. They were dropping the General Electric contract (they didn't say why), so he wouldn't have to have anything to do with the AEC or bomb making. He stayed with them till he retired.

I said, finally, "Dad, how could I not ever have heard any of this before? How come you never said anything about it?" My father said, "Oh, I couldn't tell any of this to my family. You weren't cleared."

* * *

Well, I finally started getting my clearances in 1958, ten years after my father gave his up. They turned out to be useful in the end. In 1969 they allowed me to read the Top Secret Pentagon Papers and to keep them in my safe at the RAND Corporation, from which I delivered copies of them that year to the Senate Foreign Relations Committee and later to nineteen newspapers.

But in an important sense, for a decade before that, my clearances had been my undoing. And not only mine. Precisely because we were exposed to secret intelligence estimates, in particular from the Air Force, I and my colleagues at the RAND Corporation were preoccupied in the late fifties with the urgency of averting nuclear war by deterring a Soviet surprise attack that would exploit an alleged "missile gap." That supposed dangerous U.S. inferiority was exactly as unfounded in reality as the earlier Manhattan Project fear of a Nazi crash bomb program had been, or to pick a more recent example, as concern over Saddam Hussein's supposed possession of weapons of mass destruction in 2003.

Working conscientiously, obsessively, on a wrong problem, countering an illusory threat, I and my colleagues at RAND had distracted ourselves and helped distract others from dealing with real dangers posed by the mutual superpower pursuit of nuclear weapons—dangers which we were helping make worse—and from real opportunities to make the world more secure. Unintentionally, yet inexcusably, we made our country and the world less safe.

I have known for a long time that official secrecy and deceptions about our nuclear weapons posture and policies and their possible consequences threaten the survival of the human species. To understand the urgency of radical changes in our nuclear policies that may truly move the world toward the elimination of Doomsday Machines, and ultimately to abolition of nuclear weapons, we need a new understanding of the real history of the nuclear age. I turn now to one more chapter in that hidden history.

CHAPTER 19

The Strangelove Paradox

Yes, but the whole point of the doomsday machine is lost if you
keep it a secret! Why didn't you tell the world, eh?
                                        —Dr. Strangelove

When Daniel Ford, the former executive director of the Union of
Concerned Scientists, published his well-researched book *The Button* in
1985, he could get no official comments on the question implied by his
title: "How many fingers are on the nuclear button?" Did official pre-
delegation exist—as logic suggested and various people had hinted or
speculated—or did it not? From Donald Latham, assistant secretary of
defense under Reagan for command and control systems, he received
this answer: "Well, there are contingency plans, I just really can't discuss
them." That, he noted, was about all the Pentagon would say about the
subject. Ford then quotes Desmond Ball, the extraordinarily well-
informed Australian defense analyst, as commenting to him, "This is
probably one of the most closely kept secrets."

Indeed. Going back to 1960, a quarter century before Ford's investigation, the answer to his query was given to me as a highly sensitive
secret—perhaps the most highly guarded secret in the American military system—in confidence that I would not reveal it to the U.S. public
or the world, thereby contradicting a decade of explicit denials by the

highest American authorities that any such pre-delegation existed. That confidence in my discretion was justified at that time.

But there was, and still is, a stunning paradox here. *Why* has it been kept secret at all, especially from our adversaries?

After all, the most compelling and legitimate purpose of delegation by the president has always been to assure that the Soviets (or now, Russians) could not paralyze our retaliatory forces by a "decapitating" attack on Washington, D.C., or by attacking the president wherever he might be. But even more important than establishing that reality is to make sure that the adversary also understands, recognizes, and believes that reality beyond any doubt. Otherwise, in a crisis or faced with a (possibly false) warning of a U.S. attack, any enemy uncertainty about presidential delegation could nourish hope that its best chance—perhaps its only chance—of survival was precisely to launch a decapitating attack against the U.S. capital and our major known command posts. To deter such a reckless action, surely nothing could be more important than convincing our adversary that such hopes were futile, that destroying our leadership would not prevent or even reduce the devastation they should expect. *Secrecy about this, denial of it, refusal to confirm rumors about it, could have only the opposite effect.*

Of course, there was no way that the Soviets would have been certain that such delegation existed. Even presidential statements that it did exist could be disbelieved. But a declaratory policy that it did *not* exist (as the American public was repeatedly told) and that only the president himself, or a successor brought into possession of his "football," could launch nuclear strikes, would only strengthen the hopes of Soviet planners that there was, after all, a form of preemptive attack that could allow them to survive and even "prevail." A decapitating attack, in the absence of any U.S. delegation, might actually paralyze U.S. retaliation, or at least cause a significant delay. After all, that was the logic of our own secret military planning, with its emphasis on Moscow as the highest-priority target.

Such Soviet planning was not just conjectural. As Ford put it, "Soviet strategists have written extensively about the need to bring the 'disorganization of [the enemy's] state and military command control,'" particularly for strategic weapons. He quotes a Soviet article describing this objective in detail in 1966, a time when the Soviets still had too few missiles to target all our Minuteman missiles, and yet were deploying SS-9 missiles with twenty-megaton warheads, clearly intended for the one hundred highly hardened Minuteman control centers. With such an approach, it was certain that they would also target the high civil-military command in the Pentagon and D.C. area.

Secrecy about any U.S. delegation not only encouraged such planning but also could stimulate desperate hopes in the midst of a crisis that it was actually better to execute these plans than to await a possible U.S. attack on their own command system. In other words, such secrecy lowered deterrence of a Soviet decapitating strike in a crisis.

But the situation became much worse than that under Carter and Reagan. The longstanding JCS and SAC desire to attack Moscow and the whole Soviet command and control system had remained a tightly guarded secret from the era of Eisenhower through Ford. But as early as 1977, and especially in 1978–80, there were frequent leaks and official statements that the special focus of strategic nuclear planning under President Carter—pressed by his national security assistant Zbigniew Brzezinski—was decapitation of the Soviet command system. The Reagan administration continued both the emphasis and the openness about it. In other words, secrecy about our plans to nullify Soviet decapitating attacks by delegation (which have persisted, up to the present) was now joined by *publicity* about our intentions to decapitate the Soviets. In fact, it was in the late Carter years that the term "decapitation" first acquired public currency as an official objective.

Leon Sloss, a Pentagon official, was given the task at the beginning of the Carter administration in 1977 of updating the guidance on nuclear operations. He told me years later that "The first thing I did" was to pull out of a Top Secret file-safe in the Pentagon my old 1961 draft guidance to planning for general nuclear war, finished on my thirtieth birthday. He had remembered it; he said it was the starting point for his own work. If so, he soon departed from it radically. According to that earlier guidance, an essential part of a coercive strategy, aimed at ending the war short of total annihilation on both sides, was to withhold attacks on the opponent's command structure. But as a consequence of this review, as Sloss wrote later, "increased emphasis in U.S. nuclear [weapons] employment policy was given to the targeting of enemy military forces and *political-military leadership . . . the Soviet command structure.*"

Ford quotes General Bruce K. Holloway, the former commander in chief of SAC, as writing in 1980 that U.S. war aims included "prevention of the loss of our way of life," "damage limitation," and the "degradation of the Soviet State and its control apparatus to such an extent as to make successful negotiation possible." In achieving these objectives, "the importance of crippling the [Soviet] command and the control system . . . assumes extraordinary proportions."

Nothing could so decisively *preclude* "successful negotiations" than to destroy at the outset the opposing command authorities. With whom would these "negotiations" be carried out? What ability would we have left them to control their operations, implement any "deal," or terminate their own attacks? Those were questions I had raised in 1961. Their logic was probably never accepted by SAC for a moment; certainly not by General Holloway, whose memo in 1980 Ford quotes further: "Degradation of the overall political and military control apparatus must be the primary targeting objective. Irrespective of whether we strike first or respond to a Soviet strike (presumably counterforce), it assumes the importance of absolute priority planning. Striking first would offer a tremendous advantage, and would emphasize degrading the highest political and military control to the greatest possible degree."

Obviously, the success of this would depend on the Soviets' eschewing any delegation—unlike ourselves—that would assure a devastating response to a U.S. attack on their high command. Holloway indicated explicitly his confidence that the Soviets would be more conservative in this sense than the U.S. "I am convinced that in the Soviet system there is such centralized control that it would be possible to degrade very seriously their military effectiveness for nuclear or any other kind of war if the command control system were severely disrupted. Major damage would be difficult to achieve and would require better intelligence than now possible (better reconnaissance and better clandestine inputs) but it can be done. Moreover, *it must be done, because there is no other targeting strategy that can achieve the war aims that underwrite survival.*"

In other words, the compelling incentive—in the eyes of the former CINCSAC, and certainly not only for him—to "decapitate" the Soviet system at the outset of hostilities reflects the hope that it might paralyze Soviet forces to the extent that the U.S. could survive a nuclear war, and the belief that *no other approach could do this*. Every other strategy is seen (realistically) as a "no-win" option or, more seriously, a "no-survival" approach. Nevertheless, in planning to deal with a desperate situation (and in supporting Air Force and Navy budgeting for lots of accurate missiles for an illusory goal of winning or surviving a thermonuclear war), the supposed *possibility* of averting "otherwise-certain" annihilation, no matter how slim that chance, has an attraction that tends to be irresistible.

This would not have been a big surprise to the Soviets. They undoubtedly took it for granted in our planning. McNamara had announced publicly the possibility of withholding an attack on Moscow in his Ann Arbor commencement speech of 1962, but that was, after all, only an option. Soviet military planners probably regarded it with a good deal of incredulity. Thus, at the same time in the late sixties as they were preparing for SS-9 attacks on Minuteman control centers, they were building two thousand underground bunkers for Soviet military officials and Communist Party leaders (more than one hundred thousand of them) with seventy-five relocation centers in Moscow, some of them several hundred feet deep. (Since we had not been as thorough in multiplying underground centers, there was indeed what General Buck Turgidson had feared in *Dr. Strangelove*, "a mine-shaft gap.")

But the new publicity a decade later about a renewed U.S. preoccupation with destroying these very shelters had to undermine whatever confidence Soviet leaders had in their own survival, even for long enough to order retaliation. Indeed, that was proclaimed as the very purpose of our plans and emerging military capabilities: large numbers of ICBMs each with multiple independently targetable reentry vehicles (MIRVs), allowing for a number for warheads with separate targets on each missile, with larger yield and greatly increased accuracy, for our Minuteman and sub-launched missiles (SLBMs) precisely to attack the large number of Soviet underground command posts as well as the increasing number of hardened missile sites. Moreover, the increasing capability of multiple-target, high-yield, and very accurate Trident *submarine* missiles meant that attacks on most of the Soviet command structure, as well as its missiles, could be launched so close to the Soviet Union as to give no warning, or almost none, to either the high command or the missile launch centers.

Indeed, a major rationale then *and now* (see below) for buying and deploying hosts of such warheads capable of destroying super-hardened underground command centers has been to deter Soviet (now Russian) leaders from contemplating a first strike under any circumstances by assuring them that they themselves would not survive the initial exchange, whether we struck first preemptively or not. Given these capabilities, the chance that high-level Soviet officials could actually get to their bunkers in a low-warning attack, *or* that the shelters would survive our attack, was extremely low. This evident fact, combined with the deliberate publicity given the Carter and Reagan administrations' effort to achieve decapitation, could only give a desperate sense of urgency to Soviet leaders and planners to maintain a deterrent retaliatory capability. The only ways to do that were what we ourselves had done in the era of the presumed Soviet missile superiority. They would either have to delegate authority for launch to lower commanders, and/or plan for launch on warning of attack (LOW) by high commanders: if not by computers, as some military commanders such as NORAD chief General Lawrence Kuter preferred. As Herbert York recounts:

> General Kuter told me that we had to complete the BMEWS (Ballistic Missile Early Warning System) as soon as possible, and he urged that we expand it in order to create a highly redundant capability at each site. We must expand it in order to have an absolutely reliable early warning of a missile attack. Basically, I agreed.
>
> All would have been well if he had stopped there, but he didn't. In words I can't precisely recall, he went on to say that we had to have this redundancy and the resulting high level of reliability so that, when we finally connected the warning system directly to the launch button of our own ICBMs, there would be no false alarms.
>
> I was astonished. I told him flatly that we would not automate our response, that we would not connect the warning system directly to the launch button. We would not, in sum, go to a "launch on warning" strategy. [York was mistaken in this prediction.] We would, especially, not go to one that did not have the president in the decision-making loop.
>
> Kuter coldly replied, "In that case, we might as well surrender now."

When I first read of the new emphasis on decapitation during the Carter administration, I worried that this publicity could only press the Soviets into a combination of launch on warning and delegation. Strategists like Holloway were gambling that even this pressure wouldn't lead the Bolsheviks to give up their commitment to centralized control. They were mistaken. When the Reagan administration not only continued but also reinforced this public focus, the Soviets, as I expected, worked urgently on means to counteract it. And just like the Americans, just as *unaccountably* from the point of view of deterrence, they kept these efforts effectively secret.

With the ending of the Cold War and the new possibility of open interaction between American and Soviet planners and strategic analysts, Bruce Blair—a former Minuteman control officer who subsequently became an expert in command and control issues—discovered and reported that the Soviets had responded to the threat of decapitation by designing an elaborate system to assure retaliation to an American attack that destroyed Moscow headquarters. Its code name was Perimeter; it was known informally by a Russian phrase that translates as "Dead Hand." Low-level officers in deep underground centers well away from Moscow would receive by a variety of channels several forms of evidence—seismic, electronic, infrared, radioactivity—that Moscow had suffered a nuclear explosion, along with breakage in all forms of communication to and from Moscow. In that event, they were authorized to send off ICBMs that would beep a Go signal to any ICBM sites they passed over. The Soviet rockets would not merely communicate an authorization to launch to ground officers but would actually bypass them and launch the missiles.

In an early design of the system, the signals from Moscow would launch the emergency rockets *automatically*, with no need or allowance for judgment or intervention by humans at the dispersed sites. In other words, this was, at last, the total embodiment of the Doomsday Machine, the device that Herman Kahn had speculatively imagined in *On Thermonuclear War*, whose destructive effects would be so total as to provide the ultimate deterrent while its credibility would be achieved by automaticity. There is some disagreement about whether the Soviet system was to be in continuous operation or only activated during times of crisis, when the possibility of attack seemed higher than usual, but modernized after the end of the Cold War and up to the present.

Whereas Kahn's Doomsday Machine had allowed that an automatic mechanism would be triggered, perhaps, by several near-simultaneous explosions on different cities, it appears that the Perimeter system would be activated by an attack on Moscow alone. That meant that nuclear winter, which was just coming to be understood as this system went into effect, could have been made inevitable by a single explosion on Moscow.

Stanley Kubrick presents this situation in *Dr. Strangelove* when the Russian leader informs the U.S. president that if the one American B-52 still on its way to a Soviet target (as the result of an unauthorized action by a squadron commander) is not successfully recalled—which in the film, as in real-life SAC operational planning, neither the president nor anyone else could do once the planes had been ordered to expend—its bombload will trigger an automatic Doomsday Machine in the Soviet Union that will destroy all life on earth. The precise reason the Russian leader gives for having wired up this system is to assure that an attack by the United States would be self-destructive even if it successfully destroyed Soviet command posts. Dr. Strangelove points out to the Soviet ambassador—present in the war room as a translator and conveyer of the information about the Doomsday Machine—that for purposes of deterrence it would be essential for the United States to know this in advance.

"But the . . . whole point of the doomsday machine . . . is lost . . . if you keep it a secret! Why didn't you tell the world, eh?"

The ambassador answers: "It was to be announced at the Party Congress on Monday. As you know, the premier loves surprises."

Satire, of course. But when the Soviets installed Perimeter, they had no intention of announcing it, ever. And they never did, while the USSR existed. (The Russians have now acknowledged that they still maintain it, describing it as a doomsday machine: see below.)

The designer of the secret Soviet Perimeter system, Valery Yarynich, regarded his system until his death in December 2012 (after decades of consultation on arms control in the United States) as *safer* than its alternative, which was to rely on launch on warning by high officials in Moscow only. His approach still allowed for launch on warning—as the Russian system, like ours, continues to do—in order to prevent Soviet missiles from being destroyed before they were launched and to allow them to preempt U.S. missiles promptly that had not yet been launched. But the Perimeter system was meant to remove what might present an additional pressure on Soviet commanders in Moscow to launch on warning if the warning signals *seemed* correct: that there might otherwise be no Soviet retaliation to an American attack because the commanders themselves were about to be destroyed.

However, as David Hoffman, former Moscow bureau chief for the *Washington Post* who had interviewed Yarynich many times for his book *The Dead Hand*, reported in a tribute to him on his death:

> In later years, Yarynich expressed grave doubts about the very systems of annihilation he had devoted his career to perfecting.

He once told me it was utter stupidity to keep the Dead Hand secret; such a retaliatory system was useful as a deterrent only if your adversary knew about it. More broadly, he came to doubt the wisdom of maintaining the cocked-pistols approach to nuclear deterrence, the so-called hair-trigger alert, especially after the Cold War ended. He feared it could lead to an accidental or mistaken launch. Yarynich did not keep quiet. He decided to share his insights and worries with the world.

This took courage. Even after the Soviet collapse, discussion of such topics remained guarded in Russia. In the early 1990s ... Yarynich harbored a dream that someday both the United States and Russia might share the secrets of command-and-control. He was certain it could lead to deterrence with far fewer nuclear warheads. He also favored taking missiles off launch-ready alert. He tirelessly expounded his logic, yet governments were not interested. The high priests of nuclear command-and-control could not envision opening up to each other, not here, nor in Russia.

The bottom line is that arrangements made in Russia and the United States have long made it highly likely, if not virtually certain, that a single Hiroshima-type fission weapon exploding on either Washington or Moscow—whether deliberate or the result of a mistaken attack (as in *Fail Safe* or *Dr. Strangelove*) or as a result of an independent terrorist action—would lead to the end of human civilization (and most other species). That has been, and remains, the inevitable result of maintaining forces on both sides that are capable of causing nuclear winter, and at the same time are poised to attack each other's capital and control system, in response to fallible warnings, in the delusion that such an attack will limit damage to the homeland, compared with the consequences of waiting for actual explosions to occur on more than one target.

Here, then, is the actual situation that has prevailed for more than half a century. Each side prepares and actually intends to attack the other's "military nervous system," command and control, especially its head and brain, the national command headquarters, in the first wave of a general war, however it originates. This has become the *only* hope of preempting and paralyzing the other's retaliatory capability in such a way as to avoid total devastation; it is what must above all be deterred by the opponent. But in fact it, too, is thoroughly suicidal *unless the other side has failed to delegate authority* well below the highest levels. Because each side does in fact delegate, hopes for decapitation are totally unfounded. But for the duration of the Cold War, for fear of frightening their own publics, their allies, and the world, neither side discouraged these hopes in the other by acknowledging its own delegation.

The only change in this situation has been that in the first weeks of the Trump administration, Russian news reports have begun acknowledging that the Perimeter system persists. In a February 2, 2017, article, *Pravda* revealed that the commander of Strategic Missile Forces Lieutenant-General Sergey Karakayev said five years ago in an interview in a Russian publication, "Yes, the 'Perimeter' system exists. The system is on alert. If there's a need for a retaliatory strike, the command for an attack may come from the system, not people." The *Pravda* report explained, "Nuclear-capable missile will thus be launched from silos, mobile launches, strategic aircraft, submarines to strike pre-entered targets, unless there is no signal from the command center to cancel the attack. In general . . . one thing is known for sure: the doomsday machine is not a myth at all—it does exist."

Ten days after President Trump's inauguration in 2017, *Pravda* quoted his statements that "the United States should strengthen and expand the nation's nuclear capacity" and "Let it be an arms race," and then reported that "Not so long ago, the Russian Federation conducted exercises to repel a nuclear attack on Moscow and strike a retaliatory thermonuclear attack on the enemy. In the course of the operations, Russia tested the Perimeter System, known as the 'doomsday weapon' or the 'dead hand.' The system assesses the situation in the country and gives a command to strike a retaliatory blow on the enemy automatically. Thus, the enemy will not be able to attack Russia and stay alive."

What has not changed is American preoccupation with threatening Russian command and control: as if all the above revelations, including those of Blair and Yarynich, had not occurred or were thoroughly disbelieved. The National Defense Authorization Act for Fiscal Year 2017, passed with bipartisan support and signed by President Obama on December 23, 2016, included a provision which mandated a report by the Office of the Director of National Intelligence and the Strategic command on "Russian and Chinese Political and Military Leadership Survivability, Command and Control, and Continuity of Governmental Programs and Activities." This provision of the law called for the U.S. Strategic

Command to "submit to the appropriate congressional committees the views of the Commander on the report . . . including a detailed description of how the command, control, and communications systems" for the leadership of Russia and China, respectively, are factored into the U.S. nuclear war plan. The *Pravda* news stories quoted above, both appearing in the second week of the Trump administration, were explicitly responding to these provisions of this law signed a few weeks earlier in their explanation of the continuing need for Perimeter.

Such plans and capabilities for decapitation encourage—almost compel—not only the Perimeter system but Russian launch on (possibly false) warning: either by high command (in expectation of being hit themselves imminently, and in hopes of decapitating the enemy commanders before they have launched all their weapons) or by subordinates who are out of communication with high command and have been delegated launch authority.

As General Holloway expressed it in 1980, he had confidence that with such a decapitating strategy, a U.S. first strike would come out much better for the United States than a second strike, to the point of surviving and even prevailing. He was right about the hopelessness of the alternative forms of preemption. But in reality, the hope of successfully avoiding mutual annihilation by a decapitating attack has always been as ill-founded as any other. The realistic conclusion would be that a nuclear exchange between the United States and the Soviets was—and is—virtually certain to be an unmitigated catastrophe, not only for the two parties but for the world. But being unwilling to change the whole framework of our foreign and defense policy by abandoning reliance on the *threat* of nuclear first use or escalation, policy makers (probably on both sides) have chosen to act as if they believed (and perhaps actually do believe) that such a threat is not what it is: a readiness to trigger global omnicide.

There is every likelihood that, for comparable reasons, similar secret delegation or Dead Hand systems or arrangements exist in every other nuclear weapons state—China, Britain, France, Israel, India, Pakistan, and North Korea—meaning that a Hiroshima-size explosion on any one of their capitals and/or central military headquarters is likely to lead to full-scale launching of their ready forces. The only difference is that none of these states could, at present, cause a full-scale nuclear winter, though an exchange between any two of them (except North Korea) could trigger enough global reduction in sunlight and loss of harvests for a decade to cause nuclear famine and the starvation of one to two billion people or more.

The Strangelove paradox afflicts not only the United States and Russia. Every new state that acquires nuclear weapons and comes face-to-face with the vulnerability both of the weapons systems and of the command and control apparatus confronts the same incentives, the same pressures from its military to delegate and sub-delegate authority to use them, and the same motives to keep that delegation secret from the rest of the world.

Deployment of nuclear weapons by a new state doesn't add just one new finger to a trigger on nuclear war. The world worries about the finger of an irresponsible or reckless third world leader, when the finger can just as easily be that of one of many functionaries working in a far-flung outpost for one of these leaders, new or old.

The bottom line, once again: This is not a species to be trusted with nuclear weapons. Above all, not to be trusted with a full or partial Doomsday Machine. And that doesn't just apply to "crazy" third world leaders.

CHAPTER 20

First-Use Threats

Using Our Nuclear Weapons

From an April 25, 1972, tape of Oval Office conversations, we have the following exchange between Richard Nixon and national security advisor Henry Kissinger, regarding possible American responses to an ongoing North Vietnamese offensive:

> PRESIDENT: I still think we ought to take the dikes out now. Will that drown people?
>
> HENRY KISSINGER: About two hundred thousand people.
>
> PRESIDENT [*reflective, matter-of-fact*]: No, no, no ... I'd rather use the nuclear bomb. Have you got that, Henry?
>
> KISSINGER [*like the president, low-key*]: That, I think would just be too much.
>
> PRESIDENT [*in a tone of surprise*]: The nuclear bomb, does that bother you? I just want you to think big, Henry, for Christsakes.

It was not the first time that Nixon had entertained such big thoughts. As his former chief of staff, H. R. Haldeman, reported in a memoir written as he awaited a prison term for his role in the Watergate scandal, Nixon had shared elements of his plan to end the Vietnam War during his presidential campaign in 1968.

Nixon not only *wanted* to end the Vietnam War, he was absolutely convinced he *would* end it in his first year.

. . . The threat was the key, and Nixon coined a phrase for his theory which I'm sure will bring smiles of delight to Nixon-haters everywhere. We were walking along a foggy beach after a long day of speechwriting [during Nixon's presidential campaign in 1968]. He said, "I call it the Madman Theory, Bob. I want the North Vietnamese to believe I've reached the point where I might do *anything* to stop the war. We'll just slip the word to them that, for God's sake, you know Nixon is obsessed about Communism. We can't restrain him when he's angry—and he has his hand on the nuclear button—and Ho Chi Minh himself will be in Paris in two days begging for peace."

When I read this in 1978, I had a very uneasy feeling that I might have been the source of this crazy scheme, or at least for the phrase he had coined. I had given two lectures to Henry Kissinger's seminar at Harvard in 1959, one titled "The Political Uses of Madness." It was from a series of lectures I had given that spring on bargaining theory, with the overall title "The Art of Coercion: A Study of Threats in Economic Conflict and War."

To illustrate a counterintuitive proposition in bargaining theory I had arrived at, I pointed to the difficult challenge of making a credible threat to initiate nuclear attacks on a nuclear-armed state or one of its allies. After all, this amounted to a threat of massive suicide-murder. The consequences of carrying out this threat were so fearsome that it didn't have to be very credible to be effective in achieving compliance. But at the same time, the consequences for the threateners themselves were such that it was a challenge to make their threat credible *at all*.

I had described, as an example of one possible, though dangerous, solution to this problem, Hitler's deliberate use of his reputation for madness and unpredictability—impulsiveness, recklessness, rage—to intimidate his adversaries and make his threats and ultimatums effective in the period prior to his actual invasions in World War II. Contrary to the expectations of his own generals, his blackmail had actually succeeded spectacularly in his bloodless occupation of the Rhineland, Austria, the Sudetenland, and Czechoslovakia. So the image of mad unpredictability could work. It actually had, for Hitler, but that was in considerable part because he actually *was* crazy, madly reckless and aggressive. I had never thought of it as an approach that would appeal to an American leader, nor be remotely advisable under any circumstances.

When I read Haldeman's memoir, I momentarily worried that Nixon had gotten at least the nickname for his "madman theory," and perhaps even the concept, from Kissinger—that is, indirectly, from me. To my relief, as I read the account again closely, Haldeman placed the date of this conversation with Nixon in 1968—before Nixon had met Henry Kissinger for the first time in the fall of 1969. For good or ill—and there was nothing good about it—Richard Nixon had adopted this reckless policy without inspiration from Kissinger or me.

Rather, the idea of achieving his secretly ambitious aims in Vietnam by nuclear threats had come from a more authoritative source: Dwight Eisenhower, under whom Nixon had served for eight years as vice president. As Haldeman recounted in this same passage about his madman theory, Nixon "saw a parallel in the action President Eisenhower had taken to end another war. When Eisenhower arrived in the White House, the Korean War was stalemated. Eisenhower ended the impasse in a hurry. He secretly got word to the Chinese that he would drop nuclear bombs on North Korea unless a truce was signed immediately. In a few weeks, the Chinese called for a truce and the Korean War ended." (Nixon felt that Eisenhower, as former supreme commander in Europe in World War II, did not need the hint of madness that Nixon himself did for his nuclear threats to be credible, but, according to Haldeman, Nixon "believed his hard-line anti-Communist rhetoric of 20 years would serve to convince the North Vietnamese equally as well that he really meant to do what he said.")

It was not only Nixon who believed that nuclear threats were critical to achieving the armistice in Korea that has held—uneasily, at this moment—for the last sixty-four years. Eisenhower did himself. His former White House chief of staff Sherman Adams reported asking Eisenhower later how an armistice had at last been reached in Korea. "Danger of an atomic war," he said without hesitation. "We told them we could not hold to a limited war any longer if the Communists welched on a treaty of truce. They didn't want a full-scale war or an atomic attack. That kept them under some control." His secretary of state John Foster Dulles gave this same explanation.

Whether such threats actually affected the Chinese decision makers or whether they even received them remains uncertain and controversial. What is neither uncertain nor inconsequential is that the Eisenhower administration, including Richard Nixon, regarded them as successful. In line with this belief, Eisenhower and Dulles relied on such threats repeatedly, in a series of crises. Dulles's self-congratulatory account in 1956 of the risk-taking strategy underlying the first few of these threats gave rise to the term "brinkmanship." In words that echo throughout the Cold War—in fact, words that virtually define "cold war" in a sense that is returning in the last few years—Dulles said:

> Some say that we were brought to the verge of war. Of course we were brought to the verge of war. The ability to get to the verge without getting into the war is the necessary art. If you cannot master it, you inevitably get into war. If you try to run away from it, if you are scared to go the brink, you are lost.

And as I was to discover soon after Nixon left office, this strategy did not end with Dulles and Eisenhower.

In September 1974, just after Nixon's resignation, Roger Morris, a former aide to Henry Kissinger, revealed for the first time in the magazine *Washington Monthly* that Nixon had directed plans for nuclear attacks on North Vietnam in October–November 1969. Morris had participated in an "October group" in the White House planning what his boss, Kissinger, had asked to be a "savage, brutal blow" that would bring the "little fourth-rate country" North Vietnam to its "breaking point." When I asked Morris for specifics after reading that article, he told me that he had read detailed planning folders, with satellite photographs, for several nuclear targets in North Vietnam. One of these, a trans-shipment site for materiel coming in from China, was a mile and a half from the Chinese border. A nuclear attack on this was meant to send a strong "signal" to China. A low-yield airburst nuclear weapon above this railroad spur in the jungle, the planning folder estimated, would cause only "three civilian" casualties. Another prospective nuclear target was the Mu Gia pass from North Vietnam into the Ho Chi Minh trail in Laos.

I had not known at the time about this planning going on in October 1969, just as I was beginning to copy the Pentagon Papers. I would have been astonished to learn of it, so soon in Nixon's first term, even though I was already concerned that another, eventual North Vietnamese offensive, perhaps three or four years off, might trigger use of nuclear weapons. What I had just learned from my friend Morton Halperin, a deputy to Henry Kissinger who had left the National Security Council in September, was that Nixon—contrary to all public expectations—was not planning to withdraw from Vietnam unconditionally but was threatening to escalate dramatically to achieve a quasi-victory.

Mort told me of the then-secret bombing of Cambodia that was already under way. That was precisely to demonstrate to the North Vietnamese, he said, that despite what the electorate had been led to believe, Nixon was ready to go beyond what LBJ had ever been willing to do. Other measures threatened—not in bluff—included invasion of the "sanctuaries" of Cambodia and Laos, mining of Haiphong, unrestricted bombing of cities and towns in North Vietnam up to the Chinese border, and possible invasion of North Vietnam. Warnings to the Soviet ambassador Anatoly Dobrynin as early as May, Halperin told me, had implied a readiness to use nuclear weapons if Nixon's terms were not met. But neither of us imagined then that Nixon was prepared to do this in the fall of his first year.

Nevertheless, Halperin's revelations to me of the president's secretly ambitious aims and his reliance on threats of escalation to achieve them were enough to prompt my decision to copy the Top Secret Pentagon Papers. I was sure his threats would not succeed, and would instead prolong the ground war and enlarge the air war, with heavy further casualties on both sides. If I had known then about Nixon's imminent nuclear threats and plans and had any documents on these, I would have revealed them immediately, instead of the history in the Pentagon Papers, which ended in 1968 before Nixon came to office.

Later, when the papers were published in 1971, Henry Kissinger's fear that I *did* know about Nixon's nuclear threats and plans, and might have documents to back it up, was sufficient reason for him to regard me as "the most dangerous man in America," who "must be stopped at all costs." As I mentioned in the introduction, it was the unlikely exposure of White House crimes against me—actions precisely intended to avert my revealing documents from the Nixon administration, beyond the period of the Pentagon Papers—that led to Nixon's resignation facing impeachment, making the war endable nine months later.

What had prevented Nixon's test of the madman theory from being carried out in 1969 was neither any leak of his threats and plans nor any North Vietnamese compliance with them. It was, as Nixon recounted in his memoirs, the fact that two million Americans took part on October 15 in the "Moratorium" (a general strike by another name), a nationwide weekday work- and school-stoppage protesting the war. Another demonstration, focused on Washington, was scheduled for two days in mid-November. As Nixon says, it was clear to him, given the scale of the first demonstration, that his ultimatum would fail. The North Vietnamese would not believe that he could continue such attacks in the face of this unprecedented popular resistance.

He secretly gave up his plans for attacking the North at that time. But he continued until the end of the month with a secret global alert of SAC—deliberately designed to be visible to Soviet intelligence but not to the American public, with the intent of making his nuclear threats credible to the Soviets and the North Vietnamese while keeping them unknown to the public.

That alert—which included SAC bombers flying round-the-clock missions with weapons aboard, a renewal of the air alert that McNamara had discontinued in 1968 because of an accident—was meant to convey to the Soviets, in effect: "We really are preparing to hit your ally with nuclear weapons if they don't meet our terms; don't think of making any nuclear response if we have to do that. We're poised to meet that immediately with a preemptive attack." This was, after all, exemplary of what I now understand to have been the major purpose of U.S. strategic weapons since the early fifties: to deter, with confidence, Soviet *second*-use retaliation to U.S. first use of tactical weapons against Soviet forces or their allies, by threatening that if the Soviets made a nuclear response in kind with its own tactical weapons SAC might escalate to a full first strike against the Soviet Union.

I knew none of this in 1969 or for the next five years. Neither did virtually anyone else outside a few in the White House and the Pentagon. Thus, none of the millions of people who participated in the demonstrations in 1969 were aware that they might have helped prolong a "moratorium" on U.S. nuclear attacks (though not on threats and preparations) for close to half a century more.

Within weeks of reading in 1974 Roger Morris's revelation of the first-use planning in 1969 and then hearing more about it from Morris, I mentioned what he had told me to my close friend, the Pakistani political scientist and anti-war activist Eqbal Ahmad. Eqbal informed me that he had been in Paris in December 1972, talking with the North Vietnamese negotiating team just before and during the Christmas bombing of North Vietnam that followed Kissinger's pre-election assurance that "peace is at hand." The chief negotiator Xuan Thuy, Eqbal said, had told him during that visit that Henry Kissinger had threatened North

Vietnam with nuclear attacks on twelve occasions: "*douze menaces nucleaires.*"

I said, "They were keeping a list!" He said yes, that became even clearer the next morning when he talked with Xuan Thuy's superior, Le Duc Tho. When Ahmad told him what he had heard the previous day, repeating it exactly, Le Duc Tho shook his head negatively, and said: "*Treize.*" Thirteen. "The unlucky number," he added.

To find that I had been as ignorant as every other outsider in the previous five years was no surprise to me. After all, I knew better than most how well and how long important secrets can be kept by government insiders, even from other officials. On the other hand, these were two areas—Vietnam, nuclear policy—where I thought of myself as exceptionally privy to secrets, in the know. It was something of a shock to hear as late as 1974 that I had so underestimated the nuclear dimension to Nixon's Vietnam strategy.

This news confronted me with a challenging question: If I hadn't known about *this*, what else didn't I know that I would have thought I did? How much had I been missing in my long-term preoccupation with nuclear first-strike planning, false alarms, instability, crises? Specifically, how many first-use nuclear threats by other presidents had I failed to discover or to take seriously? Those "unknown unknowns," as George W. Bush's secretary of defense Donald Rumsfeld would later call them, had suddenly become for me "known unknowns." I began an investigation that I've pursued for over four decades. Eventually it reoriented my whole understanding of the functions of our first-strike strategic forces and their relation to threats of first use of tactical weapons in support of our allies.

I began to look back on the history of U.S. first-use threats—putting together what were "alleged" or rumored threats in unclassified scholarly or journalistic works or memoirs—then reexamining episodes I had previously studied on a classified basis without fully recognizing an underlying pattern. Most histories downplayed or totally ignored these allegations or reports of nuclear threats because of a lack of documentation. Yet time after time, as documents dribbled out through declassification—often several decades after the events—what emerged was that the allegations had been sound, the threats really had occurred and had been meant to be taken seriously.

As in the case of first-strike planning and its estimated effects, or the delegation of nuclear authority, the earlier long-term paucity of documents available to investigators turned out to reflect not the absence of such threats but instead systematic, prolonged secrecy about them, even within government circles of those with clearances. Secrecy about presidential discussion of nuclear threats has been only somewhat less than that surrounding covert operations or assassination plots. But the effect on serious scholars had been to make them either altogether unaware of such threats or unduly skeptical that they reflected serious consideration at high levels.

Thus, after Harry Truman had answered a question at a press conference on November 30, 1950 (days after Marines were surrounded by Chinese Communist troops at the Chosin Reservoir in Korea), on whether there was active consideration of use of the atomic bomb in Korea by saying, "There has always been active consideration of its use," nearly all historians for decades concluded that Truman had simply made an offhand, unreflective comment that had no relation to actual decision-making.

Not so. The press conference comment probably was not a deliberate revelation by the president. (The question, evidently, had not been planted; the White House tried to walk back his statement that afternoon.) But the consideration that was going on within the JCS of the pros and cons of using nuclear attacks in various ways was active, indeed, and there was more than one occasion under Truman when some or all of the JCS actually recommended their use. All this had been concealed by secrecy (except for Truman's one breach) that was virtually complete for decades.

I well remember that 1950 press conference, when I was nineteen and expecting to be sent to Korea by the end of my junior year in college, if not sooner. (It was in that expectation that I proposed to my then fiancée that we get married before I left for the war. We did that in the Christmas break between fall and spring terms; but later that spring a new system of college deferments allowed me to graduate and pursue a year of graduate study in England before I volunteered for the Marines.) I had long wondered whether there had been more to Truman's comment than scholars had recognized. In my new study I found it noteworthy, when voluminous documentation of nuclear analyses and contingency plans finally emerged, to find that the secrecy system had been so effective and to learn both that the Joint Chiefs were ready to consider dropping atomic bombs just five years after Hiroshima and that Harry Truman didn't rule it out in internal discussion and planning even though he was less inclined than they were to do it again.

Likewise, it had become public even in 1951 that General MacArthur had advised the use of atomic weapons in Korea. (His recommendation to a member of Congress to do that, as well as expanding the war to China, led to his highly public and controversial firing by Truman.) But had Dwight Eisenhower, succeeding Truman, paid any attention to such notions (as MacArthur was still proposing)? Not only at the time but for long after, most people, including scholars, found it hard to imagine that Dwight Eisenhower (who had revealed he had opposed using the atomic bomb on Japan) was any less reluctant than Truman to make Korea a nuclear war.

Yes, Eisenhower did say in his first volume of memoirs in 1963 that he had determined a decade earlier that the war in Korea could not be allowed to "drag on," and that a conventional ground attack would be too costly: "First, it was obvious that if we were to go over to a major offensive, the war would have to be expanded outside of Korea. . . . Finally, to keep the attack from being overly costly, it was clear that we would have to use atomic weapons. This necessity was suggested to me by General MacArthur while I, as President-elect, was still living in New York."

Still, I was very struck to read, when it was declassified almost twenty years later, this account of an NSC meeting early in the Eisenhower administration on February 11, 1953:

> [The President] then expressed the view that *we should consider the use of tactical atomic weapons on the Kaesong area* [an area of approximately twenty-eight square miles, treated by the Truman administration as a sanctuary as the initial site of the armistice negotiations; according to General Mark Clark, it was "now chock full of troops and materiel"], which provided a good target for this type of weapon. In any case, the President added, we could not go on the way we were indefinitely. General Bradley thought it desirable to begin talking with our allies regarding an end of the sanctuary, but thought it unwise to broach the subject yet of possible use of atomic weapons.
>
> Secretary Dulles discussed the moral problem and the inhibitions on the use of the A-bomb, and Soviet success to date in setting atomic weapons apart from all other weapons as being

in a special category. *It was his opinion that we should try to break down this false distinction.*

The President added that we should certainly start on diplomatic negotiations with our allies. To him, it seemed that our self-respect and theirs was involved, and if they objected to the use of atomic weapons we might well ask them to supply three or more divisions needed to drive the Communists back, in lieu of the use of atomic weapons. In conclusion, however, the President ruled against any discussion with our allies of military plans or weapons of attack.[†]

Vice President Richard Nixon was, as at all NSC meetings, listening and learning. He had been in office as well in 1954–55 and again in 1958 when Eisenhower directed the Joint Chiefs to plan to use nuclear weapons, imminently, against China if the Chinese Communists should attempt to invade the island of Quemoy, occupied by Chiang's troops, a few miles off mainland China. These threats, which his mentors believed to have been successful, were among the lessons Nixon sought to apply in his own presidency, as indicated at the start of this chapter. Nixon, in short, was the not the first president to "think big." Nor was he the last.

* * *

"It has never been true that nuclear war is 'unthinkable,'" wrote British historian E. P. Thompson. "It has been thought and the thought has been put into effect." He was referring to President Harry Truman's use of atomic bombs to destroy the people of Hiroshima and Nagasaki in August 1945. What needs further attention is that the president who ordered these attacks—along with the great majority of the American public—regarded these nuclear attacks as marvelously successful. Such thoughts get thought again, and acted on.

Among military planners in the U.S. government, thinking about nuclear war has in fact been continuous over the last seventy-two years: and not only, or even mainly, with respect to deterring or responding to a Soviet nuclear attack on the United States or its forces or allies. Preparations and commitments to *initiate* nuclear war "if necessary" have been the basis of fundamental, longstanding U.S. policies and crisis declarations and actions not only in Europe but in Asia and the Middle East as well.

The notion common to nearly all Americans that "no nuclear weapons have been used since Nagasaki" is mistaken. It is not the case that U.S. nuclear weapons have simply piled up over the years, unused and unusable, save for the single function of deterring their use against us by the Soviets. Again and again, generally in secret from the American public, U.S. nuclear weapons *have* been used, for quite different purposes.

As I noted earlier, they have been used in the precise way that a gun is used when you point it at someone's head in a direct confrontation, whether or not the trigger is pulled. For a certain type of gun owner, getting their way in such situations without having to pull the trigger is the best use of the gun. It is why they have it, why they keep it loaded and ready to hand. *All* American presidents since Franklin Roosevelt have acted on that motive, at times, for owning nuclear weapons: the incentive to be able to threaten to initiate nuclear attacks if certain demands are not met.

The long-secret history of this period, extending throughout the Cold War and beyond, reveals that the assumption of a legitimate and available presidential "option" of first use—American initiation of nuclear attacks as an escalation of conventional armed conflict—is far more than purely symbolic or rhetorical. In reality, every president from Truman to Clinton has felt compelled at some point in his time in office— usually in great secrecy—to threaten and/or discuss with the Joint Chiefs of Staff plans and preparations for possible *imminent* U.S. initiation of tactical or strategic nuclear warfare, in the midst of an ongoing non-nuclear conflict or crisis.

This general proposition is, I know, unfamiliar, startling, on its face highly implausible. To make it less so, I list below most of the actual nuclear crises that can now be documented for the last half of the twentieth century; this is followed by a discussion of more recent instances of nuclear *threats* from George W. Bush to Donald J. Trump.*

1. Hiroshima and Nagasaki, August 1945 (with the threat and readiness to drop more until the Japanese surrendered).

2. Truman's deployment of B-29s, officially described as "atomic-capable," to bases in Britain and Germany at the outset of the

---

*Endnotes present the more accessible references, generally after decades of secrecy and denial, from memoirs and other public sources to recently declassified documents.

Berlin blockade, June 1948 (critical, in the eyes of the administration, to Soviet failure to challenge the blockade in the air).

3. Truman's press conference warning that atomic weapons were under active consideration (as they actually were), November 30, 1950, for Korea after China entered the war.

4. Eisenhower's secret nuclear threats against China to force and maintain a settlement in Korea in 1953.

5. Secretary of State Dulles's secret offers to French foreign minister Bidault of two (possibly three) tactical nuclear weapons in 1954 to relieve the French troops besieged by the Indochinese at Dien Bien Phu.

6. Internal agreement under Eisenhower and Dulles during the first Quemoy crisis of September 1954–April 1955 that nuclear weapons would be necessary as a last resort to defend the offshore islands of Quemoy and Matsu, communicated to the Chinese by numerous statements and moves that led, in Dulles's opinion, to the negotiated resolution of the crisis.

7. "Diplomatic use of the Bomb" (Nixon's description) to deter Soviet unilateral action against the British and French in the Suez crisis of 1956.

8. Eisenhower's secret directive to the Joint Chiefs during the Lebanon crisis in 1958 to prepare to use nuclear weapons, if necessary, to prevent an Iraqi move into the oil fields of Kuwait.

9. Eisenhower's secret directive to the Joint Chiefs in 1958 to plan to use nuclear weapons against China if the Chinese Communists attempted to invade Quemoy.

10. The 1958–59 Berlin crisis.

11. The 1961–62 Berlin crisis.

12. The Cuban missile crisis, 1962.

13. Numerous "shows of nuclear force" involving demonstrative deployments or alerts—deliberately visible to adversaries and intended as a "nuclear signal"—of forces with a designated role in U.S. plans for strategic nuclear war.

14. Much public discussion in newspapers and in the Senate of (correct) reports that President Johnson had been advised by the JCS of the possible necessity of nuclear weapons to defend Marines surrounded at Khe Sanh, Vietnam, 1968.[†]

15. Secret threats by Nixon officials to deter Soviet attack on Chinese nuclear capability, 1969–70.

16. Nixon's secret threats of massive escalation, including the possible use of nuclear weapons, conveyed to the North Vietnamese by Henry Kissinger, 1969–72.

17. Threats and nuclear-capable naval deployment in 1971 to deter (according to Nixon) a Soviet response to possible Chinese intervention against India in the Indo-Pakistani war, but possibly also, or mainly, to deter India from further military pressure on Pakistan.

18. Nixon's NSC put SAC on high alert in October 1973 to deter the Soviets from intervening unilaterally with ground forces to separate the combatants in the Arab-Israeli war, by underscoring U.S. threats to oppose them by force and expressing U.S. willingness to risk escalation to all-out nuclear war.

19. President Ford placed nuclear weapons on DEFCON 3 alert on August 19, 1976, in response to the "tree-trimming incident," a fatal skirmish in the demilitarized zone; with a U.S. show of force threatening possible use of nuclear weapons, including flying B-52 bombers "from Guam ominously north up the Yellow Sea on a vector directly to . . . Pyongyang."

20. "The Carter Doctrine on the Middle East," January 1980, as explained (below) by Defense Secretary Harold Brown, Assistant Secretary of State William Dyess, and other spokesmen.

21. Serious White House and JCS consideration, in August 1980, of the possible imminent use of tactical nuclear weapons if a secret Soviet buildup on the Iranian border led to a Soviet invasion of Iran, followed by the expression of explicit, secret nuclear warnings to the Soviet Union (a hidden episode, spelled out in a professional military journal and by articles in the *New York Times*, that remains virtually unknown to the U.S. public and even scholars, though presidential press secretary Jody Powell was quoted as describing it as "the most serious nuclear crisis since the Cuban missile crisis").[†]

22. The Carter Doctrine reaffirmed in essence, including its nuclear component, by President Reagan in January 1981.

23. Formal threats by the George H. W. Bush administration of possible U.S. nuclear response to various possible "unconscionable actions" by Iraq in Operation Desert Storm in January 1991.

24. Explicit, secret threats by the Clinton administration of nuclear use against North Korea in 1995 on its nuclear reactor program (following the near-launch of an American conventional attack in 1994).[†]

25. Public warning of a nuclear option by Clinton's secretary of defense William Perry against Libya's Tarhuna underground chemical weapons facility in 1996.[†]

It follows from this listing (and more recent threats discussed below) that there has been no seventy-year moratorium on the active consideration and use of nuclear threats to support "atomic diplomacy." Whatever the inhibitions about pulling the trigger—and the record suggests that these have been strong, even in stalemated wars like Korea and Vietnam—there is no basis whatever for speaking of a "taboo" against nuclear weapons' use, whether in threats or actual attacks. Contrary to what has often been said about nuclear weapons, there is no "tradition of non-*use*." It is fair to say that, to our extreme good fortune, there has been a long tradition of no nuclear *attacks*.

For whatever reasons, and without doubt varying ones, none of the nuclear threats or plans above since 1945 have been carried out. Does that mean they were all either bluffs or successes? Almost surely, some of them were conscious bluffs. Some others, hard to know. However, on the basis of finally released internal discussions, I definitely do not believe all of them were bluffs, in particular for Eisenhower and Nixon. I'm glad that no experience proved that to be correct. But presence on the list above reflects no judgment as to whether the president definitely intended to carry out the threat or plan "if necessary," or what he would actually have done if a threat were defied. Evidence on these matters often does exist, but it varies in strength and in no case is it conclusive one way or another; these are questions that even the presidents might find it hard to answer to themselves.

Were some successful? There's no way to know for sure. In some cases, the adversary may never have intended to act otherwise than they did; in others, there may have been a change of course for reasons entirely unrelated to the nuclear warning. Still, in several cases it is at least plausible that the threats were effective. What is more relevant here is that most of these threats were *seen* by some high administration officials as effective, whether or not their adversaries would corroborate this conclusion.

For example, fatefully, this was true of the second example in the list above, when Truman sent B-29s, publicized at the time as "atomic bombers," to Britain early in the 1948 Berlin blockade. This was almost surely a conscious bluff; the bombers initially sent had not been modified to carry atomic weapons, and none of the bombs in our relatively small arsenal then were outside the United States. But cabinet officials under Truman concluded, rightly or wrongly, that the Soviets' failure to accompany their ground blockade by cutting off our aerial resupply of West Berlin (commanded by General Curtis LeMay) with Soviet fighter planes or antiaircraft artillery based in East Germany was due to the threat represented by the B-29s, like the two that LeMay had recently sent over Hiroshima and Nagasaki. As historian Gregg Herken puts it,

> Even [Secretary of State George] Marshall—who throughout the year had been concerned that the United States not "provoke" the Russians into military action—now expressed optimism for the future. His change in attitude had been partly motivated, he confided to [Secretary of Defense James] Forrestal, by his belief that "the Soviets are beginning to realize for the first time that the United would really use the atomic bomb against them in the event of war."

Later, when Khrushchev renewed threats of blockade of West Berlin in 1958–59 and again in 1961–62, the American arsenal of now-thermonuclear weapons was no longer limited, and thousands of them were in Europe. It seems inescapable that the prolonged frustration of Khrushchev's desire to change the status of West Berlin, surrounded by Soviet divisions, must be attributed to his fear that military moves to force this risked at least the possibility of nuclear war. But the price of this particular undoubted success in keeping West Berlin from coming under the control of the Soviet satellite regime that surrounded it was the construction and maintenance of an American Doomsday Machine, eventually evoking a comparable Soviet/Russian machine, with the continuous possibility, to this day, that one or both will end most human life on earth.

What I wish to focus on here is that several presidents *believed* their threats had succeeded; and *all* of them since 1945 have acted throughout their time in office *as if* they believed that current or future first-use nuclear threats would be legitimate, could be effective, and might be necessary. That is true even of those who may have personally and privately abhorred the notion of launching nuclear weapons under any circumstances—I believe this includes John F. Kennedy and Lyndon B. Johnson (along with Robert McNamara, who served both as secretary of defense), and probably others—but who have felt obliged, partly from their personal experience in office and partly from pressure by foreign policy elites, some allies, and potential domestic rivals, to maintain and increase the credibility and effectiveness of nuclear *threats* they or others might make in the future.

In his State of the Union address in 1984, Ronald Reagan advanced the resounding and profoundly true proposition that "A nuclear war cannot be won and must never be fought." What he did not say, and like every other president, never acted as if he meant, was, "A nuclear war must never be *threatened*, or prepared for." Preparation for preemption or for carrying out threats of first use or first strike remains the essence of the "modernization" program for strategic nuclear weapons for the last seventy years—prospectively being extended by Presidents Obama and Trump to one hundred years—that has continuously benefited our military-industrial-congressional complex.

The felt political need to *profess*, at least, to believe that the ability to make and carry out nuclear threats is essential to U.S. national security and to our leadership in our alliances is why every single president has refused to make a formal "no-first-use" (NFU) commitment. They have rejected it when it has been urged, repeatedly, by China—which announced its own NFU commitment at the time of its first test in 1964, as did India at its second test in 1998—and by the Soviet Union from 1982 until 1993. In particular, Mikhail Gorbachev, on October 5, 1991, in what proved to be his last months in office, reiterated this commitment and proposed the United States join it, only to have it rejected, as usual, by the Bush administration, though a number of his other proposals on that day were accepted.

Likewise, the United States has tenaciously resisted the pleas of most other nations in the world to make a NFU pledge as an essential basis for stopping proliferation, including at the Nonproliferation Treaty Extension Conference in 1995 and the Review Conferences since 2000. Moreover, the United States has demanded that NATO continue to legitimize first-use threats by basing its own strategy on them, even after the USSR and the Warsaw Pact had dissolved (and most of the former Pact members had joined NATO). Yet this stubborn stance—along with actual threats of possible U.S. nuclear first use in more recent confrontations with Iraq, North Korea, and Iran—virtually precludes effective leadership by the United States (and perhaps anyone else) in delegitimizing and averting further proliferation and even imitation of U.S. use of nuclear weapons.

Few Americans are aware of the extent to which the United States and NATO first-use doctrine has long isolated the United States and its close allies morally and politically from world opinion. Nor are they familiar with the sharpness of the language used by large majorities in the U.N. General Assembly in resolutions condemning the first-use policies on which NATO has long based its planning and the readiness to initiate nuclear war expressed or demonstrated by every U.S. president since Truman.

U.N. Resolution 36/100, the Declaration on the Prevention of Nuclear Catastrophe, was adopted on December 9, 1981, in the wake of Reagan's endorsement of the 1980 Carter Doctrine—openly extending U.S. first-use threats to the Persian Gulf—which this resolution directly contradicted and implicitly condemned. It declares in its preamble: "Any doctrine allowing the first use of nuclear weapons and any actions pushing the world toward a catastrophe are incompatible with human moral standards and the lofty ideals of the UN."

The body of U.N. Resolution 36/100 declares: "States and statesmen that resort first to nuclear weapons will be committing the gravest crime against humanity. There will never be any justification or pardon for statesmen who take the decision to be the first to use nuclear weapons." Eighty-two nations voted in favor of this declaration. Forty-one, under heavy pressure from the United States, abstained; nineteen opposed it, including the United States, Israel, and most NATO member nations.

To say that some of the threats by the U.S. government of what the majority of nations have identified as "the gravest crime against humanity" were only implicit, as in the case of the Carter Doctrine, generally applies only to statements by the presidents themselves, who rarely spell out the nuclear nature of a threat in full explicitness even when the warning is public. That job is left to aides, other officials, and especially to journalists to whom the "real meaning" of the policy statements and deployments is authoritatively leaked. A good illustration of this was in January 1981, when Carter's outgoing secretary of defense, Harold Brown, told interviewers—in words reiterated by President Reagan a month later—that what would keep Russia (which had invaded Afghanistan in late

1979) from moving into northern Iran or other parts of the Middle East in the 1980s was "the risk of World War III." (Warning signals like these from the Reagan administration in 1981 evoked U.N. Resolution 36/100 later that year.)

But although President Carter, unlike Reagan, had not used such language explicitly a year earlier in his State of the Union message announcing his "doctrine" for the Middle East, there had been no lack of corroborating elucidations of the nuclear component to the policy. In the weeks before and after the speech, the White House almost jammed Washington talk shows and major newspaper pages with authorized leaks, backgrounders, and official spokesmen all carrying the message that the president's commitment to use "any means necessary, including military force" against a further Soviet move into the Persian Gulf region was, at its heart, a threat of possible initiation of tactical nuclear warfare by the United States.

Just after Carter's speech on January 23, 1980, Richard Burt of the *New York Times* (later a high Reagan official) was shown a secret Pentagon study, "the most extensive military study of the region ever done by the government," which lay behind the president's warning. It concluded, as he summarized it, "that the American forces could not stop a Soviet thrust into northern Iran and that the United States should therefore consider using 'tactical' nuclear weapons in any conflict there." (I well remember from my days at the RAND Corporation that classified simulation war games there in 1959–60 had all reached exactly this same conclusion.)

The 1979 study in question was known in the Pentagon as the Wolfowitz Report. (Yes, *that* Wolfowitz—Paul D.; at the time a deputy assistant secretary of defense for regional programs under President Carter; later, as deputy secretary of defense in 2001–5 under President George W. Bush, a promoter and mastermind of the invasion of Iraq.) Reportedly, the Wolfowitz study contemplated "delivering tactical nuclear warheads by cruise missiles fired from ships in the Indian Ocean."

For all the talk and posturing, for all the military analyses, plans, and recommendations, even the deployments listed above, the question remained in 1980, as before and after: Could the Russians, could anyone, come to believe that the president of the United States, if challenged, might really *carry out* such nuclear threats, accepting the prospects at best—if the war, improbably, stayed regionally limited—of annihilating the local population along with the opposing troops? Was it really conceivable that an American president could choose to order such a massacre?

It was the official function of William Dyess, assistant secretary of state for public information, to interpret Carter's meaning to the public in the week following the speech, and to address just these questions. In an arresting exchange on television one day after Burt's leak of the Pentagon study, Dyess answered both questions crisply and correctly:

> Q: In nuclear war are we committed not to make the first strike?
>
> DYESS: No sir.
>
> Q: We could conceivably make an offensive . . .
>
> DYESS: We make no comment on that whatsoever, but the Soviets know that this terrible weapon has been dropped on human beings twice in history and it was an American president who dropped it both times. Therefore, they have to take this into consideration in their calculus.

The Soviets could indeed be counted on to remember those two attacks vividly. From August 6, 1945, on, they had believed, with good reason, that these first uses of atomic weapons had been aimed for purposes of intimidation at themselves as much as at the Japanese. And beyond this, they also knew better than most a good deal about subsequent past uses of U.S. nuclear weapons. The Soviets (unlike the American public) knew this because they were made to know it by American officials—sometimes by explicit threats from the Oval Office, even when White House consideration of the use of nuclear weapons was secret from other audiences—since they or their allies or client states were the intended targets of these preparations and warnings.

Moreover, the Soviets recalled that the U.S. Strategic Air Command was established in early 1946 with the function of delivering nuclear attacks on Russia when so directed, at a time when it was publicly proclaimed by the president and high military that the Soviet Union was not expected to possess operational nuclear weapon systems for a decade or longer. SAC's *only* mission in that initial period—which included the formation of NATO—was to threaten or carry out a U.S. first strike against the Soviet Union (possibly to protect Middle East oil, as well as Berlin and Western Europe). It was not at all to deter or retaliate for a nuclear attack on the United States or anywhere else, which was not then a physical possibility.

It is not the Russians but the rest of us who need to learn these hidden realities of the nuclear dimension to U.S. foreign policy. As the last three examples in the list above indicate, from the nineties, that dimension did not disappear with the ending of the Cold War. Nor did it end with the twentieth century. Let us turn to the present one.

In 2005–2006 there were articles by the Pulitzer Prize–winning journalist Seymour Hersh and the former CIA station chief Philip Giraldi regarding U.S. contingency plans, on the directive of Vice President Richard Cheney, for a "large-scale air assault on Iran employing both conventional and tactical nuclear weapons."† On April 10, President George W. Bush described Hersh's *New Yorker* article, which had appeared that day, as "wild speculation." But on April 18, 2006, the following exchange took place in a presidential press conference, reflecting the international commentary that Hersh's report about nuclear planning aroused†:

> REPORTER: Sir, when you talk about Iran, and you talk about how you have diplomatic efforts, you also say all options are on the table. Does that include the possibility of a nuclear strike? Is that something that your administration will plan for?
>
> PRESIDENT BUSH [*emphatically*]: *All options* are on the table.

From that time on, that formula as used by others about responses to Iran's nuclear program lacked ambiguity. Others who used it during the 2008 presidential campaign included the three leading Democratic candidates for the presidency, Hillary Clinton, Barack Obama, and John Edwards;† and five of the nine Republican candidates taking part in a debate televised by CNN on June 5, 2007: Rudolph Giuliani, Governor Mitt Romney, Congressman Duncan Hunter, Virginia governor James Gilmore, and Senator John McCain. (Representative Ron Paul, at 1 percent in the polls, alone rejected it heatedly, as did, on the Democratic side, Representative Dennis Kucinich, also a 1 percenter.)

The question the Republicans were asked was "their readiness to authorize a preemptive nuclear attack on Iran if that was what it would take to prevent the Islamic Republic from having a nuclear bomb"; their repetition of the slogan about keeping options on the table was in specific response to questions about tactical nuclear weapons. Although no one noticed, except perhaps the Iranians, in taking this position they were supporting the president's *use* of our nuclear weapons in his "negotiations" with Iran.

Nor did his Democratic opponents (except for Kucinich) fail to support this use. It was reported that when the Democratic front-runner in August 2007, Hillary Clinton, was first told that her rival Barack Obama had taken the nuclear option *off* the table for attacking *Pakistan*, a "slight smile" crossed her face before she moved in confidently for the kill. So far in the campaign she had been charging Obama with being too naïve and inexperienced to be trusted with the presidency, and, as she realized immediately, he had just proved her point.

Obama had been asked by an AP reporter whether there was any circumstance in which he would be prepared or willing to use nuclear weapons in Afghanistan and Pakistan to defeat terrorism and al-Qaeda leader Osama bin Laden. As *USA Daily* reported, "'I think it would be a profound mistake for us to use nuclear weapons in any circumstance,' Obama said, with a pause, 'involving civilians.' Then he quickly added, 'Let me scratch that. There's been no discussion of nuclear weapons. That's not on the table.' . . . When asked whether his answer also applied to the possible use of tactical nuclear weapons, he said it did." (He meant for Afghanistan and Pakistan. He had elsewhere kept it on the table for Iran, like Clinton and John Edwards.) The AP account continued:

> Clinton chided her fellow senator about addressing hypotheticals.
>
> "Presidents should be very careful at all times in discussing the use or non-use of nuclear weapons . . . I don't believe any president should make any blanket statements with respect to the use or non-use of nuclear weapons," Clinton said.

So what was obvious to the then front-runner in 2007—along with the generally agreed feeling that she had won this round—is that a real president, or someone qualified to be one, would not "telegraph" that he or she *would not* use tactical nuclear weapons in unilateral operations against guerrillas inside the territory of a politically unstable, nuclear-armed ally. Indeed, as Reuters paraphrased Hillary Clinton as saying in this exchange, "presidents *never* take the nuclear option off the table." [emphasis added]

That is undoubtedly what she meant to convey. And it is, simply, a correct statement about American presidents in the nuclear era, all of them so far.

That holds not only for presidents, but also for aspirants to that office, including ambitious members of Congress. No major candidate in either party has ever been willing to undercut a current or future president's "bargaining hand" by insisting that *initiating* or *threatening to initiate* a nuclear attack is *not* a *legitimate* "option" for the president of the United States or for any other national leader—for example, Vladimir Putin.

This record was upheld in the most recent presidential campaign in 2016, during which Donald J. Trump's repeated refusal to reject the option of first use occasioned considerable unfavorable comment, even consternation. Some interlocutors almost begged him to do so, in particular Chris Matthews, in a town forum he was moderating in Green Bay, Wisconsin, on March 30, 2016:

> MATTHEWS: Can you tell the Middle East we're not using a nuclear weapon on anybody?
>
> TRUMP: I would never say that. I would never take any of my cards off the table.
>
> MATTHEWS: How about Europe? We won't use it in Europe?
>
> TRUMP: I—I'm not going to take it off the table.
>
> MATTHEWS: You might use it in Europe?
>
> [*LAUGHTER*]
>
> TRUMP: No, I don't think so. But I'm not taking . . .
>
> MATTHEWS: Well, *just say it.* "*I will never use a nuclear weapon in Europe.*"
>
> TRUMP: I am not—I am not taking cards off the table.
>
> MATTHEWS: OK.
>
> TRUMP: I'm not going to use nuclear, but I'm not taking any cards off the table.

Matthews's pursuit of this issue, like that of nearly every other interviewer, seemed to reflect the simple, widespread ignorance of the reality that Trump was taking the same position of every president since Truman, and of every major candidate in that long period, definitely including his rival Hillary Clinton. She would surely have given essentially the same answers to Matthews's questions as Trump did if she had been in that same forum, consistent with her stand in 2007. No candidate or president has ever come close to adopting and proclaiming a no-first-use policy (with Barack Obama being the only president to encourage serious internal consideration of it, especially in his last year, before rejecting it in face of opposition from his secretaries of defense, state, and energy and certain allies).

Granted, other major candidates and presidents taking the same position have aroused less unease than Donald Trump, who, along with being unusually volatile and thin-skinned, has explicitly embraced a deliberate penchant for unpredictability, evident not only during the campaign but also while president. That was already on display in his exchange in March 2016 with Chris Matthews. On the one hand, he said, "I would be very, very slow and hesitant to pull that trigger." But he followed that by asking, moments later, "Somebody hits us within ISIS, you wouldn't fight back with a nuke?"

Similarly, he said a bit further on, "I'd be the last one to use the nuclear weapon." The assurance that might have provided was undercut by the sentence (widely known to be untruthful) that immediately preceded it: "I opposed Iraq." Or this: "Look, nuclear should be off the table. But would there be a time when it could be used, possibly, possibly?" And if not, as Matthews's response seemed to suggest, "Then why are we making them? Why do we make them?"

Many mocked him for that question, though it seems a fair one. Many others shuddered at the implication that Donald Trump, presiding over a trillion-dollar makeover of our entire nuclear arsenal that he inherited as a program from Barack Obama, might feel that he could actually use some of these weapons. But *of course* he planned to use them, as he had clearly implied to Chris Matthews. He wants to use them like every other president: in "negotiation," in *threats*, in exploiting uncertainty in our opponents as to whether he might launch "a nuke" in a stalemated armed conflict or a crisis, or perhaps in pique at what he experienced as humiliating provocation. Whether he would carry out such threats in any given circumstances, or otherwise use them in attacks, remains as uncertain, and as possible, as it has been for every other president in the nuclear era.

Trump hinted strongly to Matthews, and he even came close to saying outright—"I'm not going to use nuclear, but I'm not taking any cards off the table"—that he would be bluffing. Most, if not all, of the time.

Nevertheless, the last bargaining strategy mentioned above,[†] advertising and exploiting his own unpredictability, deliberately creating uncertainty in an adversary by demonstrating impulsive, erratic, vindictive behavior—reminiscent, to many observers, of Nixon's madman theory—is especially worrisome to many in America and elsewhere because of a growing sense that this particular president actually may *be* mad.

There's ample evidence supporting that impression. Still, in some ways he has shown himself to be crazy like a fox, or he would not be president. He may yet elude his domestic pursuers and survive in office, and we and our democracy might survive that too. Or not.

Yet what seems to me beyond question is that any social system (not only ours) that has created and maintained a Doomsday Machine and has put a trigger to it, including first use of nuclear weapons, in the hands of one human being—anyone, not just this man, still worse in the hands of an unknown number of persons—*is in core aspects mad.* Ours is such a system. We are in the grip of institutionalized madness.

There is nothing new about that in human affairs. Among the aphorisms in *Beyond Good and Evil*, Friedrich Nietzsche wrote: "Madness in individuals is something rare; but in groups, parties, nations and epochs, it is the rule." We Americans do have an unusual individual in the White House at this time. But both our parties, many nations, and this epoch are on track with Nietzsche's rule. In the nuclear era, that means that we humans—above all, the nuclear weapons states and their allies—pose an imminent danger of near-extinction to ourselves and to most other terrestrial species.

That ultimate outcome is threatened above all, as revealed by the nuclear winter studies, by the arsenals and policies of the two nuclear superpowers. Let me focus on our own country's stance, as expounded by all major candidates in recent elections.

First, it should be self-evident that so long as the U.S. government seeks to maintain the credibility of its first-use nuclear threats—both in declarations and more importantly by maintaining and "modernizing" a first-strike capability aimed at Russia that supports that credibility but endangers most life—it cannot even participate in, let alone lead, a truly significant disarmament process or a campaign to delegitimize nuclear weapons' possession and use. And without U.S. leadership—requiring a *reversal of course* by our government—no significant reduction in the danger to humanity from nuclear weapons can occur.

Yet what is at issue here is more than the practical benefits of joining in the broad international consensus against initiating nuclear war, though that would seem urgent enough. It is important as well to regain a grasp of what might be called moral reality, a human perspective that transcends insiders' obsession with agency, service, party, or national advantage. Plans and doctrines for the use of nuclear weapons, and reflexive, systemic resistance to the goal of eliminating them, raise questions about who we are—as a nation, as citizens, as a species—and what we have been doing and risking, what we have a right to do, or an obligation to do, and what we should not do.

Speaking personally, I have always shared President George W. Bush's blanket condemnation, under all circumstances, of terrorism, commonly defined as the deliberate slaughter of noncombatants—unarmed civilians, children and infants, the old and the sick—for a political purpose. On its face, that position is hardly controversial. Thus, for example, the destruction of the World Trade Center buildings with their inhabitants on September 11, 2001, was rightly recognized as a terrorist action and condemned as mass murder by most of the world.

But in contrast, most Americans have never recognized as "terrorist" in precisely the same sense the firestorms caused deliberately by U.S. firebombing of Tokyo or Dresden or Hamburg or the atomic bombing of Hiroshima. These deliberate massacres of civilians, though not prosecuted after World War II like the Japanese slaughter in China at Nanking, were by any prior or reasonable criteria war crimes, wartime terrorism, crimes against humanity.

Just like the bombs that destroyed Hiroshima and Nagasaki, any future attack by a single tactical nuclear weapon near a densely populated area would kill tens to hundreds of thousands of noncombatants, as those did. Thus, virtually any threat of first use of a nuclear weapon is a terrorist threat. Any nation making such threats is a terrorist nation. That means the United States and all its allies, including Israel, along with Russia, Pakistan, and North Korea.

Indeed, going infinitely beyond any concept of terrorism or criminality, it is not merely a moral danger but a moral catastrophe that both Russia and America (with its NATO allies) are still threatening, deploying tactical nuclear weapons, carrying out exercises to execute first-use nuclear attacks against an opposing nuclear superpower "if necessary," and implying readiness to impose on the rest of humanity a near-certainty of escalation to nuclear winter and omnicide. Speaking as an American, that must cease to be the case for the United States, and it cannot wait on others or, as of 2017, come too soon.

To recover fundamental moral bearings, as well as to move urgently toward preserving human civilization and other life on this planet, the U.S. government—including the president, officials, and Congress, pressed by a popular movement and preferably backed by binding congressional legislation—should announce decisively that *there is no "nuclear first-use option" on the bargaining table* in our dealings with Russia, Iran, China, North Korea, or any other nation, because we as a people and our government recognize that nuclear first use would be a murderous, criminal action, not a legitimate "option" for the United States, Russia, or for any other country under any circumstances.

CHAPTER 21

Dismantling the Doomsday Machine

One way the RAND Corporation compensated the Air Force for the virtually complete freedom it had granted us to pursue our own self-generated research was for us to respond promptly whenever it occasionally asked us to evaluate some proposal from within the service. In 1960 my RAND secretary delivered a proposal from the Air Force for me to assess. It was, as usual, a photocopy of an original typed memo with, I believe, the title "Project Retro" from an Air Force officer. It had already gone through a number of Air Force offices. That was indicated by check marks and initials on a routing chart that was stamped on the first page, recording that it had been seen and in some way acted on by many of the agencies on the chart, Research and Development, Plans, Science and Technology, and so forth.

There was also the usual routing chart within RAND. I seemed to be among the first in the building to see it, though it wasn't obviously in my line—at first glance, it appeared to be more in the province of engineering—but I was known to be among those who were preoccupied with problems of SAC vulnerability to a Soviet surprise attack and the ability of our offensive forces to survive and retaliate.

It was a classified proposal to deal with the possibility that a Soviet attack with ICBMs could eliminate our capability to retaliate with land-based missiles, primarily Minuteman ICBMs. This was in mid-1960, before the exposure of the missile-gap myth. I had been at RAND full-time for about a year, working on problems precisely like this.

This scheme proposed in some detail to assemble a huge rectangular array of one thousand first-stage Atlas engines—our largest rocket propulsion engines, except for Titans, of which we had only a few—to be fastened securely to the earth in a horizontal position, facing in a direction opposite to the rotation of the earth.

The officer originating this proposal envisioned that if our Ballistic Missile Early Warning System (BMEWS) radars detected and reported on the huge viewing screens at NORAD a large flight of missile warheads coming across the North Pole from the Soviet Union—aimed at our missile fields in North and South Dakota, Wyoming, Montana, and Missouri—the array of Atlas engines would be fired, as near simultaneously as possible, to stop the earth's rotation momentarily.

The Soviet missiles, on their inertial path, would thus bypass or overfly their intended targets. Our land-based retaliatory force would be saved, to carry out—presumably, when things had settled down and earth was again spinning normally—a retaliatory attack against the cities and soft military targets (their missiles having already left their hardened silos) in the Soviet Union.

You didn't have to be a geophysicist, which I wasn't, to see some defects with this scheme. An awful lot of stuff would be flying through the air. Everything, in fact, that wasn't nailed down, and most of what was as well, would be gone with the wind, which would itself be flying at super-hurricane force everywhere at once. Cities on the coasts and beyond would be wiped out by giant tsunamis as the oceans redeployed onto the continents.

The Minuteman launch control officers, safe in their capsules deep underground, would have even less reason than in the foreseeable conditions of nuclear war either to launch their missiles or to come aboveground, since there would be nothing left to destroy on the surface of the Soviet Union, or the United States, or anywhere else on the planet. All structures would have collapsed, with the rubble along with all the people joining the wind and the water in their horizontal movement across the face of the earth, into space.

All this was obvious enough. My first thought was, "Pretty funny." It was the only piece of paper I had seen from the Air Force bureaucracy that showed a sense of humor. Even better, it was done perfectly straight, with no hint that it was anything but an ordinary secret official document. It looked absolutely authentic. I gave whoever had originated it (a RAND jokester?) credit.

Then I looked again at the routing slip from the Air Force. It really did appear to have gone through a number of relevant official agencies and been passed on. Half the boxes were unchecked—it hadn't gone to those divisions—but half acknowledged receipt. The signed initials were all different and looked real. No one had stopped it before it was sent to RAND, and I realized it was not a joke.

I remember sitting at my desk, looking at that document, and asking myself, for the first time: *"Could I be in the wrong line of work?"*

I did show it to a couple of RAND colleagues to see if they had the same reaction. They both were dismissive of the scheme. One engineer made some rough calculations on the back of an envelope (RAND engineers really did do this literally on occasion, though there was a blackboard in every room) and said after a few minutes, "One thousand Atlas engines wouldn't do it."

Another, a physicist, said, as I recall, "If you could actually muster enough power to stop the rotation for a second or so, it's more likely that the earth's surface would rupture from its core. The planet might break up." Yes, Project Retro could surely be filed under "Crazy."

But the truth, in retrospect, was that most of the documents I read in my national security work, including many of those I wrote myself, were only marginally, if at all, less unbalanced than Project Retro. "Unbalanced" here being a euphemism for crazy, criminally insane.

True, only Project Retro would have had the effect of wiping the surface of the earth clean of human structures, humanity, and all other terrestrial species, and dispersing the creatures of the lakes and ocean deeps to dry out, eventually, on what remained of the land.

But, as I would soon discover, the Joint Chiefs' estimates of the effects of carrying out their first strike plans, under a variety of circumstances, foresaw killing more than half a billion humans with our own weapons in a matter of months, with most of them dead in a day or two.

How to describe that, other than insanity? Should the Pentagon officials and their subordinates have been institutionalized? But that was precisely the problem: they already were. Their institutions not only promoted this insanity, they demanded it. And still do. As do comparable institutions in Russia.

RAND analysts, of whom I was one, sought to bring about less insane planning for nuclear war. We failed. That was in part because the civilian officials we were advising found it hard to get the military to adopt our proposals. But, in retrospect, our proposed strategies were totally unrealistic—as crazy as SIOP-62, SAC's own plan in 1961. Or almost as crazy. Simply improving on current SAC war plans—the secret goal that a generation of RAND analysts, from Bernard Brodie to Kaufmann to me set themselves—was far too low a bar, and still held us prisoners within the realm of madness. If RAND recommendations, including my own, had been implemented by SAC in an actual nuclear war—in the way that SAC proceeded to interpret them and execute them operationally—they would still have resulted in total global catastrophe.

To be quite plain here, I am talking about the madness of the strategy and planning I personally laid out in the spring of 1961: my draft adopted word for word by Secretary of Defense Robert McNamara as his official guidance to the JCS for their operational planning for general nuclear war. I didn't question the appropriateness and need for damage-limiting counterforce strikes against military targets. SAC planners never had any problem identifying enough "military" targets—hundreds, actually—within or in the vicinity of Moscow and *all* other cities that a presidential decision at the onset of central war to "withhold" attacks on command and control or on cities—in the interests of "intrawar deterrence," "bargaining," terminating the war, or simply limiting civilian casualties—would have been entirely vitiated. The results from either a preemptive or a retaliatory U.S. attack supposedly based on "my" guidance for "coercive war" would have been indistinguishable from those of SIOP-62.[†]

That was what Nixon and Kissinger found they had inherited from Johnson and McNamara, when they were introduced in 1969 to estimates of eighty to ninety million deaths from immediate effects of the "smallest" attacks available to them. Obviously these estimates reflected attacks that burned all the major urban areas, even when population was not targeted "*per se.*" (No one knew then that these firestorms would cause global nuclear winter, as had actually been true not only in the sixties but ever since large numbers of atomic bombs had become available in the early fifties for use against cities.)

Both the predicted results and the actual, unrecognized climatic effects remained at these same catastrophic levels when Nixon and Kissinger left office, and throughout the Cold War, despite efforts as delusional and abortive as mine and McNamara's by defense secretaries and their aides under Ford, Carter, and Reagan to compel SAC to provide operational plans for "limited nuclear options" in war with the Soviet Union.

Not that I or anyone else would ever have been blamed for the omnicidal results if our plans were actually carried out, in the way and on the scale that SAC prepared to carry them out. No one would be left to hold anyone accountable, since the result would have been the near extinction of our species.

*   *   *

Here is what we know now: the United States and Russia each have an actual Doomsday Machine. It is not the same relatively cheap system that Herman Kahn envisioned (or Stanley Kubrick portrayed), with their warheads buried deep and set to explode in their own territories, producing deadly global fallout. But a counterpart nevertheless exists for each country: a very expensive system of men, machines, electronics, communications, institutions, plans, training, discipline, practices, and doctrine—which, under conditions of electronic warning, external conflict, or expectations of attack, would with unknowable but possibly high probability bring about the global destruction of civilization and of nearly all human life on earth.

These two systems still risk doomsday: both are still on hair-trigger alert that makes their joint existence unstable. They are susceptible to being triggered on a false alarm, a terrorist action, unauthorized launch, or a desperate decision to escalate. They would kill billions of humans, perhaps ending complex life on earth. This is true even though the Cold War that rationalized their existence and hair-trigger status—and their supposed necessity to national security—ended thirty years ago.

Does the United States still need a Doomsday Machine? Does Russia? Did they ever?

Does the existence of such a capability serve any national or international interest whatsoever to a degree that would justify its obvious danger to human life?

I ask the questions not merely rhetorically. They deserve sober, reflective consideration. The answers do seem obvious, but so far as I know they have never been addressed. There follows another question: Does any nation on earth have a *right to possess* such a capability? A right to threaten—by its simple possession of that capability—the continued existence of all other nations and their populations, their cities, and civilization as a whole?

Robert F. Kennedy's *Thirteen Days*, based on his personal diaries and recollection, offered an account of the Cuban missile crisis that he drafted in the summer and fall of 1967. RFK's murder in 1968 prevented him from rewriting and completing it prior to publication. At the end of the book, Theodore Sorensen, who edited the memoir, added this note:

> It was Senator Kennedy's intention to add a discussion of the basic ethical question involved [in the crisis]: what, if any, circumstance or justification gives this government or any government the moral right to bring its people and possibly all people under the shadow of nuclear destruction?

I know of no other occasion on which a former official, in or out of office, ever raised this particular question of moral right, whether in memos, internal discussions, or memoirs. But once posed in these terms, is it really so hard a question to answer?

Arguments made for the necessity or desirability of continued possession of *some* nuclear weapons by nuclear weapon states (NWS) do not remotely apply to maintaining doomsday arsenals on the massive scale of the superpowers—thousands of first-strike weapons each. That's true even when these pro-nuclear arguments do seem plausible to many as reasons for maintaining a small deterrent force.

Thus, for example: "You can't uninvent nuclear weapons." That has been a widespread and effective argument against a total unilateral abolition over the past seventy years. True, you can't eradicate the knowledge of how to make nuclear weapons and delivery systems. But you *can* *dismantle* a Doomsday Machine. And that, at minimum, is what we must hasten to do. There is no need or justification for us to wait for the Russians to do it to theirs first or in step with us, though that global imperative applies just as well to them.

This implies moving in the opposite direction from the programs of Presidents Obama, Trump, and Putin to reconstruct their entire machines, with their first-strike characteristics, with "modernized" replacement components.[†] In reality, such a program seems nothing other, in either country, than a further subsidy to the military-industrial-legislative complexes that each of them have or are: a boon to profits, jobs, votes, campaign donations (kickbacks). Good, solid, traditional political incentives, but very far from legitimate justifications for maintaining or rebuilding a Doomsday Machine.

No state ever set out intentionally to acquire a doomsday capability. Nor does the existence of one such machine compel or even create a tangible incentive for a rival or enemy to have one. In fact, having two on alert against each is far more dangerous for each and for the world than if only one existed. If the two existing machines were dismantled (in terms of their doomsday potential), there would never be any strategic rationale for anyone to reconstruct that capability, any more than there was a conscious intention in the first place.

The good news is that dismantling the Doomsday Machine in one country or both would be relatively simple in concept and in physical operation (though politically and bureaucratically incredibly difficult). It could be accomplished quickly, easily within a year. But it would mean—and here's where institutional resistance would be strong—giving up certain infeasible aims and illusory capabilities of our nuclear forces: in particular, the notion that it is possible to limit damage to the United States (or Russia) by means of a preemptive first strike, targeted on the adversary's land-based missiles, its command and control centers and communications, its leadership ("decapitation"), all other military targets and war-supporting resources, including urban-industrial centers, transportation, and energy.

In other words, it would mean totally discarding the present strategy and criteria for covering targets in our strategic nuclear war plans and discarding most of the forces deployed to carry out these aims and plans. This would mean dismantling *all* the land-based missile forces (Minuteman missiles), most or all strategic nuclear bombers, most of the current fourteen Trident submarines, and most of the warheads on remaining submarine-launched ballistic missiles in remaining Tridents.

Actually, there were sound, almost equally compelling reasons to dismantle all the above items no later than half a century ago, when the feasibility of a "damage-limiting" strike against a large Soviet force of hardened missile silos and sub-launched missiles became a delusion and hoax. That was true even before there was any awareness of the dire danger of triggering a nuclear winter.

But that potentially widespread awareness today gives every person, institution, and nation in the world an unprecedentedly compelling and urgent basis for demanding that such capabilities and planned "options" be immediately dismantled.

However low the probability might be of the United States or Russia carrying out its current strategic contingency plans against the other with the effect of causing nuclear winter and near human extinction, it never will be zero, so long as Doomsday Machines of the present type exist.

Just how high does such a risk have to be to make the prospect of it intolerable? What risk of nuclear winter happening—whether by panicked reaction or unstable leadership or unauthorized action—is "acceptable" as the price of maintaining our current strategic forces, and of any benefits that can supposedly be claimed for that? Five percent over the next forty years? One percent? Three in a million?

Why is anything other than *zero* remotely acceptable? Fortunately, it *can* be zero. The major risks could even be eliminated by executive decision alone, in constitutional principle: though in practice, politically, there would have to be considerable support for this in Congress and the public, and in the military-industrial complex, reluctant as the latter would be. Although Donald J. Trump seems more willing to use presidential power than his predecessor, even beyond constitutional limits, the likelihood has always been slim that he would use it in this direction, and now even less than before talk of impeachment commenced. The same appears to apply to Putin. Nevertheless, it is true for both superpowers: the current danger of Doomsday *could* be *eliminated* without the United States or Russia coming close to total nuclear disarmament, or the abandonment of nuclear deterrence, either unilaterally or mutually (desirable as the latter would be).

Just for contrast, the risk that one city will be destroyed by a single (perhaps terrorist) nuclear weapon in the next year or the next decade *cannot*, unfortunately, be reduced to zero. But the danger of near-extinction of humanity—a continuous possibility for the past sixty-five years—*can* be reduced to zero by dismantlement of most existing weapons in both the United States and Russia (and smaller dismantlement in all the other NWS).

This dismantlement of the Doomsday Machines is not intended as an adequate long-term substitute for more ambitious, necessary goals, including total universal abolition of nuclear weapons. We cannot accept the conclusion that abolition must be ruled out "for the foreseeable future" or put off for generations. There will not be a truly long-run human future without it. In particular, it seems more naïve than realistic to believe that large cities can coexist indefinitely with nuclear weapons. If human civilization in the form that emerged four thousand years ago (in Mesopotamia, Iraq) is to persist globally even another century or two, a way must be found to make the required transformations ultimately practical.

Thus, it is urgent for the nuclear weapon states to acknowledge the reality that they have been denying, and the non-nuclear weapon states have been proclaiming, for almost fifty years: that in the long run, and that time has arrived, effective nonproliferation is inescapably linked to nuclear disarmament. Eventually, indeed fairly soon, either all nations forgo the right to possess nuclear weapons indefinitely and to threaten others with them under any circumstances, or every nation will claim that right, and actual possession and use will be very widespread.

Abolition of nuclear weapons must come in stages, but if proliferation in the near future is to be averted, a real commitment to total abolition of nuclear weapons—banning and eliminating their use and possession— as the truly reigning international goal is no longer to be delayed or equivocated. We must begin now the effort to explore and to help bring about conditions that will make a world of zero nuclear weapons feasible. Thus, it is extremely deplorable that the nuclear weapons states and their allies, led by the United States, boycotted the recent negotiations at the United Nations toward a treaty banning nuclear weapons, even if none of them are yet ready to join the more than 120 nations that adopted the treaty on July 7, 2017.

But what I am proposing is an effort to mobilize international support for a shorter-run program to avert as quickly as possible an imminent and continuous threat to human survival. The logic of this program is relatively simple to comprehend. What needs to be done to reduce the danger is easily specified in terms of concrete steps.

The threat of full nuclear winter is posed by the possibility of all-out war between the United States and Russia. Since the end of the Cold War, probably the greatest remaining risk of this annihilating outcome is by a preemptive attack by one side or the other triggered by an electronic false alarm (which has repeatedly occurred on both sides) or an accidental detonation (which was a remote but real risk in a number of previous accidents).[†] The risk is not negligible of such an attack being triggered by an apocalyptic terrorist group, with the capability of creating a nuclear explosion in Washington or Moscow.

The danger that either a false alarm or a terrorist attack on Washington or Moscow would lead to a preemptive attack derives almost entirely from the existence on both sides of land-based missile forces, each vulnerable to attack by the other: each, therefore, kept on a high state of alert, ready to launch within minutes of warning.

The easiest and fastest way to reduce that risk—and indeed, the overall danger of nuclear war—is to dismantle entirely (not merely "de-alert") the Minuteman III missile force (currently scheduled for "refurbishment"[†]), the U.S. land-based leg of the nuclear "triad." Former secretary of defense William Perry has argued precisely that, as has James E. Cartwright, former commander of the Strategic Command and vice chairman of the JCS. A second stage would be to reduce the Trident submarine-based ballistic missiles (SLBM) force to give up its capability to target and destroy the entire Russian land-based missile force (on which the Russians choose to rely far more than does the United States). Having first deprived the Russians of their high-priority, time-urgent *targets* for those forces by dismantling the U.S. Minuteman silos and their control centers, the remaining incentive for the Russians to launch their ICBMs on warning—to avert their being destroyed by U.S. SLBMs—would be eliminated. Launch on warning would no longer be susceptible of being rationalized strategically on either side.

All of the above propositions apply with equal force to the current, vulnerable opposing offensive nuclear forces of India and Pakistan, with the potential global catastrophe of their mutual launch roughly half the scale of the full nuclear winter produced by a United States/Russian nuclear war. The world's interest in reducing these forces and avoiding their hair-trigger alert status—likewise for all currently expanding and "modernizing" nuclear arsenals—is wholly comparable and secondary only to the mutual confrontation of current superpower forces.

To suggest that these are relatively simple steps for the superpowers and others neglects the challenge of fundamentally altering the doctrine and strategy that have shaped the buildup of our strategic forces over the past sixty-five years. Contrary to public understanding, that strategy has not been a matter of deterrence of nuclear attack on the United States, but rather the illusionary one of improving first-strike capability. Specifically, this has involved the goal of "damage-limiting" to the United States in the event of a U.S. preemptive strike against Soviet/Russian nuclear capability, triggered by a warning of impending attack, possibly in the context of escalation of a conventional or limited nuclear war.

That strategy remains in force, although, as noted, the objective of limiting damage to the United States in large-scale nuclear war, or of keeping such a war with a nuclear state limited, has been essentially a hoax, infeasible to achieve for about fifty of those years—ever since the Soviets acquired SLBMs and a large force of hardened ICBMs. Even striking first, it has not been feasible to avoid the effective total destruction of U.S. society (even earlier, that was not feasible for Western Europe), by blast, heat, radiation, and fallout alone from Soviet/Russian retaliation.

Now, in light of the phenomenon of nuclear winter precipitated from cities burning from our U.S. attacks alone (aside from Soviet retaliation), there can no longer be any fig leaf of pretense that a "damage-limiting" first strike by either side would be anything less than suicidal—as Alan Robock and Brian Toon have put it, "self-Assured Destruction" (SAD)—or, in fact, *omnicidal*. The changes I am describing mean giving up the pretense, and the supposed political and alliance advantages of maintaining the pretense, that it is possible for either superpower to limit damage to anyone or to everyone by attacking the other with nuclear weapons, whether first or second or in any circumstances or manner whatever.

The sole purpose of U.S. nuclear weapons should be to deter nuclear attack on the United States and its allies. That sole purpose can and should be accomplished with radically lowered numbers of U.S. nuclear weapons, almost entirely SLBMs, ICBMs having been dismantled as they should have been generations ago. This shift would not totally eliminate the dangers of nuclear war, but it would abolish the threat of nuclear winter.

Unfortunately, there continues to be little awareness of the recent scientific confirmation of the thirty-year-old nuclear winter "hypothesis" and its implications for our existing strategic nuclear war plans. To be sure, these actual plans remain Top Secret, but a great deal of testimony by officials, former insiders, and well-informed researchers makes clear that they have much the same character and the same opacity to civilian superiors even within the government as during the time when I had direct knowledge of them.

But I can't expect enough others to find my judgment adequately credible to motivate a broad and urgent movement for change without more authoritative confirmation. It is therefore a priority of mine—and, I hope, of readers of this book—to encourage pressure on Congress (and potential whistleblowers and other witnesses) and on other legislatures both in nuclear and non-nuclear weapons states to *investigate* the questions and issues I have raised, both in the United States and worldwide.

After all, not one of these legislatures (starting with our own) has ever successfully demanded or been told the truth of nuclear targeting or of the prospective consequences of nuclear war, whether relatively limited and small or all-out.[†]

It is the long-neglected duty of the U.S. Congress—preferably with the expert help and authority of the National Academy of Sciences, in part on a classified basis for details of actual weapons assignments against targets, yields, height of burst, numbers of detonations—to test the now-confirmed scientific findings regarding nuclear winter against the realities of our secret war plans. On that basis, Congress and the NAS can and must investigate the foreseeable human and environmental consequences of implementing the various "options" in those plans.

But past experience makes clear that Congress will not hold real investigative hearings, using committee subpoena powers, to penetrate the curtains of secrecy around these matters without a new level of pressure from American citizens. It is a major purpose of this book to help inspire that pressure, though it's obvious that will require a major change in public mood and priorities, and, if such pressure is to be effective, a still greater change in the composition of the present Congress.

My own experience of the last half century tells me that such a change in public awareness and resulting pressure on Congress will not occur without revelations by patriotic and courageous whistleblowers. We have long needed and lacked the equivalent of the Pentagon Papers on the subject of nuclear policies and preparations, nuclear threats, and decision-making: above all in the United States and Russia but also in the other nuclear weapons states.

I will always deeply regret that I did not make known to Congress, the American public, and the world the extensive documentation of persistent and still-unknown nuclear dangers that was available to me half a century ago. Those in nuclear weapons states who are now in a position to do more than I did then to alert their countries and the world to fatally reckless secret policies should take warning from the earlier silence by myself and others—and do better.

I would say to them: Don't do what I did. Don't wait to tell the truth to the public and legislatures, with documents, until you've lost your access or (in my case) the documents themselves. Above all, to paraphrase an infamous statement by a former secretary of state, don't wait until the "smoking gun" about your own country's reckless nuclear threats and policies is a mushroom cloud.

Given such revelations and corresponding investigations by legislatures in this country and other nuclear weapons states, it seems to me reasonable to hope that new public awareness of the now-secret realities would make the prevailing establishment consensus on the need and *legitimacy* of threatening and preparing to bring about total omnicide unsustainable. It should be commonly recognized that no stake whatever, no cause, no principle, no consideration of honor or obligation or prestige or maintaining leadership in current alliances—still less, no concern for remaining in office, or maintaining a particular power structure, or sustaining jobs, profits, votes—can justify maintaining *any risk whatever* of causing the near extinction of human and other animal life on this planet.

Omnicide—threatened, prepared, or carried out—is flatly illegitimate, unacceptable, as an instrument of national policy; indeed, it cannot be regarded as anything less than criminal, immoral, evil. In the light of recent scientific findings, of which the publics of the world and even their leaders are still almost entirely unaware, that risk is implicit in the nuclear planning, posture, readiness, and threats of the two superpowers. That is intolerable. It must be changed, and that change can't come too soon.

The steps I have indicated are only a beginning toward the ultimate delegitimation of nuclear weapons and nuclear threats. But none of the necessary changes can occur without an informed public, suitably alarmed by a situation that properly evokes horror, fear, revulsion, and incredulity, accompanied, hopefully, by the determination of the highest order and urgency to eliminate it.

Yet these reactions have been suppressed by a practice, when the reality is revealed and discussed at all, of maintaining a quasi-academic tone, an "objective," dispassionate, non-evaluative discourse regarding what the planning and practice has been and the bureaucratic or political reasons behind it, without any appropriate evaluation of the nature or consequence of these decisions and actions. That has contributed to the lack of an adequate political response, even when some aspects of past realities are occasionally exposed.

Moreover, the warnings and demands of activists are almost entirely ignored in mainstream media and politics and academic discussion as being non-expert and emotional rather than rational, failing to give appropriate weight to the complexities, the competing moral considerations and priorities that must drive reasonable and responsible policy-making.

What is missing—what is foregone—in the typical discussion and analysis of historical or current nuclear policies is the recognition that what is being discussed is dizzyingly insane and immoral: in its almost-incalculable and inconceivable destructiveness and deliberate murder-ousness, its disproportionality of risked and planned destructiveness to either declared or unacknowledged objectives, the infeasibility of its secretly pursued aims (damage limitation to the United States and allies, "victory" in two-sided nuclear war), its criminality (to a degree that explodes ordinary visions of law, justice, crime), its lack of wisdom or compassion, its sinfulness and evil.

And yet part of what must be grasped—what makes it both under-standable, once grasped, and at the same time mysterious and resistant to our ordinary understanding—is that the creation, maintenance, and political threat-use of these monstrous machines has been directed and accomplished by humans pretty much the way we think of them: more or less ordinary people, neither better nor worse than the rest of us, *not* monsters in either a clinical or mythic sense.

This particular process, and what it has led to and the dangers it poses to all complex life on earth, shows the human species—when organized hierarchically in large, dense populations, i.e., civilization—at its abso-lute worst. Is it really possible that ordinary people, ordinary leaders, have created and accepted dangers of the sort I am describing? Every "normal" impulse is to say "No! It can't be that bad!" ("And if it ever was, it can't have persisted. It can't be true now, in our own country.")

We humans almost universally have a false self-image of our species. We think that monstrous, wicked policies must be, can only be, conceived and directed and carried out by monsters, wicked or evil people, or highly aberrant, clinically "disturbed" people. People not like "us." That is mistaken. Those who have created a continuing nuclear threat to the existence of humanity have been normal, ordinary politicians, analysts, and military strategists. To them and to their subordinates, Hannah Arendt's controversial proposition regarding the "banality of evil" I believe applies, though it might better have been stated as the "banality of *evildoing*, and of most evildoers."

After all, we Americans have seen in recent years human-caused catastrophes reflecting governmental or corporate recklessness far greater and more conscious and deliberate than our public can easily imagine or is allowed to discover in time. Above all, the invasion of Iraq and the occupation of Afghanistan, but also the failure to prepare for or respond to Hurricane Katrina, the Gulf oil spill, and financial disasters affecting millions: the savings-and-loan scandal, Internet and housing bubbles, criminal fraud, and the meltdown of the banking and investment system.

Perhaps reflection on these political, social, and moral failures—preceding though amplified by current premonitions of disastrous decision-making during the tenure of Donald Trump—will lend credibility to my basic theme, otherwise hard to absorb: that the *same type* of heedless, shortsighted, and reckless decision-making and lying about it has characterized our government's *nuclear* planning, threats, and preparations, throughout the nuclear era, risking a catastrophe incomparably greater than all these others together.

I well know that it is entirely unrealistic to hope that the present Congress (not to speak of the present president), dominated by the current Republican Party, or for that matter a Congress returned to the control of Democratic members mainly of the sort we have seen in the last generation, would respond to demands for *any one* of the measures I have proposed above:

- a U.S. no-first-use policy
- probing investigative hearings on our war plans in the light of nuclear winter
- eliminating our ICBMs
- forgoing delusions of preemptive damage-limiting by our first-strike forces
- giving up the profits, jobs, and alliance hegemony based on maintaining that pretense
- otherwise dismantling the American Doomsday Machine

Both parties as currently constituted oppose every one of these measures. This mortal predicament did not begin with Donald J. Trump, and it will not end with his departure. The obstacles to achieving these necessary changes are posed not so much by the majority of the American public—though many in recent years have shown dismaying manipulability—but by officials and elites in both parties and by major institutions that consciously support militarism, American hegemony, and arms production and sales.

Tragically, the news is equally bad when it comes to the prospects of reversing American energy policy in time and on a scale to avert catastrophic climate change. Much the same institutions and elites tenaciously obstruct solution to this other existential challenge; they are, indeed, inordinately powerful. And yet, as demonstrated by the downfall of the Berlin Wall, the nonviolent dissolution of the Soviet empire, and the shift to majority rule in South Africa, all unimaginable just thirty years ago, such forces for sustaining an unjust and dangerous status quo are not *all*-powerful.

Is it simply quixotic to hope to preserve human civilization from either the effects of burning fossil fuels or preparing for nuclear war? As Martin Luther King Jr. warned us, one year to the day before his death, "There is such a thing as being too late." In challenging us on April 4, 1967, to recognize "the fierce urgency of now" he was speaking of the "madness of Vietnam," but he also alluded on that same occasion to nuclear weapons and to the even larger madness that has been the subject of this book: "We still have a choice today: *nonviolent coexistence or violent coannihilation.*"

He went on:

> We must move past indecision to action. . . . If we do not act, we shall surely be dragged down the long, dark, and shameful corridors of time reserved for those who possess power without compassion, might without morality, and strength without sight.
>
> . . . Now let us begin. Now let us rededicate ourselves to the long and bitter, but beautiful, struggle for a new world.

Glossary

AEC	Atomic Energy Commission
BMEWS	Ballistic Missile Early Warning System
BNSP	Basic National Security Policy (civilian guidance for war planning)
CINCPAC	Commander in Chief, Pacific Command
DAC	Democratic Advisory Council
DARPA	Defense Advanced Research Projects Agency
ExComm	Executive Committee of the National Security Council (Cuban missile crisis)
FOIA	Freedom of Information Act
GEOP	General Emergency Operations Plan (PACOM general war plan)
ISA	International Security Affairs (OSD)
JCS	Joint Chiefs of Staff
JSCP	Joint Strategic Capabilities Plan
LOW	launch on warning
LST	landing ship, tank
NIE	National Intelligence Estimate
NSC	National Security Council
ONR	Office of Naval Research
OSD	Office of the Secretary of Defense
PACAF	Pacific Air Forces
PACOM	Pacific Command
RAF	Royal Air Force
SAC	Strategic Air Command
SAMs	surface-to-air missiles
SAP	special access programs
SIOP	Single Integrated Operational Plan
Westpac	Western Pacific

Notes

Introduction

6 Many of these other documents See National Security Study Memorandum 1 (NSSM-1), Vietnam Options paper, and others: ellsberg.net/Vietnam.

6 the command and control of nuclear weapons See my essay of August 1960, "Strategic Objectives and Command Control Problems," ellsberg.net/RAND, written as a RAND internal document but widely circulated at the time within the defense establishment as an early, unclassified exposition of "the problems of command and control," then not widely understood.

6 including some on nuclear policy National Security Study Memorandum 3 (NSSM-3), 1969, still not declassified despite frequent FOIA requests by the National Security Archive.

6 I drafted the Top Secret guidance For full text and accompanying notes, see ellsberg .net/BNSP.

6 at the highest civilian supergrade level GS-18, civilian protocol equivalent between major general and lieutenant general in military rank. When I transferred to the State Department in 1964, it was at the equivalent rank FSR1, Foreign Service Reserve-1.

7 I told just one person Daniel Ellsberg, *Secrets: A Memoir of Vietnam and the Pentagon Papers* (New York: Penguin, 2003), chapter 7, "Vietnam: The Lansdale Team," 102–108.

8 A separate, secret grand jury James Goodale, *Fighting for the Press: The Inside Story of the Pentagon Papers and Other Battles* (New York: CUNY Journalism Press, 2013), 174–179.

8 President Nixon had secretly been informed Daniel Ellsberg, *Secrets*, 426–443.

9 These crimes against me Daniel Arkin, "Daniel Ellsberg: Nixon White House Wanted to 'Shut Me Up' With Assault," NBC News, June 19, 2017, www.nbcnews.com/politics/politics -news/daniel-ellsberg-nixon-white-house-wanted-shut-me-assault-n774376, with link to Nick Akerman, Watergate Special Prosecutors's Office, "Investigation into the Assault on Anti-War Demonstrators on the Capitol Steps on May 3, 1972," June 5, 1975.

9 During the next thirteen days See Daniel Ellsberg, *Secrets*, chapter 29, "Going Under-ground," 387–410.

10 National Security Archive National Security Archive, George Washington Univer-sity, nsarchive.gwu.edu/nsa/the_archive.html. See many references below.

10 scores of important subjects Among these are my forty years of anti-nuclear activism from the end of the Vietnam War in 1975 to the present, including many of my some eighty-seven arrests for nonviolent civil disobedience (one on the Greenpeace ship *Sirius* in Lenin-grad harbor in 1982 protesting Soviet nuclear testing; most recently on August 9, Nagasaki

Day 2017, protesting the continued design of nuclear weapons at the Lawrence Livermore National Laboratory, Livermore, California); the history of nuclear weapons accidents and false alarms that have greatly contributed to the dangers of the nuclear era; and the alarming relevance of the recently revealed nuclear crisis of 1983 (unperceived at the time on the U.S. side: see references below) to current circumstances of renewed cold war and mutual costly "modernization" of U.S. and Russian strategic forces with preemptive first-strike characteristics, along with new capabilities for cyberwarfare.

11 **recently declassified documents** Among the most important of these are a series of electronic briefing books from the National Security Archive: "Newly Declassified Documents on Advance Presidential Authorization of Nuclear Weapons Use," National Security Archive electronic briefing book, August 30, 1998, nsarchive.gwu.edu/news/predelegation /predel.htm; "First Declassification of Eisenhower's Instructions to Commanders Predelegating Nuclear Weapons Use, 1959–1960," National Security Archive Electronic Briefing Book No. 45, May 18, 2001, nsarchive.gwu.edu/NSAEBB/NSAEBB45/; "The Creation of SIOP-62: More Evidence on the Origins of Overkill," National Security Archive Electronic Briefing Book No. 130, July 13, 2004, nsarchive.gwu.edu/NSAEBB/NSAEBB130/index.htm; "New Evidence on the Origins of Overkill First Substantive Release of Early SIOP Histories," National Security Archive Electronic Briefing Book No. 236, originally posted November 21, 2007, updated October 1, 2009, nsarchive.gwu.edu/nukevault/ebb236/index.htm; " 'It Is Certain There Will Be Many Firestorms': New Evidence on the Origins of Overkill": National Security Archive Electronic Briefing Book No. 108, January 14, 2004, nsarchive .gwu.edu/NSAEBB/NSAEBB108/index.htm.

11 **Lacking that, I have tried in many ways and venues** In addition to many lectures, interviews, and articles (for which see ellsberg.net/articles), this includes testimony in some of my trials for civil disobedience protesting nuclear weapons. In particular, in my trial in Golden, Colorado, November 27, 1979, for four arrests for obstructing the railroad tracks at the Rocky Flats Nuclear Weapons Production Facility, which was then producing components for the neutron bomb, I revealed much of the substance—then Top Secret—of the early chapters of this book, in hopes that making this public under oath in a criminal trial, subject to perjury, would add authority to my revelations. See my testimony in *A Year of Disobedience and a Criticality of Conscience* by Joseph Daniel, to which I also contributed a preface and afterword (Boulder, CO: Story Arts Media, 2013). Among articles, see in particular "Roots of the Upcoming Nuclear Crisis (or, Dr. Strangelove Lives: How Those Who Do Not Love the Bomb Should Learn to Start Worrying)," David Krieger, ed., *The Challenge of Abolishing Nuclear Weapons* (New York: Routledge, 2011), 45–76.

11 **the open literature** See in particular the publications of Hans M. Kristensen, director of the Nuclear Information Project at the Federation of American Scientists, including "US Nuclear War Plan Updated Amidst Policy Review," April 4, 2013, fas.org/blogs/security /2013/04/oplan8010-12/. Joseph Trevithick, "Here's America's Plan for Nuking Its Enemies, Including North Korea," *Warzone*, April 7, 2017, www.thedrive.com/the-war-zone/9056 /heres-americas-plan-for-nuking-its-enemies-including-north-korea.

13 **"If we have them, why can't we use them?"** Harper Neidig, "Scarborough: Trump Asked Adviser, Why US Can't Use Nuclear Weapons," *The Hill*, August 3, 2016, thehill.com/blogs /ballot-box/presidential-races/290217-scarborough-trump-asked-about-adviser-about -using-nuclear.

14 unless, evidently, he were the first See the important and timely essay, bringing up to date many of the issues raised in this book, by Bruce Blair, "What Exactly Would It Mean to Have Trump's Finger on the Nuclear Button? A Nuclear Launch Expert Lays Out the Various Scenarios," *Politico Magazine*, June 11, 2016, www.politico.com/magazine/story/2016 /06/2016-donald-trump-nuclear-weapons-missiles-nukes-button-launch-foreign-policy -213955.

16 Meanwhile, frequent leaked reports in the American press William M. Arkin, Cynthia McFadden, Kevin Monohan, and William Windrem, "Trump's Options for North Korea Include Placing Nukes in South Korea," NBC News, April 7, 2017, www.nbcnews.com /news/us-news/trump-s-options-north-korea-include-placing-nukes-south-korea-n743571; William M. Arkin, "North Korea Has at Least One Thing Right About America's Plans for War," Vice News, March 15, 2016, news.vice.com/article/united-states-plans-for-war-with -north-korea.

16 Dead Hand David E. Hoffman, *Dead Hand: The Untold Story of the Cold War Arms Race and Its Dangerous Legacy* (New York: Anchor Books, 2010). For description and further references to the Dead Hand system, see chapter 19, "The Strangelove Paradox."

16 Thanks to revelations from the former Soviet Union See especially Aleksandr Fursenko and Timothy Naftali, *"One Hell of a Gamble": Khrushchev, Castro, and Kennedy, 1958–1964* (New York: W.W. Norton & Co., 1997). Aleksandr Fursenko and Timothy Naftali, *Khrushchev's Cold War: The Inside Story of an American Adversary* (New York: W.W. Norton & Co., 2006); Sergei N. Khrushchev, *Nikita Khrushchev and the Creation of a Superpower* (University Park, PA: Penn State University Press, 2000); Sergo Mikoyan, *The Soviet Cuban Missile Crisis: Castro, Mikoyan, Kennedy, Khrushchev, and the Missiles of November,* ed. Svetlana Savranskaya (Palo Alto, CA: Stanford University Press, 2012); General Anatoli I. Gribkov and General William Y. Smith, *Operation Anadyr: U.S. and Soviet Generals Recount the Cuban Missile Crisis* (Chicago: Edition Q, 1994). Michael Dobbs, *One Minute to Midnight: Kennedy, Khrushchev, and Castro on the Brink of Nuclear War* (New York: Alfred A. Knopf, 2008). I've benefited from long conversations with Sergei Krushchev, Sergo Mikoyan, and Timothy Naftali.

16 The strategic nuclear system is more prone to false alarms See the account by a former CIA officer Peter Vincent Pry, *War Scare: Russia and America on the Nuclear Brink* (Westport, CT: Praeger, 1999). Also Schlosser, *Command and Control*; see references immediately below on 1983.

16 Later studies have confirmed Scott D. Sagan, *The Limits of Safety: Organizations, Accidents, and Nuclear Weapons* (Princeton, NJ: Princeton University Press, 1993). See also Eric Schlosser, *Command and Control: Nuclear Weapons, the Damascus Accident, and the Illusion of Safety* (New York: Penguin Press, 2013), especially on the 1979 and 1980 false alarms. See several important books from Bruce G. Blair, including *Strategic Command and Control: Redefining the Nuclear Threat* (Washington, D.C.: Brookings Institution Press, 1985); *The Logic of Accidental Nuclear War* (Washington, D.C.: Brookings Institution Press, 1993); *Global Zero Alert for Nuclear Forces* (Washington, D.C.: Brookings Institution Press, 1995).

16 false alarms in . . . 1983 On the recently confirmed 1983 Soviet war scare, including especially dangerous false alarms, see the work of former CIA analyst Benjamin B. Fischer, "A Cold War Conundrum: The 1983 Soviet War Scare," first published in CIA, *Studies in Intelligence*, 1996. See also Benjamin B. Fischer, "The Soviet-American War Scare of the

1980s," *International Journal of Intelligence and Counterintelligence* 19 (2006): 480–518. And in particular, especially relevant to current concerns about cyberwarfare in service of decapitation, which may give rise to mutual fears encouraging preemption: Benjamin B. Fischer, "Canopy Wing: The U.S. War Plan That Gave the East Germans Goose Bumps," *International Journal of Intelligence and Counterintelligence* 27 (2014): 431–464.

For the definitive confirmation of the seriousness of this crisis on the Soviet side—a very highly classified study done in 1990 that was finally declassified twenty-five years later, in 2015, see "The 1983 War Scare Declassified and For Real: All Source Intelligence Report Finds US-Soviet Relations on 'Hair-Trigger' in 1983," edited by Nate Jones, Tom Blanton, and Lauren Harper, National Security Archive Electronic Briefing Book 533, October 24, 2015, nsarchive.gwu.edu/nukevault/ebb533-The-Able-Archer-War-Scare-Declassi fied-PFIAB-Report-Released/. For further documentation and analysis, see Nate Jones, ed., *Able Archer 83: The Secret History of the NATO Exercise that Almost Triggered Nuclear War* (New York: New Press, 2016). The Reagan policies that frightened the Soviets were extensively documented at the time, including through extensive interviews, in Robert Scheer's *With Enough Shovels: Reagan, Bush, and Nuclear War*, updated edition (New York: Vintage Books, 1983).

17 the phenomena of nuclear winter For some of the original studies, see R. P. Turco, et al., "Nuclear Winter: Global Consequences of Multiple Nuclear Explosions," *Science* 122 (1983): 1283–1292. Carl Sagan, "Nuclear War and Climactic Catastrophe: Some Policy Implications," *Foreign Affairs* 62 no. 2 (1983/84): 257–292; see also expanded version in Lester Grinspoon, ed., *The Long Darkness: Psychological and Moral Perspectives on Nuclear Winter* (New Haven, CT: Yale University Press, 1986), 7–62. Paul R. Ehrlich, et al., *The Nuclear Winter: The World After Nuclear War* (London: Sidgwick & Jackson, 1985). Carl Sagan and Richard Turco, *A Path Where No Man Thought: Nuclear Winter and the End of the Arms Race* (New York: Random House, 1990).

17 the most recent scientific calculations Steven Starr, "The Ban Treaty Must Address the Scientifically Predicted Consequences of Nuclear War," Bulletin of the Atomic Scientists, May 19, 2017, thebulletin.org, gives a good list of some of most recent literature on the subject. See Owen B. Toon, et al., "Atmospheric Effects and Societal Consequences of Regional Scale Nuclear Conflicts and Acts of Individual Nuclear Terrorism," *Atmospheric Chemistry and Physics* 7 (2007); Alan Robock, et al., "Climatic Consequences of Regional Nuclear Conflicts," *Atmospheric Chemistry and Physics* 7 (2007); Michael Mills, et al., "Massive Global Ozone Loss Predicted Following Regional Nuclear Conflict," *Proceedings of the National Academy of Sciences* 105, no. 14 (2007): 5307–5312; Michael J. Mills, et al., "Multi-decadal Global Cooling and Unprecedented Ozone Loss Following a Regional Nuclear Conflict," *Earth's Future* 2 (2014), 161–176; Andrea Stenke, et al., "Climate and Chemistry Effects of a Regional Scale Nuclear Conflict," *Atmospheric Chemistry and Physics* 13 (2013): 9713–9729; Alan Robock, et al., "Nuclear Winter Revisited with a Modern Climate Model and Current Nuclear Arsenals: Still Catastrophic Consequences," *Journal of Geophysical Research* 112 (2007).

18 Gorbachev has reported Alan Robock, "Nuclear Winter," *Wiley Interdisciplinary Reviews: Climate Change* 1 (May/June 2010): 425, climate.envsci.rutgers.edu/pdf/WiresCli mateChangeNW.pdf. "Mikhail Gorbachev, then leader of the Soviet Union, described in an interview in 1994 how he felt when he got control of the Soviet nuclear arsenal, 'Perhaps there was an emotional side to it. But it was rectified by my knowledge of the might that had been accumulated. One-thousandth of this might was enough to destroy all living things on earth. And I knew the report on nuclear winter.' And in 2000 he said, 'Models made by Russian and American scientists showed that a nuclear war would result in a nuclear winter that would be extremely destructive to all life on Earth; the knowledge of that was a great stimulus to us, to people of honor and morality, to act in that situation.'"

18 Reagan, who made a similar attribution *New York Times*, February 12, 1985, "Interview with the President on a Range of Issues," www.nytimes.com/1985/02/12/world/transcript -of-interview-with-president-on-a-range-of-issues.html.

"Or now, as a great many reputable scientists are telling us, that such a war could just end up in no victory for anyone because we would wipe out the earth as we know it. And if you think back to a couple of natural calamities—back in the last century, in the 1800s, just natural phenomena from earthquakes, or, I mean, volcanoes—we saw the weather so changed that there was snow in July in many temperate countries. And they called it the year in which there was no summer. Now if one volcano can do that, what are we talking about with the whole nuclear exchange, the nuclear winter that scientists have been talking about?" In contrast with Gorbachev, Reagan drew from this not only the desirability of eliminating all nuclear weapons but also necessity of conducting space tests of his Strategic Defense Initiative (SDI, Star Wars), which, in abandoning the Anti-Ballistic Missile Treaty with the Soviets, prevented an agreement with Gorbachev at the Reykjavik Summit on mutual nuclear abolition.

18 Kahn had said he was sure Herman Kahn, *On Thermonuclear War* (Princeton, NJ: Princeton University Press, 1960), 144–156. Herman Kahn, "'A Doomsday Machine'—Last Word in the Arms Race?," *US News & World Report* (May 1, 1961): 61, 64.

19 John Somerville later termed "omnicide" John Somerville, "Nuclear 'War' is Omni- cide," *Peace Research*, April 1982.

19 so was Herman Kahn in 1960 *On Thermonuclear War*, 523–524, "The Doomsday Machine . . . will not always be a completely academic notion. While it does not seem tech- nically feasible today, unless R&D is controlled, it most likely will be technically feasible in 10 to 20 years. A central problem of arms control—perhaps the central problem—is to delay the day when Doomsday Machines or near equivalents become practical, and when and if Doomsday Machines or near equivalents are feasible to see to it that none are built." In 1983 scientists discovered that an American Doomsday Machine capable of producing nuclear winter had existed at the time Kahn published this statement in 1960 and has existed ever since.

Chapter 1: How Could I?

27 premises of this last justification For the debate on the "decision" to drop the atomic bomb, see Gar Alperovitz, *Atomic Diplomacy: Hiroshima and Potsdam: The Use of the Atomic Bomb and the American Confrontation with Soviet Power* (New York: Penguin Books, expanded and updated edition, 1985; first published 1965); Gar Alperovitz, *The Deci- sion to Use the Atomic Bomb* (New York: Vintage Books, 1986); Martin Sherwin, *A World Destroyed: Hiroshima and Its Legacies* (Stanford, CA: Stanford University Press, 2003; first published 1975); Barton J. Bernstein, ed., *The Atomic Bomb: The Critical Issues* (New York: Little, Brown and Company, 1976); Stewart L. Udall, *The Myths of August: A Personal*

Exploration of Our Tragic Cold War Affair with the Atom (New York: Pantheon, 1994); Leon V. Sigal, *Fighting to a Finish: The Politics of War Termination in the United States and Japan, 1945* (New York: Cornell University Press, 1998); Kai Bird and Lawrence Lifschultz, eds., *Hiroshima's Shadow: Writings on the Denial of History and the Smithsonian Controversy* (Stony Creek, CT: The Pamphleteer's Press, 1998); J. Samuel Walker, *Prompt and Utter Destruction: Truman and the Use of the Atomic Bombs Against Japan*, 3rd revised edition (Chapel Hill: University of North Carolina Press, 2016). Particularly pathbreaking, along with many of these other studies, is the more recent work of Tsuyoshi Hasegawa, *Racing the Enemy: Stalin, Truman, and the Surrender of Japan* (Cambridge, MA: Belknap Press, 2005), and Tsuyoshi Hasegawa, ed., *The End of the Pacific War: Reappraisals* (Stanford, CA: Stanford University Press, 2007). Scott D. Sagan and Benjamin A. Valentino, "Revisiting Hiroshima in Iran: What Americans Really Think about Using Nuclear Weapons and Killing Noncombatants," *International Security* 42, no. 1, (Summer 2017): 41–70.

28 "the world was headed for grief" Leo Szilard, *Leo Szilard: His Version of the Facts*, ed. Spencer R. Weart and Gertrud Weiss Szilard (Cambridge: The MIT Press, 1980), 55.

28 "a black day in the history of mankind" Ibid., 146.

29 war-winning weapon For one of the most illuminating discussions of hopes for the bomb in the post–World War II world, see Greg Herken, *The Winning Weapon: The Atomic Bomb in the Cold War, 1945–1950* (New York: Alfred A. Knopf, 1981).

32 I knew what I wanted to work on Daniel Ellsberg, "Decision-making Under Uncertainty: The Contributions of von Neumann and Morgenstern," (honors thesis, Harvard University, 1952). Daniel Ellsberg, "Classic and Current Notions of 'Measurable Utility,'" *Economic Journal* 64 (1954): 225–50.

32 That included situations of conflict Daniel Ellsberg, "Theory of the Reluctant Duelist," *American Economic Review* vol. 46 (1956): 909–23. I might note that although I was often described later as a "game theorist," my initial contribution in my thesis and this article based on it was a *critique* of the von Neumann and Morgenstern solution to rational strategy in "two-person, zero-sum games," the foundation of classical game theory. That was possibly the first—and for many years one of the only—critical, skeptical accounts of that theory.

32 invent better ones Daniel Ellsberg, "Risk, Ambiguity, and the Savage Axioms," *Quarterly Journal of Economics* 75 (1962), 643–69. Much extended in 1962 Ph.D. thesis, *Risk, Ambiguity and Decision* (Garland, NY: 2001; Kindle edition: Routledge, 2015).

34 "a guided missile to any spot on earth" World Circling Space Ship, www.astronautix .com/w/worldcirclingspaceship.html.

35 Earlier studies assumed only a minor role Albert Wohlstetter, Fred S. Hoffman, and Henry S. Rowen, "Protecting U.S. Power to Strike Back in the 1950's and 1960's," staff report, R-290, (Santa Monica, CA: RAND Corporation, September 1, 1956). Top Secret, declassified circa mid-1960s. albertwohlstetter.com/writings/19560901-AW-EtAl -R290.pdf.

37 An article on the new "military intellectuals" "The Military Intellectuals," *London Times Literary Supplement*, August 25, 1961.

38 a study of how the Japanese had achieved a surprise attack Later published, having taken years and intense lobbying to get cleared, as *Pearl Harbor: Warning and Decision* (Palo Alto, CA: Stanford University Press, 1962).

39 "cannot ensure a level of destruction" Wohlstetter, et al., staff report R-290, 100.

Chapter 2: Command and Control

41 I joined a few others See my "Strategic Objectives and Command Control Problems," August 12, 1960, ellsberg.net. This was written as a RAND internal document, but it was unclassified and widely circulated outside RAND in command and control circles.

42 "planning on strategic warning *is* dangerous" Albert Wohlstetter, Fred S. Hoffman, and Henry S. Rowen, "Protecting U.S. Power to Strike Back in the 1950's and 1960's," staff report, R-290 (Santa Monica, CA: RAND Corporation, September 1, 1956). Top Secret, declassified circa mid-1960s. albertwohlstetter.com/writings/19560901-AW-EtAl-R290.pdf.

42 I conjectured—as was later borne out See the Mark Machina compilation, "Further Readings on Choice Under Uncertainty, Beliefs and the Ellsberg Paradox," a selective listing as of 2001 from "450 scholarly articles that reference Ellsberg (1961)" [my 1961 article "Risk, Ambiguity and the Savage Axioms"] in my *Risk, Ambiguity and Decision* (Garland, NY: 2001; Kindle edition: Routledge, 2015), xxxix–xlviii.

43 "The first BMEWS radar complex" Eric Schlosser, *Command and Control: Nuclear Weapons, the Damascus Accident, and the Illusion of Safety* (New York: Penguin Press, 2013), 255.

45 President Reagan once made a public statement "On the Record; Reagan on Missiles," *New York Times*, October 17, 1984.

46 I had raised this question Daniel Ellsberg to Albert Wohlstetter and Frank Eldridge, "Subject: Strains on the Fail-Safe System," RAND Memo M-5 039, July 1958, ellsberg.net; copies to Harry Rowen, Alain Enthoven, Ed Oliver, Jay Wakeley, Dick Mills, R. B. Murrow, C. J. Hitch, Bill Jones.

57 I had come across a SAC manual Ibid. "Strains on the Fail-Safe System."

58 "Spark Plug procedures are the only method" Quoted sentences in this paragraph and the next are from my notes on the GEOP (General Emergency Operations Plan, the PACOM general war plan).

61 operators of the Minuteman missiles had circumvented John H. Rubel, *Doomsday Delayed: USAF Strategic Weapons Doctrine and SIOP-62, 1959–1962* (Lanham, MD: Hamilton Books, 2008), 14–15.

62 "the locks had been installed" Bruce Blair's Nuclear Column, Keeping Presidents in the Nuclear Dark, "Episode #1: The Case of the Missing 'Permissive Action Links,'" February 11, 2004, Center for Defense Information, web.archive.org/web/20120511191600/http://www .cdi.org/blair/permissive-action-links.cfm.

65 assured the practical inability of the president Noam Chomsky brought to my attention a memoir by a SAC pilot, Major Don Clawson, who during 1961–1962 flew fifteen air alert (CHROME DOME) missions in B-52s carrying two nuclear HOUND DOG missiles and four other nuclear weapons. In several passages, Clawson substantiates that the looseness of control that I found in the Pacific was virtually identical to SAC procedures, even during the Cuban Missile Crisis. In a section titled "Incredible Reliance on Crew Integrity," Clawson writes "The total reliance on the B-52 combat crew force's integrity amazes me even today. Obviously if the crew had the ability to deconstruct and verify a simple, in the clear message, they also had the ability to construct a valid message. Each aircraft had the means of transmitting such a message that would only require authentication to execute the entire Airborne Alert Force, with no recall possible . . . In spite of the contention shown in motion pictures such as *Dr. Strangelove* and *Thirteen Days* that there was an electronic interlock on the B-52 inhibiting the crew from arming and dropping the weapons, there was no such system. All the crew needed was a message in the proper format and authenticated with material hanging around each of the primary crew-members' neck's . . . A rogue crew or crew-member could have easily and quickly composed an authentic message and broadcast it on HF radio, which would have required all SAC elements to keep rebroadcasting it. There was a two-man policy in effect requiring two people be in place at a time when the activity involved nuclear weapons, but when flying Airborne Alert, we sometimes did not have a third pilot, which meant that there was frequently only one pilot in the cockpit when the other was sleeping. The crews were fully aware of this situation; in face we discussed it from time to time." Major Don Clawson, USAF Ret., *Is That Something the Crew Should Know? Irreverent Anecdotes of an Air Force Pilot* (London: Athena Press, 2003), 105–106. In line with my own earlier concerns, Clawson, in retirement, wrote to the former Secretary of Defense, Robert McNamara, in December 2001 (in a letter included at the end of his book), asking: "Did you as Secretary of Defense realize that any one of the primary crew-members on the airborne alert B-52s could construct a valid, authenticated message? This message could have been broadcast using the high frequency radio, on the aircraft, and execute the entire B-52 airborne alert force with no possibility of a recall of the airborne aircraft. Was this possibility ever discussed?" Clawson received no response.

Chapter 3: Delegation

69 At that time, no system of Permissive Action Links (PALs) Peter Douglas Feaver, *Guarding the Guardians: Civilian Control of Nuclear Weapons in the United States* (Ithaca: Cornell University Press, 1992).

Chapter 4: Iwakuni

78 As Admiral Eugene LaRocque later testified U.S. Congress, Joint Committee on Atomic Energy, *Hearing before the Subcommittee of Military Applications, Proliferation of Nuclear Weapons* (Washington, D.C.: U.S. Government Printing Office, 1974), 93rd Congress, 2d Session, September 10, 1974, 18.

Chapter 6: The War Plan

94 "In general war, Annex C will be executed" All quotes from my notes, 1960. Emphasis added.

100 "The meeting took place near mid-December 1960" John H. Rubel, *Doomsday Delayed: USAF Strategic Weapons Doctrine and SIOP-62, 1959–1962* (Lanham, MD: Hamilton Books, 2008), 23–39. Rubel was at the time Deputy Director of Defense Research and Engineering, later sole director and Assistant Secretary for Research and Engineering.

103 Kistiakowsky reported to him David Alan Rosenberg, "The Origins of Overkill: Nuclear Weapons and American Strategy, 1945–1960," in Steven E. Miller, ed., *Strategy and Nuclear Deterrence: An International Security Reader* (Princeton, NJ: Princeton University Press, 1984), 118.

Chapter 7: Briefing Bundy

108 Some forty years later On the issue of delegation, see the National Security Archives Electronic Briefing Books on the subject, specifically "Newly Declassified Documents on Advance Presidential Authorization of Nuclear Weapons Use," National Security Archive Electronic Briefing Book, August 30, 1998, nsarchive.gwu.edu/news/predelegation/predel .htm; see also Peter J. Roman, "Ike's Hair-Trigger: U.S. Nuclear Predelegation, 1953–1960," *Security Studies* 7, no. 4 (Summer 1998): 121–64. Eisenhower's permission of sub-delegation appears in "First Declassification of Eisenhower's Instructions to Commanders Predelegating Nuclear Weapons Use, 1959-1960," National Security Archive Electronic Briefing Book No. 45, May 18, 2001, nsarchive.gwu.edu/NSAEBB/NSAEBB45/.

109 inside Raven Rock mountain See also the highly revealing book by Garret M. Graff, *Raven Rock: The Story of the U.S. Government's Secret Plan to Save Itself—While the Rest of Us Die* (New York: Simon & Schuster, 2017), which came out too recently to be adequately reflected in the account presented here.

113 refused to send combat troops to Vietnam Daniel Ellsberg, *Papers on the War* (New York: Simon & Schuster, 1972), especially chapter 1, "The Quagmire Myth and the Stalemate Machine," in particular, 52–71.

Chapter 8: "My" War Plan

123 *we could not afford to deprive the Soviets* Joint Staff and USAF planners were not merely skeptical of and resistant to the proposal to have a withhold option for Moscow in initial attacks, they could scarcely imagine postponing an opportunity to "decapitate" Soviet central command at the outset of general war. The question I raised repeatedly to such officers was: How long would fighting against Japanese forces have continued, beyond August 1945, if the first, second, or third atomic bomb had been targeted on Tokyo (as some had proposed) and killed the Emperor, precluding his order to surrender?

That seemed to be an unanswerable challenge to them in discussion, and indeed, according to Desmond Ball in *Politics and Force Levels*: "Moscow was taken off the list of initial targets in late 1961" (191). But later accounts (see pages 299–308 in same text, and General George Lee Butler's memoirs) indicate that neither my argument nor the option of withholding against Moscow were ever taken seriously by SAC (or by civilian officials who publicized an emphasis on decapitation under presidents Carter and Reagan). Desmond Ball, *Politics and Force Levels: The Strategic Missile Program of the Kennedy Administration* (Berkeley: University of California Press, 1981); George Lee Butler, *Uncommon Cause: A Life at Odds with Convention* (Denver: Outskirts Press, 2016).

123 as Fred Kaplan has ably shown Fred Kaplan, *The Wizards of Armageddon* (New York: Simon & Schuster, 1983), 203–19, 260–62.

125 my first draft of the general war section of the BNSP For full text, see ellsberg.net /Pentagon. This applies as well to the other memos by me mentioned or quoted in this chapter.

128 roughing out "options" in line with my guidance Ball, *Politics and Force Levels*, 190–191. William Burr, "New Evidence on the Origins of Overkill," National Security Archive Electronic Briefing Book No. 236, November 21, 2007, updated October 1, 2009, nsarchive2.gwu.edu//nukevault/ebb236/index.htm.

128 The final version For texts of all these memos and drafts, see ellsberg.net/BNSP.

128 my draft portion of the proposed BNSP President Kennedy chose, eventually, not to issue a presidential BNSP in 1961 nor in his remaining years in office (rejecting, also, a long proposed draft BNSP by Walt Rostow in 1962). According to Desmond Ball, Richard Neustadt "managed to persuade President Kennedy that a BNSP would limit his flexibility," an opinion shared by McGeorge Bundy. Ball, *Politics and Force Levels*, 190n40.

128 a critical influence on U.S. strategic war planning Fred Kaplan traces this lineage of later directives and guidance back to "McNamara's SIOP-63 guidance of 1961–62" and the earlier RAND studies repeatedly in *The Wizards of Armageddon*, in particular pages 383–84 for the Carter administration and page 389 for Reagan.

Chapter 9: Questions for the Joint Chiefs

131 my rough notes on questions for them See ellsberg.net/Pentagon.

132 an attack intended to maximize population loss My draft of April 1961 (see ellsberg .net)—which was sent without change to the JCS in May by Gilpatric, for McNamara, as Secretary of Defense Policy Guidance for war planning—stated: "It is in the interest of the United States to achieve its wartime objectives while limiting the destructiveness of warfare, whether it be nuclear or non-nuclear, local or global. Specifically, the United States does not hold all the people of Russia, China, or the Satellite nations responsible for the acts of their governments. Consequently, it is not an objective of the United States to maximize the number of people killed in the Communist Bloc in the event of war."

141 revealed in *Whole World on Fire* Lynn Eden, *Whole World on Fire: Organizations, Knowledge, and Nuclear Weapons Devastation* (Ithaca, NY: Cornell University Press, 2004).

141 This would reduce sunlight and lower temperatures See endnotes in the introduction referencing scientific studies from 1983 and especially since 2007.

143 such catastrophic "major attack options" Fred Kaplan, *The Wizards of Armageddon* (New York: Simon & Schuster, 1983); Janne E. Nolan, *Guardians of the Arsenal: The Politics of Nuclear Strategy* (New York: Basic Books, 1989); Janne E. Nolan, in *An Elusive Consensus: Nuclear Weapons and American Security after the Cold War* (Washington, D.C.: Brookings Institution Press, 1999); General Lee Butler, *Uncommon Cause: A Life at Odds with Convention*, vol. II (Denver, CO: Outskirts Press, 2016); Janne Nolan, "Cold Combat: The Memoir of a Nuclear Convert," *Bulletin of the Atomic Scientists* 73, no. 3 (2017), 192–195.

144 A few years after leaving the White House McGeorge Bundy, "To Cap the Volcano," *Foreign Affairs*, October 1969, quoted in Herbert F. York, *Race to Oblivion: A Participant's View of the Arms Race* (New York: Simon & Schuster, 1970), 168.

144 In the last year in the Cold War Herbert F. York, "'Remarks' About Minimum Deterrence," paper presented at the Lawrence Livermore National Laboratory workshop "The Role of Nuclear Weapons in the Year 2000," October 22–24, 1990. This paper was reprinted in Herbert F. York, *Arms and the Physicist*, as "Minimum Deterrence," (Melville, NY: American Institute of Physics, 1995) 273–277.

144 total of 63,836 weapons Max Roser and Mohamed Nagdy, "Nuclear Weapons," (2016), Our World in Data, ourworldindata.org/nuclear-weapons/. See also Hans M. Kristensen and Robert S. Norris, "United States Nuclear Forces, 2017," *Bulletin of the Atomic Scientists*

73, no. 1 (2017): 48–57, and Hans M. Kristensen and Robert S. Norris, "Russian Nuclear Forces, 2017," *Bulletin of the Atomic Scientists* 73, no. 2 (2017): 115–126.

Chapter 10: Berlin and the Missile Gap

145 Khrushchev renewed an ultimatum Important accounts of the Berlin Crisis include Michael Beschloss, *The Crisis Years: Kennedy and Khrushchev, 1960–1963*, (New York: HarperCollins, 1991); Marc Trachtenberg, *History and Strategy* (Princeton, NJ: Princeton University Press, 1991), especially chapter 5, "The Berlin Crisis," 169–234; Marc Trachtenberg, *A Constructed Peace: The Making of the European Settlement, 1945–1963* (Princeton, NJ: Princeton University Press, 1999); Aleksandr Fursenko and Timothy Naftali, *Khrushchev's Cold War: The Inside Story of an American Adversary* (New York: W. W. Norton & Co., 2006). And for a bold, fascinating argument about the centrality of Germany to the origins of the Cold War and U.S. nuclear strategy, see Gar Alperovitz and Kai Bird, "The Centrality of the Bomb," *Foreign Policy* no. 94 (Spring 1994): 3–20; Gal Alperovitz and Kai Bird, "A Theory of Cold War Dynamics: U.S. Policy, Germany, and the Bomb," *The History Teacher* 29, no. 3 (May 1996): 281–300.

147 When JFK asked Acheson privately McGeorge Bundy, *Danger and Survival: Choices about the Bomb in the First Fifty Years* (New York: Random House, 1988), 375.

148 Thirty years later, McNamara revealed Robert McNamara, *In Retrospect* (New York: Vintage Books, 1996), 345: "In the early 1960s . . . In long private conversations, first with President Kennedy and then with President Johnson, I had recommended, without qualification, that they never, under any circumstances, initiate the use of nuclear weapons. I believe they accepted my recommendations. But neither they nor I could discuss our position publicly because it was contrary to established NATO policy." See also James G. Blight, Bruce J. Allyn, and David A. Welch, *Cuba on the Brink: Castro, the Missile Crisis, and the Soviet Collapse* (New York: Pantheon, 1993), 262. Also, McNamara interview by Deborah Shapley, *Promise and Power: The Life and Times of Robert McNamara* (Boston: Little, Brown and Company, 1993), 595–596.

151 The words "less than ten million deaths" Three years later in *Dr. Strangelove*, General "Buck" Turgidson, to the President, after recommending a first strike on the Soviet Union: "Mister President, I'm not saying we wouldn't get our hair mussed, but I'd say no more than 10 to 20 million tops, depending on the breaks." Stanley Kubrick, Terry Southern, and Peter George, *Dr. Strangelove or: How I Learned to Stop Worrying and Love the Bomb*, directed by Stanley Kubrick. Los Angeles, CA: Columbia Pictures Corporation, 1964, www.visual-memory.co.uk/amk/doc/0055.html.

152 50 to 100 ICBMs as of mid-1961 "The Soviet ICBM Program—Evidence and Analysis," *Foreign Relations of the United States, 1961–1963*, Volume VIII, National Security Policy, ed. David W. Mabon (Washington, D.C.: Government Printing Office, 1996), Document 29, June 7, 1961, history.state.gov/historicaldocuments/frus1961-63v08/d29.

153 McNamara told the president Desmond Ball, *Politics and Force Levels: The Strategic Missile Program of the Kennedy Administration* (Berkeley: University of California Press, 1980), 246.

154 "death-beam gap" John Pike, "The Death-Beam Gap: Putting Keegan's Follies in Perspective," October 1992, www.fas.org/spp/eprint/keegan.htm.

158 McNamara had said in February that there was no gap Desmond Ball, *Politics and Force Levels*, chapter 4, "The Kennedy Administration and the Demise of the 'Missile Gap,'" especially 90–94.

162 "believes that Soviet determination" "Soviet Capabilities for Long Range Attack," *Foreign Relations of the United States*, National Intelligence Estimates and Related Reports and Correspondence, 1950–1985 (Washington, D.C.: Government Printing Office), 20, June 7, 1961, research.archives.gov/id/7327101.

166 It was correct, as Horelick and Rush themselves acknowledged Arnold L. Horelick and Myron Rush, "Deception in Soviet Strategic Missile Claims, 1957–1962," R-409-PR, Rand Corporation, May 1963. See also Arnold L. Horelick and Myron Rush, *Strategic Power and Soviet Foreign Policy* (Chicago, IL: University of Chicago Press, 1965).

168 bluffing his own Warsaw Pact allies See "Khrushchev's Secret Speech on Berlin, August, 1961," Cold War International History Project, www.mtholyoke.edu/acad/intrel /khrush.htm [quote from this on the web].

Chapter 11: A Tale of Two Speeches

169 One of the memos I gave him Links to my memos on ellsberg.net. (These read very badly to me, now. They are definitely part of my "confessions.")

173 Gilpatric gave the speech on October 21, 1961 Speech text: Roswell L. Gilpatric, Deputy Secretary of Defense, Speech Before the Business Council at the Homestead, Hot Springs, Virginia, nsarchive2.gwu.edu/NSAEBB/NSAEBB56/BerlinC6.pdf. Joseph A. Loftus, "Gilpatric Warns U.S. Can Destroy Atom Aggressor: Puts Nuclear Arms in 'Tens of Thousands'—Doubts Soviet Would Start War," *New York Times*, October 22, 1961. See also "First-Strike Options and the Berlin Crisis, September, 1961: New Documents from the Kennedy Administration" National Security Archive Electronic Briefing Book No. 56, edited by William Burr, released September 25, 2001, nsarchive2.gwu.edu/NSAEBB /NSAEBB56/.

174 "addressed a meeting of the Business Council" Michael Beschloss, *The Crisis Years: Kennedy and Khrushchev, 1960–1963* (New York: HarperCollins, 1991), 332. Italics in original.

175 "The President, Bundy, Rusk, and McNamara collaborated with Gilpatric" Ibid., 329–330.

176 "the Gilpatric speech seemed to be Kennedy's response" Seymour Hersh, *The Dark Side of Camelot* (Boston: Little, Brown and Company, 1997), 262. See also Aleksandr Fursenko and Timothy Naftali, *Khrushchev's Cold War: The Inside Story of an American Adversary* (New York: W. W. Norton & Company, 2006), 399–400.

176 "By asking Gilpatric to make this speech" Beschloss, *The Crisis Years*, 331–332.

176 "The thirty-megaton blast and Malinovsky's tough language" Ibid., 332.

177 "Khrushchev almost certainly wondered" Ibid., 351.

178 McNamara had decided for this occasion Robert McNamara, Speech to NATO Ministerial Meeting, Athens, Greece, May 5, 1962, nsarchive2.gwu.edu//NSAEBB/NSAEBB159 /usukconsult-16c.pdf.

181 A scholar as authoritative as Richard Rhodes Richard Rhodes, *Dark Sun: The Making of the Hydrogen Bomb* (New York: Simon & Schuster, 1995), 570.

184 Ann Arbor speech Robert McNamara, Speech, Ann Arbor, Michigan, July 9, 1962 roberts mcnamara.com.files.wordpress.com/2017/04/mcnamara-1967-22no-cities22-speech-p.pdf.

184 "what McNamara said irritated the Soviet leader" Fursenko and Naftali, *Khrushchev's Cold War*, 442.

185 Ten days later, Khrushchev attacked *Pravda*, July 11, 1962, quoted in Arnold L. Horelick and Myron Rush, *Strategic Power and Soviet Foreign Policy* (Chicago, IL: University of Chicago Press, 1965), 91.

Chapter 12: My Cuban Missile Crisis

188 We have an unusual record of the Cuban missile crisis Timothy Naftali and Philip Zelikow, eds., *The Presidential Recordings of John F. Kennedy, Volume I-III: The Great Crises* (New York: W. W. Norton & Co., 2001).

188 "I'll be quite frank" Timothy Naftali and Philip Zelikow, eds., *The Presidential Recordings of John F. Kennedy, Volume I-III: The Great Crises: September–October 21, 1962* (New York: W. W. Norton & Co., 2001), 464.

190 The deployment obviously did confront Kennedy My notes from my internal study in 1964 of the Cuban crisis (see ellsberg.net) record that Adam Yarmolinsky told me that at the time McNamara told him about the presence of the Soviet missiles, about 7:30 A.M. on October 16, 1962, McNamara's reaction to the impending crisis was: "This shows how stupid it was to draw that line; I advised against it." According to Yarmolinsky (May 16, 1964) McNamara thought, that Tuesday morning in 1962, "there might not have had to be a crisis if JFK hadn't drawn the line." I noted that Adam (in 1964) "thinks it unlikely that JFK would have made the firm, precise commitment he did if he had thought there was much chance it might be called. He made it public only for political reasons."

193 Dean Acheson, for one, did not In an interview, Theodore Sorensen, who served as White House Counsel to the President during the period of the Cuban missile crisis, noted: "I remember very clearly when we brought in former Secretary of State Dean Acheson to talk to our group, expert on the Russians, expert on the Cold War, and he recommended the air strike. And someone said, 'Mr. Secretary, if we bomb these Soviet missiles in Cuba, what will their reaction be?' And he said, 'I know the Soviets very well,' he said, 'they will feel compelled to bomb NATO missile bases in Turkey.' And somebody else said, 'And then what would we do?' 'Oh,' he said, 'under our NATO covenants, we would obligated to bomb Soviet missile bases inside the Soviet Union.' 'Oh, and then what will the Soviets do?' 'Well,' he said, 'by that time we hope cooler heads will prevail and people will talk.' There was a real chill in that room." See interview with Theodore Sorensen: nsarchive2.gwu.edu//coldwar/interviews/episode-10/sorensen2.html.

194 "almost maudlin" Dean Acheson, "Dean Acheson's Version of Robert Kennedy's Version of the Cuban Missile Affair: Homage to Plain Dumb Luck," *Esquire*, February 1969, 44.

Chapter 13: Cuba: The Real Story

200 "the Saturday before the Sunday" Interview with Robert McNamara, *War and Peace in the Nuclear Age: Europe Goes Nuclear*, February 20, 1986, (thirty-six minutes in), open vault.wgbh.org/catalog/V_DF35A31CD90545FE83A077DE010DD044.

202 It was not until 1975–76 James G. Hershberg, "Before 'The Missiles of October': Did Kennedy Plan a Military Strike Against Cuba?," in James A. Nathan, ed., *The Cuban Missile Crisis Revisited* (New York: St. Martin's Press, 1992), 237–280. (An earlier version of this chapter was first published as an article in *Diplomatic History* 14 (Spring 1990): 163–198.)

202 about to "lose Cuba" In his memoirs Khrushchev wrote, "While I was on an official visit to Bulgaria, for instance, one thought kept hammering away at my brain: what will happen if we lose Cuba?. . . It was during my visit to Bulgaria that I had the idea of installing missiles with nuclear warheads in Cuba without letting the United States find out they were there until it was too late to do anything about them." Nikita Khrushchev, *Khrushchev Remembers*, with an introduction, commentary, and notes by Edward Crankshaw, trans. and ed. Strobe Talbot (New York: Bantam Books, 1970), 546.

203 The morning after the president's speech on October 22 Aleksandr Fursenko and Timothy Naftali, *"One Hell of a Gamble": Khrushchev, Castro, and Kennedy, 1958–1964* (New York: W. W. Norton & Co., 1997), 249–250.

203 But, as the Soviet Ambassador Anatoly Dobrynin See the discussion of the controversy about whether this meeting ever took place, in Sheldon M. Stern, *Averting 'The Final Failure': John F. Kennedy and the Secret Cuban Missile Crisis Meetings* (Stanford, CA: Stanford University Press, 2003), where he concludes "The historical jury is still out," 289–290, 368–372.

204 The initial inferences drawn were that Dean Acheson, "Dean Acheson's Version of Robert Kennedy's Version of the Cuban Missile Affair," *Esquire*, February 1969, 144.

205 A different light was shed on this seven years later Robert F. Kennedy, *Thirteen Days: A Memoir of the Cuban Missile Crisis* (New York: W. W. Norton & Company, 1971), 84–87.

205 published in *Time* in 1982 Dean Rusk, et al., "Essay: The Lessons of the Cuban Missile Crisis," *Time*, September 27, 1982, 85–86.

208 "The President was not optimistic, nor was I" Kennedy, *Thirteen Days*, 108–09. Ellipsis in original.

208 "It was we who gave the order to fire" Tad Szulc, *Fidel: A Critical Portrait* (New York: William Morrow and Company, 1986), 584.

209 First, that the number of Soviet troops Blight, et al., *Cuba on the Brink*, 250–251; Svetlana Savranskaya and Thomas Blanton, "Last Nuclear Weapons Left Cuba in December 1962," National Security Archive Electronic Briefing Book 449, December 11, 2013, nsarchive.gwu.edu/NSAEBB/NSAEBB449/; Sergo Mikoyan, *The Soviet Cuban Missile Crisis: Castro, Mikoyan, Kennedy, Khrushchev, and the Missiles of November*, ed. Svetlana Savranskaya (Stanford, CA: Stanford University Press, 2010), 266.

209 So far as we knew, Khrushchev had *never* sent In fact, Khrushchev had deployed twelve medium-range ballistic missiles to East Germany in December 1958, in line with his threat to turn over allied access to West Berlin to the East Germans by the end of the year. This meant he had missile warheads within range of London and Paris, which he had claimed falsely during the Suez crisis of 1956. But although his purpose was presumably to give substance to threats of nuclear war if the U.S. should maintain its rights of access by force, Khrushchev kept this deployment secret not only from the U.S. and NATO but also his own Presidium and even Walter Ulbricht, the head of the East German satellite state. This deployment, which he withdrew in 1959, remained totally unknown to the West until

2001. See Aleksandr Fursenko and Timothy Naftali, *Khrushchev's Cold War* (New York: W. W. Norton & Co., 2006), 194, 208–209, 211–213, 442.

210 "It would have been an *absolute disaster* for the world" James G. Blight, et al., *Cuba on the Brink: Castro, the Missile Crisis, and the Soviet Collapse*, fortieth anniversary ed. (New York: Rowman & Littlefield, 2002), 379.

210 "A smell of scorching hung in the air" James G. Blight and Janet M. Lang, *The Armageddon Letters: Kennedy/Khrushchev/Castro in the Cuban Missile Crisis* (New York: Rowman & Littlefield, 2012), 275.

211 At that same moment, as the quarantine became effective Scott D. Sagan, *The Limits of Safety: Organizations, Accidents, and Nuclear Weapons* (Princeton, NJ: Princeton University Press, 1993), 62–71.

212 "These few minutes were the time" Kennedy, *Thirteen Days*, 47–48.

212 "Isn't there some way we can avoid" Ibid., 48.

212 "We had come to the time of final decision" Ibid., 47–48.

213 "The meeting droned on." Ibid., 49–50.

214 Shumkov wondered whether the destroyer Svetlana V. Savranskaya, "New Sources on the Role of Soviet Submarines in the Cuban Missile Crisis," *Journal of Strategic Studies*, 28, no. 2 (2005) 233–259; Peter A. Huchthausen, *October Fury* (Hoboken, NJ: John Wiley & Sons, Inc., 2007).

214 "When they blew up those grenades" Aleksandr Fursenko and Timothy Naftali, *Khrushchev's Cold War: The Inside Story of an American Adversary* (New York: W. W. Norton & Company, 2006), 487, citing a BBC Scotland interview with Shumkov.

214 "Shumkov cut him off" Huchthausen, *October Fury*, 210.

215 "aimed exclusively at uncovering violations" Savranskaya, "New Sources on the Role of Soviet Submarines in the Cuban Missile Crisis," quoting Dubivko, "In the Depth of the Sargasso Sea" 321n32.

215 "For some time we were able to avoid them" Document #7, Recollections of Vadim Orlov (USSR Submarine B-59), "We Will Sink Them All, But We Will Not Disgrace Our Navy," Alexander Mozgovoi, *The Cuban Samba of the Quartet of Foxtrots: Soviet Submarines in the Caribbean Crisis of 1962* (Moscow: Military Parade, 2002). Translated by Svetlana Savranskaya in *The Underwater Cuban Missile Crisis: Soviet Submarines and the Risks of Nuclear War*, National Security Archive Electronic Briefing Book No. 339, edited by Thomas Blanton, William Burr, and Svetlana Savranskaya, October 24, 2012, nsarchive.gwu.edu/NSAEBB/NSAEBB399/.

216 "Maybe the war has already started up there" Recollections of Vadim Orlov, "We Will Sink Them All, But We Will Not Disgrace Our Navy," in Mozgovoi, *The Cuban Samba of the Quartet of Foxtrots*.

217 "The Man Who Saved the World" This is also the title of the PBS documentary in 2012, quoting Thomas Blanton of the National Security Archive. The film ends with Arkhipova's statement of pride.

218 "easily" been mistaken "for a nuclear bomber" Premier Khrushchev's communiqué to President Kennedy, accepting an end to the missile crisis, October 28, 1962, in *The Cuban Missile Crisis, 1962: A National Security Documents Reader*, eds. Laurence Chang and Peter Kornbluh (New York: New Press, 1998), 238.

218 "There's always some son-of-a-bitch" Roger Hilsman, quoted in Michael Dobbs, *One Minute to Midnight: Kennedy, Khrushchev, and Castro on the Brink of Nuclear War* (New York: Alfred A. Knopf, 2008), 269–270.

218 "The generals are itching for a fight." Evan Thomas, *Robert Kennedy: His Life* (New York: Simon & Schuster, 2000), 227.

219 "The thought that disturbed him most" Kennedy, *Thirteen Days*, 84.

219 "Mr. President, we and you ought not now to pull" Khrushchev letter to Kennedy, October 26, 1962, State Department translation, in Chang and Kornbluh, *The Cuban Missile Crisis*, 198.

221 "When I asked the military advisors if they could assure me" Norman Cousins, "Editorial: The Cuban Missile Crisis: An Anniversary," *Saturday Review*, October 15, 1977.

Chapter 14: Bombing Cities

225 Where did the road to doomsday begin? For a partial list of readings I've consulted on the origins of bombing in general and the Anglo-American bombing of Germany and U.S. bombing of Japan in particular, in addition to those already cited herein, see the following: Conrad C. Crane, *Bombs, Cities, and Civilians: American Airpower Strategy in World War II* (Lawrence: University Press of Kansas, 1993); Richard Overy, *The Bombers and the Bombed: Allied Air War Over Europe, 1940–1945* (New York: Viking, 2013); Hermann Knell, *To Destroy a City: Strategic Bombing and Its Human Consequences in World War II* (Cambridge, MA: Da Capo Press, 2003); Randall Hansen, *Fire and Fury: The Allied Bombing of Germany, 1942–1945* (New York: NAL Caliber, 2009); Alexander McKee, *Dresden 1945: The Devil's Tinderbox* (New York: Dutton, 1982); Ronald Schaffer, *Wings of Judgment: American Bombing in World War II* (New York: Oxford University Press, 1988); A. C. Grayling, *Among the Dead Cities: The History and Moral Legacy of the WWII Bombing of Civilians in Germany and Japan* (New York: Walker & Company, 2006); Keith Lowe, *Inferno: The Fiery Destruction of Hamburg, 1943* (New York: Scribner, 2007); Jorg Friedrich, *The Fire: The Bombing of Germany, 1940–1945* (New York: Columbia University Press, 2006); Erik Markusen and David Kopf, *The Holocaust and Strategic Bombing: Genocide and Total War in the Twentieth Century* (Boulder, CO: Westview Press, 1995); Susan Griffin, *A Chorus of Stones: The Private Life of War* (New York: Anchor Books, 1993); Sven Lindqvist, *A History of Bombing* (New York: New Press, 2001); John Dower, *War Without Mercy: Race and Power in the Pacific War* (New York: Pantheon, 1986); Charles Griffith, *The Quest: Haywood Hansell and American Strategic Bombing in World War II* (Alabama: Air University Press, 1999); Haywood S. Hansell, *The Strategic Air War Against Germany and Japan* (Washington, D.C.: Office of Air Force History, United States Air Force, 1986); Tami Davis Biddle, *Rhetoric and Reality in Air Warfare: The Evolution of British and American Ideas About Strategic Bombing, 1914–1945* (Princeton, NJ: Princeton University Press, 2002); Robert Pape, *Bombing to Win: Air Power and Coercion in War* (Ithaca: Cornell University Press, 1996); Mike Davis, "Berlin's Skeleton in Utah's Closet," in *Dead Cities: And Other Tales* (New York: New Press, 2002), 65–84.

226 "The ruthless bombing from the air of civilians" Franklin D. Roosevelt, "An Appeal to Great Britain, France, Italy, Germany, and Poland to Refrain from Air Bombing of Civilians," September 1, 1939, www.presidency.ucsb.edu/ws/?pid=15797.

226 **"conduct hostilities with a firm desire"** John Finnis, et al., *Nuclear Deterrence, Morality and Realism* (New York: Oxford University Press, 1987), 39.

227 **Britain introduced these three principles** Ibid., citing Sir John Slessor, *The Central Blue: Recollections and Reflections by Marshal of the Royal Air Force* (London: Cassell and Co., 1956), 213; "Protection of Civilian Populations Against Bombing From the Air in Case of War," League of Nations Resolution, September 30, 1938, www.dannen.com/decision /int-law.html#d.

227 **"the first terror bombing of a civilian population"** Barbara Tuchman, *Stilwell and the American Experience of China, 1911–1945* (New York: Macmillan, 1971), chapter 5.

227 **his manuscript in English didn't surface** See Herbert Mitgang, "Article Hemingway Wrote for Pravda in '38 Is Published in English," *New York Times*, November 29, 1982. It was published in *Pravda* on August 1, 1938, under the title "Humanity Will Not Forgive This!" The text was published in 1982 by William Braasch Watson, who provided an introduction.

239 **"an absolutely devastating, *exterminating attack*"** Finnis, et al., *Nuclear Deterrence, Morality and Realism*, 44. Emphasis added.

240 **"We will pay back a hundredfold"** F. M. Sallagar, *The Road to Total War: Escalation in World War II*, R-465-PR (Santa Monica, CA: RAND Corporation, April 1969), 111.

241 **"You know, there aren't too many bombs within that circle"** Freeman Dyson, *Disturbing the Universe* (New York: Harper & Row, 1979), 26.

242 **"If there was to be any strategic bombing at all"** Sallagar, *The Road to Total War*, 128.

242 **"Bomber Command, as represented by its Commander-in-Chief"** Ibid.

242 **"to employ a high proportion of incendiaries"** Ibid., 129.

243 **the American Jesuit John Ford and the British pacifist Vera Brittain** John C. Ford, S.J., "The Morality of Obliteration Bombing," *Theological Studies* 5, no. 3 (September 1944): 261–309; Vera Brittain, *Seeds of Chaos* (London: New Vision Publishing Co., 1944); Vera Brittain, *One Voice: Pacifist Writings from the Second World War* (London: Continuum, 2005). Another strong critic was the Anglican Bishop George Bell. See Andrew Chandler, "The Church of England and the Obliteration Bombing of Germany in the Second World War," *The English Historical Review* 108, no. 429 (1993): 920–946.

244 **"The primary object of your operations"** Ibid., 155–56.

244 **The primary targets listed were four important cities** Ibid., 156. On this directive, Sallagar comments: "There could be little question but that the intent was to launch a concentrated air offensive against German cities."

244 **"Ref. the new bombing directive"** Ibid., 157.

245 **"a pregnant date in air history"** Ibid.

245 **"a bombing directive had singled out the parts of cities"** Ibid.

Chapter 15: Burning Cities

247 **"Bodies were frequently found"** Robert N. Neer, *Napalm: An American Biography* (Cambridge, MA: Belknap Press, 2013), 63.

248 "Nobody understands to this day" Freeman Dyson, *Weapons and Hope* (New York: HarperCollins, 1984), 117.

248 "The Dresden fire storm was the worst" Freeman Dyson, *Disturbing the Universe* (New York: Harper & Row, 1979), 28.

248 a surrealistic account of the Dresden attack Kurt Vonnegut, *Slaughterhouse-Five* (New York: Delacorte Press, 1969).

249 "long-awaited decision to adopt deliberate" John W. Dower, *Cultures of War: Pearl Harbor/Hiroshima/9-11/Iraq* (New York: W. W. Norton & Company, 2010), 175.

249 On February 3, 1945, General Spaatz Michael S. Sherry, *The Rise of American Airpower: The Creation of Armageddon* (New Haven, CT: Yale University Press, 1987), 260–264. Sherry's book is particularly perceptive on the downslide toward area bombing and firebombing.

250 "Our policy never has been to inflict terror" Neer, *Napalm*, 65.

250 "It seems to me" Frederick Taylor, *Dresden: Tuesday 13 February, 1945* (London: Bloomsbury, 2005), 432. Emphasis added.

250 "assume that the view under consideration" Ibid., 432. Emphasis added.

251 American bombardiers weren't hitting See Malcolm Gladwell, "The Strange Tale of the Norden Bombsight," TED talk, July 2011, www.ted.com/talks/malcolm_gladwell?language=en.

253 "Incendiary projectiles would burn the cities" Michael S. Sherry, *The Rise of American Air Power: The Creation of Armageddon* (New Haven, CT: Yale University Press, 1987), 31, 58. See also Neer, *Napalm*, 66 (with references).

253 "There won't be any hesitation about bombing civilians" Dower, *Cultures of War*, 168. See also Sherry, *The Rise of American Air Power*, 109.

254 "no evasive action" became the rule Curtis LeMay, World War II Database, ww2db.com/person_bio.php?person_id=509.

254 His memoir, *Mission with LeMay* General Curtis E. LeMay, *Mission with LeMay: My Story*. With MacKinlay Kantor (New York: Doubleday and Company, 1965).

256 "Plenty of strategic targets right in the primary area" LeMay, *Mission with LeMay*, 349–352. Some thought paragraphs have been omitted.

257 "Drafts from the Tokyo fires" Ibid., 352.

258 "Contrary to supposition" Ibid., 253.

260 the *New York Times* was reporting Warren Moscow, "51 Square Miles Burned Out In Six B-29 Attacks on Tokyo," *New York Times*, May 30, 1945, A1, 4.

260 "only in the eleventh paragraph" Dower, *Cultures of War*, 183. See also Sherry, *The Rise of American Air Power*, 109.

260 or a night's troubled sleep Peter J. Kuznick, "The Decision to Risk the Future: Harry Truman, the Atomic Bomb and the Apocalyptic Narrative" *Asia-Pacific Journal* 5, no. 7 (July 2007), apjjf.org/-Peter-J.-Kuznick/2479/article.html (and see footnote 6).

261 "It is probable that more persons were killed in one six-hour period" United States Strategic Bombing Survey, *Effects of the Incendiary Bomb Attacks on Japan: A Report on Eight Cities*, Report 90, Dates of Survey: October 3, 1945–December 1, 1945. Washington, D.C.: Physical Damage Division, April 1947.

261 written for Stimson by McGeorge Bundy See James Hershberg's account of the genesis of this propaganda piece in his outstanding biography of Conant (who pressed Stimson to publish it and supervised Bundy in drafting it), *James B. Conant: Harvard to Hiroshima and the Making of the Nuclear Age* (New York: Knopf, 1993), 289–394.

262 "It is my opinion" William D. Leahy, *I Was There: The Personal Story of the Chief of Staff to Presidents Roosevelt and Truman Based on His Notes and Diaries Made at the Time* (New York: Whittlesey House, 1950), 441.

262 "we scorched and boiled and baked" LeMay, *Mission with LeMay*, 387.

262 The judgment that the bomb had not been necessary For references, see Oliver Stone and Peter Kuznick, *The Untold History of the United States* (New York: Simon & Schuster, 2012), 176–177.

263 "Based on a detailed investigation" United States Strategic Bombing Survey, Pacific War, July 1, 1946, 26, www.anesi.com/ussbs01.htm#hindsigh.

263 "There are no innocent civilians" Sherry, *The Rise of American Air Power*, 287. Interview June 29, 1981 (cf. 392).

Chapter 16: Killing a Nation

266 attack fifteen "key Soviet cities" Richard Rhodes, *Dark Sun: The Making of the Hydrogen Bomb* (New York: Simon & Schuster, 1995), 23–24. See also Gregg Herken, *Brotherhood of the Bomb* (New York: Henry Holt and Co., 2002), 142.

266 President Harry Truman himself wasn't formally briefed David Alan Rosenberg, "U.S. Nuclear Stockpile, 1945 to 1950," *Bulletin of the Atomic Scientists* 38, no. 5 (1982): 26. Rosenberg got these numbers declassified for the first time in 1982.

266 considered as "laboratory weapons" David Alan Rosenberg, "American Atomic Strategy and the Hydrogen Bomb Decision," *Journal of American History*, June 1979, 66.

267 "Atomic bombs in numbers" Ibid., 67.

267 capability for "killing a nation" Ibid., 67–68. And see Edward Kaplan, *To Kill Nations: American Strategy in the Air-Atomic Age and the Rise of Mutually Assured Destruction* (Ithaca, NY: Cornell University Press, 2015).

267 hit twenty cities with fifty bombs Rosenberg, "American Atomic Strategy," 68. See also Rosenberg, "U.S. Nuclear Stockpile," 26.

267 There were fifty bombs in the arsenal Gregg Herken, *The Winning Weapon: The Atomic Bomb in the Cold War 1945–1950* (New York: Knopf, 1981), 271.

267 strikes on seventy Soviet urban areas Rosenberg, "American Atomic Strategy," 70.

267 might kill 2.7 million people Ibid., 73.

268 in the stockpile by January 1, 1951 Rosenberg, "U.S. Nuclear Stockpile," 26.

268 Groves had overlooked Herken, *The Winning Weapon*, 341.

269 identified 409 airfields David Alan Rosenberg, "The Origins of Overkill: Nuclear Weapons and American Strategy, 1945-1960," *International Security* 7, no. 4 (Spring 1983): 35. Rosenberg's articles, this one in particular, are fundamental to published accounts of early nuclear war planning, based on declassified documents (many of which Rosenberg first revealed). For other important accounts see Fred Kaplan, *The Wizards of*

Armageddon (New York: Simon & Schuster, 1983); Marc Trachtenberg, *A Constructed Peace: The Making of the European Settlement, 1945–1963* (Princeton: NJ: Princeton University Press, 1999); Scott D. Sagan, *Moving Targets: Nuclear Strategy and National Security* (Princeton, NJ: Princeton University Press, 1989); Janne E. Nolan, *Guardians of the Arsenal: The Politics of Nuclear Strategy* (New York: Basic Books, 1989); and Desmond Ball and Jeffrey Richelson, eds., *Strategic Nuclear Targeting* (Ithaca, NY: Cornell University Press, 1986).

271 He told Gordon Dean . . . to "keep them confused" Adam Clymer, "A-Test 'Confusion' Laid to Eisenhower," *New York Times*, April 20, 1979 (citing Gordon Dean's diary for May 27, 1953).

271 Eisenhower had been "appalled" David Alan Rosenberg, "The Origins of Overkill: Nuclear Weapons and American Strategy, 1945–1960," in Steven E. Miller, ed., *Strategy and Nuclear Deterrence: An International Security Reader* (Princeton, NJ: Princeton University Press, 1984), 118.

271 "And we call ourselves the human race!" William Burr, "Studies by Once Top Secret Government Entity Portrayed Terrible Costs of Nuclear War," National Security Archive Electronic Briefing Book No. 480, posted July 22, 2014, nsarchive.gwu.edu/nukevault /ebb480/.

271 President Nixon in 1969 William Burr, "The Nixon Administration, the 'Horror Strategy,' and the Search for Limited Nuclear Options, 1969–1972," *Journal of Cold War Studies* 7, no. 3 (Summer 2005): 34.

271 His national security assistant Ibid., 35.

272 In 1973, midway in his abortive search William Burr, "To Have the Only Option That of Killing 80 Million People is the Height of Immorality," National Security Archive Briefing Book No. 173, November 23, 2005, nsarchive.gwu.edu/NSAEBB/NSAEBB173/. See also William Burr, "'Is This the Best They Can Do?': Henry Kissinger and the US Quest for Limited Nuclear Options, 1969–75," in *War Plans and Alliances in the Cold War: Threat Perceptions in the East and West*, eds. Vojtech Mastny, Sven G. Holtsmark, and Andreas Wenger (New York: Routledge, 2006), 118–140.

272 as General Lee Butler . . . has revealed George Lee Butler, *Uncommon Cause: A Life at Odds with Convention* (Denver: Outskirts Press, 2016), 6–17.

272 At the same time As I mentioned in the introduction, Edward Teller, the "father of the H-bomb," was apt to emphasize that the thousands of thermonuclear weapons in both arsenals, no matter how they were used, could kill *"at most a quarter* of the earth's population." He said this once in answer to a question I posed at a 1982 public hearing by a committee of the California legislature in Los Angeles on the pros and cons of a bilateral nuclear weapons freeze. He was dismissing the possibility of "omnicide," though I had not raised that term in my prior statement. He had insisted that he speak after me, with no rebuttal, but I couldn't resist questioning his assurance on this point, which he offered. Killing nearly everyone, he repeated, was *"impossible."* Teller's oral emphasis in both cases.

272 "only the extermination of our civilization" Edward Thompson, "Notes on Exterminism, the Last Stage of Civilization," *New Left Review* I, no. 121 (May–June 1980): 23, 29.

272 as something that needed to be resisted Daniel Ellsberg, *Papers on the War* (New York: Simon & Schuster, 1972), 10–12:

"In my opinion this war, even at this late stage, needs not only to be resisted; it remains to be understood.

"I am speaking of the limitations not only of public awareness but of the best analyses by 'experts'—former officials, radical critics, journalists, or academic specialists. No one known to me—and that includes myself—seems to possess as yet an adequate comprehension of the forces, institutions, motives, beliefs, and decisions that have led us as a nation to do what we have done to the people of Indochina as long as we have. No one seems to have an understanding fully adequate, that is, either to wage successful opposition against the process or effectively change it; or even adequate to the intellectual challenge of resolving the major puzzles and controversies about the way the process works today and has worked for the past quarter century. . . .

"One problem is that few of the analysts personally command experience or data concerning more than a few of the many dimensions of this process. Another is the relative lack of specialized studies in some of these areas, e.g., on the domestic politics of U.S. foreign policy. Above all, crucial data on the bureaucratic decision process have been closely guarded, limited to a few analysts—I was one—and publicly lied about.

"I repeat the premise: efforts at better understanding cannot be put off till the triumph of resistance, the end of the war (any more than continued resistance can await a perfect understanding).

"It was in this belief that I undertook, beginning in the fall of 1969, to reveal to the Congress and the American people the documents and analyses that came to be known as the Pentagon Papers."

All this applies—as I knew at the time—to our nuclear policy as well. As I've described in the introduction, it was my intention as I wrote this in 1972 to contribute to public understanding of the nuclear era by releasing the "other Pentagon Papers" on nuclear matters after my first trial.

Chapter 17: Risking Doomsday I

275 July 7, 1942 Gregg Herken, *Brotherhood of the Bomb* (New York: Henry Holt, 2002), 65–67.

276 "Certainty is a state of mind" Nuel Pharr Davis, *Lawrence and Oppenheimer* (New York: Simon & Schuster, 1968), 131–32.

276 "I'll never forget that morning" Arthur H. Compton, *Atomic Quest: A Personal Narrative* (New York: Oxford University Press, 1956), 127–28. Emphasis added.

277 "Actually, Professor Heisenberg" Richard Rhodes, *The Making of the Atomic Bomb* (New York: Simon & Schuster, 1987), 405, citing Albert Speer, *Inside the Third Reich* (New York: Macmillan, 1970), 227.

278 "these bombs must *never* be made" Compton, *Atomic Quest*, 128. Emphasis added.

278 "scientists discussed the dangers of fusion" Pearl S. Buck, "The Bomb—The End of the World?" *American Weekly*, March 8, 1959, 9–12.

279 "Once Bethe's calculations had relegated atmospheric ignition" Peter Goodchild, *Edward Teller: The Real Dr. Strangelove* (Cambridge: Harvard University Press, 2004), 66. Emphasis added.

279 "The impossibility of igniting the atmosphere" Ibid.

280 Accounts agree that when General Groves Davis, *Lawrence and Oppenheimer*, 235.

281 "In the final weeks leading up to the test" Goodchild, *Edward Teller*, 103–04. Emphasis added.

281 "Before the Trinity test" Thomas Powers, "Seeing the Light of Armageddon," *Rolling Stone*, April 29, 1982, 62. Emphasis added.

282 "Still alive . . . No atmospheric ignition." Davis, *Lawrence and Oppenheimer*, 239.

282 "The whole world has gone up in flames." James Hershberg, *James B. Conant: Harvard to Hiroshima and the Making of the Nuclear Age* (New York: Knopf, 1993), 232, citing a Conant speech of September 25, 1954.

284 "They're going to take this thing over" Davis, *Lawrence and Oppenheimer*, 241.

284 Oppenheimer had estimated that the first bomb Rhodes, *The Making of the Atomic Bomb*, 648.

284 According to Albert Speer Ibid., 405.

285 "the nearest thing to Doomsday" William L. Laurence, "Drama of the Atomic Bomb Found Climax in July 16 Test," *New York Times*, September 26, 1945.

Chapter 18: Risking Doomsday II

286 "the fission bomb was all well and good" Peter Goodchild, *Edward Teller: The Real Dr. Strangelove* (Cambridge: Harvard University Press, 2004), 63.

286 "Hans Bethe recalled talking to his wife" Goodchild, *Edward Teller*, 64.

287 "the cities of the United States" Leo Szilard, et al., "A Petition to the President of the United States," U.S. National Archives, Record Group 77, Records of the Chief of Engineers, Manhattan Engineer District, Harrison-Bundy File, folder #76, July 17, 1945, www.dannen.com/decision/45-07-17.html.

289 "that by one means or another, the development of these weapons" "The GAC Report of October 30, 1949" in Herbert York, *The Advisors: Oppenheimer, Teller, and the Superbomb* (Stanford, CA: Stanford University Press, 1989), 158.

289 "Reprisals by our large stock of atomic bombs" Ibid., 160.

289 "The majority feel that this should be" Ibid., 159.

290 "We base our recommendation on our belief" Ibid., 159–160.

290 "By its very nature it cannot be confined" E. Fermi and I. I. Rabi letter dated October 30, 1949, "An Opinion on the Development of the 'Super,'" in York, *The Advisors*, 161–162.

291 "to continue with its work on all forms of atomic energy weapons" York, *The Advisors*, 69.

291 "that enough be declassified about the super bomb" "The GAC Report of October 30, 1949," in York, *The Advisors*, 159.

293 The poet Allen Ginsberg and I Joseph Daniel, Keith Pope, Allen Ginsberg, LeRoy Moore, *A Year in Disobedience and a Criticality of Conscience* (Boulder, CO: Story Arts Media, 2013). See ellsberg.net.

294 That was the same factor Oppenheimer . . . predicted Gregg Herken, *Brotherhood of the Bomb* (New York: Henry Holt and Co., 2002), 67. Oppenheimer described a bomb—igniting

two to three tons of liquid deuterium—with an explosive yield of one hundred million tons of TNT, destroying some 360 square miles.

294 There were tears in his eyes His anguish was not misplaced. See Arjun Makhijani, Howard Hu, and Katherine Yi, eds., *Nuclear Wastelands: A Global Guide to Nuclear Weapons Production and Its Health and Environmental Effects* (Cambridge, MA: The MIT Press, 1995). See also Mike Davis, "Dead West: Ecocide in Marlboro Country," *New Left Review* I/200, (July–August 1993): 49–73. Reprinted in Mike Davis, *Dead Cities: And Other Tales* (New York: New Press, 2002), 33–64.

295 "a weapon of genocide" Fermi and Rabi, "An Opinion on the Development of the 'Super'," and "The GAC Report of October 30, 1949" in York, *The Advisors*, 161–162, 158, 160.

Chapter 19: The Strangelove Paradox

297 "This is probably one of the most closely kept secrets." Daniel F. Ford, *The Button: The Pentagon's Command and Control System—Does It Work?* (New York: Simon & Schuster, 1985), 141.

298 deploying SS-9 missiles with twenty-megaton warheads Ibid., 122–24.

299 frequent leaks and official statements . . . decapitation "Jimmy Carter's Controversial Nuclear Targeting Directive PD-59 Declassified," National Security Archive Electronic Briefing Book 390, September 4, 2012, nsarchive.gwu.edu/nukevault/ebb390/.

299 The Reagan administration continued "Reagan's Nuclear War Briefing Declassified: Kremlin Leaders Among Prime Targets in War Plan," National Security Archive Electronic Briefing Book No. 575, December 22, 2016, nsarchive.gwu.edu/nukevault/ebb575-Reagan -Nuclear

299 "increased emphasis in U.S. nuclear [weapons] employment policy" Leon Sloss and Marc Millot, "U.S. Nuclear Strategy in Evolution," mimeograph, December 12, 1983, 14; cited in Ford, *The Button*, 28. Emphasis added.

300 "the importance of crippling the [Soviet] command" Ford, *The Button*, 129.

300 "I am convinced that in the Soviet system" Letter from Bruce Holloway to Dr. Francis X. Kane, TRW, Inc., March 31, 1980, cited in Ford, *The Button*, 128.

301 they were building two thousand underground bunkers Ibid., 124.

301 increasing capability of multiple-target The hard-target-kill capability of SLBMs has in the last eight years—during the Obama administration—been enormously increased by introducing enhanced-accuracy "super-fuzes" for warheads: Hans M. Kristensen, et al., "How U.S. Nuclear Force Modernization is Undermining Strategic Stability," Bulletin of the Atomic Scientists, March 1, 2017, thebulletin.org/how-us-nuclear-force-modernization -undermining-strategic-stability-burst-height-compensating-super10578.

301 a major rationale then *and now* Anthony Capaccio, "U.S. Reviews Nuclear Strike Survival for Russia and China," *Bloomberg*, January 29, 2017, www.bloomberg.com/news /articles/2017-01-30/nuclear-strike-survival-for-russia-china-get-new-u-s-review.

302 "General Kuter told me that we had to complete the BMEWS" Herbert York, *Making Weapons, Talking Peace* (New York: Basic Books, 1987), 183–84.

304 "the premier loves surprises" Stanley Kubrick, Terry Southern, and Peter George, *Dr. Strangelove or: How I Learned to Stop Worrying and Love the Bomb*, directed by Stanley

Kubrick. Los Angeles, CA: Columbia Pictures Corporation, 1964, www.visual-memory.co
.uk/amk/doc/0055.html.

304 The designer of the secret Soviet Perimeter system Valery E. Yarynich, *C3: Nuclear
Command, Control, Cooperation* (Washington, D.C.: Center for Defense Information, 2003).

304 However, as David Hoffman David Hoffman, "Valery Yarynich, the Man Who Told of
the Soviets' Doomsday Machine," *Washington Post*, December 20, 2012.

306 "Yes, the 'Perimeter' system exists" "Russia's Secret Shield, aka Perimeter, Dead
Hand," *Pravda*, February 2, 2017, www.pravdareport.com/russia/politics/02-02-2017/136776
-perimeter-0/.

306 Ten days after President Trump's inauguration "Russia Tests Doomsday Weapon, US
Tests Russia's Ability to Survive," *Pravda*, January 30, 2017, www.pravdareport.com/hotspots
/conflicts/30-01-2017/136733-doomsday_weapon-0/.

306 National Defense Authorization Act for Fiscal Year 2017 In particular, Section 1647,
and c, on STRATCOM.

308 the starvation of one to two billion people or more Alan Robock and Owen Brian
Toon, "Self-Assured Destruction: The Climate Impacts of Nuclear War," *Bulletin of the
Atomic Scientists* 68, no. 5 (2012): 666–74; Ira Helfand, "Nuclear Famine: Two Billion People
at Risk?" *International Physicians for the Prevention of Nuclear War*, November 2013. See
Owen B. Toon, et al., "Consequences of Regional-Scale Nuclear Conflicts," *Science* 315, no.
5816 (2007): 1224–1225, calculating the possible reduction in sunlight—and its effects on
global harvests and growing seasons—of a conflict between India and Pakistan involving
only fifty Hiroshima-size fission weapons on each side. See also Alan Robock and Owen
Brian Toon, "Local Nuclear War, Global Suffering," *Scientific American* 302 (January 2010):
74–81, climate.envsci.rutgers.edu/pdf/RobockToonSciAmJan2010.pdf. Ira Helfand, M.D.,
International Physicians for the Prevention of Nuclear War, has calculated that these
climatic effects on global food supplies could starve to death up to two billion of the world's
most undernourished people: "Nuclear Famine: Two Billion People At Risk? Global
Impacts of Limited Nuclear War on Agriculture, Food Supplies, and Human Nutrition,"
2nd edition, 2013 www.psr.org/assets/pdfs/two-billion-at-risk.pdf.

Chapter 20: First-Use Threats

310 "Nixon not only *wanted* to end the Vietnam War" H. R. Haldeman, *The Ends of Power*
(New York: Times Books, 1978), 82–83. Emphasis in original.

310 Art of Coercion lectures: See ellsberg.net/Doomsday/Art of Coercion and Daniel Ellsberg, "The Theory and Practice of Blackmail," in Oran R. Young, ed., *Bargaining: Formal
Theories of Negotiation* (Urbana: University of Illinois Press, 1975), 343–363.

310 Hitler's deliberate use of his reputation for madness "The Political Uses of Madness,"
ellsberg.net/Doomsday/Art of Coercion.

311 his "madman theory" The first extensive investigation and discussion of Nixon's
threats, plans, and secret nuclear alert in the fall of 1969 and Nixon's madman strategy
appeared in Seymour Hersh's amazingly revelatory book, *The Price of Power: Kissinger in
the Nixon White House* (New York: Summit Books, 1983). Subsequently, see Scott D. Sagan
and Jeremi Suri, "The Madman Nuclear Alert: Secrecy, Signaling, and Safety in October
1969," *International Security* 27, no. 4 (Spring 2003): 150–183, and William Burr and Jeffrey

P. Kimball, *Nixon's Nuclear Specter: The Secret Alert of 1969, Madman Diplomacy, and the Vietnam War* (Lawrence: University Press of Kansas, 2015), greatly extending earlier articles by Burr and Kimball. See also "Nixon, Kissinger, and the Madman Strategy during Vietnam War," National Security Archive Electronic Briefing Book No. 587, May 29, 2015, nsarchive.gwu.edu/nukevault/ebb517-Nixon-Kissinger-and-the-Madman-Strategy-during-Vietnam-War/; "Nixon's Nuclear Ploy: The Vietnam Negotiations and the Joint Chiefs of Staff Readiness Test, October 1969," National Security Archive Electronic Briefing Book No. 81, December 23, 2002, nsarchive.gwu.edu/NSAEBB/NSAEBB81/index.htm; "Nixon White House Considered Nuclear Options Against North Vietnam, Declassified Documents Reveal: Nuclear Weapons, the Vietnam War, and the 'Nuclear Taboo,'" National Security Archive Electronic Briefing Book No. 195, July 31, 2006, nsarchive.gwu.edu/NSAEBB/NSAEBB195/index.htm.

311 **Nixon "believed his hard-line anti-Communist rhetoric"** Ibid.

311 **"That kept them under some control"** Sherman Adams, *Firsthand Report: The Story of the Eisenhower Administration* (New York: Harper & Brothers, 1961), 48–49.

312 **"Some say that we were brought to the verge of war"** James Shepley, "How Dulles Averted War," *Life*, January 16, 1956, 78.

313 **"the most dangerous man in America"** Seymour Hersh, *The Price of Power: Kissinger in the Nixon White House* (New York: Summit Books, 1983), 385.

313 **What had prevented Nixon's test** Richard Nixon, *RN: The Memoirs of Richard Nixon* (New York: Grossett and Dunlap, 1978), 401–03. See also Hersh, *The Price of Power*, 130.

315 **I began to look back at the history of U.S. first-use threats** For an early important account, see Sidney Lens, *The Day Before Doomsday: An Anatomy of the Nuclear Arms Race* (Garden City, NY: Doubleday, 1977).

316 **Thus, after Harry Truman had answered** Harry S. Truman, "The President's News Conference," November 30, 1950. Gerhard Peters and John T. Woolley, The American Presidency Project, www.presidency.ucsb.edu/ws/?pid=13673. Also Truman's memoirs, vol. II, *1946–52: Years of Trial and Hope* (New York: Signet, 1965), 450–51; and Dean Acheson, *Present at the Creation* (New York: W. W. Norton & Company, 1969), 472–85.

317 **Yes, Eisenhower did say in his first volume of memoirs** Dwight D. Eisenhower, *The White House Years, 1953–1956: Mandate for Change* (Garden City, NY: Doubleday, 1963), 178, 180.

317 **account of an NSC meeting early in the Eisenhower administration** S. Everett Gleason, "Memorandum of Discussion at the 131st meeting of the National Security Council," February 11, 1953. Top Secret, Eyes Only (declassified). Eisenhower Library, Eisenhower papers, Whitman file, history.state.gov/historicaldocuments/frus1952-54v02p1/d46. Emphasis added.

318 **"the President ruled against any discussion with our allies"** The corresponding discussion in Eisenhower's memoirs does raise the subject of allied attitudes (and perhaps, implicitly, those of the American public as well) in remarks that may well express the attitudes of some later Presidents (e.g., Richard Nixon, then Eisenhower's vice president) when they contemplated presenting a U.S. nuclear first use to allies and the American public as a *fait accompli*:

"If we decided upon a major, new type of offensive, the present policies would have to be changed and the new ones agreed to by our allies. Foremost would be the proposed use of atomic weapons. In this respect American views have always differed somewhat from those of some of our allies. For the British, for example, the use of atomic weapons in war at that time would have been a decision of the gravest kind. *My* feeling was then, and still remains, that it would be impossible for the United States to maintain the military commitments which it now sustains around the world (without turning into a garrison state) did we not possess atomic weapons and the will to use them when necessary. But an American decision to use them at the time would have created strong disruptive feelings between ourselves and our allies. *However, if an all-out offensive should be highly successful, I felt that the rifts so caused could, in time, be repaired.*" Emphasis added. Eisenhower, *The White House Years, 1953–1956: Mandate for Change*, 180.

318 when Eisenhower directed the Joint Chiefs Morton Halperin, *The 1958 Taiwan Straits Crisis: A Documentary History*, RAND Corporation Research Memorandum RM-4900-ISA, December 1966 (redacted, formerly Top Secret), www.rand.org/content/dam/rand/pubs /research_memoranda/2006/RM4900.pdf. For passages and pages omitted from the RAND publication, and for my own notes on the crisis as a consultant to Halperin's study, see ells berg.net/Doomsday/Quemoy.

318 "It has never been true that nuclear war is 'unthinkable'" E. P. Thompson and Dan Smith, eds., *Protest and Survive* (New York: Penguin, 1980), 42.

319 The long-secret history of this period In my essay "Call to Mutiny," introduction to *Protest and Survive*, E. P Thompson and Dan Smith, eds. (New York: Monthly Review, 1981), I presented a list of eleven cases, plus a reference to nineteen nuclear "shows of force" listed by Barry Blechman and Stephen Kaplan, *Force without War: U.S. Armed Forces as a Political Instrument* (Washington, D.C.: Brookings Institution Press, 1978). Six presidents and thirty-six years later, many other cases have surfaced, thanks to FOIA and such windfalls as the Nixon tapes. Joseph Gerson's outstanding analysis, *Empire and the Bomb: How the U.S. Uses Nuclear Weapons to Dominate the World* (London: Pluto Press, 2007) adds some examples not listed here: see his Table 1.1, pp. 37–38, which also illustrates that the Soviets, Chinese, Israelis, Pakistanis, and Indians have all used their bombs in the same ways as the U.S., though much less often. See also Konrad Ege and Arjun Makhijani, "U.S. Nuclear Threats: A Documentary History," *Counterspy* (July–August 1982) and Richard K. Betts, *Nuclear Blackmail and Nuclear Balance* (Washington, D.C.: Brookings Institution Press, 1987).

319 Truman's deployment of B-29s Gregg Herken, *The Winning Weapon: The Atomic Bomb in the Cold War, 1945–1950* (New York: Knopf, 1980), 256–74.

320 Eisenhower's secret nuclear threats Eisenhower's memoirs, vol. I, *The White House Years, 1953–1956: Mandate for Change*, 178–81. See also Alexander L. George and Richard Smoke, *Deterrence in American Foreign Policy* (New York: Columbia University Press, 1974), 237–41.

320 Secretary of State Dulles's secret offers Prime Minister Bidault in the film *Hearts and Minds*, and in Roscoe Drummond and Gaston Coblentz, *Duel at the Brink* (New York: Doubleday, 1960), 121–22. See also Richard Nixon's memoirs, *RN: The Memoirs of Richard Nixon* (New York: Grosset & Dunlap, 1978), 150–55.

320 Internal agreement under Eisenhower and Dulles Richard K. Betts, *Nuclear Blackmail and Nuclear Balance* (Washington, D.C.: Brookings Institution Press, 1987), 54–62, Dulles's quote on page 61. See also Robert S. Norris and Hans M. Kristensen, "U.S. Nuclear Threats: Then and Now," *Bulletin of the Atomic Scientists* 62, no. 5 (2006): 70.

320 "Diplomatic use of the Bomb" Richard Nixon, "A Nation Coming into Its Own," *Time*, July 29, 1985.

320 prevent an Iraqi move into the oil fields of Kuwait Blechman and Kaplan, *Force without War*, 238, 256.

320 use nuclear weapons against China Morton Halperin, *The 1958 Taiwan Straits Crisis: A Documentary History*, RAND Corporation Research Memorandum RM-4900-ISA, December 1966 (redacted, formerly Top Secret), www.rand.org/content/dam/rand/pubs /research_memoranda/2006/RM4900.pdf. For passages and pages omitted from the RAND publication, and for my own notes on the crisis as a consultant to Halperin's study, see ells berg.net/Doomsday/Quemoy.

320 1958–59 Berlin crisis Nixon, "A Nation Coming into Its Own."

320 1961–62 Berlin crisis See chapter 10, "Berlin and the Missile Gap." Also Blechman and Kaplan, *Force without War*, 343–439.

320 The Cuban missile crisis, 1962 See chapter 12, "My Cuban Missile Crisis" and chapter 13, "Cuba: The Real Story."

320 Numerous "shows of nuclear force" Blechman and Kaplan, *Force without War*, 47–49, with a table listing nineteen such incidents between November 1946 and the worldwide SAC alert of October 1973.

320 defend Marines surrounded at Khe Sanh, Vietnam, 1968 Herbert Schandler, *The Unmaking of a President* (Princeton, NJ: Princeton University Press, 1977), 89–91. See also General Westmoreland's memoirs, William C. Westmoreland, *A Soldier Reports* (New York: Doubleday, 1976), 338. "If Washington officials were so intent on 'sending a message' to Hanoi, surely small tactical nuclear weapons would be a way to tell Hanoi something, just as two atomic bombs had spoken convincingly to Japanese officials during World War II, and the threat of atomic bombs induced the North Koreans to accept meaningful negotiations during the Korean War. It could be that use of a few small tactical nuclear weapons in Vietnam—or even the threat of them—might have quickly brought the war there to an end."

320 deter Soviet attack on Chinese nuclear capability Nixon, "A Nation Coming into Its Own."

321 Nixon's secret threats of massive escalation H. R. Haldeman's memoirs, *The Ends of Power* (New York: Times Books, 1978), 81–85, 97–98; and Richard Nixon's memoirs, *RN*, 393–414. See also Seymour Hersh, *The Price of Power: Kissinger in the Nixon White House* (New York: Summit Books, 1983); Larry Berman, *No Peace, No Honor: Nixon, Kissinger, and Betrayal in Vietnam* (New York: Free Press, 2001); John A. Farrell, *Richard Nixon: The Life* (New York: Doubleday, 2017).

321 deter India from further military pressure Nixon, "A Nation Coming into Its Own."

321 Nixon's NSC put SAC on high alert in October 1973 Nixon, "A Nation Coming into Its Own."

321 President Ford placed nuclear weapons on DEFCON 3 Norris and Kristensen, "U.S. Nuclear Threats," 70, quoting Major General John K. Singlaub, *Hazardous Duty: An American Soldier in the Twentieth Century* (New York: Summit Books, 1991) cited in (and see also) Richard A. Mobley, "Revisiting the Korean Tree-Trimming Incident," *Joint Force Quarterly* (Summer 2003): 110–111, 113–114. I am indebted to Norris and Kristensen for their references to this incident, the first one known to me involving the brief Ford administration.

However, it might be more accurate to regard it as a "show of force," like those listed by Blechman and Kaplan in *Force without War*, than as a nuclear threat.

321 "The Carter Doctrine on the Middle East" References in text.

321 Serious White House and JCS consideration, in August 1980 The August 1980 White House discussion was reported by Richard Halloran in "Washington Talk; How Leaders Think the Unthinkable," *New York Times*, September 2, 1986, based on interviews and an account of the secretary of defense and JCS involvement by Benjamin F. Schemmer: "Was the U.S. Ready to Resort to Nuclear Weapons for the Persian Gulf in 1980?" *Armed Forces Journal International* (September 1986). This latter highly significant and authoritative account, including named sources, has been almost entirely ignored in the literature, except for Halloran's story, likewise ignored. Schemmer quotes White House officials as describing this virtually unknown 1980 crisis as "the most serious nuclear crisis since the Cuban Missile Crisis." Administration officials regarded the explicit threats to the Soviets as successful. See also, AP, *Rocky Mountain News*, August 27, 1986, citing NBC News, August 26: "NBC quoted intelligence sources as saying that that the Soviet Union was thought to be on the verge of attacking the oil-rich Persian Gulf in August 1980, while Iran was holding American hostages. NBC quoted General David Jones, who was chairman of the Joint Chiefs at the time, as saying 'there was no way the United States had the conventional capability to stop the Soviets if they had wanted to make a major move into Iran . . . The case was then, as it is to a large extent now, that if the Soviets decided to move in a major offensive into that region [as the White House feared at that moment, eight months after the Carter doctrine had been announced] then you would probably have to consider the use of nuclear weapons to stop them, Jody Powell, Carter's press secretary at the time, told NBC.'" Note that these accounts came out, to little notice, in 1986, six years after a reported nuclear crisis took place during the 1980 presidential campaign. It had been kept totally secret and unreported at the time and—as is typical of presidential memoirs except for Eisenhower's—is not mentioned in President Carter's subsequent memoirs.

321 The Carter Doctrine reaffirmed in essence References in text.

321 Formal threats by the George H. W. Bush administration Norris and Kristensen, "U.S. Nuclear Threats," 71, and William M. Arkin, "Calculated Ambiguity: Nuclear Weapons and the Gulf War," *Washington Quarterly* 19, no. 4 (Autumn 1996): 2–18. Both of these provide many more references.

322 Explicit, secret threats by the Clinton administration Norris and Kristensen, "U.S. Nuclear Threats," 70, citing congressional testimony by General Eugene Habiger, commander of the U.S. Strategic Command (Stratcom), before the U.S. Senate Armed Services Committee, March 13, 1997. "Asked what 'sort of deterrence' he thought U.S. nuclear weapons played in preventing WMD from being used by rogue states, Habiger responded, 'In my view, sir, it plays a very larger role . . . [The threat of U.S. nuclear use] was passed to the North Koreans back in 1995, when the North Koreans were not coming off their reactor approach they were taking.'" Habiger subsequently explained [in conversation with Kristensen, August 12, 2004] that the message passed on to North Korea had been explicit (70).

322 Public warning of a nuclear option by Clinton's secretary of defense Norris and Kristensen, "U.S. Nuclear Threats: Then and Now," citing Robert Burns, "U.S. Libya," Associated Press, April 23, 1996, and "Nuclear Weapons Only Option for USA to Hit Buried

Targets," *Jane's Defence Weekly*, May 1, 1996, 3. As the latter headline indicates, this episode under Clinton aired the "need" for bunker-buster nuclear weapons against hardened underground sites that might harbor WMDs (or rogue statesmen like Saddam Hussein) that had been publicized in the Gulf War. This purported need arose again in the Iraq War, and has since 2004 led to plans for possible nuclear strikes against underground nuclear energy installations in Iran. That exemplifies the "nuclear option" that the president and most recent Democratic and Republican presidential candidates, with the possible exception of Barack Obama but including Hillary Clinton and Donald Trump, insist must be on the table in negotiating with *everyone*, in particular in 2017 under Trump, with North Korea.

322 "atomic diplomacy" The term introduced by Gar Alperovitz in his pathbreaking work, *Atomic Diplomacy: Hiroshima and Potsdam* (New York: Vintage Books, 1965).

322 a "taboo" against nuclear weapons' use Nina Tannenwald, *The Nuclear Taboo: The United States and the Non-Use of Nuclear Weapons Since 1945* (Cambridge, Cambridge University Press: 2008).

322 "tradition of non-*use*" T. V. Paul, *The Tradition of Non-Use of Nuclear Weapons* (Stanford: Stanford Security Studies, 2009).

323 "Even [Secretary of State George] Marshall" Herken, *The Winning Weapon*, 274.

324 In his State of the Union address in 1984 George P. Shultz and James E. Goodby, *The War That Must Never Be Fought* (Hoover Institution, 2015), xii.

324 India at its second test See the important study by Achin Vanaik, *After the Bomb: Reflections on India's Nuclear Journey* (New Delhi: Orient Blackswan, 2015).

324 the Soviet Union from 1982 until 1993 Serge Schemann, "Russia Drops Pledge of No First Use of Atom Arms," *New York Times*, November 4, 1993.

325 U.N. Resolution 36/100 Declaration on the Prevention of Nuclear Catastrophe, U.N. General Assembly 91st plenary meeting, December 9, 1981, www.un.org/documents/ga/res/36/a36r100.htm.

326 "the American forces could not stop a Soviet thrust" Richard Burt, "Loading For Bear; 'One-and-a-Half War' Strategy Now Means Just What It Says Money Is a Critical Obstacle," *New York Times*, February 2, 1980.

326 "delivering tactical nuclear warheads by cruise missiles" Joshua M. Epstein, *Strategy and Force Planning: The Case of the Persian Gulf* (Washington, D.C.: Brookings Institution Press, 1986), 16, citing Kenneth Waltz, "Strategy for the Rapid Deployment Force," *International Security* 5 (Spring 1981): 64n20.

327 Dyess answered both questions *Newsmakers*, NBC, February 3, 1980.

328 In 2005-2006 there were articles Philip Giraldi, "Deep Background," *American Conservative*, August 1, 2005. Seymour Hersh, "Last Stand," *New Yorker*, April 10-17, 2006 and "The Iran Plans," *New Yorker*, July 10-17, 2006. Giraldi said the tactical nuclear weapons were for "suspected nuclear-weapons-program development sites" that were "hardened or are deep underground and could not be taken out by conventional weapons." Hersh also reported, along with his accounts of the detailed discussions and planning, high-level military skepticism about the feasibility and consequences of the planned air attack, and very strong opposition to the "nuclear option" by the Joint Chiefs of Staff (JCS). As a result, he reported in July 2005, the White House had reluctantly "dropped its insistence that the plan for a bombing campaign include the possible use of a nuclear device to destroy Iran's uranium-enrichment plan at Natanz," although a former senior intelligence official told him, "Bush and Cheney were dead serious about the nuclear planning" and "the civilian hierarchy feels extraordinarily betrayed by the brass."

328 But on April 18, 2006 Quoted in Scott Sagan, "The Case for No First-Use," *Survival* 5, Number 3 (2009), 174, with my emphasis added, as indicated in original video. See original video of White House Office of the Press Secretary, "President Bush Nominates Rob Portman as OMB Director and Susan Schwab for USTR," April 18, 2006. When used by politicians about Iran in 2006–2008, the phrase "all options" evidently meant "all except for direct negotiations with Iran, regular diplomatic relations, assurances against American attack, or expanded trade." Obama broke with that tradition with the Iran nuclear deal, and has been heavily criticized for doing so by Trump, who has threatened to rip up the Iran deal, and resumed the earlier restricted meaning of "all options" with regard to North Korea, and perhaps with Iran.

328 Others who used it during the 2008 presidential campaign Thus, for example, Edwards at the Herzliya Conference in Israel in January 2007: "To ensure that Iran never gets nuclear weapons, we need to keep ALL options on the table. Let me reiterate—ALL options must remain on the table." Emphasis his, in his written transcript. Ron Brynaert, "Edwards: 'Iran Must Know World Won't Back Down,'" Raw Story, January 23, 2007.

328 five of the nine Republican candidates taking part in a debate Republican Presidential Debate, CNN, June 5, 2007, transcripts.cnn.com/TRANSCRIPTS/0706/05/se.01.html.

329 "I think it would be a profound mistake" Dennis Conrad, Associated Press, August 2, 2007.

329 "presidents *never* take the nuclear option off the table" Steve Holland, "Obama, Clinton in New Flap, Over Nuclear Weapons," Reuters, August 2, 2007. Clinton was "extending their feud over whether Obama has enough experience to be elected president in November 2008."

330 "I would never take any of my cards off the table" "Full Transcript: MSNBC Town Hall with Donald Trump Moderated by Chris Matthews," March 30, 2016, info.msnbc .com/_news/2016/03/30/35330907-full-transcript-msnbc-town-hall-with-donald-trump -moderated-by-chris-matthews.

331 Barack Obama being the only president Bruce Blair, "How Obama Could Revolutionize Nuclear Weapons Strategy Before He Goes," *Politico Magazine*, June 22, 2016, www .politico.com/magazine/story/2016/06/barack-obama-nuclear-weapons-213981. David E. Sanger and William J. Broad, "Obama Unlikely to Vow No First Use of Nuclear Weapons," *New York Times*, September 5, 2016, www.nytimes.com/2016/09/06/science/obama-unlikely-to -vow-no-first-use-of-nuclear-weapons.html.

332 the last bargaining strategy mentioned above Donald Trump could cite the authority of STRATCOM, Strategic Command, "Essentials of Post-Cold War Deterrence," the successor to SAC, in 1995: "Because of the value that comes from the ambiguity of what the US may do to an adversary if the acts we seek to deter are carried out, it hurts to portray ourselves as too fully rational and cool-headed. The fact that some elements may appear to be potentially 'out of control' can be beneficial to creating and reinforcing fears and doubts within the minds of an adversary's decision makers. This essential sense of fear is the working force of deterrence. That the US may become irrational and vindictive if its vital interests are attacked should be a part of the national persona we project to all adversaries." Obtained under FOIA by Hans Kristensen, www.nukestrat.com/us/stratcom /SAGessentials.PDF.

332 reminiscent, to many observers, of Nixon's madman theory James Hohmann, "The Daily 202: Donald Trump embraces the risky 'Madman Theory' on foreign policy," *Washington Post*, December 20, 2016. See also Nicole Hemmer, "The 'Madman Theory' of Nuclear War Has Existed for Decades. Now, Trump Is Playing the Madman," *Vox*, January 4, 2017, www.vox.com/the-big-idea/2017/1/4/14165670/madman-theory-nuclear-weapons -trump-nixon. Excerpt from Trump interview on *Face the Nation*, January 3, 2016, www .youtube.com/watch?v=QVTAaJ1fzfc.

333 Speaking personally, I have always shared See my articles, "Ending Nuclear Terrorism: By America and Others," in Richard Falk and David Krieger, eds., *At the Nuclear Precipice: Catastrophe or Transformation* (New York: Palgrave Macmillan, 2009), 83–96; "U.S. Nuclear Terrorism," in Karen Lofthus Carrington and Susan Griffin, eds., *Transforming Terror: Remembering the Soul of the World* (Berkeley: University of California Press, 2011), 19–25.

Chapter 21: Dismantling the Doomsday Machine

338 The results from either a preemptive or a retaliatory U.S. attack Though the framework of "withhold" options for cities and central command in Moscow remained in place for decades on paper, the reality at the operational level and the point of impact remained that of SIOP-62, totally negating these "options." General George Lee Butler (USAF, Ret.), the last commander of SAC and the first commander of its successor the Strategic Command, makes that clear in his unprecedentedly candid memoirs. For a description of the planning process as it existed in the Eighties, Butler gives space in his memoir to Franklin C. Miller, who eventually served under seven defense secretaries and as the NSC's senior director for defense policy and arms control. Miller reports that when he became director of strategic forces policy in the Office of the Secretary of Defense (OSD) in 1981, he found a situation unchanged from what I had discovered a generation earlier:

"The first issue we took on had its origins in Secretary of Defense Robert McNamara's 1962 speech to the American Bar Association in Chicago [a Kaufmann-drafted precursor to the Athens and Ann Arbor speeches]. McNamara argued that the President should have the option, in a major counter-military strike, to spare ('withhold') attacks on certain Soviet cities in the hope of sending a signal of restraint to the Kremlin. This was incorporated into formal plans. At some point, presumably in the 1970s, the war planners at the JSTPS [the Joint Strategic Target Planning Staff, which produced the SIOP] (without informing the Joint Staff or OSD, much less the White House staff) had decided to define a 'city' in such a manner that had the President ordered a strike that included the cities withhold, all of those cities would nevertheless have been obliterated."

Similarly, though Presidential Guidance was "not to rely on launch on warning of attack," while allowing preplanning of the "option" to do so, "It was disturbing to discover during our involvement in the LUA [launch under attack, an alternative description of launch on warning] debate that, despite Presidential guidance, the JSTPS resented our involvement in what they considered a strictly military issue, in part because no senior officer there could believe a President would not choose to direct a launch on warning/ under attack."

Finally, when Miller accompanied Secretary of Defense Cheney to a briefing on the SIOP in 1989 (the year the Berlin Wall came down), Cheney "was astonished at the number of weapons directed to the general area of Moscow."

So much for my success in 1961–62, nearly thirty years earlier, in trying to modify SAC war plans. Reading Butler's disillusioned and, for me, disillusioning memoir last year (it came out as an ebook, self-published, in 2016), I reflected that perhaps, even so, I had brought about one single change in the prevailing preparations for general war. McNamara's had directed, based on my draft, that there should be a "withhold option" on attacking China in the event of armed conflict with the Soviet Union, rather than automatic annihilation of China in any such war. That was my special contribution, from my knowledge of PACOM plans; all the other elements of the strategy were familiar at RAND. Nothing else we had proposed in 1961, so far as I could see, seemed to have survived even a decade bureaucratically.

Still, that alone could have seemed to me potentially a great achievement—saving a hundred million lives in China in the event of a decapitating attack on Washington!—if not for what I now knew about nuclear winter. However, just months after reading the Butler/ Miller revelations last year, I was staggered to read a 1968 document sent to me in October by a former SAC officer, Joel Dobson, who had come across it on the National Security Archive website in a briefing book I hadn't seen. It recorded notes of a meeting of President Lyndon Johnson with his secretaries of defense and state, Clark Clifford and Dean Rusk, the JCS and their chairman General Earle Wheeler, Walt Rostow, and others, in the Cabinet Room on October 14, 1968.

The memo was a single page, headed Eyes Only For the President, originally Top Secret, (finally declassified after several appeals, apparently in 2010, some nine years from the time the National Security Archive first requested it), The notes read:

> Secretary Clifford: There have been instructions issued on authority to release nuclear weapons in the event the President has been killed or cannot found. This is to prevent a breakdown in the chain of command.
> The project's code-name is "Furtherance."
> We recommend three major changes:
> (1) Under the former orders, a full nuclear response against both the Soviet Union and China was ordered if we were attacked. Under the change, the response could go to either country—not both. There could be a small-scale or accidental attack. We do not recommend full attack at all times. This would permit a limited response.
> (2) Instructions on the response to a conventional attack would be conventional, not nuclear as is now in the plan.
> (3) There was only one document of instructions beforehand. Now there would be two documents.
> (4) We all recommend this.
> Walt Rostow: We think it is an essential change. This was dangerous. We recommend going forward.
> (General Wheeler and all the JCS concurred.)

October 1968. Ten years after I had first seen the Pacific Command war plans, almost eight years after I had reported on them to McGeorge Bundy and had drafted for McNamara's signature a directive—which he sent to the JCS—to *exclude automatic attack* on China in the event of our armed conflict with the Soviet Union. So far as I had ever known, over the last half century, that 1968 "change" had been ordered by the secretary of defense and embodied in war plans a full seven years before this presidential meeting.

338 That was what Nixon and Kissinger found William Burr, "The Nixon Administration, the 'Horror Strategy,' and the Search for Limited Nuclear Options, 1969–1972," *Journal of Cold War Studies* 7, no. 3 (Summer 2005): 34. William Burr, "To Have the Only Option That of Killing 80 Million People is the Height of Immorality," National Security Archive Briefing Book No. 173, November 23, 2005, nsarchive.gwu.edu/NSAEBB /NSAEBB173/.

338 efforts as delusional . . . defense secretaries and their aides See closing chapters 25 and 26 of Fred Kaplan's *The Wizards of Armageddon* (New York: Simon & Schuster, 1983), 356–391.

340 "It was Senator Kennedy's intention" Theodore C. Sorensen, editorial note in Robert F. Kennedy, *Thirteen Days: A Memoir of the Cuban Missile Crisis* (New York: W. W. Norton & Company, 1969), 98.

340 the programs of Presidents Obama, Trump, and Putin William J. Broad and David E. Sanger, "U.S. Ramping Up Major Renewal in Nuclear Arms," *New York Times*, September 21, 2014. Kingston Reif, "Trump Continues Obama Nuclear Funding," *Arms Control Today*, July/August 2017, www.armscontrol.org/act/2017-07/news/trump-continues-obama-nuclear -funding.1080/00963402.2017.1290375. President Trump is now signing contracts for replacement of the entire nuclear triad, in advance of his end-of-the-year review of strategic policy. David E. Sanger and William J. Broad, "U.S. To Overhaul Nuclear Arsenal Despite the Risk," *New York Times*, August 28, 2017.

343 We must begin now the effort to explore The far-sighted article by Randall Forsberg, "The Freeze and Beyond: Confining the Military to Defense as a Route to Disarmament," *World Policy Journal* 1, No. 2 (Winter 1984): 285–318, an early exposition of the important concepts of "non-offensive defense" and "cooperative security," is still highly relevant, as is John D. Steinbruner, *Principles of Global Security* (Washington, D.C.: Brookings Institution Press, 2000), and John D. Steinbruner and Nancy Gallagher, "Prospects for Global Security," *Daedalus* (Summer 2004): 83–103.

343 more than 120 nations that adopted the treaty United Nations General Assembly, Treaty on the Prohibition of Nuclear Weapons, July 7, 2017 undocs.org/A/CONF.229/2017/8. See also Aria Bendix, "122 Nations Sign 'Historic' Treaty Banning Nuclear Weapons: While the Treaty Faces Many Barriers to Implementation, It Signifies a Profound International Statement," *Atlantic*, July 8, 2017, www.theatlantic.com/news/archive/2017/07/122-nations -approve-historic-treaty-to-ban-nuclear-weapons/533046/.

343 an accidental detonation Eric Schlosser's brilliant investigation of the Titan II accident at Damascus, Arkansas, on December 18, 1980, reveals that this incident could have resulted in a nuclear explosion possibly triggering an all-out war. Eric Schlosser, *Command and Control: Nuclear Weapons, the Damascus Accident, and the Illusion of Safety* (New York: Penguin, 2013). See also Milton Leitenberg, "Accidents of Nuclear Weapons and Nuclear Weapon Delivery Systems," *SIPRI Yearbook of World Armaments and Disarmament 1968–69* (Stockholm: Almqvist & Wiksell, 1969), 259–270, and Milton Leitenberg, "Accidents of Nuclear Weapons Systems," *World Armaments and Disarmament, SIPRI Yearbook 1977* (Cambridge, MA: MIT Press, 1977), 52–82. See also "Every Nuclear Tipped Missile is an 'Accident Waiting to Happen,'" National Security Archive Electronic Briefing Book No.

442, posted October 7, 2013, edited by William Burr, nsarchive2.gwu.edu/nukevault
/ebb442/

344 dismantle entirely Five years ago David Krieger and I urged just that (not for the first time) and spelled out the reasons for it, after being arrested with thirteen others at Vandenberg Air Force base protesting the imminent test flight of a Minuteman III. David Krieger and Daniel Ellsberg, "For Nuclear Security Beyond Seoul [Nuclear Security Summit], Eradicate Land-Based 'Doomsday' Missiles," *Christian Science Monitor*, March 27, 2012. See ellsberg.net.

344 currently rescheduled for "refurbishment" "The other contracts the Pentagon announced last week are for replacements for the 400 aging Minutemen intercontinental ballistic missiles housed in underground silos. The winners of $677 million in contracts— Boeing and Northrop Grumman—will develop plans for a replacement force . . . Mr. Perry, who was defense secretary under President Bill Clinton, has argued that the United States can safely phase out its land-based force, calling the missiles a costly relic of the Cold War. But the Trump administration appears determined to hold on to the ground-based system, and to invest heavily in it. The cost of replacing the Minutemen missiles and remaking the command-and-control system is estimated at roughly 100 billion." Sanger and Broad, "U.S. To Overhaul Nuclear Arsenal Despite the Risk."

344 Former secretary of defense William Perry has argued William J. Perry (secretary of defense 1994–1997), "Why It's Safe to Scrap America's ICBMs," *New York Times*, September 30, 2016, www.nytimes.com/2016/09/30/opinion/why-its-safe-to-scrap-americas-icbms.html. Also James E. Cartwright (General, USMC, Ret., commander of U.S. Strategic Command 2004–2007, Vice Chairman of the JCS 2004–2011) and Bruce G. Blair, "End the Policy for First-Use of U.S. Nuclear Weapons, *New York Times*, August 14, 2016, www.nytimes .com/2016/08/15/opinion/end-the-first-use-policy-for-nuclear-weapons.html. Also Tom Z. Collina, *Arms Control Today*, May 21, 2012, "Former Stratcom Head Calls for Cuts," www .armscontrol.org/act/2012_06/Former_STRATCOM_Head_Calls_for_Cuts.

344 On the Russian buildup: Hans M. Kristensen and Robert S. Norris, "Russian Nuclear Forces, 2017" *Bulletin of the Atomic Scientists* 73, no. 2 (2017): 115–126.

345 as Alan Robock and Brian Toon have put it Alan Robock and Brian Owen Toon, "Self-Assured Destruction: The Climate Impacts of Nuclear War," *Bulletin of the Atomic Scientists* 68, no. 5 (2012): 66–74.

346 After all, not one of these legislatures On the inability of Senator Robert Kerrey, then ranking member of the Senate Intelligence Committee, to get access to targeting lists of the SIOP, see Brett Lorrie, "A Do-It-Yourself SIOP," *Bulletin of the Atomic Scientists* 57, no. 4 (2001): 22–29.

350 As Martin Luther King Jr. warned us Rev. Dr. Martin Luther King Jr., "Beyond Vietnam," Riverside Church, April 4, 1967, kingencyclopedia.stanford.edu/encyclopedia /documentsentry/doc_beyond_vietnam/. Emphasis added.

Acknowledgments

395 that statement (in part) I urge readers to look for the whole statement on ellsberg.net, the ending of my preface to Joseph Daniel's *A Year of Disobedience a Criticality of Conscience* (Boulder, CO: Story Arts Media, 2013). 80–81.

396 "increasing levels of cancer, leukemia, and genetic mutation" This was neither rhetorical nor exaggeration. Carl Johnson, MD, director of the Jefferson County Health Department where Rocky Flats was located, found that nearness to the Rocky Flats plant correlated both to plutonium contamination and incidence of cancer, a study later published in 1981 in *Ambio*, the journal of the Royal Swedish Academy of Sciences. His results were confirmed by Karl Morgan of the Department of Energy's Oak Ridge National Laboratory, known as the "father of health physics," who along with Alice Stewart, British epidemiologist and renowned expert on the harmful effects of low-dose radiation, testified at our late trial in November 1979. Johnson was forced out of his job by real-estate interests in Jefferson County. (See *A Year of Disobedience and a Criticality of Conscience*, 55, 57, 112–113, also on ellsberg.net).

After a surprise FBI raid on Rocky Flats in 1989 to collect evidence of environmental lawbreaking at the plant, and a runaway grand jury whose sealed report calling Rocky Flats "an ongoing criminal enterprise" for its violations and recommending criminal indictment and trial of several high-ranking Rockwell and DOE officials was leaked to the press, production at Rocky Flats was "suspended" and, in fact, permanently ended, the entire facility razed. (See LeRoy Moore, "Local Hazard, Global Threat" in *A Year of Disobedience and a Criticality of Conscience*, 106–135, on the health findings, the cover-up, and legal disputes—which continue to this day—over inadequate cleanup and protection of the public against development interests in Jefferson County adjacent to Rocky Flats.)

Acknowledgments

Without the encouragement, support and guidance of my son Robert Ellsberg, this project could not have been completed. When Robert found me effectively stuck a year and a half ago, he put aside or added to his own work schedule to devote long intervals in which he acted as a combination of coach, motivational trainer, editor, and work manager. (My thanks go as well to his partner, Monica Olson, who lent her enthusiastic support to his doing this.)

On several final chapters—in particular, those on Cuba and the last one on agenda—where I felt overwhelmed confronting a multiplicity of memos and drafts and couldn't see how to boil them down, he cut and pasted from my own files to put together drafts that allowed me to move ahead. Toward the end he talked with me almost every day, setting goals and keeping my spirits up, counseling what to keep in and what to cut or leave out. In short, he applied his professional art as a gifted editor to serve his father in what was literally a labor of love.

This book has been a very long time in gestation: really, the whole of the nuclear era so far, since I first heard of U-235 in the fall of 1944. During that long period, every person mentioned in this book in whatever connection, including references, has contributed to my present and still-evolving understanding of nuclear danger. I am grateful to every one of them for that. That definitely includes my former RAND and Pentagon mentors, colleagues, and friends, however much our views and concerns diverged in later years.

It also includes, above all, mentors, colleagues, and friends of the last fifty years who have shared both of my dual commitments to the antiwar and anti-nuclear movements: Gar Alperovitz, Noam Chomsky, Jim and Shelly Douglas, Douglas Dowd, Mort Halperin, David Hartsough, Randy

Kehler, Peter Kuznick, Steve Ladd, Robert Lifton, Greg Mitchell, Robert Musil, Cody Shearer, Gary Snyder, Norman Solomon, Janaki Tschannerl, Brian Willson, and Howard Zinn. I treasure what I have learned from each of these, far beyond anything I learned at Harvard.

I've also cherished my contacts, however brief in some cases, with the many thousands of people who have been in jail with me for actions of nonviolent civil disobedience protesting our nuclear policy or wrongful interventions. That applies especially to the members of the Rocky Flats Truth Force (including Frank Cordaro, Jay Dillon, Marion Doub, Evan Freirich, Elena Klaver, Patrick Malone, LeRoy Moore, Chet Tchozewski, and Roy Young). For me this all started under the influence of Janaki Tschannerl, Randy Kehler, and Bob Eaton, who inspired in me (along with the writings of Barbara Deming) the thought of truth-telling as a form of Gandhian nonviolent resistance.

In that same spirit, I want to pay tribute to fellow whistle-blowers: in particular to Mordechai Vanunu (a prophet of the nuclear age, who suffered the greatest personal price so far, for his revelations of the Israeli nuclear program—including ten and a half years in solitary confinement—and who is still in internal exile in Israel), Frank Serpico (perhaps the first modern whistle-blower, who also paid a heavy physical price), and my more recent heroes, Chelsea Manning and Ed Snowden. Likewise, with my admiration and appreciation for their truth-telling: William Binney, Tom Drake, Sibel Edmonds, Melvin Goodman, Frank Grevil, Katharine Gun, John Kiriakou, Edward Loomis, Ray McGovern, Jesselyn Radack, Coleen Rowley, Thomas Tamm, Russell Tice, J. Kirk Wiebe, Joseph Wilson, and Ann Wright (and others, less personally known to me).

In this context, Morton Halperin deserves special mention as one of the very few friends from my years at RAND and the Pentagon—where all my associates held security clearances—whose friendship survived my release of the Pentagon Papers and who supported my act. (Almost the only others were Bernard Brodie, Tom Schelling, and Melvin Gurtov.) Becoming an absolutely crucial member of my defense team, Mort willingly risked his own future clearance and career. Ever since then, he has been an indefatigable critic of wrongful interventions and defender of whistle-blowers' legal rights. (He was one of the very first to argue publicly for "no first use" of nuclear weapons, from 1960.)

I'm deeply grateful for friendship and support for my work that has included but gone well beyond warm hospitality: Markell Brooks, Daidie Donnelly, Judy Ehrlich, Jodie Evans, Verona Fonte, Rick Goldsmith, Hilary and Danny Goldstine, Claire Greensfelder, Susan Griffin, Edie Hartshorne, Martin and Dorothie Hellman, Sy and Liz Hersh, Barbara Koeppel, David and Carolee Krieger, Peter and Simki Kuznick, Joanna Macy, Jeffrey and Leila Masson, Julia Pacetti, Lynda and Stewart Resnick, Peter Dale Scott (my close friend and mentor since the Pentagon Papers trial) and Ronna Kabatznick, Bert Schneider, Lloyd and Marva Shearer, Stanley and Betty Sheinbaum, Jeremy Sherman and his parents Gordon and Kate, Dan Smith and Joan Marler, Lee Swenson and Vijaya Nagarajan. Every year since 1982, the many participants in Robert Lifton's annual Wellfleet seminar have provided me with a welcome, quasi-academic intellectual community.

I have benefited from research grants from the W. Alton Jones Foundation and the John D. and Catherine T. MacArthur Foundation and award money from the Right Livelihood Foundation (2006). Moreover, I was enabled to work on this book at writing retreats at the Mesa Refuge (Pt. Reyes Station, California) and the Carey Institute for Global Good (Renssalaerville, New York). David Krieger's Nuclear Age Peace Foundation, of which I am a Senior Fellow, has been a conduit for vital financial support for my work (in particular from Markell Brooks). They all have my great thanks.

Likewise, David Krieger and his colleagues at NAPF—along with long-time stalwarts of nuclear abolition including my friends Helen Caldicott (who revived Physicians for Social Responsibility), Alice Slater (Abolition 2000), Jackie Cabasso, John Burroughs, and Andrew Lichterman (Western States Legal Foundation), Bruce Blair (Global Zero), Jonathan Granoff (Global Security Institute), Aaron Tovish (Mayors for Peace), and Alyn Ware (Parliamentarians for Nuclear Nonproliferation and Disarmament)—for keeping alive the cause of total elimination of nuclear weapons. All of these organizations deserve the attention and support of readers of this book, as do ICAN (International Campaign for the Abolition of Nuclear Weapons), Federation of American Scientists, Arms Control Association, Greenpeace and International Network of Scientists and Engineers for Global Responsibility, Arjun Makhijani's Institute for Energy and Environmental Research, and the Campaign for Nuclear Disarmament. I have learned a great deal over the last forty years from all those named above, and particularly from my friend Christopher Paine (National Resources Defense Committee).

My younger son, Michael, played a crucial part in encouraging and helping me to write the book proposal that I turned over to my outstanding agent, Andy Ross, and that helped sell this book. Andy Ross's tenacity made sure that—after seventeen rejections, on commercial grounds—this manuscript found the perfect home at Bloomsbury, thanks to editor Peter Ginna (who has, of course, my thanks). At Bloomsbury, my wonderful editor Nancy Miller's continued enthusiasm, through long delays and extensions, has kept me going, and her careful work has greatly improved the text, as has the meticulous copyediting by Laura Phillips and her crew. My assistant Nomi Yah has been indispensable for thirteen years. Michael Mack, a Macintosh wizard, has surmounted numerous computer crises. Tom Reifer, Allen Pietrobon, and William Burr have supplied uncountable numbers of reference articles.

Invaluable comments and corrections have been provided by readers of parts or all of this manuscript: David Barash, William Burr, Linda Burstyn, Martin Hellman, Frank von Hippel, Judith Lipton, Benoit Pelopidas, Ted Postol, Alan Robock, Eric Schlosser, Daniel U. Smith, Norman Solomon, Trevor Timm, Brian Toon, and Aaron Tovish. Several of these have gone over the entire manuscript so generously and meticulously that I do not see how in good conscience, if I identified them, they could escape all responsibility for any remaining errors. (I've always wanted to write that.) I am grateful to Alan Robock and Brian Toon for sharing all their papers on nuclear winter with me, including some not yet published, and for answering patiently all my questions.

Since this is my final book—so I hope (my wife assures me I am not alone in that)—I want to take more space than usual to acknowledge my profound debt and gratitude to those who have been with me for the long haul, my family (which has virtually come to include Tom Reifer).

To start with Tom: In January 1984, when I asked a question in the first session of a course I was teaching on nuclear policy at UC Irvine, exactly one member of the class of four hundred undergraduates raised his hand, and he answered correctly. I was impressed and asked his name. When I found that Tom was also the only student, so far as I could tell, who was reading all the voluminous optional reading I had recommended, I admitted him to the graduate seminar I was conducting on the same subject. The other members were all graduate students or faculty. It soon became clear that he was the outstanding discussant.

What I didn't know at the time was that he wasn't enrolled at Irvine or any other university; he was sixteen years old, a school dropout who never formally graduated from high school. He had been a runaway from an abusive home since he was thirteen, until his sister had recruited him off the streets into the movement started by Randy Kehler and Randall Forsberg for a bilateral nuclear weapons freeze. But after assisting me in that course (and during it, passing a high school equivalency test, and earning a letter of commendation from me) he went on to get a BA and MA at UC Santa Cruz in sociology and a PhD at SUNY Binghamton. Tom is now a full professor of sociology at the University of San Diego. His pathbreaking thesis, drawing on world systems theory, will be published—after a gestation period comparable to that of this book—as "Lawyers, Guns and Money: Wall Street and the American Century."

Tom has been a close friend for most of the third of a century since he took my course, but for the first ten years or so he was, in effect, my student; for the last twenty years, more of a mentor. This text reflects at least a thousand hours of intense discussion with him over the last three decades, and not only about nuclear policy (I'm greatly indebted to Kerstin Lanham for her generous readiness and extraordinary facility to transcribe many of those dialogues for me). Imagine what it has meant to me to have had round-the-clock assistance from him in recent months just to complete the references and notes in this book!

Next, my older children, Robert Boyd and Mary Carroll Ellsberg. I couldn't tell them why I was away from home so much in Washington in their early youth, because they weren't cleared. Nor did they know the substance of the Pentagon Papers they spent a night helping me copy: Robert, at thirteen, collating, and Mary, who was ten, cutting Top Secret off the tops and bottoms of the pages with a scissors. (I wanted them to see that I was doing something, calmly and deliberately, that I thought was right, whatever they might hear if I went to prison shortly as I expected.)

They weren't scarred by that experience, evidently. They both went on to fulfill a father's highest hopes for careers of right livelihood. Robert, a born editor and inspiring author, has been for years the editor-in-chief and publisher of Orbis Books, the publishing house of the Maryknoll order. Mary, after working, at considerable risk, in the Sandinista literacy and health campaigns in Nicaragua, earned a PhD in public health from Umeå University in Sweden with an epidemiological study in Nicaragua of violence against women, a subject on which she has become a world-wide authority. She is now Director of the Global Women's Institute and Professor of Global Health at George Washington University.

In my first book in 1972 I acknowledged my wife, Patricia, as my partner, lover, and closest friend. That remains true forty-five years later.

It's fifty-two years from our first date on April 16, 1965, when she had made me an offer I couldn't refuse: to accompany her the next day to the first SDS rally against the Vietnam war. (It was my first Saturday off from the Pentagon in nine months, spent working dutifully six and a half days a week on the escalation of the war.) Two nights after that I was in love with her, as I've been ever since.

Patricia was an unindicted co-conspirator for the final copying and release of the Pentagon Papers. (Unindicted, it turned out, because she had never been fingerprinted, unlike me and my co-defendant Tony Russo; the FBI couldn't identify her prints on the Papers.) That occupied the first year of our marriage, followed by two years on trial and two more years of antiwar activism.

She didn't know in the first years of our marriage what's revealed in my introduction here, about the "other Pentagon papers" on nuclear matters, with my expectation of another trial and almost certain life imprisonment. Or, absent that outcome (thanks to tropical storm Doria) the prospect after the war of forty more years of preoccupation and activism on what was, to her, a whole new obsession of mine. She surely deserved to know all that when she accepted my proposal in 1970, but I couldn't tell her without incriminating her further.

Since 1975 Patricia has had to live with my on-and-off engagement with this book. That's been true for the entire life of my youngest son, Michael Gabriel (now forty), who like his mother has endured endless monologues on this and other grim subjects. Publication day will be a glorious liberation for both Michael and Patricia (though Michael will be taking on the task of managing my related website). That Patricia has remained my loving partner throughout this interminable pursuit is . . . a miracle, the kind that gives me hope for this world.

One of the most challenging days for our marriage was the first birthday of my youngest son Michael, May 12, 1978. Instead of being at home with them in San Francisco to observe the occasion, I was sitting with Robert—by then the editor of the *Catholic Worker*—who had come out to Colorado to join me on the railroad tracks at the Rocky Flats Nuclear Weapons Production Facility, awaiting what was to be my fourth arrest there and his first.

As we traveled in a police van to jail, in handcuffs, Robert looked out at the tracks we were passing and said, "You know, there should have been people sitting on the tracks at Auschwitz."

Mary had come out to the tracks while her brother was in jail, and she was shocked to see his appearance in court for sentencing on May 27. He had spent sixteen days on a water fast, most of it in solitary confinement (separated from the rest of us until that morning), and he had to leave the courtroom at one point, dizzy and nauseated, But she then heard him, as we all did, deliver in a strong voice his stunning address to the court, handwritten the night before.

The last words in this book go to Robert from that statement (in part):

> By sitting on railroad tracks at Rocky Flats—one dozen, two dozen, even a hundred people—we ourselves may not actually be able to stop the production of plutonium triggers there. But we are trying to show that we as a people, if we wish and if we are determined, have that power—the power to change ourselves and history—we as a people can close Rocky Flats, and in fact that is what we must do. We do not deny that the goal of world-wide disarmament is a complicated one and filled with risks, but it is time that we begin accepting the risks of peacemaking as we have for so long lived under the risks of war . . .
>
> For us, the choice is clear.
>
> Rocky Flats is the Auschwitz of our time. Behind that barbed wire and those locked doors, intelligent, decent family men in their white suits and their security badges are implementing the technological preparations for the Final solution to the Human Problem. In each bomb prepared at Rocky Flats is another Holocaust—perhaps for the children of Moscow, Peking, Hanoi—those who build them don't know.
>
> At one of the German concentration camps—I believe it was Dachau—the American troops who liberated it forced the townspeople to tour the camp—to the huddled, emaciated survivors, the piles of corpses, the ovens that had disposed of the dead. And of course they were numbed and shocked and they said, "We didn't know—we didn't know what was in those boxcars—we didn't know what came out of those chimneys."
>
> We would like to spare the people of this county, this state, and our country, that kind of experience—so we are shouting, we are trying to warn the people what kind of cargo over those

railroad tracks in sealed boxcars is killing and mutilating your unborn children by increasing levels of cancer, leukemia, and genetic mutation—even if the bombs never go off.

And we are doing more than that. There are people right now who are blocking those tracks. There is a group of people— someday they will be thanked, now they are jailed—who are saying, "Build your bombs, continue our business as usual in this death camp—but I'm sorry that I must withdraw my consent—you will have to do it over our bodies."

They are saying, no longer should nuclear bombs be made in this country without Americans being arrested. And when I heard that in Colorado there were people who were willing to say this and act on it, I had to come here—because I knew these were people I wanted to know and to join and be with.

As Robert said the last words, he turned around, away from the judge, and thanked the defendants who filled the small courtroom for giving him the chance to be in their company. We all stood up and met that with shouts and applause, and the judge, who had warned us against demonstrations, ordered the marshals to clear the courtroom.

Index

A NOTE ON THE AUTHOR

In 1961, Daniel Ellsberg, a consultant to the Department of Defense and the White House, drafted Secretary Robert McNamara's plans for nuclear war. Later he leaked the Pentagon Papers. He lectures and writes on the dangers of the nuclear era and the need for whistle-blowing. A Senior Fellow of the Nuclear Age Peace Foundation, Ellsberg is the author of *Secrets* and the subject of the Oscar-nominated documentary *The Most Dangerous Man in America*. He is also a key figure in Steven Spielberg's upcoming film about the Pentagon Papers, *The Post*, scheduled to be released in December 2017. He lives in Kensington, California, with his wife, Patricia.